Date Due

AP 23 '96			
MR 12 '98			

Keepers of the Culture

The Power of Tradition in Women's Lives

Janet Mancini Billson

LEXINGTON BOOKS
An Imprint of The Free Press
New York   London   Toronto   Sydney   Tokyo   Singapore

Library of Congress Cataloging-in-Publication Data

Billson, Janet Mancini.
    Keepers of the Culture: the power of tradition in women's lives / Janet Mancini Billson.
        p.   cm.
    Includes index.
    ISBN 0-02-903512-0
    1.   Women—Canada—Social   conditions.   2.   Minority   women—Canada—Social
Conditions.   3. Minority Women—Canada—Social Life and customs.   4. Sex role—Canada.
I. Title.
HQ1453.B55   1995   95-3611
305.42'0971—dc20   CIP

Lexington Books
An Imprint of The Free Press
A Division of Simon & Schuster Inc.
866 Third Avenue, New York, N. Y. 10022
Printed in the United States of America

printing number

1 2 3 4 5 6 7 8 9 10

For my grandmothers,
Tabatha Myers Billson and Ilyh Wood Ramey,
who lived the traditions . . .
For my mother,
Kathleen Billson Ramey,
always my best teacher . . .
For my daughter, Kyra Mancini,
who remembers the old while creating the new . . .

And for my husband,
Norman T. London,
who sits beside me in love and work.

The Woman's Part

Art Solomon
Ojibway Elder

"The woman is the foundation on which
nations are built."
She is the heart of her nation.
If that heart is weak the people are weak.
If her heart is strong and her mind is clear
then the nation is strong and knows its purpose.
The woman is the centre of everything.

But equally, women must honour men
if not, then everything is out of balance
and we can have nothing but chaos and pain.
These are the first elements that must be
put back together
or nothing, but nothing
can come right again.

Excerpted from "a voice of many nations," Native Women's Association of Canada, Ottawa.

Contents

Preface

S cholarship, like all passion, never occurs in a vacuum.[1] Passion is *for* something. My passion is for writing about women and power: how women and men work out their power arrangements within the context of intimate relationships, and how that varies across cultures. Between 1986 and 1994 I made several journeys across Canada, staying in cultural communities of native, minority, and immigrant women. I interviewed more than 250 women in order to learn more about these issues that face all women.

I went back to Canada as a sociologist committed to documenting the changes in male and female roles during the past hundred years. I also returned to Canada as a woman on my own journey to rediscover my roots, to meet women like those with whom I would have been friends and neighbors had I not left Canada as an adolescent. In every community, I requested and received permission to conduct interviews. Everywhere I was welcomed into the homes and lives of women whose day-to-day existence was often very different from my own.[2] The journey helped me grow both as a social scientist and as a woman.

Shulamit Reinharz and Barbara Du Bois argue that "passionate scholarship" requires us to ground theory in the language and experience of women.[3] Because we are the expert witnesses about our own lives, I worked with women in these communities as consultants: Iroquois (Six Nations) women of Ohsweken, Ontario; Blood (Kainai) women of Standoff, Alberta; Inuit women of Pangnirtung, Baffin Island, Northwest Territories; Jamaican women of Toronto; Mennonite women of Elmira, Ontario; Chinese women of Vancouver; and Ukrainian women of Saskatoon, Saskatchewan. A second volume of *Keepers of the Culture* will address issues of women who are more assimilated into the mainstream of Canadian society (for example, women from Canada's two "founding cultures," French and British).

For this book, I facilitated discussions among women whose voices are seldom heard, including rural, urban, and small-town women, women of color, indigenous women, immigrant women, and women of dissimilar religious, educational, and economic backgrounds. I invited members of each community to work with me and to develop a plan that would bring many different voices into our conversations. They included married, single, divorced, and widowed women; employed, unemployed, and self-employed women; homemakers, business executives, artists, and welfare recipients; older and younger women; women who are community leaders and those who do not get involved; and financially stable and poverty-stricken women.

Often the line between interviews and participant observation is not clearly drawn. In the chill of an Arctic summer I went seal hunting with Inuit women of Baffin Island, who live in a geographic isolation penetrated by soap operas from Detroit. We went fishing by the dim light of the midnight sun and made bannock (pan-fried bread) for tea. In cosmopolitan Vancouver I ate noodle soup for breakfast and spoke with immigrant women from mainland China who were sold into servitude as children only fifty years ago and whose granddaughters are completing professional university degrees. I discussed the roots of domestic violence[4] with Ukrainian prairie women who remember living in underground sod houses; we stuffed cabbage rolls and made pies while singing traditional songs about women from "the old country." I spent a night in a tipi with a Blood Indian medicine woman and witnessed the band's annual Sun Dance ceremony. I danced to reggae music at Toronto's Caribana Ball. I went shopping with Mennonite women at Saturday market, and I attended a forest pageant produced by the Six Nations.

In order to take the clearest possible social photograph of each community, I used a combination of qualitative and quantitative methods: intensive tape-recorded interviews of women individually and in focus groups; participant observation in their communities; analysis of statistical, demographic, and historical data; and taking photographs. I met local families and attended local events considered by women to be important to women.

Keepers of the Culture reflects a collaborative effort between the women of these communities and myself as "midwife."[5] I encouraged the women to speak out, feel safe, tell the truth, and be self-reflective. I listened passionately as they attempted to untangle the interwoven power relations between women and men and how, sometimes inexplicably, these relations change over time. I asked my collaborators to go beyond their own experiences to discuss the general strengths, problems, and needs of women in their community. Group sessions inspired debate and alternative explanations of how things became the way they are now.

We operated as partners in discovering and analyzing the realities of women's lives. As intellectual midwife, I stimulated discussion of sources of strength for both women and men, the way power was distributed between the sexes traditionally and how it plays out now, how men and women seem to have gotten off track with each other, and how the current generation's future will contrast with the lives of their parents and grandparents. We journeyed together into the past, struggling to analyze the sources of gender oppression in each community. Women reflected on their own relationships with men, talked about raising their daughters and sons, and predicted what power relations might look like for these children as they grow up. I asked the same sequence of questions in every community and crafted additional questions to address specific issues or unique histories. The discussions were tape-recorded and transcribed.[6]

As the project moved toward completion in each community, our understanding of women's power and roles became progressively refined and verified. Conceptualization began not in the privacy of my study, but during the interviews and informal conversations.[7] We worked collaboratively, like detectives trying to unravel a mystery that affects all of us. The women in each locale helped interpret and analyze these changes, and they have reviewed the draft of their chapter before it became a part of this book.

Though I set out on this journey to talk to women, I also spoke with a few men in each community. Invariably they confirmed the women's view of major issues and gender relations, including the nature and type of women's oppression by men. Their recollections of male roles in past generations are closely interwoven with women's perceptions. For example, when I asked them to describe the hardest part of their lives, women in the native communities portrayed men as not doing well in education and employment, turning more and more to drugs and alcohol, and beating women as a way to soothe the pain and regain some semblance of power. Most men unhesitatingly and without my prompting painted the same picture; some realities are too obvious to ignore.

Everywhere I saw firsthand the massive changes that have taken place for both women and men, changes that are important to chronicle as part of our social history. For example, gender roles turned upside down among Blood Indian couples as they shifted from hunting and gathering to agriculture to welfare dependency or wage-earning jobs, or among the Inuit as they left the land to live in settlements. Women are freer to make their own choices, yet bound by the double and triple responsibilities of being homemaker, mother, and employee. Many of the changes are exhilarating and empowering; others are draining and confusing. I will explore these contradictions in the case studies of women in seven communities later in this book.

Canadian sociologist Dorothy Smith says that a woman conducting research on women is "a member of the same world she explores, active in the same relations as those for whom she writes. Like Jonah, she is inside the whale."[8]

I am, in critical ways, an insider—a sister traveler on the journey through life as a woman. I am embedded in the same everyday contexts as the women I interviewed, although the details of our circumstances may differ greatly. This truth was expressed over and over during my journeys as the communities and I tried to make sense out of what it means to be a woman, and to explore together the complex relations between men and women.

In equally important ways, though, I am outside the whale. I am not Chinese or Inuit; I am not living below the poverty level; I am not a widow or a young woman facing little prospect of receiving an education. No researcher can be entirely like those she seeks to understand, if only because of the mandate she imposes on herself to try to stand outside at the same time as she explores inside. Doing this kind of research is always problematic. It is not easy to live both inside and outside the whale.

Inside the whale, I experience the frustrations of encountering male power—and I also experience the joys of feeling close to a father, husband, son, brothers, and uncles. Outside the whale, I read that women have been oppressed and subordinated in all cultures since the first woman was dragged into a cave thousands of years ago. I wonder, as a theorist and realist, whether this can possibly be true. There must be exceptions. Inside the whale again, I call upon my personal knowledge of women who are strong, vibrant, and certainly not oppressed in spite of a male-dominated society.

Each of us lives both inside and outside the whale in our own way. If women are to become united for positive social change, though, we must expand our awareness of each other's realities, opportunities, and dreams. If this book does justice to the trust hundreds of women and men have placed in me, all the work will have been well worth our collective energies. Like the research process, writing the book was a journey of discovery and self-discovery. By challenging some of our most basic assumptions about how women and men relate to each other, I hope to inspire readers to embark on a similar voyage of their own.

Keepers of the Culture is only one small step toward improving mutual understanding among women who live very different lives by virtue of our diversities in race, ethnicity, and social class, as well as how we spend our individual days and nights. But every step counts.

Acknowledgments

W ithout the cooperation of hundreds of women across Canada, this project could not have been undertaken. *Keepers of the Culture* was not written by the women in the seven communities, but it is written from their perspectives, with their permission and collaboration, and with their feedback. As much as possible in writing these pages I used the words of women who participated in the project to explore issues facing all women today. The women, whom I view as consultants, read these pages before you did; their concerns, additions, rewordings, and corrections were integrated into the final draft, as I promised all participants from the very beginning. Each community has received multiple copies of the book for their libraries and collective use.

Although their names and identities have been changed within each chapter, I want to acknowledge the women and men who served as consultants for their communities by listing their names here. In this way, they can be recognized (with their permission) for their invaluable contributions. I am deeply indebted to their willingness to facilitate the interview process and to open their homes and their hearts to us. Many others preferred to remain anonymous; they know that their ideas were equally appreciated. Those who read the final draft of their community's chapter deserve special thanks.

Iroquois Women of the Six Nations, Ohsweken, Ontario
Reva J. Bomberry, Wilton C. Bomberry, Patricia Commandant, Beatrice Harris, Lori Hill, Sherry Hill, Susan J. Hill, Elva Lickers, Bill Montour, Kim Montour, Janice Porter, Caren Smith, Karen Williams, and others.

Blood Women of Standoff, Alberta
Carole Benner, Henry Big Throat, Irene Bullshields, Edna Eagle-bear, Bernice Firstcharger, Georgette Fox, George Goodstriker, Leeann Healey, Jan Healy, Shirley Healy, Lenore Heavy Runner, Margaret Hindman, Sybille Manneschmidt, Corrine Many Bears, Gerri Many Fingers, Bernice Medicine, Esther Scalplock, Carrie Lyn Soup, Beverly Tailfeathers, Carrie Tailfeathers, Esther Tail-feathers, Ken Tailfeathers, Olivia Tailfeathers, Rick Tailfeathers, Carol White Quills, and others.

Inuit Women of Pangnirtung, Baffin Island, Northwest Territories
Annie Akpalialuk, Apea Akpalialuk, Eena Alivaktuk, Meeka Alivak-tuk, Jeannie Alivaktuk, Roposie Alivaktuk, Alan Angmarlik, Rev. Ben Arreak, Mary Arnakak, Meeka Arnakak, Lynn Cameron, Qat-soo Eevik, Glenn Hanna, Chamberlain Jones, Irene Jones, Martha Kakee, Jukeepa Kanayuk, Annie Martha Keenainak, Simeonie Keenainak, Jonah Kilabuk, Reepa Kilabuk, Peah Kisa, Saila Kisa, Eena Kullualik, Geela Maniapik, Corol McKillican, Rick McKilli-can, Iola Metuq, Lena Metuq, Johnny Mike, Loie Mike, Annie Okalik, Kudloo Pitseolak, Leah Qappik, Peepeelee Qappik, Peter Qappik, Sheila Qappik, Mary Shukulak, Peona Shukulak, Geela Sowdluapik, Saila Sowdluapik, Niomie Veevee, Pauloosie Veevee, Rosie Veevee, and others.

Jamaican Women of Toronto
Brenda Charles, Norma Forbes, Errol Gibbs, Maryane Gibbs, Madeline Harris, Eileen Lawson, Lynn Lewis, Romeo Kaseram, Marcia McGhee, Juliette Phillips, Florine Powell, Marjorie Rain-ford, Sandra Rainford, Dagneline Rente, Susan Roberts, Bernadine Stewart, Elva Waldron, Percy Waldron, and others.

Mennonite Women of Elmira, Ontario
Susanna Bauman, Delphine Frey, Lucille Frey, Marie Frey, Edward Gingerich, Marlene Gingerich, Ammon Martin, Dorene Martin, Florence Martin, Janella Martin, Leighton Martin, Lovina Martin, Sandra Martin, Dolores Harms Penner, E. Paul Penner, Janet Plen-ert, Stephen Plenert, Kay Shantz, Larry Shantz, Marilyn Shantz, Ronald Shantz, Marie Weber, and others.

Chinese Women of Vancouver, British Columbia
Wendy Au, Winnie Chang, Yvonne Chang, Nancy Chin, Jenny

Chiu, Emily Chow, Annie Choy, Christine Choy, Ansar Cheung, Lam Yan Chung, Anita Fung, Toy Lin Gom, Wai Ching Hong, Ariana Huang, Jocelyn Hsiung, Eliza Ip, Helen Lam, Lena Lee, Mandy Lee, Elli Li, Sui Ling Li, Alexina Louie, Centina Lowe, Wendy Liu, Cathy Lu, Mu Lueng, Sofia Lui, Celina Luk, Yau Luli, Alice Man, Hung Yin Poon, Vinsy Taam, Man Che Tam, Conwan Ting, Esther Tom, Choi Wong, Oi Mei (Amy) Wong, Saintfield Wong, Evans Wu, Maple Wu, Ping Tai Wu, Angela Yap, Lam Sheong Yee, Linda T. O. Yen, Lou Gon Zing, and others.

Ukrainian Women of Saskatoon, Saskatchewan
Rose Bazowsky, Mary Beally, Olga Bilek, Loraine Bobowski, Sherri Bobowski, Rose Borsa, May Boychuk, Lena Bukurak, Melania Burianyk, Nell Burianyk, Anna Cholod, Mary Cooper, Bill Diakiw, Bella Dobni, Anna Dorosh, Margaret Ezak, Marilyn Feschuk, Mary Grebatin, Toni Horachek, Helen Hnatiuk, Helen Hnatyshyn, Rose Kaminsky, Cecilia Kachkowski, Mary Kalist, Lorraine Kenaschuk, Mary Keneschuk, Kathy Kendall, Rose Kerelchuk, Theresa Kindrachuk, Ann Kozakavich, RoseAnne Kowalsky, Nick Kostenuik, Dorothy Kucey, Mary Kuchapski, Michael Kuchapski, Mary Labach, Minnie Lemko, Pauline Lucyshyn, Helen Maksymiuk, Rev. William Makarenko, Olga Masnick, Vera Nokony, Sophie Ochitwa, Pauline Ostapowich, Anna Papish, Dorothy Prior, Olga Pilipow, Alice Prociuk, Irene Horhota Ritch, Doris Ryk, Vivian Sarchuk, Olga Satzewich, Orest Sirman, Peter Sirman, Mary Sopatyk, Savella Stechishin, Mary Talarkski, Josie Talpash, Mary Tkachuk, Theresa Turchyn, Elizabeth Wachniak, Ann Werezek, Ann Wojcichowsky, Tom Yakimchuck, Caroline Zabediuk, and others.

Many others helped in organizing the research and managing the data. The Scientific Research Institute of the Northwest Territories and the Hamlet Council of Pangnirtung approved the Inuit research segment; Pangnirtung Secretary Manager Alan Angmarlik smoothed the way and helped me find accommodation with an Inuit family, Rosie and Pauloosie Veevee. Chief Bill Montour of the Six Nations Reserve and Chief Roy Fox of the Blood Reserve graciously introduced me to women leaders and opened many doors. In all the communities, countless public officials answered questions about resources, statistics, and further contacts.

My daughter and chief research assistant, Kyra Mancini, helped conduct interviews with Inuit women, coded the Inuit data, and transcribed interviews for many of the communities. Every step of the way she has been my intellectual companion. I am grateful to her and to research assistants Nina Alesci, Martha Stapleton, Fran Taylor, and Joyce Turner, who transcribed and/or coded data for various communities. I could never have coped with the mountains of words generated by so many interviews. Each of these women painstakingly worked with the data, struggling to transform the words into manageable form.

Colleagues C. Margaret Hall (Georgetown University), Emily Stier Adler and Carolyn Fluehr-Lobban (Rhode Island College), Shulamit Reinharz (Brandeis University), and Ruth M. Wallace (George Washington University) have read sensitively through portions of the manuscript. Their grounded approach to feminism helped inspire the project's initial conceptualization, and their insights improved the final product. Many others—too many to mention here—have discussed the project, referred contacts, or commented on earlier papers that this project generated, but I especially want to thank Diddy Hitchins (University of Alaska-Anchorage); Lorna Irvine and Paula Gilbert (George Mason University); James Houston; Graham Johnson (University of British Columbia); Jeanne Kissner and Richard Beach (SUNY-Plattsburgh); David Flaherty, Carl Grindstaff, Will McEachern, Robin McGrath, and Lynn Wilson (University of Western Ontario); Mary McIntosh (United States Information Agency); Jane Szurek (Rhode Island School of Design); Margaret Brooks Terry (Baldwin-Wallace College); Barrie Thorne (University of Southern California), and Gail Tyerman (Canadian Foreign Service) for their enthusiastic encouragement. Robert Highley and my son, Mark F. Mancini, kept the computer singing, for which I am eternally grateful!

One of the joys of doing the research for *Keepers of the Culture* was that it involved a special kind of contact with my extended family, who live in Ontario, Alberta, and British Columbia. My parents, Kathleen and Clifford Ramey of London, provided a way station on many cross-country trips and organized the community review process, which involved a massive mailing during the summer of 1994. My brothers, Robert B. Ramey and James C. Ramey, were instrumental in arranging logistics for the Blood and Chinese interviews, respectively. Aunts, uncles, and cousins (especially Dorothy and Gordon Johnston, Richard and Janet Billson, Blanche Shepherd, and Victoria Shepherd) made the journeys easier by providing contacts and lodging. Our family works with love and caring, even across great distances and the separation of years. Thank you!

When I first brought the idea for this book to Lexington Books, Margaret Zusky became an instant advocate. From day one, she has been a thoughtful critic, a stalwart supporter, and a sympathetic reader. When it all seemed overwhelming, Margaret spurred me on to bring the project to fruition. A superb editor and a good friend, she too is a keeper of our culture. I am grateful also to the Free Press editorial staff, especially Susan Arellano, Carol Mayhew, and Nancy Ethridge, for helping bring the book to fruition.

I am deeply indebted to the Canadian government for its support of *Keepers of the Culture* through Faculty Enrichment and Faculty Research Grants in 1986 and 1988; also to the Rhode Island College (RIC) Faculty Research Committee for grants between 1986 and 1991; and to the RIC Faculty Summer Stipend Program, 1988. They literally made the journeys possible.

And for bringing me home to the study of Canada, I want to thank my husband, Norman T. London. From hiking with us into Auyuittuq National Park in the Canadian Arctic to helping rescue me from hypothermia, spending countless nights alone while I wrote this book, cooking and keeping the home fires burning, and commenting on the final draft, he has been there every moment.

1

The Tapestry of Women's Lives

The First Flight

We take off from Boston's Logan Airport almost two hours late. Finally, I feel excited, anticipating the sisters I will meet on this journey in the years ahead. Why did I do this? Why Canada? Why women? Who am I trying to comprehend—myself? My mother and aunts? Or those strange women who do not know me now, have never even heard of me, but who will open up their doors, their lives, and their hearts to me?

I count the years away and realize I have now lived twenty-seven years in the United States, only 17 in Canada. I am a marginal person, split in half and a little more than half. I live with it every day and every night, waking up at three in the morning with tears streaming onto my pillow, once again dreaming that someone I love in Canada is sick or dying. Twenty-seven years . . . I miss home.

Nationalism is not the issue for me. The beauty and the familiarity of those Canadian places where I lived and traveled as a child still speak to my heart. The soaring trees of Vancouver Island, slender and delicate, that march majestically from the mountain tops down to the sea. The grain elevators, wearing bittersweet orange or mustard yellow, that stand guard over tiny prairie towns surrounded by vast, undulating fields of wheat. The dead flat tablelands and gray stone villages of Southern Ontario. The flash of maple leaves in a Quebec

1

fall. The burnished red sands of Prince Edward Island's mist-shrouded shores. The endless tundra and ice of Canada's North.

Truly I am, like native people, a North American, a daughter of both lands. It is only the political border—so easily crossed, but so psychologically powerful—that creates this marginality of mine. I don't have to accept that border. I can be of both sides, or forget the notion of sides entirely. I can think instead, as the old maps show, of one continent divided by the north-south sweeps created by geology: the Cascades, the Rockies, the Great Plains, and the Appalachians. So that is the answer—I am going to speak with my North American sisters. I have never liked politics anyway.

All my other trips to Canada since I left as a young woman have been fleeting passages through places, not to them. This time I will encounter Canada's people as well as her scenery. This time I will stay awhile in the towns, the villages, the settlements. I am going back to learn more about being a woman—the part about how men have power so easily, and how women find their own unique strength in culture and community. And I am going back to heal the great divide inside my heart.

Culture is at the heart of being a woman. The tapestry of women's lives is woven on the loom of culture, often producing a rough and prickly cloth that is hard to wear and restricts our freedom. Ironically, though, culture also provides the loom from which new tapestries are woven—soft and gentle weavings in which the light and dark areas are counterbalanced, and that enable women to move out from under the mantle of oppression.

As we leave a century marked by dramatic social earthquakes, we must pause to document the impact of rapid social change on women in a variety of cultural contexts, and how women are contributing to this change. In *Keepers of the Culture* you will meet women from different cultural communities in Canada, all of which also exist in the United States, in their homelands, and in many other parts of the world. All belong to native, minority, and/or immigrant cultures: Iroquois, Blood, Inuit, Mennonite, Chinese, Jamaican, and Ukrainian. They will tell their stories about the remarkable changes in women's roles and social position, the nature and extent of women's power, and how women keep and re-shape traditional culture as they face the special problems of today's complex world.

The roots of tradition are being bent, twisted, and sometimes ripped out of the cultural landscape by bewildering social transformations. Today fewer than a third of North Americans live in the Ozzie-and-Harriet model of family life: Mom, Dad, and two children, with Dad working outside the home and making major decisions while Mom "keeps the home fires burning" and plays a subordinate role. Other models of male-female relations prevail: The flexibility of gender roles, innovative ways of holding families together, and unexpected definitions of what makes a good woman or a good man weave their way through the tapestry of women's lives.[1]

Many changes are for the better. Yet contemporary mainstream society is toxic for women in many circumstances, especially when being female combines with minority status, poverty, and old age. In part this is because messages from a distant era regarding appropriate female and male behavior persist long after we recognize that they are detrimental to the survival and health of women or of society as a whole. Because of this cultural lag, women's contemporary identities become stuck in traditional gender definitions, some of which are oppressive to women.[2] Liberation—in other words, discarding restricted definitions of what it means to be female—comes slowly when men continue to benefit from women's powerlessness.

Women in these communities, however, derive satisfaction from shaping and reshaping the very cultures that have shaped them. In every community I visited, women speak of their key role as "keepers of the culture."[3] Evelyn Beck describes Ukrainian women as "kinkeepers." Blood and Iroquois medicine women are "faithkeepers." A Jamaican woman refers to herself as a housekeeper, not in the sense of being a domestic (as so many professional Jamaican women were classified when they immigrated to Canada), but to convey an image of herself as homemaker—literally, keeper of the house.

In the Mennonite and Ukrainian communities, the traditional female role as keeper of the culture is highly respected, even revered, especially as it is displayed through the socialization of children.

Regard for women's conservational role thus helps to counterbalance traditional male dominance. In other communities, such as the Jamaican, Inuit, Blood, and Iroquois, the impact of rapid social change on male roles has been devastating; women's attention to keeping together family, culture, and faith has been critical to the survival of both genders.[4]

Many women in these cultures have not embraced the women's movement wholeheartedly, have approached it on their own terms, or have rejected it completely. Where women are appreciated, respected, trusted, and admired because of their integrative role—where it is truly recognized how critical that role is—then a balance of power is created that makes women either feel liberated "in their own way" (and therefore disinterested in the women's movement) or suspicious that the movement will destroy their "place" or their culture. Where the culture defines the female role positively, women may be loathe to adopt what they perceive as an alienating lifestyle.

Rediscovering and redefining culture has been a source of both power and pain for women. Until we grasp how culture shapes the female experience, our ability to understand each other and to create a cohesive women's movement will suffer. The assumption that being female overrides culture, race, or ethnicity is a questionable one that dampens the effort to improve women's status.[5] From the variegated strands of female identity, women can weave a successful movement.

Culture and the Logic of Oppression

This book draws upon the tradition in feminist sociology that analyzes power differentials between men and women from an historical and cross-cultural perspective.[6] Culture is the way of life—the values, beliefs, and customs—that distinguishes one group from another. Power is the ability to influence or control others, oneself, and resources such as time, money, and property. Culture binds individuals together in community, providing the moral and social justification for (among other things) perpetuating oppression of women or rejecting it. It is the vehicle through which the most uncomfortable tensions between men and women eventually, or explosively, resolve into new rules governing their relationships.

The ingredients of a "good woman" and a "good man" follow remarkably different cultural recipes that in turn affect role expectations, work opportunities, and the ability to make choices.[7] In most traditions males enjoy broader powers and fewer restrictions; women's power and status are defined not only as different from men's, but as inferior. The logic of women's oppression intricately connects power and culture, because culture defines who will have what kind of power and under what circumstances. Blueprints for identity and preferred behavior pass from generation to generation, reproducing personal and political ideologies that maintain power for the dominant sex. The old model of male superiority is often cruel and restrictive, resulting in women's economic, political, and educational isolation, which in turn undermines their position in the community and chances of achieving their—our—dreams.

Men's privilege and women's subordination cut across cultures, although in varying degrees. From an early age, people teach children to recognize and perpetuate power differences between males and females. Limits on where females can go and what they can do reinforce these differences, making it easier for men to achieve their goals and have their needs met. Barriers to equality begin to have negative consequences for both women and men, causing anger and pain. Because men typically control most meaningful forms of power, women begin to wish for more power—even equality. The movement toward equality can create a backlash or amplify oppressive acts.[8] Women strive harder for equality, and a vicious cycle is created.

This logic flows inexorably to one conclusion: Patriarchal domination of women exacts a high price from both sexes. Gender inequality is expressed in a variety of powerful ways, hurts women deeply, and it constricts men's growth as well. Traditions die hard. The way of life of mother and father is written large across the lives of daughter and son: their choices in mates, the way they raise their own girls and boys, and what they expect their futures to bring. On the individual level, females establish a negative identity in response to language and important social signs that define girls (and then women) as inferior: Names, titles, styles of dress, ornamentation, gestures, and modes of interaction all contribute to a sense of being "other,"[9] somehow less than males.

Laws and customs dictate who may go where in each community. All societies bring men and women together for sexual relations and allow them to mingle within the context of home and family. Outside the family, societies vary markedly in the degree of spatial segregation of the two sexes. Social life is often segregated into separate arenas, as in the Inuit women's club (the *quitak*) or the Mennonite custom of men and women sitting on opposite sides of the aisle in church. Men-only and women-only activities exist in every culture.

The time-honored segregation of sexes supports men's power advantage in property, income, influence, and privilege: If the bastions of male socializing and politicking (such as men's clubs and legislative bodies) do not include women, then women find themselves unable to influence formal or informal decisions. In fact, differential access to space is a key battleground of the women's movement, as shown by organized attempts to break down male control over certain occupations—law, medicine, mechanics, engineering, social clubs, political organizations, and even the front line of military operations.

Unequal access to space, decision making, and power has meant that women still do not garner their fair share of resources. In North America, about 45 percent of married women stay home without a salary to rear children and keep house; those women who work outside the home earn about 70 cents for every dollar earned by men in comparable jobs. Like such ancient customs as female infanticide, contemporary issues such as pay equity and comparable worth suggest the bias toward greater value being placed on males, as well as men's greater power.

On the community level, male control of economic and political resources disempowers women, resulting in significant gaps between two "gender classes." Unfortunately, men also often exercise power over women through desertion, failure to pay child support, battering, blocking mobility up the career ladder, and failure to acknowledge women appropriately for their contributions.

What are the consequences of unequal distribution of power between men and women? Male stress and earlier death echo problems of female depression. Domestic violence leaves women wounded and men shamed. Restricted opportunities in education and work distort men's perceptions of themselves and feed into women's poor self-esteem.

Inequality and power imbalances rob women of opportunities to engage in political leadership, economic stability, and meaningful work. Women spend far too much personal and political energy seeking approval; their potential as full-blown humans remains untapped.[10] Women and even young girls experience pain and anger at some level because they feel undervalued.

The dynamic is similar to that found in other dominant-subordinate relationships, such as that between whites and blacks in North America. The tensions created by forces of domination in society replicate themselves in the most minute expressions of male and female behavior. Women respond to male dominance in the same ways that other minority and oppressed groups respond, from outright rebellion and organizing social movements to passive resistance, accommodation, "passing," retreating, manipulating, and submission.

Oppression of women, whenever and wherever it exists, is oppressive and toxic for men as well. Men historically have enjoyed superior power, but feel emotionally constricted. They often find it difficult to participate fully in loving, open, and uninhibited interpersonal relationships. The volatile combination of male anger, guilt, and ambivalence and female anger, frustration, and fear damages male-female relationships. Power struggles block freedom of emotional expression and stunt independence and creativity. Alcoholism, child abuse, marital alienation, and loss of love endlessly interconnect with imbalanced gender relations.

The Cat's Cradle of Women's Experience

This argument sketches out the premises surrounding universal subordination of women. As a feminist, I believe this to be a compelling argument. Virtually every woman has at some time in her life felt disempowered by sexism. Those who have personally escaped oppression know someone else who has been hurt by male domination in politics, the workplace, the community, or the family. Certainly the rule of men (patriarchy) and freedom for women (liberation) are incompatible ideas.

In our commitment to liberate women—perhaps in an attempt to build sisterhood—feminists have found it useful to assume that women across time and cultures have been more or less equally oppressed by men. We have also assumed that women equally define gender (rather than class, race, or religion) as the central basis for oppression in their lives. As the women's movement matures, however, we are realizing that the assumption of universal subordination leaves women in a precarious place—always on the bottom of a bad arrangement—that may not be an accurate depiction of women in all cultures.[11]

Instead, our social world constantly regenerates like a cat's cradle, in new but always interwoven patterns of culture, oppression, and liberation. Having acknowledged the tragic pervasiveness of women's oppression, we must be careful to document cultures that elevate women to higher status (at least in some arenas), celebrate our strengths and contributions, and venerate our knowledge and wisdom. This reexamination of the complexities of women's lives forces us to confront several crucial questions:

- How have women's roles and social positions been transformed during the last 100 years, a period of explosive change in most parts of the world?
- Are women everywhere oppressed by the rule of men?
- Where women are oppressed and powerless relative to men, how did that happen?
- Are some cultures more supportive of women's equality?
- Are women more powerful in some arenas, places, or times than in others?
- What are the cultural elements that make it easier for us to regain our power and to live equally within our communities and families?
- Who has control over resources; the power to define roles, position, and identity; and the right to make and enact decisions?
- Are there cultures that promote women's power and domination of men?

In order to answer these questions, I interviewed the women you will meet in these pages. They are the true experts about their lives.

Invitation to the Journey

The book's core chapters sketch the distinctive interplay of power, culture, and change. Although I used the same structure across chapters in order to highlight social changes over the last century, I have allowed the special circumstances facing women in each community to dictate the shape of their chapter. Profiles of individual women enrich our understanding of issues facing the entire community. (Of course, the names used are fictitious, and I have changed identifying details.) Women's voices that are seldom heard float across these pages, echoing the voices of their unheard sisters. As Jamaican Makeda Silvera writes, "You, we must challenge the limits of a horizon which superficially frees some women but leaves the masses of women under the tyranny of silence."[12]

Common threads run through our lives, threads that have more to do with being a woman than with living in a particular culture. They are equally worth unraveling. The last three chapters—Common Pain (Chapter 9), Uncommon Strength (Chapter 10), and Diversity and the Future of the Women's Movement (Chapter 11)—outline themes that tie women together, regardless of culture. They remind us that, as in a tapestry, separate strands eventually produce identifiable patterns. To be successful, the women's movement must be able to work with the "whole cloth" of women's experience. I hope *Keepers of the Culture* will bring us closer to that place.

My field notes start and end each chapter, to serve as a transition from one community to the next. They may help provide a sense of my experience as both stranger and friend, researcher and woman. I begin with women who historically enjoyed broad powers: the Iroquois women of the Six Nations.

Preparing for the Inner Journey

Today was my first day in the field, arranging interviews that I will do later in Vancouver. This part of the continent is lovely, so lovely: tall trees, lush growth everywhere, the jagged mountains, the sea. I miss the West, and regard it with great awe, as did Canadian artist Emily Carr.

I was very moved by a video about Carr's life in British Columbia, shown by friends at a gathering to welcome me. Ultimately she was included by critics as the lone, peripheral female figure alongside Canada's most famous artists, the all-male Group of Seven. Like Carr, I have something deep inside me waiting to come out.

The years are slipping by, and I recognize that I have always focused my energies and time on men or children or community groups. How many years have I been distracted away from my own voice? And now, how to focus? This trip is a new beginning. I want to celebrate Canada; but most of all, I want to celebrate women.

Can I make a "great" contribution? Do I have to be "Small," the nickname Carr gave herself? I am in a unique position to do this. I was born in Canada and educated in the one-room schoolhouses of Southern Ontario and the high schools of Victoria and Vancouver, but I have acquired objectivity by virtue of my years away. Conversely, it is a long way from Virginia (where I live now) to Mud Street School or Granville Street, but my view of the world is rooted in being a girl and a young woman in Canada.

I am a feminist, but not so radical that I cannot hear the voices of women who dislike feminism. I am a sociologist, but first I am a woman who has been on her own journey through marriage and children, divorce and remarriage, and the pains and joys of blending and reblending families.

And I am a writer. This project will require discipline, commitment, and hard work. I must watch and listen and feel with the women before I can paint their portraits with words. I must listen as they speak to me and to each other. I must use their words beside mine, not mine instead of theirs.

I am introduced by a contact to her husband as someone "doing a study of women in Canada." He replies, "Oh, I used to do a lot of that when I was younger." She looks embarrassed but laughs. I ask what he found. He says, "Your book wouldn't be big enough to hold it all." He is a victim of multiple sclerosis; his wife has gone back for teacher certification and now supports the family. She calls it role reversal. He adds, "You should talk to the men, too." I do. Tomorrow I head back East to begin the interviews with women and men of the Six Nations Reserve.

2

Clan Mothers and Sky Walkers

Iroquois Women of the Six Nations, Ohsweken, Ontario

Mohawk women have traditionally been strong, involved in politics and religion in our own way. But now with all the changes around us and the changes within society itself, the younger women are beginning to lose touch. Being out in the work force and trying to maintain certain traditions, it's a hard decision to make.

—Gracie

En route to the Six Nations Reserve

It is a dry, hot afternoon in August 1949. I am eight years old. In the back seat of my father's 1947 Studebaker, I sip ginger ale to keep from getting carsick as we bounce along a "corduroy" dirt road that cuts through the checkerboard Ontario countryside. We are just a few miles from our army camp home outside of Hagersville (population 1,825), but we have never come this way on our Sunday drives. Suddenly, my father's voice drops to a near whisper: "This is the Six Nations Reserve . . . We're going to drive through it." Shivers spread across my back as I think about the "cowboy and Indian" movies I have seen. "This is Tonto's home," my father adds reassuringly, and I realize we will be safe after all. Mohawk Jay Silverheels, who plays the Lone Ranger's brave and loyal companion, is one of my Hollywood heroes.[1]

Another childhood idol, poet E. Pauline Johnson (Tekahionwake), was born here, too. My mother keeps Flint and Feather *on the night stand next to her bed.[2] Arrows and feathers are engraved into the dark wine leather binding, and a Victorian photograph of the beautiful*

11

young Johnson graces the book's preface. My mother has read many of the poems to me, and I have begun to read others myself. At school, I am proud to memorize "The Song My Paddle Sings" ("Dip, dip / While the waters flip / In foam as over their breast we slip") and "Lullaby of the Iroquois" ("Little brown baby-bird, lapped in your nest / Wrapped in your nest / Strapped in your nest").

Forty years later I drive into the reserve in my own car. It is late July, hot and dry. Everywhere the soil has cracked open like the glazing on an old piece of china. A plume of dust follows my car. I stop at a variety store, buy a can of ice-cold pop, and relive that day in 1949. It hits me that my father drove through the reserve to prove that it was safe: to teach me that the people who were not allowed in the bars and restaurants on the "right" side of the track in Hagersville were not monsters or villains. They were ordinary people with ordinary lives; yet, because of their culture, they were somehow different and to be respected for their difference. It was a lesson that stuck in my mind.

This day I drive along every road in the reserve, miles and miles of criss-crossing gravel lanes that intersect in the tiny village of Ohsweken. I pass a library, a modern band administration building, two restaurants, a post office, a huge community center/gym, a branch of Mohawk Community College, a craft shop, and a multitude of houses—including the magnificent mansion, Chiefswood, where Pauline Johnson grew up. Tiny log cabins from the nineteenth century dot the countryside, along with bales of hay and modern ranch or split-level homes. A granite monument in the village center remembers the Iroquois men who died in World War II.

I sit at a table in the Village Inn and sip ginger ale to calm my stomach, overwhelmed with a sense of elation that I have explored the reserve by myself. I dig into a bowl of Indian corn soup and feel welcomed by my old neighbors. Had I not moved to Canada's west coast at the age of thirteen, I would have gone to Hagersville High School in 1955 with the women I will interview. The waitress tells me that she used to play in the badminton tournament in the army camp's drill hall every Christmas. I spent my whole childhood playing badminton there. Now the hangars are used for a flea market; the waitress goes there almost every weekend. This morning I went to see the barracks where I had lived, now just an indentation in the ground blanketed with weeds and crabgrass. Jay Silverheels and E. Pauline Johnson are dead. Flint and Feather *now sits next to my bed, a treasured gift from my mother, every poem an old friend. Soon the book will go to my daughter. The Iroquois would remind me that life, like nature, always comes full circle.*[3]

"In the beginning there was no earth, only a vast ocean, with fish below and sea-birds flying over its surface. Far above, in the Sky-World, lived the gods who were like people—like Iroquois."[3] Among them was a pregnant woman who asked her husband to indulge her strange food cravings. She demanded bark from the roots of the sacred "tree of life" in the center of the universe. The obedient husband began digging into the tree's roots and, to his horror, inadvertently poked a hole in the Sky-World's floor.

Curious to see what lay below, the wife peered into the hole, but slipped through it (or was pushed by her disgusted husband), falling, falling, falling through the sky. She grabbed at strawberry plants and tobacco leaves as she fell. The seabirds, seeing her plight, made a raft with their wings to save her from drowning. The water animals also watched her spin toward the ocean floor and convinced the turtle to let her stand on his back. A beaver, a loon, and a seagull dived to the ocean's depths, searching for earth to heap on the turtle's back, but after many valiant attempts, it was an otter who returned successfully, clutching a bit of dirt. He seemed dead, so the other animals sang and prayed and breathed air into his watery lungs until he revived. The woman planted the soil on the turtle's back, creating a place for plants and roots to flourish. Thus "earth world" was created.

This Iroquois legend speaks at once of the long-standing powers of women and their intimate connection with the bounty of the earth. Today, on the remnant of their sweeping empire that stretched from the Adirondacks to the Genesee River, Iroquois women are still strong, although in different ways. Now it is the men who are "sky walkers" (ironworkers), and few women coax plants or roots from Mother Earth.

Mohawk lawyer Patricia Monture-Okanee reminds us that "First Nations [aboriginal] people are not homogeneous . . . we are distinct nations with distinct experiences. We have separate ways."[4]

Still, women of the Six Nations—the Mohawk, Cayuga, Onondaga, Oneida, Seneca, and Tuscarora Indians—share centuries of history as part of the traditional League of the Iroquois, founded in the middle of the fifteenth century by Hiawatha, the great Onondaga architect of a complicated social and political confederation of several tribes. Designed to end a long history of feuds and wars,[5] the League was anchored in a "carefully designed constitution embodying the principles of health, peace, justice, righteousness, order, and force (or power)."[6] Their ancestors can be traced to at least 500 B.C. and possibly earlier; the distinctive Iroquois culture—with its wooden longhouses that held several families each—had developed by A.D. 1000. The great longhouses, which were managed by the women, protected families through long winters and hot summers.

The Mohawks, called "the people of the flint" and "keepers of the eastern door," were, with the Onondagas, the most famous and powerful of the Iroquois; the Seneca were "keepers of the western door." By the sixteenth century the League's 50 clan-based chiefs (or *royaners*[7]) and their families lived in well-developed Iroquois towns scattered around the Genesee River and Finger Lakes region in the western part of what later became New York, and as far east as the Hudson River. In 1722, in order to reduce factional conflict and to create a larger, more cohesive group, the Five Nations became the Six Nations with the addition of the Tuscarora.[8]

Women of the Six Nations Reserve[9] experience incongruous positions in gender and ethnic stratification. As Iroquois women, they continue to enjoy high status and respect; as Indian women within the North American context of white domination, they suffer from low status and lack of respect. This dissonance frustrates and surprises some Iroquois women, and it makes them even more determined to assert their position as leaders among their people. It is difficult for contemporary Iroquois women, who are used to being accorded high regard within their own community, to go outside the reserve where they experience the double oppressions of race and gender common in mainstream society. A woman who lives on the reserve and works in an urban office dominated by white males articulates this incongruity:

> I think differently. Being a Cayuga woman is a frame of mind. You
> know what you set out to accomplish and how to accomplish it. It is all

up to the individual. I am a very stubborn person, and I may not fall in line with what is expected of me. I find it very difficult, especially in business—and let's face it, it is mostly males that you are talking to—and they don't hold the same amount of respect for you as they would another male. It is not just the fact that I am an Indian. It's because I am female, too.

Out of Tradition

TRADITIONAL ROLES: "BACKBONE OF THE SOCIETY"

"Traditionally, the man was supposed to shelter the woman; as the stronger person, he did the hunting and fighting," a cultural worker says. "Yet, if you look at natural ways of life, for instance birds, the raising of the young birds is with both male and female. They both go out and bring food to the young. They both build nests. In native society we learned from the animals."

Prior to reserve life, women were in a "constant round of caring for the children, cooking, minding the houses—and moving them when the time came—gathering shellfish, tanning skins."[10] They gathered berries, nuts, and firewood. At festivals and ceremonies, men sang and danced; women danced gentle, shuffling steps that urged Mother Earth to yield generous harvests of "our life supporters," the "three sisters" of corn, beans, and squash.[11] These dances persist today in a rich panoply of seasonal festivals. Men crafted longhouses and canoes from bark and wood. The man's primary role took him away from his family for long periods of hunting, fighting, or "dealing with the public" in treaty negotiations. He returned with small game like rabbits, squirrels, fowl, birds, and fish. Occasionally, the hunt produced deer for food and skins.

Expert horticulturists, the women maintained gardens and later played a large role in farming. Women hoed, planted, tended, and harvested communal fields in a cooperative manner under the supervision of a "chief matron" who was wise and experienced in agriculture.[12] Men who traveled great distances with warring parties avoided hunting in order to shield their location; they depended entirely upon the dried food women prepared for the journey.

Prior to contact with Europeans, Iroquois women were expert potters, using the vessels for cooking and storing dried food in *graniers*, or underground pits. They also achieved fame for their beautiful, intricate embroidery, first with porcupine quills and later with glass beads. Although weaving was not well developed among the Iroquois, women made bags from elm bark and sandals, moccasins, dolls, table mats, and small baskets from corn husks.[13]

Women looked after the fields while the men were away. Women and older people were responsible for protecting the village against intruders. More fundamentally, women took charge of child rearing and discipline, and they passed on core values and beliefs from one generation to the next—a solemn responsibility that contributed to the community's very survival. Iroquois women maintained the household and "had all the say," an Onondaga elder, Sadie, recalls:

"Woman has got to keep everything . . ."
The men had it relatively easy—all they had to do was hunt and protect the camp. In a way, today that's what it's like, but instead of hunting, men are out working. My great-grandmother was a gentle old lady, a powerful old lady. She told me to remember what she taught me about the woman's part—marry, have children, and look after my family well. She said, "When I am gone who is going to tell you? You don't got nobody else to tell what is right and wrong." So I put that in my head. I learned the hard way from my great-grandmother. I kept that in here [pointing to her heart]. I'll keep that because she always said, "You remember those things."

Woman has got to keep everything. She has got to keep dinner, washing, scrubbing, washing clothes, and all that stuff. Keep the house clean. Those days we didn't have no running water. Draw your water, warm it before you wash clothes—my husband used to get water and wood. It took a long time to do anything, but I managed. Maybe that is why I am still healthy and I am not on medication yet. I worked hard in my life. I scrubbed the kids' clothes for school, I made lunch; they come back from school, I had supper on. That was a lot of work, caring for ten of them. I always says, "Well, that's what you are here for—I don't care how many kids you got, you got to look after them."

When we had Longhouse [the traditional religion], not just on the weekends but anytime when they let us know when they are going to have green corn dance or vegetable dance or midwinter and social dances and all that, we get ready and go. I live in seniors' housing now, so my life is easier. I made my funeral clothes—see, I keep them in this suitcase under the bed. I sewed them and embroidered them. But I still enjoy all I have been doing.

TRADITIONAL POWERS: "MY HEART IS NOT ON THE GROUND"

Of the cultures in this book, the Iroquois had the most clearly woman-centered traditional system, one of the few in the world that closely approximates a *matriarchate* (a society ruled by women). Women's power to select and depose male chiefs balanced male authority. Traditional society was matriarchal-like (although Iroquois women did not hold political office, they held key decision-making powers), matrilineal (lineage and clan membership passed through the woman to her children), and matrilocal (newly married couples usually established households in the wife's community). In fact, according to some reports from the nineteenth century, an Iroquois woman "had a freer, more influential place in the world she lived in than her European counterpart did in hers."[14] As we shall see later, Iroquois women's central role and their historical power continue to influence contemporary male-female relationships.

The extent of Iroquois women's traditional power has been the subject of considerable scholarly debate since the nineteenth century, when early reports described far-reaching female authority and others supplied contradictory evidence. Cara Richards reviewed historical documents in key decision-making areas: the fate of captives; choice of mate and form of marriage; and custody of children after separation. She concludes that not only did Iroquois women have substantial power in these areas, but their power *increased* over time (and male power decreased). This in part explains some of the controversy; observers writing in different eras recorded an evolving situation.[15] Although Richards argues that this pattern refutes earlier claims that the Iroquois were an aboriginal matriarchate (that is, from the very beginning of their tribe), the roots of female power in this culture reach back into prehistory and many authorities reaffirm the matriarchate hypothesis.[16]

Reminding us of a Hopi prophecy—"A Nation is not conquered / Until the hearts / of its women / are on the ground"[17]—Monture-Okanee writes that "the woman is central in the First Nations philosophy, because we are the ones who bring forth life. That is why we are respected. . . . My heart is not on the ground."[18]

Because theirs was a matrilineal and matrilocal society, Iroquois women named and raised the children. Women owned the houses, belongings, and fields; men owned only their weapons and personal belongings. Women exerted great influence behind the scenes, even deciding whether captives would be adopted, tortured, or killed.[19] Essentially, the clan mothers both symbolized and enforced the core values of group sharing and cooperation in order to ensure group survival as opposed to individual prosperity. (Like the Inuit, Iroquois are expected to take no more than they need and to share freely.) Older women served as marriage brokers; their advice was sought in the event that a couple faced marital problems; and their permission was required for divorce. Upon divorce, a woman possessed sole rights to the house and children: Her husband left in shame with the clothes on his back and his weapons.

In relating the *Rites of Condolence* upon the death of a chief, Horatio Hale in 1883 devotes several paragraphs to confirming women's authority:

> The common notion that women among the Indians were treated as inferiors, and made "beasts of burden," is unfounded so far as the Iroquois are concerned. . . . The work of the community and the cares of the family are fairly divided. . . . The household goods belonged to the woman. On her death, her relatives, and not her husband, claimed them. The children were also hers; they belonged to her clan, and in case of a separation they went with her. She was really the head of the household; and in this capacity her right, when she chanced to be the oldest matron of a noble family, to select the successor of a deceased chief of that family, was recognized by the highest law of the confederacy. . . .
>
> Casual observers have been misled by the absence of those artificial expressions of courtesy which have descended to us from the times of chivalry, and which, however gracious and pleasing in witness, are, after all, merely signs of condescension and protection from the strong to the weak. The Iroquois does not give up his seat to a woman, or yield her precedence on leaving a room; but he secures her in the possession of her property, he recognizes her right to the children she has borne, and he submits to her decision the choice of his future rulers.[20]

Hale contends that complete equality of the sexes in social estimation and influence flowed through narratives of the early missionaries who recorded native reports and confederation rules.

Judith Brown also argues that Iroquois women's traditional powers were strong and that they derived from female control of agricultural production. Essentially, women owned the land (that is, people related through the female ties to collectively held land), the implements, and the seed; therefore they also owned the bountiful harvests of a highly organized and efficient system. "Iroquois women maintained the right to distribute and to dispense all food, even that procured by the men. This was especially significant as stored food constituted one of the major forms of wealth for the tribe. . . . Iroquois matrons [clan mothers] were able to make available or to withhold food for meetings of the Council and for war parties, for the observance of religious festivals, and for the daily meals of the household."[21]

Economic powers led to and reinforced women's political powers, the right of clan mothers to select the chiefs and council members, to decide the fate of captives, to support or deflect war, and to influence treaties. The base of their power was the clan system. Each nation was divided into clans named after animals—bear, turtle, eel, deer, wolf, hawk, eagle, and so forth:[22]

> The whole thing we set up to keep track of family lines and avoid intermarriage. A person of the turtle clan couldn't marry another person of the turtle clan. It doesn't matter whether this turtle clan is Iroquois or Sioux or another tribe, because you would be marrying your brother or your sister—they are still turtles. Women are the clan carriers. My mother was bear and my father was turtle, so we are bear because we follow Mother's side of the clan.

The eldest woman of each clan served as its head, or clan mother. These women chose the fifty chiefs, who were supposed to lead rather than command, as Hale reports:

> The first members of the council [in the mid-fifteenth century] were appointed by the convention . . . but their successors came in by a method in which the hereditary and the elective systems were singularly combined, and in which female suffrage had an important place. When a chief died or . . . was deposed for incapacity or misconduct, some member of the same family succeeded him. Rank followed the female line; and this successor might be any descendant of the late chief's mother or grandmother—his brother, his cousin or his nephew—but never his son. . . . In [a] family council the "chief matron" of the fami-

ly, a noble dame whose position and right were well defined, had the deciding voice.[23]

Chiefs essentially served at the pleasure of the clan mothers, who could depose them if they did not look after the best interests of the community as a whole.[24] If the women did not like the way a man conducted himself, they could "remove his horns"—the symbol of his leadership—by asking him to step down; as a matter of respect, he was expected to do so. If he refused to step down, the other chiefs would ask him to give up his power. If he still refused, he could be killed or driven out of the band in order to preserve cohesion. Says a teacher: "They have never gone past the clan mothers asking the chief to step down, but those provisions are there in case." Words like *respect* and *dignity* pepper this discussion.

Not surprisingly, many contemporary Iroquois women mention their mother as the most important person in their lives. As one of them, Sunny, says, "I am not sure why really. I just know she is the most important one. I would do anything for my mother. I don't know whether it is something that I have been taught or what. It is just a feeling that I have."

The Turning Point: The American Revolution

As a Mohawk teacher puts it, "Your American Revolution could probably be looked at as a civil war for the natives, because families split right down the middle—half fought for the Americans and half fought for the British."[25] As early as the 1600s, the Iroquois had become deeply involved in the emerging North American fur trade and had developed a reputation as respected warriors throughout the Great Lakes and St. Lawrence River regions. The French in Lower Canada (now Quebec), also major players in the fur trade, had built alliances with many tribes that were old enemies of the Iroquois. The Iroquois Wars of the mid-seventeenth century (complicated by the rivalries between the French and the English, with whom the Iroquois traded at Albany, New York) included several attacks and counterattacks between the French and the Iroquois. On the heels of war and disease, the Iroquois negotiated treaties with both the French and the English in 1701 in an effort to establish neutrality within the context of increasing European settlement and economic activity.[26]

During the American War of Independence, however, many Iroquois supported the Loyalists, fighting on the side of the English from 1777 to 1779: "The Mohawk lost their homes to neighbouring rebel settlers, and most Seneca, Onondaga and Cayuga towns were burned in 1779. In turn the Iroquois and their allies, under the leadership of Joseph Brant and others, repeatedly attacked and burned rebel forts and settlements, driving the frontier East to Schenectady, New York."[27] After the American Revolution, the League of the Iroquois fell apart; those who fought on the British side eventually were rewarded for their loyalty with several thousand acres of prime land along the pastoral Grand River in Southern Ontario. The Six Nations Reserve lies near what is today the bustling market town of Brantford, named after the famed Iroquois Joseph Brant, who led them in battle against the Americans and then to the Grand River site; his sister, Mary Brant, was also influential in leading the Mohawks to support the British. The reserve was officially constituted in 1847 with about two thousand Iroquois. Today, with its heart at the tiny village of Ohsweken, the reserve is home to about seven thousand Iroquois of thirteen nations (or subnations).

In the early reserve period, contact with British culture resulted in transfusions of patriarchal ways into the Six Nations culture. Male and female roles began to change with the move toward an administrative chief and inheritance traced through the male side. The society, which had been based on hunting and gathering as well as horticulture, moved toward agriculture. Like the Bloods, the Six Nations were taught farming and expected to relate well to this transformation of their economic base, a Mohawk historian explains: "When we came to Canada, the roles changed slightly. For instance, you would never have found a man helping a woman pulling corn. Then once they came up into this area, after the European contact, there were many men in agriculture. Roles would have changed slightly as far as warring goes, too. There was more peace at that time."

Another major change occurred in 1924 when Canada abolished the jurisdiction of the hereditary council and authorized the election of a council by male suffrage only—a total abnegation of the traditional female power in Iroquois society. This created a shadow government, however, since the hereditary chiefs continued to meet—at first clandestinely, then openly. Today the traditional hereditary political system of clan mothers coexists with an electoral system in which reserve members elect an administrative chief. Similarly, two streams of spirituality flow through Iroquois life—the traditional Longhouse religion and more than a dozen denominations of Christianity. With these changes, Iroquois culture reeled from contact with whites, as depicted in *"The Corn Husker,"* a poem by E. Pauline Johnson about her foremothers:

> Hard by the Indian lodges, where the bush
>   Breaks in a clearing, through ill-fashioned fields,
> She comes to labour, when the first still hush
>   Of autumn follows large and recent yields.
>
> Age in her fingers, hunger in her face,
>   Her shoulders stooped with weight of works and years,
> But rich in tawny colouring of her race,
>   She comes a-field to strip the purple ears.
>
> And all her thoughts are with the days gone by,
>   Ere might's injustice banished from their lands
> Her people, that to-day unheeded lie,
>   Like the dead husks that rustle through her hands.[28]

Although the Iroquois fared well in agriculture early in this century, distributing their wheat and other crops through Brantford's market, eventually farming fell to the vagaries of the Great Depression, as happened also to Blood farmers. As urbanization spread throughout North America, the warriors of early times turned their skills toward ironworking. The women still garden and can food, but look primarily to off-reserve employment to support themselves and their families.

Into the Twentieth Century

CONTEMPORARY ROLES: "ANCHOR OF THE FAMILY"

Patricia Monture-Okanee captures the traditional women's role when she talks about her duties as a contemporary Mohawk woman: "As a Hadenosaunee woman, I also have the responsibility to teach my son, and the men, and my nieces, and my nephews, and my sisters, and all the little ones here on Turtle Island" (North America).[29] This remains the Iroquois woman's key role: keeper of the culture, the faith, and the home. But the outside world has changed around her, as has life on the reserve.

Today no more than a handful of farms remain, engaging perhaps 3 percent of the reserve's population in raising cattle, wheat, soybeans, or hogs. Most Six Nations men go off reserve to work in a variety of construction-related jobs. The most prestigious iron-workers—"sky walkers" or "high-riggers"—have developed a fine reputation in construction all over North America. Women work on or off the reserve in clerical and social service positions. Unemployment is much lower here than on the isolated Blood reserve in southern Alberta. Ohsweken is only a few minutes from Brantford; twenty minutes from Hamilton, a major steelworking city; and an hour from Toronto, Ontario's capital with over a million residents and diverse industries. Although men have been the primary wage earners, over the years Six Nations women have picked cherries and tobacco in order to earn extra money for their children's school clothes, and many women now work outside the home in clerical, semiprofessional, and professional positions (either part- or full-time).

Traditional images of the "good woman" and the "good man" continue to shape the lives of the Iroquois. The good woman is the anchor of her family, the keeper of the faith and the culture. And she is strong. In addition to being a good wife, mother, and home-maker, she must be honest, refrain from gossiping, and be a responsible, mature person who is loving but also willing to take charge. Because of the drinking problems that have plagued the community, "It would be frowned upon to consume alcohol beverages." A good Iroquois woman, true to traditional values, would feel responsibility toward all of the people, not just for her own family: "You are supposed to think about others before you think about yourself. If someone needs something, then you offer your services or food, whatever. You open your homes to them. We look for that kind of person."

Descriptions of women's contemporary role are surprisingly consistent with recollections and reports of their traditional role. The Longhouse religion taught that a woman's role was to marry and have children—a pressure that persists today, as a single woman points out: "You know I should be married and have all my kids. Otherwise, that is something that is frowned upon." Says another, "All I know is you are supposed to get married and have babies. You are supposed to be more family oriented than anything because a woman is the center of a family." Phoebe, a tourism director in her thirties, puts it this way:

> A woman is the backbone of society. There is a certain role that she is expected to play. Women are the faith keepers, and as far as political goals, the clan mothers would be still be the ones who keep the chiefs in line. The woman is not only supposed to be responsible for carrying on a family line, but she has to raise the children. She has her household chores—the cooking, the sewing, basically the same things we used to do a long time ago. Many women would carry on most of the stuff because it was handed down to them.

As with Inuit women, whose role traditionally centered on preparation of skins and making clothing to protect their families, Iroquois women held responsibility for sewing. Also like Inuit women, today many Iroquois women reject traditional mandates, as Phoebe explains: "I hate sewing. I would do mending, but give me a pattern and I can mess it up. A long time ago, a few years ago, the woman wouldn't have had any choice if she wanted to keep her children properly clothed. She would have to go out and buy the material and make the clothing."

The good man is responsible toward his family, bringing home money to help support the children. Unfortunately, that is not always the case for some families, which creates bitterness among women. Sunny describes the ideal man as "basically the same thing as a woman, except with different responsibilities. The woman would be the disciplinarian in a family, whereas the man wouldn't, but the qualities would be the same." Leigh notes that traditionally, men would not have been so active in the domestic sphere:

> Now it's more open—the man will help his wife. Our men cook, clean, do the laundry, anything—step in if needed. If I have the day off and my husband is at work, I will take major responsibility, but the reverse is also true. We chip in with the household chores, everything. I enjoy cooking supper and making my husband's life comfortable; he also

does the same for me. . . . He's not above cooking a meal himself—he's a good cook, he does all the canning. He has no qualms about helping me with dishes every night, and I do the same for him. Sometimes I cut the grass, I go out and do his chores, because he has a lot of meetings at night. My fathers and brothers never touched a dishcloth. Forget it! They wouldn't look at a dish. In my husband's family, the men had to do dishes, too. He hates doing dishes, but he does them.

Although some men were allowed to avoid household chores in childhood, now most seem willing to pitch in even if they dislike it, Leigh adds. Some men change diapers, even "messy ones." Lianne remembers when her husband had to change their baby: "She messed her diaper and he had a tea towel tied around his nose! It was the first time he had done it, and he didn't even know how to put the disposable diaper on her. He didn't know that you pull out these tabs, and his brother had to help him do it. He couldn't stand the smell; he was almost getting sick!"

Although helping with domestic chores may be more acceptable for men here, some women feel angry at the lack of sharing in relationships, as Tonya explains:

> It makes me angry that there seems to be a more overwhelming responsibility on the woman. I work all day, I go home, fix supper, wash the baby. I don't sit down until eight o'clock. There are people who will just let it go, but I like to keep up. Probably I'll just keep the anger inside—or I'll say something, but it always comes out wrong, because it's anger at that point; it's not constructive. It's just really frustrating. I really enjoy working here; I wouldn't want to work anywhere else. I enjoy my family—so what do you do?

In spite of the necessity and reality of wage-earning work, however, the contemporary Iroquois woman shares with her ancestors of centuries gone by an abiding sense of duty in being a "keeper of the faith." A Cayuga woman, Gracie, age thirty-three, gives us a glimpse into this key role as she describes the ancient responsibilities that may be an onerous challenge in today's world:

> *"I'm supposed to become a Keeper of the Faith . . ."*
> Being Cayuga and female means a lot of responsibility. The women in our society are the faith keepers. We have knowledge of the religion and political beliefs that are passed down from generation to genera-

tion by certain families. My mother participates in ceremonies and cooks for them. I will be expected to do the same.

There are four major ceremonies in each of the seasons and minor ceremonies throughout the year, but the commitment is not just for when you are attending ceremonies, it is also in your personal life. You have to uphold this within your community, so you can't act out of role. You have to conduct yourself that way at all times. I don't know whether I am ready for it or not, because I would have to take time off from my job to do this. Materialistic wealth is secondary to the religion. It is a difficult decision for me to make, but I am more like a traditionalist rather than orthodox. You try to maintain the traditions while leading a modern lifestyle.

Deciding to be a faith keeper means a commitment that will be with me for the rest of my life. My mother is getting too old to carry it on, so I will take it over when I am ready. I am going through the learning process right now that usually goes to the oldest daughter. I am not the oldest, but I am more inclined to follow the traditional teachings than my sisters. I will probably take my mother's position within the Longhouse.

If I make the commitment, I will be in a learning process until the other women feel that I have learned enough, that I am behaving correctly. I will have to earn their respect. If they tell me to do something, I will have to do it and not ask why, just do it. It is taken for granted that I will take over my mother's position. They all pitch in with teaching me, even the men. It is not something that just your mother teaches you. It is the whole religion that teaches you.

BECOMING A WOMAN, BECOMING A MAN

Male or female, growing up on the Six Nations Reserve reminds you above all that you are a native person. As Gracie explains, "They tell you that if you're born an Indian it doesn't matter which way you go, which path you follow. You are still an Indian and that is that. There is always that Indian-ness there." For those who follow the Longhouse religion, emphasis is placed on raising daughters to be leaders and decision makers. For others, more stress is placed on treating males and females equally. Lianne is raising her daughter, now twelve, to become a strong woman: "My daughter is more dominant than the boys. She can tell them and they listen to her. One of the boys is quite a bit older, but she still has that influence. . . . My husband says she is just like me." Leigh fights her traditional woman-as-responsible upbringing:

> In my family, your wifely duty was to make sure you had supper on the table. If you were tired, well that was just too bad. I think I've still got that in me, but I'm fighting it. I'm consciously aware of how my ma was brought up, so I don't want to be that way because I don't think it's right. If you're tired, you're tired. Who can fault you? If you're looking after your kids all day or if you put in a hard day's work, you're human, take a rest. With my mother, she's boss, but she believed that if your man worked all day, no matter what kind of day you had, his supper was always on the table waiting for him, ready to eat.

Molly's mother did seasonal tobacco work: "It's hard, dirty, sweaty work, so I can't see where my dad's was any more physical than hers, but she would still have the meal on the table for him when he got home." She also resists the mandate to care for her husband no matter what, although she was raised this way. She is concerned about men who abuse both alcohol and women on the reserve, and she tries to raise her sons to respect women, take responsibility around the house, and avoid alcohol and hitting women: "I don't think I can keep it from him; I teach him that there's something other than this kind of life style. All I can do is encourage him, because I wouldn't want to see him like that either."

As time slips by, the ancient molds of male and female behavior are cracking. Children who are raised by television, public schools, and movies slip away from traditional authority. The Iroquois were a very family-oriented and loving people whose values have changed through the impact of non-native society, Lianne theorizes: "Hollywood has done a great deal to disrupt the harmony within native society. Indians were always portrayed as drunk or as people who didn't say too many words. You always see the male abuse the woman. You always see the woman as fat and dumb, lazy. The male as unintelligent, vicious." Such images haunt those who believe that assimilation might bring greater rewards and less pain than preservation of their own culture. Elders remember being whipped for speaking their own language in school:

I wasn't really encouraged to learn my own culture or language, even though my mother can speak fluent Cayuga. You don't want to do that because when you go off reserve, you are going to face a lot of prejudice, so you are better off to become more non-native than Indian. That is the general feeling of the community. You were better off not to be Indian, and it had an effect on the people themselves.

In traditional times women taught children the old ways. Now that they work outside the home, an elder, Eliza, worries about who will teach children the culture:

We're losing the languages. I used to speak five different [Iroquoian] languages when I was small. I spoke Mohawk all the time. . . . When my family grew up, they all got married and went on their own. They come back on the weekends for two or three hours just to make sure that we are okay. It isn't close like in the old days. Maybe we will just lose our own religion in time. I think that is just what is going to happen. These old folks told us way back that it would gradually go down. It is happening. It is happening! My own daughters, too. They can't say I never told them. Who is going to tell them what is right and wrong when I am gone? They are going to feel it. Now they are teaching these little ones how to speak their own language. It's the mother's fault because they don't make them.

An Onondaga elder, Eva, who is seventy-nine, laments the loss of discipline she sees among today's children:

"I Listened to My Grandmother . . ."
My grandmother raised me. She always said before we went to Longhouse, "This is what you've got to put on," so I have Indian clothes. She made pan bread to take in a basket, so I know how to make this bread. She'd say, "I want you to go to wash before we go," so that is what I had to do. "When we go in I want you to stay inside. I mean what I said. You stay in there until it is over." Then we are free. I couldn't come out because men are standing up, talking and preaching. I couldn't talk to any people that were sitting next to me. People like for me to behave, so I had to do that.

Now I see kids at Longhouse, they gab, they don't even listen to what the men are talking about. They don't have too much respect, because the mothers don't tell them like they should. When I raised my twelve, I teach them respect for Longhouse. My grandma always tells me, "You tell them kids to sit down and behave. No running in and out of that door. You make them go to the washroom before they come in and sit till its over." So that is what I done. You ask my daughter, she will tell you that is how I brought them up, every one of them. They say, "Ma, how come we have to sit like that?" "Well," I says, "that's the way I was brought up. I respect my grandmother, and I expect you to do the same thing." These kids are in there banging the doors, running around. They don't care.

Children learn by watching their parents and other family members. The mother has a more clearly defined and intensive role in raising both boys and girls until they reach puberty, at which time the father is expected to take more interest in raising his sons. Some fathers still teach their sons how to hunt, fish, and trap in the traditional manner, or they might play football with them or teach them to drive. Mothers teach their daughters domestic skills and, in some families, crafts.

Mothers of the younger generation, who were taught very little (if anything) about sex, are trying to educate their daughters more openly. When Nola talked with her daughter for the first time about sex, she explained that a good sexual relationship takes time: "You can have a million one-night stands, but to have a good sexual relationship you need to get to know your partner, you need to trust your partner, you have to be able to be free and open. I always got the feeling that my mother thought sex was dirty." Her own mother never discussed sex with her; Nola learned from her sisters or friends at school. She talks frankly with her eight-year-old daughter, but at the child's level: "She told me where a baby came from. She already knew about it. I didn't tell her."

CONTEMPORARY POWERS: "BOSSY WOMEN"

"Women are still the mainstay and center of the household," reminds an elder woman: They have a lot of input. Much of the final say comes from the woman."[30] "Around here," says Molly, forty-two years old and a homemaker, "most of the women are in control of everything—the household, the kids, the shopping, the decision making, the finances, work, everything. And the man just works." She believes that "Indian women, not just Six Nations, are more independent than non-natives. More aggressive." Throughout history, Iroquois women have enjoyed a "very prominent place," she adds. Beyond the home, they often had the final say in whether to pursue war or peace and other significant public matters: "It was deemed to be their right and duty, when in their opinion the strife had lasted long enough, to interfere and bring about a reconciliation."[31] This carries over into modern times as "very aggressive and independent" women. When Molly thinks of who is boss in her family, her mother instantly comes to mind:

> I have a little old lady for a mother and she is absolute, positive boss over all her sons and grandsons. As big as they are, her word is law, more so than grandfather's. He has respect, but she rules. There's a big difference. You'll find that in most families. My word is law in my home . . . it's expected to be that way. It's not just me saying that. My kids have grown up seeing that's the way you treat your mother. I always say I'm pulling rank on them and that's that. Most of the families I know, it's the mother that gets that respect.

This high level of authority, as mentioned earlier, stems in part from the extended absence of males from the household historically. Today, as men work in construction, the same situation often occurs. Joanne's father worked in the United States all her life, and the only time she saw him was on weekends: "My mother had complete control over the family while he was gone. There was always the little bit of argument if we wanted to do something—'Come on mom, come on mom.' We'd bug her until she'd give in." When Joanne's father returned on weekends, he would reinforce his wife's discipline. Nonetheless, Joanne's mother ran the household and made most major decisions. Now Joanne has major control in her marriage, especially over her daughter: "My husband has *no* control over our three-year-old. He tries hard, but she's got him wrapped right around her finger. He'll reinforce what I say if she's doing something. He'll say, 'Your mom said. . . .' But if it comes down to the actual disciplining, I do it . . . and she knows it." Joanne is pleased that her husband and daughter have a caring relationship. Leigh and her siblings similarly were raised and disciplined by her mother:

> *"Still don't question it!"*
> Our dad left so early . . . but when he was around, it was the same way. He would reinforce the discipline. Whatever she said went, and you

just didn't question it. That was the ultimate. If it went too far he would step in; we knew he loved us, but there was no close-knit loving relationship with him. How much of a relationship can you develop on a weekend? Very little, so our relationship with him was kind of distant. We were all very close to our mother, and she was and still is the boss. She's the authority and don't you question it, because she knows best or supposedly knows best. Still don't question it!

My mother raised me to look after myself and to be the boss of the family. She said, "There's no questions about that, and don't you dare let no man tell you what to do." So you have some pretty bossy women in my family. Out of seven sisters, five are bossy women. I say "bossy" because we *are* bossy. You know, it sounds harsh, but that's just the way we are. Our men are almost followers. My situation is kind of different because my man is stronger. Whatever I say doesn't necessarily go, but I still feel like I'm in control—I wish my husband could hear this!

Similarly, Phoebe admits that she has found herself in trouble because she is a very outspoken person: "If I believe in something strongly enough, I will fight for it. It doesn't matter whether I am arguing against men, women, or their position. If I feel that I am right, I will fight for it. That behavior is looked upon as my being just a troublemaker or plain old stubborn."

"In my family I don't think it has been like that," Faye, a woman in her fifties, says. Her father worked in Hamilton and was home by five o'clock every night. She and her sisters felt the influence of both her father and her brothers. Carla, forty-four, also saw a different marriage. Her mother adored her father; if they fought, the children never saw it ("the perfect marriage"). On weekends, her father was the king returning triumphant: "I saw mother do everything for him, so I've always been ready to please a man. I spoiled my husband so bad, I became a rug! Now I'm coming out of the rug bit—where I made every excuse for him, you know, because he was a man. I've had to learn how to stand up for myself." At the same time, Faye recognizes that both she and her mother always found ways to get around their men: "The end result was always what we wanted anyway, but you have to sort of work around him and make it so it's his idea."

Are there ways in which men are superior to women? "Physically—we'll give them that! That's the only way!" Yet women respect men for their well-developed strength and their ability to do high-risk, high-rise construction work. As Sonya says,

> I put in a forty-hour week and my man puts in a forty-hour week, but I know darn well his is hard physical work, and mine is mental. So when we get home at night, even though I'm mentally tired or bored, I prepare the meal without thinking about it. I wouldn't ask him to do it because he's too tired. If he had a different job, it might change, but I have sympathy for how hard he works. When it comes to dishes, sometimes he helps me. If he didn't work, I'd insist that he get up here and help me.

Nola, a professional woman in her late thirties, agrees: "I'm also a go-getter, and I expect my husband to be just as hard a worker. I think it's just the fact that women have more say; we have more input into all concerns of the family."

Women's traditionally broad powers have narrowed somewhat to the domestic sphere, although many women work outside the home now. Iroquois women protect their power and want to buttress their self-esteem, self-confidence, and self-respect. Says a child care worker:

> I think men like challenge in a woman. They don't like them to be a doormat, they don't like them to say "yes sir, no sir." If he doesn't find challenge at home, he'll find it somewhere else. Women have to become more outspoken, more readily able to look after themselves, and more knowledgeable. They should be able to sit down and carry on an intelligent conversation. Men like and respect that in their wife.

The only way in which women are inferior is that often they make less money than men. While that does not appreciably change women's decision-making prerogative, it sits uncomfortably for those who see themselves as "women's libbers."

Women who work outside the home usually control their own income and perhaps also the family checkbook. In fact, this is the only group in which, when asked who controls the checkbook, several women laughed and said, "We do—who else would?" In the average home on the Six Nations Reserve, decision making might be shared or by consensus, but, as one woman puts it, "Let's face it; the woman would have more influence." Does this bother the men?

"Right now I don't think it bothers them, because it is a way of life. It's in them." Male-female power relations may change some day in reaction to the dominant male image portrayed by the media.

Even in families in which men hold sway, the tasks of running the house, handling the money, and disciplining the children rest mainly with the woman. Decisions about the children's health and education would be made by the woman after consulting with her male partner: "They would talk about it, but everything is more or less left up to mom." What kind of decisions would the male make, then? "Probably not that many within the house itself." Men do make the final decisions regarding the purchase of automobiles. Gardening is usually shared work: "Mom would look after her part. We always had a garden, and everybody worked on that, but farm animals were Dad's responsibility."

There can be an underside to female authority in the domestic sphere. Because she is "in charge," the woman may also end up being a slave to her man. For example, Ellen believes that men think of themselves as king of the household: "But they don't do anything. The king just sits there. You look after the kids, you cook the meals, you wash the floors, you maintain the household, but he's the king." Furthermore, in the public sphere men still hold superior influence and power, both economically and politically, "mostly because they are the wage-earners." When men provide for women and children, "everyone depends on them, because they have the money. It's that dependency that gives them power to run the whole show."

For younger women in their twenties and thirties, the pressure (as in other cultures) is toward egalitarianism. Many women are striving for equality in their domestic relationships with men— which, for Iroquois women, ironically means "giving" men more power. These women see balanced power relations as being more positive than either female dominance or male dominance. As Ellen says, when children are small, the mother takes more responsibility and has more authority: "I suppose as my son gets older it's going to become more of a shared thing, too. He'll look to both of us, hopefully, but right now he's attached to me because he's so little; he's pretty well in my hands." Leigh believes that female dominance worked in the past, given the traditions, but it has not been

easy for her to take real power, although her husband acts as
though he thinks she is boss. Now, the non-native influence serves
as the catalyst for shifting power relationships:

"Men get some crazy ideas lately!"
Things are changing and for the better, because with women's lib I
think equality is really important. I sort of backed down from my
stance as the boss, because it has to be a two-way street. If you want to
take control, there's going to be problems. You're going to have a man
who is not happy because he wants to be told what to do all the time.
I've changed since I married; I found out that you compromise and you
have to equal out your relationship to make things work, so we do a lot
of compromising. We do a lot of sharing. I like it that way, he likes it
that way, and we're both happy.

It's more of a partnership rather than a monarchy where one is
"queen bee." The men hear that the white man's the king of the house,
and they're wondering why they're not! You know, they get some crazy
ideas lately! It's more equalizing, society is changing, but I still believe
that Indian women are way ahead on the women's lib part of things.
Along with me changing, he's changing, so we're both changing in the
right direction and it's good for both of us. After fifteen years of marriage, I've become more assertive and independent—sure, because I've
seen liberated women on TV, but also because my girlfriends nag me:
It's our tradition, right?

I had to change for my own survival. I don't know whether I wanted
it or not, but I was forced into it. Now I'd never go back to being nobody's doormat. He likes the more independent woman—I'm not a
soppy little kid hanging all over him, depending on him to breathe. He
couldn't stand that . . . The responsibility was too much for him.

Sherri, age seventeen, wants to be "a career woman" and to
share power with her husband. She also expects to run the household and to make domestic decisions, and that her husband would
help clean and do housework. Tammy, who is sixteen, wants to
marry a man who will be able to make decisions ("I don't think I'd
want to do it all"). Her parents share decision making: "My mother's white, so she's not had the same traditions." Even though their
ancestors were powerful women, teenage girls believe that males
have more power because "they are tougher." They pick fights and
bully the girls; they see it as their prerogative to sleep with any girl

they choose; and they engage in physical abuse: "The boys push the girls around quite a bit. Most of the Indian girls grow up tough, too, so they can push right back."

Love, Marriage, and Divorce: The Legacy of the Indian Act

The Indian Act of 1876 left a legacy that plagues Iroquois (and other Canadian Indian) women more than a hundred years later. First, it attempted to determine a native woman's identity within her tribe: When a Six Nations woman married a man from another nation, she was expected to change to his nation (for example, a Mohawk woman would have to change to Cayuga). Second, the act declared that an Indian woman who marries a non-native man must forfeit her Indian status—she is known then as a "nonstatus Indian."[32] These patriarchal artifacts produced by contact with Euro-Canadian society have greatly complicated love and marriage for Iroquois women: "The Indian Act changed us from a matriarchal to a patriarchal society."

For almost a century Six Nations women were forced to become a member of their husband's nation, controverting the traditional practice of tracing lineage through the woman's side. Now, many contemporary women heartily resist the old rules. For example, when Leigh, a Lower Mohawk, married a Barefoot Onondaga man, she did not change her tribal identity: "As far as I'm concerned, I'm Lower Mohawk." She and her friend laugh about their assertiveness:

> I still refer to myself as Mohawk, too. I can't get used to myself being an Onondaga. They give you a band number with your husband's number. His was Barefoot Onondaga XXX. When we got divorced they still listed me as Barefoot Onondaga YYY, whatever it is. Legally I am still Onondaga, but I still think of myself as a Lower Mohawk.

Similarly, her friend, who has a degree in business management, is listed as an Oneida Indian: "My band number would be Oneida XXX, but whenever anyone asks me what nation I belong to I always say Cayuga, because that is what I was born. Since I am a traditional person, I was raised that you follow the mother's line. My mother is Cayuga as her mother before her, and so on and so on.

Because my dad was Oneida, we were just listed under him. It doesn't matter what the government says; we do it our own way. . . . That's invading our culture."

A far more devastating situation resulted from the laws governing racial intermarriage. The Indian Act created a disparity between the genders that does not fit with Iroquois matriarchal tradition, because while a native woman who married a white man was forced to leave the reserve and lose all her rights, an Indian man who married a non-native lost no rights. The native woman lost her claim to reserve housing and her share of the band's annual royalties, she was no longer considered a full Indian, and—most importantly for the survival of the line, traced through the woman's side—her children were not considered Indian.

In 1986 the Canadian Parliament passed Bill C-31, which allowed reserves to decide whether they wanted "nonstatus" women back on the reserve lists. This legislation tried to correct the old discrimination against women created by the Indian Act (which the United Nations Human Rights Commission determined to be a direct abrogation of human rights), but Bill C-31 ignited a burning controversy of its own, and the native community remains divided on the issue.

Troubling uncertainties remain. Some women on the Six Nations Reserve believe that it is only fair that nonstatus women should be able to return to the reserve. Others feel that women who married out knew they would lose their status, so they should be prepared to pay the price. Still others feel that marrying a non-native threatens the culture and dignity of Indian life. Molly places all women's issues into the context of this debate and dilemma:

"I knew I'd never marry a white man . . ."
For me, right now at this time in native person's history, I have a very hard time with membership in the band and self-control. I was raised in a traditional Indian-thinking family. We were never prejudiced toward a non-native, but at the same time I wouldn't marry one. I wouldn't even consider marrying one. I have a lot of strong Indian thoughts, where marrying non-native is not Indian. . . . But at the same time, everything's changing, and you have to get rid of that old way of thinking.

Passing Bill C-31 was not a popular decision everywhere. How the hell did that get in? Nobody I talked to wanted it, and we're the most liberal reserve! You go to the other reserves, they're more militant, more against it than we are!

With women's lib and being an Indian woman, I still feel that you go with your man. I keep my own name and I keep my own band, but if I chose to marry a white person, I would go and become a white person. I would sever, not all ties, because I'd still have my family, but I wouldn't expect to be able to live beside my sister. That would be gone. Growing up, I knew I'd never marry a white man. It was pounded into my head. I want my children to marry Indians, I want my grandchildren to be Indians.

Molly did not vote on band membership for women who "marry out" because she was brought up Confederacy (the traditional political system) rather than Council (the contemporary political system). Her brother and grandfather were both chiefs, "so my thoughts run that way." Yet, the elected council makes decisions that affect the whole reserve: "How can I sit here and lip off about something when I didn't participate? I feel myself torn. Now the most important issues in our whole native life are slapping us in the face." Her mother may have been able to ignore the political dilemma, even though it has been obvious that Six Nations people (like other native people in North America) have been losing touch with traditional culture and adopting some of the more destructive features of mainstream culture. "No one has done anything about it and maybe it's too late to do anything. I'm really having a hard time trying to keep up the traditional way and not fall into the elective way, but at the same time knowing that you've got to do something. We can't just sit here anymore and let them do things to us."

On the other side of this issue, which has divided the native community, Nola argues that the old legislation was grossly unfair to women. She notes that many more native men marry white women than native women marry white men:[33]

> The thing that bothers me is that the men get away with it! They can marry the white woman and bring her to the reserve. I think they should both be off the list. Instead of it turning to the woman's advantage and saying, well, if a man can bring his non-native wife to live on the reserve, an Indian woman can bring her non-native husband—I agree with it not being fair—I think they should both go off, because now it's a hell of a mess.

At the heart of this debate are fears about the very survival of Indian culture and traditions. Says a craftswoman, "To me it's not prejudice. . . . We're looking at a race of people here, a proud race." Cultural survival sometimes looms larger than love and marriage, or family ties. Linda, a thirty-two-year-old teacher's aide, loves her sister and her nieces and nephews but she would fight to keep her sister off the reserve:

> My second to the oldest sister married a non-native. She was my father's favorite. She married a non-native and that was it, "Go!" She wanted him to give her away, and he just said, "No. I don't want no more to do with you." She was banished from the family. She got married at a justice of the peace and was gone for years. When she finally came home, he said, "You're my daughter and I love you, but you still go live over there. You don't come back here expecting the same rights. You're part of us, but you're not; you can't live next door to me. I don't love you that much."

An elder adds her voice:

> My son found a girl, started fooling around. He says, "Ma, I am getting married." I don't care as long as she is an Indian woman. I always said never marry different kind. Marry your own kind. But I got two girls married different kind [non-natives]. It kind of makes me feel funny, you know, when we get together. Well, how come they got these two? Different coloring. I believe my own religion, and I was told to tell them to marry their own color as long as it is an Indian. They were talking about this Indian girl marrying white, and she wants to come back. She can't! She made herself her own bed over there, why should she come back? She should have thought of that before she married out.

In spite of these legal and social complications, Iroquois women greatly value marriage and consider it to be a natural part of the woman's journey through life. Even younger women feel pressure to conform to the traditional woman's role as homemaker, mother, and spiritual leader. Phoebe, a graduate of the Mohawk College Social Services Program, is married with three children. She does not wear a wedding ring, having been married in the Longhouse way, and she feels strongly committed to her role as "keeper of the culture." Sunny, age thirty-two, affirms the role but resists expectations that she will marry soon:

"When I'm through living my life . . ."

I am looking at my life as well as what is expected of me. By now I should have been married. This is expected, and I didn't follow through. I am a stubborn person. I didn't want anybody. I knew I wasn't going to be happy married and raising kids. I want to go in different directions. I want to see what life is all about before I settle down—then I'd know it would be a wise decision. I wasn't willing to sacrifice myself for my culture, for my people, so to speak.

I think people just gave up on me. Now if I get married, fantastic. If I don't, fine, but I always said I wasn't going to get married until I was thirty-five. I have seen and learned a lot of things. I am happy, except when someone starts bugging me about when I am going to get married. I might have to go to another reserve to marry, because right now all the good guys are taken. If I marry someone from another reserve, he would have to come here and live, though. I wouldn't go there to live.

Marriage may be a strongly held value, but things don't always run smoothly, as elder Mabel, who is seventy, knows. She met her husband while they were playing baseball on a warm summer evening:

We got married when I was eighteen. He asked me to marry him, but it took me a while because I was thinking about this married life. My mother always said, "Don't get married young." I said yes, though. I got five boys and six girls. I made more decisions than he did, but he was out working all the time as an ironworker, and I was always home with the kids. He left me when the last baby was two months old. I don't know how long before another guy come along and said, take this and buy something for the table. We've been together thirty years, common law. I brought my children up, and this man helped me out.

For contemporary women, marriage often conflicts with a career outside the home. Elda, a planner with a degree in environmental studies, is a Mohawk who was born and raised on the reserve. Her commitment to her marriage is unquestioned, but her commitment to helping redevelop her lifelong home is equally strong. Elda says her mother "pushed us towards a career as well, so I think she wanted us to have the best of both worlds." Now the older woman questions Elda's successful career, because it has meant putting her two-year-old into day care: "Sometimes she has a conflict in herself. She was all for me going to school, getting my degree—she pushed everyone of us in that direction, not forcefully, but just encouraged us." Yet Karen's mother holds fast to the traditional image of what a mother should be like: "With the baby, if I'm not doing something the way she did it, she'll let me know."

Having the best of both worlds means entering the entangled world of double shifts: one outside the home, and one inside. Perhaps even more than their counterparts in other communities, Six Nations women generally believe that they should have the same opportunities as men; this belief is matched by the overriding reality that a woman must achieve in both spheres in order to be truly respected and fulfilled. She ends up trying to juggle the two and not getting as much support as she needs from her husband or partner. The stress amplifies if a child or the mother becomes ill, sick time is depleted, or child care problems arise.

In the Longhouse religion, divorce does not exist. Even though rings are not exchanged, Leigh notes, "you are still married for life." Separation is frowned upon even if the relationship does not work out; the couple is expected to strive harder. Both man and woman will talk to a family member, traditional chief, or elder and get back together. Some do not talk it through: "Once you are brought up that way, it's inside of you and it's something that you don't throw out the window. You just expect your marriage will last forever." Although Christian denominations dislike divorce, the rates are higher among women in these churches.

Challenges Confronting Women

With modern life has come the same litany of social problems experienced by Blood, Inuit, and other native people in North America. As Iroquois families attempt to redefine themselves in terms of traditional versus nontraditional, native versus mainstream culture, identity confusion is bound to occur. Nontraditional families especially face disturbingly high rates of alcoholism, spousal assault, and child abuse.[34] Like other native women, Iroquois women are more likely than white women to have low and insecure incomes, to be on welfare and/or unemployed, to have lower educational levels, and to live in substandard housing (although Iroquois fare better than the Blood and Inuit, for historical reasons as well as because of their proximity to major urban employment areas).

DISCRIMINATION

As with other native and visible minority groups in this book, Iroquois women confront the devil of discrimination—first as native people, and again as women. "The first time I actually experienced discrimination was when I was about twelve years old," recalls Phoebe, "and it has been there since." Phoebe still feels she has to tread lightly on both racial and gender counts in order "to avoid being walked all over," although she thinks discrimination may be fading a little:

> It could be just my point of view that has changed, my understanding of different peoples. I took a course on world religions; that helped me understand why people may think the way they do. Reading newspapers helped me see how native people are portrayed. I started developing empathy, seeing why people would think this way about Indian people. That is probably why I am in tourism. It's one way I feel I can help alleviate the problem.

Women resist the traditional homemaker imperative, yet face discouragement and discrimination when they try to break into mainstream society as career women. Nola explains:

> Women aren't happy at home anymore because there's so much advancement in everything, including equipment, that they have spare time on their hands. They're not having as many kids anymore. They have three kids, and before you know it, they're all in school, so you've got the day to clean up your house—wow, that must be really exciting! Women become totally bored and lose respect for themselves. Women become depressed, lonely, and frustrated and proceed to have marital and child care problems; those erupt into family problems. They're looking for something more challenging. I can't really say being a housewife isn't challenging, because I don't have firsthand experience, but they are looking for another outlet for their own personal self.

Such an outlet may be hard to find for women born in the 1950s and earlier, who seldom finished high school. "I'm thirty-seven and in my age group, the dropout rate was fantastic—"and it still is," says Nola. "Maybe two would graduate from high school. Everybody quit. Then along comes Sue, who's five years younger than I am and she just about made it and along comes Leigh who's ten years younger, and she made it." Most of Nola's friends are homemakers who lack the self-confidence to complete their educations or find a job: "They're bored, and that boredom causes problems in the family" as the empty-nest syndrome takes over. Depression, drinking, affairs, and deepening loss of self-confidence are frequent companions of middle age for this generation.

VIOLENCE, LIBERATION, AND ALCOHOL

One of the most intransigent problems facing native people (including the Six Nations), and one that affects women's lives in a multitude of ways, is alcohol and drug abuse. According to an addictions counselor, both men and women on the reserve are influenced by non-native values and lifestyles that contradict Iroquois traditions. The two cultural streams are basically incompatible. He believes that Iroquois are going through a transition that is difficult to cope with—and that sometimes leads to alcoholism and wife-battering: "Any problem in today's society, whether it is on reserve or off reserve, you can trace back to alcoholism. Whether it was because your parents were alcoholics or you were influenced by your uncle or aunt, it can all be traced . . . it is the underlying cause of just about every problem we face today."

The Ontario Native Women's Association report on family violence draws this disturbing profile: "The incidence of abuse for First Nations women in Ontario is eight times the national average. Eight out of ten First Nations women currently living in this province are survivors of either child sexual abuse, incest, rape, or a battering relationship."[35] Both male and female counselors on the Six Nations Reserve link violence against women with alcohol, female aggression, and male failure. Elly, a crisis center worker, offers an analysis that sounds very similar to the Inuit and Blood situations in terms of women adapting more readily to social change and taking on more power relative to men. Iroquois women's power is rooted in traditional authority as well as in the groundswell of contemporary women's liberation, Elly explains:

> Indian women have been more aggressive, and they've gone out into the mainstream—the majority of the graduates and the majority of the

employed are women. Our men are going through a transition where their roles aren't quite as clear. The woman is so independent, and she's sitting there saying, "No, I don't have to put up with this." Pretty soon the fisticuffs start flying, and she's hitting back as much as he's hitting her. It's only that he's so physical that it shows on her. Don't ever think that he's the only one throwing the punches. Often the woman throws the *first* punch. She'll go on the attack, then it escalates and because he's stronger, she ends up on the bottom, looking like the abused one.

A school secretary confirms this view. "The reason we fought was because I was the aggressive one. I'd just as soon hit him over the head with a frying pan as look at him because he made me mad. My son, he swore he'd never hit a woman, and he was living with a girl who would just as soon knock him on his rear as look at him. He wouldn't fight back, so he was always having black eyes and bruises, and he left her because she punched him—gave him a black eye—and he pushed her away." He told his mother that he had come so close to hitting her that he had to leave, because he knew it was going to come to that eventually. Adds another counselor who insists that she herself will not take abuse from her husband, "It is the women—boy, the women are aggressive! The women are strong, and yet physically the man is superior. In nine cases out of ten, the women hit the men first."

David, a counselor, confirms this image of domestic violence: Men do the most harm and usually trigger the violent encounter, especially after abusing alcohol and because of low self-esteem or even jealousy of women's success. Sometimes the woman's anger and pain boil over, however, and she strikes the first blow. "It's very degrading for a man to have his wife beat him up," David adds, "but if he comes home drunk and passes out, she beats the living daylights out of him. Usually she's been drinking, too, and raises holy heck in the family." "Unfortunately, violence is a common scenario here, " Rita admits.

Women who are victims receive support from their families and work toward building independence in case they need to make a break. As among other native groups, children are favored so much that violence (when it occurs) tends to be directed toward women: "We're not perfect people by any means, but child abuse is not quite as prevalent as abuse of women. I lived with a man after I got divorced, and I used to get beat up. My children hate him because we fought so much, but they admit that he always treated them well, sometimes better than I did."

Rape, including marital rape, occurs on the reserve just as it does in other communities. Like incest and battering, rape is seldom discussed openly, although attempts have been made to start an incest support group. People are not ready to come and talk about the darker side of family life or about sex—yet. "It's getting better," says a crisis center worker who does front-line duty with abused women. "Women will talk about it, but I don't think they're ready to admit they were raped by their husbands. They'll just sit there and not say anything, or they'll deny it. Things are definitely changing, but it's slow." Girls between nine and twelve are most vulnerable to rape, says Nola. "By the time they become teens, they're pretty and they're interested in sex. The preteens don't have the confidence to tell. They think it's them; they're the ones at fault. We have to be more open with our children, have them more aware that sex shouldn't be a dirty word."

Liz, fifty-six, tells why she left her husband and shares the problems she faces with her son:

"I wonder why they drink in the first place . . ."
It was too much. Every night my husband stopped in town. I have supper on at six o'clock. I would say, "Why don't you come home and eat, change your clothes, then go back out?" No. He stopped in town until closing time. He and his buddies come back and sit in the kitchen with a box of beer, so I get my kids and send them to bed.

I really don't ask why he did it, but he can't say that I left my kids. I don't care where I went, I took them. My little ones are more important than that man drinking. I never drank until after the baby got big. Oh, I had good parties here and there, but I didn't drink my head off until I don't know what I am doing. Not that way. The boys are drinking and doing drugs more than the girls. They don't do as well in school as the girls do. They aren't getting as much education or as many jobs as the girls. It seems like the men are weak; they aren't trying. Maybe it is the drink holding them back—they drink so much. Otherwise, maybe they would be all right.

I don't know where the heck the teenagers get pot. I had an argument with my own boy about it. His welfare check would keep us all winter, but when he gets the check, he goes out and buys pot. He comes back two or three days later looking for something to eat. I say, "If I see those packages, it is going in the woodstove." I shove it in the fire. "That is not for us, you know; I don't want none of that stuff in the house." But I wonder why they drink in the first place. That is what I can't understand. I heard one person say, "Oh, I can't quit." I smoked one cigarette right after another. I quit when I said I was going to: "I did it—I don't see why you can't. There is no such thing as you can't quit."

Nola believes that boredom leads people to seek stimulation through the bottle: "And not from other women necessarily, but from men! They need excitement. They want somebody they can exchange views and talk intelligently with, and it's usually done over a bottle of beer." The consequences can be devastating for a family. Leigh tells about the impact of her father's drinking:

My father was an ironworker and an alcoholic. He fooled around on my mother; just name it, he did it. I always said I'd never marry an ironworker, I'd never marry an alcoholic. And here I am, I married an ironworker and my husband likes to drink. I hate drinking, but I find myself being pulled into that old pattern. It's self-defeating. I like to drink once in a while, but it's not a necessity for me. My husband's drinking created a problem for us. He smashed up our truck—nearly killed himself. That had to happen before he said, look, I think I might be drinking too much. It happened in my mother's family, and I vowed it would never happen to me. It is a problem in every aspect of your life when alcohol is present. It's always been present, too.

What could help the Iroquois not become so dependent on alcohol? Some women believe that alcohol relieves the stress of being a "sky walker," climbing up high scaffolding and handling huge pieces of steel that can kill you with the slightest error. Alcohol serves as an outlet and a way to relax for men who "lead such a dangerous life, high up on iron all the time." Others think that this explanation is a cop-out: "There are other stressful events in your life, but you don't need alcohol to relieve that stress; it's an excuse to be away from home." One woman argues that men need to become more confident and feel better about themselves: "They're insecure, so alcohol is a crutch that helps them feel good about themselves. I think they have an ego problem, because when they're out, what do they do? Not necessarily just having a good time with men. There is a lot of adultery . . . Oh, God, it's just incredible!" For the woman who believes in trust and loyalty as a key part of marriage, infidelity deals a painful blow.

Being sucked into drinking (and overdrinking) is easy for women who are partners of alcoholics. By accepting men's alcohol abuse, they make things worse: "Sure, I'll sit and have a beer with you, or I'll bring you a six-pack home. Put your feet up, you've had a hard day; here's your drink," one woman says wryly. Women and their children fall victim to the pattern of scapegoating and neglect that alcohol triggers.

In a culture that clearly placed women in the home (albeit with special political and religious powers), some men become upset with working wives who seem not to be taking their rightful place, David says: "With the wife working, drinking problems can happen. If the man isn't comfortable with himself to start off with, it builds insecurities. The male ego is very, very fragile. It can be broken very easily, even though the male is going to put on this front that you didn't hurt him. There is an old saying that you never show your enemy that they hurt you. That's how the male ego works." An alternative explanation suggests that native men succumb to the justifiable anger and frustration produced by the legacy of discrimination and blocked opportunities that go hand in hand with reserve life and minority status. Seeing women finish school and "make it" in the world of work may simply rub salt into old wounds. Another woman takes "a daring position" regarding male alcoholism: "Maybe I'm a feminist in saying that men are just weak, but I don't see how they can let themselves get that way without trying to control it."

Edith, age forty-two, recounts theories of biological intolerance, peer pressure, and lack of male role models because fathers are away so much, but feels that male alcoholism is caused primarily by outside pressures: "You can talk about removing the discriminatory sections of whatever act, but if you're an Indian and you look it, you just can't ignore that. My husband looks real Indian—I don't believe I said that!—but you're not going to remove the visible part of being an Indian when you're off the reserve." When her husband travels to the United States to play sports, people hurl racial insults at him. By succumbing to the media image of the flashy, beer-drinking sports figure, he has brought his marriage to the brink of collapse: "You see the commercials on TV? Sports with beer—that's in his soul. There's no way I want to put myself and my child through that. If it's social, fine; I don't want any part of this uncontrolled drinking."

A crisis center worker speculates that alcohol's attractiveness may stem in part from legislation that prohibits the sale of alcohol on the reserve. Inevitably, bootleggers find a way to bring liquor inside the reserve boundaries, and the forbidden-fruit aspect of alcohol makes it even more desirable: "Almost because you can't have it, you want it." Teenage girls confirm that many of their friends, especially boys, start drinking as early as eleven. One confirms that her little brother started hanging around the fourteen-year-olds: "They start into a bad scene around here. Never was a lot of police, so they don't really have to worry much." Poor grades stimulate early drinking, drinking produces poor grades: "Some stop when they are older, but many just keep doing it." The problem, more obvious among the young boys, is more related to alcohol than drugs.

David paints a clearer picture of the ages and types of addictions found among clients at the reserve's alcohol and drug abuse treatment center. Tragically, the age at which serious substance abuse problems begins to appear is steadily dropping:

> We see about 20 percent alcoholics, another 20 percent drug abusers, and about 60 percent cross addictions. We are just at the tip of the iceberg. With our prevention work, we are getting younger clients. Four years ago, most were over thirty; now they are in their twenties. We are also getting more kids between thirteen and twenty, especially around seventeen, eighteen, and nineteen.

These younger males approach manhood with few real choices ahead of them. They find themselves confronting failure to complete high school and the likely prospect of unemployment.

Alcohol abuse presents another thorny problem for Six Nations women. Because of the stigma attached to a woman who fails to meet her responsibilities, it takes longer for her to reach out for help than it will for males. This reversal of the typical pattern of help-seeking reflects the power and authority accorded women in Iroquois culture, as Rita points out:

> A woman has almost as much power as a man does, and today she is supposed to be a supermom—getting a job and raising a family, doing the housekeeping and the cooking. Sometimes the only way she can deal with these pressures is either drinking or prescription drugs, because her inner needs aren't being met. She can't do all the things she's been told she has to do. She can deal with the pressures by turning to the bottle. She has insecurities, feelings of low self-esteem—"I am not good enough"—[and] a woman will hold those feelings in more than a man. A male will usually take it out on something or someone, by fighting or in physical work. A woman still has that taboo against getting too physical, so her emotions stay pent up inside. It's too devastating for her to admit, "I don't feel like I am a very good mother."

Ironically, for these women whose culture has afforded them relatively high power, the price of perceived failure is high. Addiction counselors attempt to help women realize that their feelings of low-self esteem are not unusual and that they can feel better about themselves again. "Trying to reach that person is where we are having problems today," a counselor notes.

As in other communities, substance abuse among women may take a different form, observes Rita, a counseling center assistant: "Many times they are addicted to drugs from doctors, usually Valium. A few doctors will say, 'Here's your prescription . . . I will collect my money,' because they don't have time to see how her spiritual life is going, or her social life." Some women slide down this slope toward addiction because doctors represent professional expertise.

The reserve offers several alcohol-related programs that address substance abuse and various social problems, but few that provide basic economic stability: "If you go through the village and you look at all the facilities we have here, they're all social service oriented. We hardly have anything that is economic. We're getting into private enterprise, but most of it is social service, welfare, crisis services, alcohol and drug programs—it's a social service community." A battered women's shelter, although perhaps useful in some cases, adds to the list of services that deal with the symptoms, rather than with the causes of women's pain.

Toward the Twenty-First Century

THE ROAD TO EQUALITY

Women of the Six Nations Reserve and Mennonite women consistently describe themselves as *not* oppressed. While Mennonite women do not see themselves as oppressed because women's work and role are highly valued in their culture, Iroquois women do not see themselves as oppressed because their tradition defines them as powerful and deserving of respect. Since cultural definitions of gender penetrate deeply into women's self-perceptions, Iroquois women were surprised that other native women (such as the Blood and Inuit) do not have the same matriarchal power base, as Molly remarks:

> I just took it for granted that all Indian people basically had this. Even now that we are considered a "patriarchal society," we haven't changed that much. Even if we still had the same role as we did two-hundred years ago, I wouldn't feel oppressed because I would know that this is my *responsibility* as a woman. I would have been taught that. Do we need liberating? I don't think so. I've chosen to "liberate" myself by delaying the decision to be a wife and mother until I am ready for it, even though I get some pressure to conform. I'm still respected as a woman, and I'm still given the responsibility of the religion.

Iroquois women tend to see themselves as relatively powerful, and not especially in need of liberation. This is true in spite of the social and interpersonal problems that face women everywhere (battering, rape, incest, and so forth). Women in this culture can always reflect back to their traditional powers—to the historical definitions of women as strong leaders, and to the legacy of the clan mothers. In a sense, they have an inherent "cultural right" to be strong, assertive, and capable women. Do Iroquois women need liberating? Phoebe answers for her sisters: "I wouldn't think so, not here. Not on the reserve, within our own community. Many of us are hard to swallow when we go off reserve because of things that we are used to here. No, I don't think we are oppressed."

Most of the women I interviewed on the Six Nations Reserve—from teens to elders—have heard of women's liberation, embrace it in at least the most general terms, and feel that it fits in nicely with their traditional powers and roles. Although they have not had formal "women's lib meetings," they have had informal meetings in which they "sit around and discuss these things." For the most part, they enthusiastically support issues such as child care, pay equity, educational and career opportunities for women, and basic rights. The movement has definitely influenced the way women think about their lives, says an eighteen-year-old commerce student: "Even on the reserve, where the woman's place is supposed to be in the home, it's changing. We're being affected whether we want to be or not. We get information from TV, radio, the newspaper, from your friend across the street who's out working, from your sisters, whatever. It's looking right at us!" The messages women send their daughters about being female are inevitably shaped by mainstream media biases:

> We see the same television commercials, read the same magazines with all these nice slim, independent-looking women. Our men are admiring them, wanting us to be like the one that advertises for that cigarette [Virginia Slims]—"You've come a long way baby"—you know. We see how women are finally sticking up for themselves and we're becoming independent, so that's what we want to be, but men want us to be like the women they're admiring in these magazines. Incest and rape—you see commercials on TV now: "Tell someone." They're street-proofing our kids. We all see it, the same way everyone off the reserve sees it. Everyone's coming out of their closet off the reserve; we're coming out of our closets. It's going in the same direction, but it's much more open.

Because Iroquois society locates women's major responsibility in the home, some women feel constricted in their ability to change. The woman is the backbone of the family; she helps teach and discipline children, perpetuating positive native values. If she leaves her family to work in a paid position, "then she is in conflict again because of her role. Inside she is fighting with what society is saying on the outside, that today's woman has to go out and have a career."

Timing may be the answer: career first, family second.[36] For example, elder women say they want their granddaughters to finish high school (and perhaps go to college), study hard, and travel before they settle down. Says one, "I keep telling them not to get married. Get yourself a job. Work so you have money coming in; buy what you want. When you get about thirty or thirty-five, then think about settling down." Rita adds, "Once you settle down that means you have to stay home, look after the house. That is the way." Elders frown upon their daughters and granddaughters leaving small children with baby-sitters: "They should be home looking after them. It is the man's place to work and support the family." The traditional view carries enormous weight in a culture that venerates the wisdom and authority of elder women.

In addition to mainstream messages about women having careers for self-fulfillment and liberation, many Iroquois women work for financial reasons: "Women are forced to go out when they would much rather be home, which creates a whole new ball game." Finding a path that balances old and new messages about womanhood can be a tricky business. Iroquois women try to conceive of liberation within the context of their culture. Molly elaborates:

> If I had turned my back on my culture and said, okay, I don't want to have anything to do with anything, then it might have been more difficult for me. That was a choice that I made anyway. I could have joined the Christian religion, as many of my friends have—which is their choice—but I chose to follow the Longhouse religion. It was *my* choice, and in return I expected a chance to grow and to explore on my own. A long time ago you wouldn't have had a choice, really. You would have just been told and you did it. Now we emphasize choice *and* responsibility."

WOMEN'S EMPOWERMENT

Monture-Okanee observes that native women "must be provided room to speak and the power to define. We are capable speakers and do not need someone else to speak for us."[37] The women who speak through this chapter do so eloquently, confirming her view. They see themselves as strong, competent, and self-sufficient. Generational differences exist, but the dual themes of responsibility and choice run through their lives. Katie, age twenty-two, describes with great respect how her life differs from her mother's because of choices she is making for herself:

> Mother was always involved with the kids, because that was her life—raising all nine of us, looking after the house. *My* life, I was drawn into a whole different setting. Maybe it was because I came from such a large family and I wanted to do things differently—almost opposite to

what she did. I wanted to have independence and freedom, which she probably felt she had when she was having the kids. Maybe that was her idea of it. When I was growing up we were independent. We had to be, once we got past that stage where we could be on our own and she could be confident that we would be all right. It was just, "See ya later, Mom, we'll come back at suppertime." It was really, really, really free.

Part of doing things differently is seeking formal higher education, which empowers women to lead, parent, and change the face of the reserve. When asked to describe the most significant event in her life, Nola immediately replies, "My graduation from college. The high school system was so awful and boring, I hated it, so when I graduated from college it was a milestone and an achievement." In the old days, native education meant attending residential school for a few years, a mixed blessing at best. Like the Blood Indians and Inuit, older Iroquois women have vivid memories of being punished for speaking their own language, of sexual abuse, and of extreme structure and discipline.[38]

With a tradition of homemaking for women and construction for men, parents have not placed heavy emphasis on education until recently. Now, however, women are completing high school, and many are going on to college to study nursing, teaching, or social work. Because Hamilton lies less than a half hour away, it is easy to live on the reserve and attend McMaster University or Mohawk Community College. (The latter operates a tiny branch at the edge of the reserve.) Yet rates of higher education completion are low. In Canada as a whole, "1.9 per cent of Registered Indian people have a university degree, compared to 10 per cent of the general population. Just over 20 per cent of First Nations people have any post-secondary school education at all, yet 40 per cent of the non-First Nations population" do.[39] As Monture-Okanee points out, "The continual denial of our experience at every corner, at every turn, from education at residential schools through to universities, is violence."[40] Iroquois women who have earned professional degrees are, indeed, pioneers for their people, breaking into new territory that will open doors for their families and daughters in the next century. They understand clearly that higher education can elevate their social and economic status.

Young men work side by side with their fathers, learning construction from an early age; their rates of high school and college completion are lower than that of young women. Tammy says that once Iroquois boys enter high school, their performance begins to lag behind the girls and they start to drop out: "I don't think they want to be there. They have an image to live up to—if they do too well, they're looked down on as being too smart. I don't think they want to do really well. They want to seem to come up cool and care less. So their grades go down and they start into the drug scene."[41] This produces a higher unemployment rate for males than for females (in part, like the Inuit, because construction work is more seasonal than women's occupations). Employers often view women as more reliable, probably because of lower rates of alcohol and drug abuse. Women are "not afraid" to go back to school.

DREAMS FOR THEIR DAUGHTERS

Younger women and teens dream of education, careers, going to England, becoming an artist or going into business, perhaps moving to Toronto and finding a good job—"moving around a bit." Some speak of reserve life as too confining and want to raise their children elsewhere; in this context, they do not talk about what leaving might mean for maintaining their Indian identity. Most add that "eventually" they would like to "settle down and have children."

Teenage girls are not sure that traditional definitions fit modern lifestyles. Says Tammy, "I don't like that old role. I think women should be treated equally with men, have jobs like the men, and bring home stuff for the family." The domestic imperative does not appeal to her. Rather, she and her friends want an "equal partnership" when it comes to child care and housework. The traditional expectations that women will stay home and raise children, though, have by no means disappeared among the younger generation. Rachel, who is twenty, thinks about taking correspondence courses to finish her high school diploma and says she and her friends do not feel any pressure toward having a career: "On the reserve, they think more about getting married and settling down and taking care of the house."

Elda feels her role in planning and development will allow her to shape the community in a way that clan mothers did long ago, but through a different vehicle: "I know it's crystal-balling to say this, but I dream of developing a long-term comprehensive plan which includes all of the human, physical, and financial resources available on the reserve; which includes all people, all the land ... that's what I've aimed at since I started to work here. I think we'll move in that direction." Her optimism spreads among her female colleagues: "We put up the flats out here, and then started working together to get the apartments built as well as the houses and the subdivisions." Power and voice come in many forms.

One mother in her thirties would like to see her daughter "get a good education and become a nurse or something—but I would like to see her married with a family; to be happy and healthy; and to respect people." Elder women envision a "modern" sequence of freedom and independence followed by commitment and responsibility. For the daughters of contemporary Iroquois women, these should be viable dreams.

The Last Night

Tonight is the annual Forest Pageant held in the reserve's outdoor amphitheater. Thunderstorms and heavy rains delay the performance by an hour, but I am happy to sit under a tree and watch the crowd filter into this sylvan setting. The theater follows the contours of a deep bowl-shaped depression in the woods, around a small spring-fed pond known as Sour Springs. The seats are cut into the slope; directly opposite is a clearing that serves as the main stage, and on the right is the staging area. The actors include men and women of all ages in traditional Iroquois dress. They begin at nightfall and perform under floodlights and by the light of a bonfire as the gloom gathers around us.

A wooden concession stand near the entrance serves popular food: corn and kidney bean soup, Indian tacos, and ham on a scone. Indian craft stands also flank the entranceway. A tour bus full of English tourists joins the audience.

The pageant begins with a young man, perhaps in his thirties, who wears a red jacket over his buckskin leggings. He portrays the famous Seneca chief, Red Jacket. A woman's voice begins the play with a narrative to the effect that, although Chief Red Jacket was not the most illustrious of the Iroquois leaders, his life contributed understanding into the Indians' plight and he fought hard to pre-

serve Iroquois land in upstate New York prior to the American Revolution. Chief Red Jacket approaches the pond's edge, faces the audience, and delivers a long prayer in Iroquois. Then two bonfires are lit—one on center stage, one on the staging area—casting an eerie orange glow on actors and audience alike.

The story tells how traders, who were plying the Indians with alcohol (mainly rum), came with their wives to upstate New York around the Finger Lakes, where the Six Nations originated. Then came the missionary and his wife, plying their Christian beliefs. President Washington was trying to get the Six Nations to leave their individual lands and villages and go together to one reservation, where he said they would prosper. Chief Red Jacket adamantly refused to agree to this scheme, which would disrupt their well-established communities. The debate went back and forth between Chief Red Jacket and the government agent, who pointed out that there would be many more immigrants coming ("his people") and they would need the land to farm.

Chief Red Jacket's wife was angry that he went off to so many council meetings and government negotiations. In his absence, she turned to the Christian faith, forsaking her traditional religion. When he returned from a meeting, Chief Red Jacket found that she had left him and taken their children with her.

The chief then lived alone in the woods, suffered greatly, turned to rum, and for several months was a desperate man. A young brave journeyed to call him to council and found him talking to himself in the middle of the woods, having hallucinations and delusions. The young man said, "Perhaps the people do not want you back as chief." That shook Chief Red Jacket so much that he threw away the bottle of rum and the medal President Washington had given him, saying, "I must return to work with my people." When he returned to the council meeting, he realized he was very ill and would not live much longer. He briefly reunited with his wife and children, then died.

The moral of the story is clear: Alcohol and the white man's religion had robbed the chief of his pride, self-esteem, and faith. The pageant does not really blame the white people, however. It was Chief Red Jacket's personal responsibility that he had succumbed to the rum; he had lost control. He had given up his spirit, and only he could regain his spirit.

The attentive audience applauds and as I turn to leave, I notice an elder woman with tears in her eyes. They match mine, and many others. It all seemed so long ago—more than two hundred years. But as I climb down the bleachers toward the exit and walk past the corn soup and hamburgers, I realize that this morality play was for both then and now. I wonder how much longer this story will be necessary.

3

Manly-Hearted Women
The Blood Women of Standoff, Alberta

I would like my daughter to get the best education so she can be independent and support herself. I hope she will maintain ties with our parents and learn Blackfoot. We want her to go to university someday, but first we would like her to know that she is Indian and not be shy or ashamed of it. Many Indian people are succeeding today, and she can be one of them.

—Connie

En Route to the Blood Reserve

Draped alongside the Rocky Mountains in southern Alberta, the Blood Reserve pushes south across golden plains toward the Montana border. The Blood lands sprawl on either side of Route 3, with only 353,000 acres left of the vast territory these people once dominated. Several years earlier, driving from Calgary to Glacier International Peace Park three hours south, my eyes caught the sign: "Welcome to the Blood Reserve—population 5,781." I could not stop that day, but the lonely beauty of the distant mountains beckoned me to return.

Now I am on my way to interview Blood women, with permission from the chief and council tucked carefully into my pocket. It is a typical warm prairie night. Fields fly by, left and right, as I shepherd my brother's old pickup truck into the gathering gloom of dusk. The sun slips out of sight behind the foothills, throwing gilded peaches and roses across the sky. I pull the truck onto an old side road and climb along a ridge.

The prairie grass waves, catching the gold of sunset. I sit in the darkening silence with a shawl around my shoulders and suddenly can almost sense what it must have been like to live out on the

plains before the arrival of white settlers. On the horizon the skele-
tons of old sweat houses perch on the slope like rib cages of long-ex-
tinct dinosaurs. Chief Mountain, a holy place for the Bloods,
emerges from a long line of peaks in the distance as the last rays of
sun play across the foothills. Slowly, the sun spreads its glow across
huge billowing clouds—turning them into another mountain
range—then dusk slips into night.

The next morning Harold takes me on a tour of the reserve. He
explains the medicine wheel dangling from a friend's windshield: "It
is a symbol like the cross. It signifies unity: a complete circle, Moth-
er Earth to the greater world and back. We are all its servant. We be-
lieve in a circular existence. We come from Mother Earth when we
are born. When we die we are back in the Mother Earth." Mother
Earth.

H ate Woman listened to her husband, a Blood warrior named
Weasel Tail, sing words that were supposed to comfort her as
he left with a war party in the mid-nineteenth century: "Girl I love,
don't worry about me! I'll be eating berries coming home."[1] But
Hate Woman insisted on accompanying her husband on raids; if he
was going to be killed on a war party, she wanted to be killed, too.
Although some of the men disliked her presence, she stayed by her
husband's side through perilous raids against the enemy: Sitting
Bull's Sioux (exiled in Canada after defeating Custer), the Crees,
the Crows, and the Gros Ventres. Hate Woman deftly wielded a
six-shooter, stole her share of ponies from other tribes, and finally
was honored by the men, who asked her to recount her exploits at
Sun Dance (a ceremony that renews spiritual connections to the
Great Spirit and celebrates the virtue of women, as well as the
transformation of men into warriors).[2] Although she was one of
only a handful of women who broke out of the traditional female
role, Blood women still tell her story today.

Kanai—"many chiefs"—was their name before their ancient enemies, the Crees, called them Blood people, because they used the
color red for ceremonial purposes.[3] They were a powerful and ad-
venturous group of hunters and gatherers: seven bands roaming the
plains in search of the buffalo that clothed and fed them, and

camping in closed circles of white tipis made by women. The Bloods form part of the Blackfoot Confederacy, which also includes the Peigan (Pikuni) and Blackfoot (Siksika) Indians in Alberta and the Blackfeet in Montana.[4]

The Bloods went from a nomadic hunting and gathering society to a reserve-based agricultural society in one generation. As with the Inuit and Iroquois, economic circumstances changed drastically with the coming of white people. Population declined as the whiskey trade and such "white" diseases as smallpox mercilessly struck the Bloods.[5] To satisfy the burgeoning fur trade, they hunted the buffalo herds—which previously blackened the Plains like a giant, undulating fur robe—until the animals virtually disappeared in the 1880s. White settlers encroached on traditional Blackfoot lands. These pressures led the Bloods to sign Treaty Number Seven with the Canadian government in 1877. With other tribes of the Blackfoot Confederacy, the Bloods once had controlled 50,000 square miles; the treaty reserved a total of 1,433 square miles for the Indians, less than 3 per cent of the ceded land.[6]

The treaty gave the 2,200 Bloods the rights to "annual treaty of $5 to each person, $15 to minor chiefs, and $25 to head chiefs; to receive a bonus of $12 at the original treaty; to have their share of $2,000 a year for ammunition; a uniform every three years for chiefs; a Winchester rifle, flag and medal for chiefs at the treaty signing; to send teachers among them; and to provide certain farming tools and cattle."[7] Their lives changed forever.

Out of Tradition

TRADITIONAL ROLES: "HEAVY BURDENS"

Prior to contact with European settlers, the Bloods traveled freely between what are now southern Alberta and northern Montana. Men were chiefs, warriors, buffalo hunters, negotiators, and traders. The courage of warfare was a central part of male identity, as men protected the camps from traditional tribal enemies. Equally, a man's self-esteem derived from providing for his family through participation in pony raids or buffalo hunting parties.[8]

In their quest for large game, males spent long periods away from home; females processed food, tanned buffalo hides, made clothing, maintained order and culture in the men's absence, and cared for young children, the elderly, and pack dogs.[9] Women sewed skins into clothing and managed the practical details of everyday life. Experts at drying and preserving berries, buffalo meat, small game, and fish, Blood women also made utensils and produced arts and crafts. Although traditional roles emphasized the man as provider and the woman as sustainer, both males and females acted as producers, processors, and consumers as survival needs dictated. Schneider, in her detailed study of roles among various Plains Indian tribes, reports that men may have worked on clothing (for example) when they were away from camp for long periods, while women took up some of the "male" tasks at home.[10]

Because of the short summers and early frosts of the northern Plains, Blood women were not horticulturists like their more southerly cousins. Rather, they gathered berries and hunted small local game. In the "dog days" (prior to the acquisition of horses around 1730), Blood women reportedly led a particularly hard life. Each time the group moved to more bountiful hunting grounds, women were responsible for transporting all of their family's worldly possessions, even if it meant carrying heavy burdens on their backs. They devised an ingenious sledge, the *travois*, by tying two long tipi poles together at one end and loosely connecting them through the middle section. Skins, cooking gear, clothing, and tipis—which women constructed and reconstructed with each move—were piled high on the *travois*. Dogs and later horses pulled the *travois*, although women also were known to place the poles over their shoulders and drag them along the ground. As they inevitably became stooped and stiff with age, women more often than men were abandoned to face death alone as the tribe moved camp.[11]

Women occasionally accompanied men on buffalo hunts in order to help regulate herd movements. A Blood elder describes a typical method of hunting buffalo during the dog days:

> After swift-running men located a herd of buffalo, the chief told all the women to get their dog *travois*. Men and women went out together. . . . The women were told to place their *travois* upright in the earth, small end up. The *travois* were so spaced that they could be tied together to form a semicircular fence. Women and dogs hid behind them while two fast-running men circled the buffalo herd. . . . Barking

dogs and shouting women kept the buffalo back. The men rushed in and killed the buffalo with arrows and lances.[12]

Sometimes the men would drive an unsuspecting herd over a cliff, riding their horses hard to keep the buffalo moving toward the edge. Women waited below as the huge animals floated through the air, crashing to certain death. They began processing the kill immediately, then hauled meat and hides back to the encampment. Women used every part of the buffalo—even the brains, which they mixed with ash to soften the thick skins.

Grinnell, however, indicates that buffalo hunting was usually the male preserve: "The man who was to call the buffalo arose very early, and told his wives that they must not leave the lodge, nor even look out, until he returned."[13] Women's duty was to pray for a successful hunt and to dress the meat after the kill.

As with the Inuit and Iroquois, though, women's skills and knowledge were equally important to the group's survival. While Blood women's sense of pride and self-esteem centered on domestic duties, their much-acclaimed skills in dressing buffalo hides and making saddles brought respect to them and wealth to their people during the height of the buffalo period in the late 1870s. Blood women produced literally thousands of buffalo robes.[14] In fact, Ewers argues, "The women who dressed buffalo robes for market played an even more important role in the fur trade than did their husbands who killed the buffalo. Theirs was harder work than buffalo hunting." One hunter could keep several wives supplied; one woman could dress twenty-five to thirty hides per winter.[15] Lewis points out that this role increased women's economic importance.[16] Blood women were considered "excellent workers" and valuable wives; ironically, though, because the buffalo hide trade was in the hands of men (both native and white), women actually fell to a more dependent position, and their status declined.[17]

For decades Blood and other Indian women were stereotyped as "squaws," an insulting term that defined them solely as appendages of their husbands, mere property placed on earth for men's pleasure. Blood women continue to confront this old stereotype. In a story that links the nineteenth and twentieth centuries, Freda, age forty-four, talks about the transition to modern life through the experience she knows best, childbirth:

"Miscarriage"

My mother had twelve children who lived and four or five miscarriages. When she was a young woman, she miscarried at about three months and was bleeding very badly; the family called in a medicine woman, who gave her herbs that didn't seem to help. Someone asked if it might be the afterbirth, and the medicine woman said "No, a fetus that age doesn't have an afterbirth." My mother grew worse and was hemorrhaging badly. They decided to take her to the hospital, even though she was afraid to go. If she had gotten there a half hour later she would have died because she had lost so much blood; of course it was the afterbirth.

In the early 1970s, I lost my fourth child. When I started to lose it, we didn't have a car, so me and my husband walked from our house up to the main road to hitchhike to the hospital. I was very weak and frightened from losing blood. Then a pickup truck with two white men crossed over the center line and squished us up against the ditch. The men leaned out and said to my husband, "Are you going to let us have her?" He yelled at me in Blackfoot, "Just run, just run, get out of the way!" I was so weak that I fell into the ditch. Just then another car came along, so the men drove away. We rested along the roadside for another half hour before someone finally stopped for us.

Freda arrived at the hospital exhausted and weak, but most of all frightened and reminded indelibly of how her position as an Indian woman in white society did not parallel the centrality of her place in Blood society.

TRADITIONAL POWERS: "AN INTEGRAL PART"

In spite of women's hard work and the relative complementarity of male and female roles, men in prereserve Blood society were defined as the major provider and "boss."[18] (This is in stark contrast to Iroquois women, who traditionally enjoyed substantial political power, choosing chiefs and council members.) Some outside observers saw Blood women as slaves whose husbands had "absolute power" over them; Blood men were "the undisputed lords of their households."[19] Men made primary decisions about when and where to move, at least in part because they were the acknowledged experts on game movements. Traditional male power was rooted in a machist, patriarchal-like and patrilineal social order that was reinforced by contact with white men from European heritages that valued men and devalued women, as evidenced in the nineteenth-century legislation that discriminated against Indian women.

Infidelity was cause for cutting off a woman's nose or ear, or even her death. In part because lineage and inheritance flowed through the male side, male jealousy was pronounced.[20] Polygamy was not uncommon: Because of high loss of male lives in warfare, at times women outnumbered men by two or three to one. Multiple wives became a status symbol and, because of women's centrality in hide production, an indication of male economic success.[21]

The image of Blood women as subordinate to men, however, may be vastly overdrawn. Although women did not have visible political power, and men did have the right to make decisions concerning war and migration, some women say that men would not have made any of those decisions without consulting their wives and also the camp's senior holy woman. "A long time ago," women say, Blood men had a slight edge in authority, but women played "a valuable and integral part of Blood society."[22] They enjoyed considerable influence and power. They did not generally take part in tribal affairs, but women could own property, receive and exercise medicine power, and give names to children.[22] The Bloods were matriarchal religiously and patriarchal politically; people remember a certain balance and egalitarianism similar to the Inuit, though perhaps not as well developed.

A few Blood women were extremely powerful compared to their sisters and to many men. Those who were designated as "sits-beside-me wife" enjoyed more power and status than other wives. This is similar to the Inuit concept of a leader of the men and a leader of the women (with the leader of the men being defined as the ultimate, general authority).[23] Native anthropologist Beatrice Medicine argues in *The Hidden Half* that other powerful roles were open to women. She documents "warrior" and "manly-hearted woman" roles among the Peigan of Alberta (and implies their existence among their Blood neighbors).[24] Hungry Wolf also documents the acceptance of Running Eagle, a Blackfoot woman, into full warrior status.

Esther Goldfrank, who wrote an extensive anthropological report on the early reserve period, claims that nine women on the Blood Reserve were "manly-hearted"—women who were ambitious, bold, accorded special privileges, and respected. She also contends that female independence and aggressiveness were so typical among the Blood that it may not have been as necessary to especially designate certain women as manly-hearted.[25]

Traditionally, all religious power passed through the women to the men. The women's spiritual society, the Mo'to'kiiks, and the men's Horn society represent a balance of power, because the Horn society cannot exist without the blessing of the Mo'to'kiiks. Women play a major role in Blood religion. They "put up" a Sun Lodge at the annual Sun Dance and keep the medicine bundles, roles they continue to play today.

The Turning Point: Mother Earth Wrong Side Up

The Bloods initially coped well with the constraints of reserve life, even in the face of a short growing season and recurrent droughts. Some men objected to farming—turning Mother Earth "wrong side up"—which was traditionally the preserve of Blood women. Since authorities thought men should perform the manual labor and leave women to do lighter housework chores, gender roles began to shift. Goldfrank maintains that stripping away old values and replacing them with new ones represented a conscious program instigated by the Canadian government, which "had no compunctions about destroying any part of the old Blood culture [that] conflicted with its own administrative aims or ethical standards."[26] Reserve life posed an enormous threat to traditional social cohesion and values. Mary, who is seventy-four, remembers her parents' lives during the waning agricultural period, when times were hard and welfare had not yet come to the reserve:

"They have to provide for their family . . ."
My mother worked really hard. She had thirteen children and two or three miscarriages. Our brother lived for only a year, but the rest of us

survived. Mother used to go out and chop wood and carry water. She worked really hard. She would carry water from down the hill. She'd wash, she'd clean. We would have to carry our water from a wagon here in Standoff.

There was no welfare back then, so my dad was always out trying to get money for different things. We had cattle and chickens and horses. He used to work his own field, 110 acres. In the fall when he harvested, he'd usually take a load of grain down. He would never take money, he would just exchange it for flour, hundreds of pounds of flour. So he thinks about things, how to be prepared for wintertime.

I remember when one family was out of flour, our dad would give us some flour to take to Standoff, and they would give us stuff to take back. Dad would make this box, it holds so many dozen eggs, and when that box was full he brought it to the Standoff store, and if the people at the store wouldn't take it he'd go out in the community for anyone who wanted to buy the eggs. He was really doing good and busy, because there was no welfare. He had to find ways, you know, to feed his family and clothe his children. In the summertime he and a lot of the husbands on the reserve would go out haying, because they say they have to provide for their family. It was fun to see all these people hauling hay. They cut hay and then they load up and take it off the reserve. Sometimes I would go out with my dad and my younger brother to help them load up the hay. It kept everybody busy.

Welfare did a lot of damage, but if you just stop welfare, it hurts a lot of people, because especially younger people, they depend on it now. Sometimes I think about when I was a little girl. Although times were hard, getting food for the family kept the husbands busy; they weren't so free.

Unfortunately, agriculture failed for many reasons, including the Great Depression and government mismanagement of livestock and feed. By World War II the Bloods had drifted into the economic instability and anomie that haunt reserve Indians in North America. The negative impact of contact with whites did not become manifest until the 1950s, when exceptionally high rates of social pathology emerged in the form of suicide, alcoholism, drug abuse, fatal accidents, divorce, desertion, domestic violence, and murder. During a period of affluence for mainstream white society, the Bloods experienced a downward spiral of social and economic woes that were inextricably rooted in discrimination and prejudice. With their economic, religious, and cultural foundation in jeopardy or destroyed, the Bloods searched for meaningful ways to provide for their families and regain their traditional pride.

In the late 1960s, this search focused on efforts to establish self-government and promote economic development.[27] Hope surged with a new town site at Standoff in the 1970s, the expansion of Blood Band (tribe) Farms, and the discovery of oil on the reserve. But economic underdevelopment, in spite of Blood efforts to stimulate new enterprises, has plagued this reserve as it has others. Unemployment stands in the 80 percent range. At least 70 percent receive some kind of welfare or government transfer payment. Ironically, the band now leases most of its farmlands to whites. Blood-owned Kainai Industries ("100 percent Canadian owned"), which produces modular homes for export to other reserves and communities, employs only forty to one hundred men annually, as contracts arise; few women find work in this construction business.

As with other native communities that are relatively distant from urban centers, economic viability presents on the Blood Reserve complex and frustrating dilemmas. Better education and training cannot guarantee jobs on the reserve. Yet those who leave for the cities (especially men) miss their families and become depressed; many lack an adequate support network.[28]

Today the Bloods live in small ranch houses on the reserve at Standoff. Tiny cabins dot the plains from an earlier era, abandoned because they lack modern facilities. Modern prefabricated homes manufactured by Kainai Industries form the core of Standoff village. Horses and abandoned automobiles scattered among the houses symbolize the competing cross-currents of old and new lifestyles. The reserve includes a supermarket, a rodeo ring, two hangars, a sports complex, a hospital and dental area, a swimming pool, a bank, a pharmacy, a post office, a restaurant, a co-op garage, a small church, two elementary schools, a junior high school, a high school, and a museum-library called the Ninastako Center.

The reserve is dry—as is the closest town, Mormon-dominated Cardston—but it was not always so. In fact, Gladys, age seventy-seven, argues that when electrification came to the reserve around 1964 and alcohol arrived in 1966, she observed a transformation in her husband, who no longer had to bring water or chop wood for fuel. With time on his hands and ready availability of alcohol, "at that point he began to drink." Now residents drive an hour to Lethbridge or across the border into Montana to find alcohol. The relatively short trip is frequently made by those who still have not found a new source of meaning to their lives.

Into the Twentieth Century

CONTEMPORARY ROLES: "TURNING THE WORLD UPSIDE DOWN"

Blood women, on the whole, seem to have adapted more easily and quickly than men to the rapid social change created by cultural contact with another, more dominant culture, and to the shift from nomadic to reservation life. Native women have lower rates of alcohol and drug abuse; lower rates of death by suicide, accident, firearms, and murder; and lower rates of school dropout and involuntary unemployment. Subjective reports of women and men interviewed for this book support these objective indicators.

Modernization has taken its toll on the identity of men, who discovered that equally important and meaningful work outside the home did not replace their traditional role. As the male roles of hunter, warrior, pony raider and breeder, farmer, and rancher have disappeared one by one, women have found themselves in positions of increasing responsibility. As with Inuit men, the Blood man's confidence in his ability to make a major contribution to his family's well-being (as traditional values dictate) has been severely undercut. And as with Inuit and Jamaican women, the Blood woman's burden doubles when she must rely solely or primarily on herself for food and shelter—"turning the world upside down," as elder Agnes says.

In an economy based on welfare and irregular wages, many Blood women are the main providers for their families, and many men are taking primary responsibility for child care, cooking, and cleaning—a dramatic reversal of the traditional pattern. During the agricultural and ranching period, occasionally a Blood man would help his wife, but usually he was too busy to tend the children or the house. Now, when a Blood woman works, her mother or sister might take care of the children, but increasingly her male partner takes significant homemaking responsibility (including child care). It is difficult to find exact statistics on the extent of this role reversal because of considerable part-time, seasonal, and sporadic employment, but both men and women perceive it as a growing phenomenon. When asked who is more likely to be the major provider, most Bloods I interviewed said it is the woman.

The contemporary Blood woman's role, then, takes two forms: being responsible to her family and community, and being a nurturing friend. A "good woman" has a stable marriage or relationship, education and a job, and a good personality. She should be friends with everyone and be there to listen if someone needs to talk. Helping the people in her community (regardless of their social position) and going to church are also desirable qualities.

Women define a "good man" as having "more or less the same qualities, but a little stronger." He should face his responsibility of supporting a family, insists Rhonda, age thirty-seven:

> Some men will accidentally get different girls pregnant. It happens a lot. They won't own up to their responsibility, to say that's their child. Sometimes it bottles up inside them, and then they explode. That's when they start drinking. Many young guys are alcoholics.

Perhaps the most interesting question at the heart of role reversal is this: Why have women adapted more easily to reserve life than have men? Both genders experience discrimination based on race and class; on the reserve, some status distinctions have also emerged. Both also have suffered the indignities of living on the edge of patriarchal, white-dominated society. Women have pursued education and fallen prey less often to alcohol, Rhonda hypothesizes. "It seems like more men are alcoholic because they are bored and depressed." She draws a direct connection between alcohol abuse and employment problems for men. Women drive the school buses, a job men rarely win "because they drink too much and they lose their licenses. That rules out a whole line of jobs where responsibility and soberness are important." Channeling men into trades for which there is little demand may be another explanation. For the men, says Delphine, a Blood employment counselor, "Everybody was trained more or less in the same area when they left school, so they can't expand into anything else." This helps identify the root of male frustration, she adds:

A woman could find a job as a secretary if there is nothing else available; she can always find something that she could do with her skills . . . from high school typing or secretarial classes, so she could fit in. Men have only carpentry or menial skills that don't get them jobs right away. All the jobs are filled, so there is no place for them to go unless someone is fired or quits, then maybe they will be next in line.

Another explanation may lie in Louise Spindler's hypothesis that the persistence of the "manly-hearted woman" image makes it easier for Blood women to take public roles.[29] Margaret, an elder in her eighties, says women have no choice. She remembers that when things were hard her husband did not mind her taking a "minor job" part-time during fall harvest, "but as soon as we finish that, from there on he won't have me work. He would rather support us than [have] me bringing in money." Margaret sees a different situation for young women today who work at full-time jobs: "She stays there all day and has to get a baby-sitter. Her husband will be drinking around while she is supporting them. She has to, because right now you cannot control that liquor."

The insulating value of the domestic role adds another factor. Since the failure of agriculture and the shift to service jobs and welfare dependency, the man's work has all but disappeared, but the woman's work remains. The persistence of women's domestic role (in addition to their new public roles) appears to have provided some protection against the social pathologies that typically erupt with rapid social change.[30] With increasing opportunity, Blood women have not necessarily moved away from their traditional domestic role when they work outside the home or attend university, which creates a double burden for them. In addition to wage-earning jobs on the reserve, women work in the domestic sphere at their traditional duties, continuing to carry major responsibility for homemaking and child care. Vicki, who at age twenty-four finished university and works full-time as a nurse while managing a home and three small children, understands this well: "You know, the house still has to be run. The children still have to be cared for. When we go away during the day to work outside the home, most of us still have to do the inside work when we come home." Ironically, this double role and double burden may be significant in preserving female identity and insulating women from the dramatic changes that have created such havoc among men.

Rosa, a sixty-four-year-old mother of three, said that her husband's role changed dramatically when electrification came to the reserve, whereas hers remained the same. Finding firewood and bringing water were no longer major, time-consuming chores. Although she was cooking with electricity instead of coal oil, she was still cooking; similarly, although she was doing laundry with water from a tap instead of a pump or a well, she was still doing laundry. Marianne, who is in her thirties, took a teacher's aide course and works at the kindergarten level. She explains how she manages her time:

> We still have to do our work at home. Sometimes I didn't go to bed until eleven when they were small, just to get my work done. Now, I put a wash in as soon as I get home and run upstairs and do the supper. Of course, they helped when they got old enough. It was difficult, but I was too busy to feel depressed about my divorce.

A health worker, Joyce says that most men find it difficult to adjust to a new female role, even if they know the family needs their income: "The men think that women should just stay home and take care of the house and the family—not even have a career or work." Men seem to be jealous of women working outside the home, says her co-worker, Leona: "Indian men are really insecure when it comes to that—there are a lot of marital problems." This echoes the traditional value placed on female fidelity and male jealousy.

The comments of a young clerical worker are typical: "My husband was raised to have the wife stay at home, but that is not the way I was raised." She and her family had to leave the reserve because her father was an alcoholic, and her mother had to clean hotel rooms ("We saw her do that"). At fifteen she held her first summer job. After marriage, with a limited budget from her husband's poorly paid job, she offered to work: "I wanted to get a job as a salesperson in a store or whatever, but my husband didn't allow it until we found ourselves getting nowhere. We wanted things, so finally he allowed me to go to work; it was his permission, essentially."

Lois, a craftswoman in her forties, thinks more men are warming up to the homemaking role. She cites the case of her daughter, Betty, age twenty-two, who married at sixteen. At first she worried that Betty was not developing appropriate attitudes. Betty's husband was attending university, but he was not doing very well. Betty did not seem to take adequate care of their baby or the house. She was not a good cook or attentive to her husband; yet she was very happy. This worried Lois, who felt Betty's "maternal instinct had something wrong with it." When her husband dropped out of university, Betty began taking courses and was often the best in the class. Her husband runs the house: "He doesn't cook, but he keeps it going, and takes care of the baby; he is very happy—he likes doing it. He is more loving and attentive to the baby than my daughter ever was." She sees this as an increasingly frequent occurrence, especially among young couples.

BECOMING A WOMAN, BECOMING A MAN

The fact that more and more Blood men take care of their children on a routine basis may have an enormous impact on future development of male and female identity. Historically, young boys and girls learned the male or female roles at the side of their same-sex parent. Young boys absorbed all the intricacies of making hunting and warring weapons simply by working with their fathers from an early age. They played games that paralleled their father's real-life tasks. They also walked out onto the plains in their early teens for a few nights of solitude to give their growing minds an opportunity to have a dream or vision, from which they discovered their spirit helpers and adult name. Sun Dance also afforded a significant opportunity for young braves to demonstrate their strength and prove that they had reached manhood. By the age of thirteen or fourteen they were ready to apprentice to their fathers on warring parties.[31] Courage and strength of character were the most heralded qualities for men.

Elders or holy men and women took young children under their wings, teaching them the oral traditions they could discover only through listening and watching carefully. Both boys and girls learned about the significance and meaning of nighttime ceremonies, Sun Dance, and other rituals; the lessons were liberally sprinkled with legends and true stories about adventures long ago. A deep respect for nature in all its manifestations lay at the core of these teachings: "Sun is our father. The warm love that he sends to our mother, Earth, brings life and makes everything grow."[32] For example, Wallace Many Fingers, Jr., describes the symbolism of

Sun Dance, "the most important event in the lives of all members of the Blood tribe":

> There are four directions and four colours; blue, red, yellow and white. Indian spiritual life revolves around [them]. According to our elders, the foundation of the Indian way is based on relationships and certain fundamental values; respect, caring, sharing and strength. Each corner of the circle represents the foundations of the Indian ways. In the middle of the circle is the fire . . . listening. All the Great Spirit's people are at the center of the universe.[33]

Beverly Hungry Wolf remembers becoming a woman by living with her grandmother in the wild: "I got my education from my culture. My teachers were my grandmothers, and I am really thankful for that."[34] The one she lived with was Mrs. Old-Man-Spotted; when her husband died, they hacked off the old woman's little fingers and her hair as visible signs of her grief.[35] This memory was burned forever in the young girl's mind.

When Beverly's education began, her grandmother said, "In the future you won't be sorry that you learned about these things, so don't mind me bossing you around."[36] She taught Beverly the old tribal songs and how to cook, sew, do beadwork, and make willow backrests and other furnishings for a tipi. Toy tipis and dolls helped her learn the woman's arts. Little boys hunted gophers and squirrels to provide the girls with skins for their doll clothes and rugs for the miniature tipis; like children everywhere, they mimicked in fantasy the realities of the adult world around them. Their summer camping trips into the mountains to find wood for the winter afforded schooling close to the source of survival—Nature herself.

Girls learned to follow mouse trails through the snow to find their tiny nests and the certain treasure that lay there: lily roots. They hunted for wild duck eggs and roasted "wild things" over an open fire. Beverly learned how to fetch clean water from creeks and to melt snow in wintertime. She learned how to identify kinni-kinnick berries, serviceberries, and chokecherries, which the girls ate fresh or dried and pounded into little cakes. How to find and prepare wild tomatoes (rosehips) and countless other plants, roots, and herbs formed part of her knowledge base. She smoked small game like rabbits and remembers that women back then even knew how to cure cancer ("the big boil") with roots and herbs. "We didn't hardly know about candy or liquor," Beverly says, "and those are two things that spoil the young people today."[37]

Annie, age seventy-one, talks about life during the early part of this century, when children were educated at the residential schools built at the edge of the reserve. She could see her parents only at Christmas and in the summers, and she was punished for speaking Blackfoot, but Annie remembers an Anglican minister-teacher who helped children learn agricultural roles:

> I was just wishing he would be alive today to teach our children the way he taught us. When you leave the school and get married, you won't have difficult times—how to clean a home, how to cook—he taught us a lot of things, that old guy. Same thing with the boys. Today, our kids go to day schools. They don't know nothing. They don't know how to work. They don't even know how to dig a hole, our boys. But myself, I taught my kids what I was taught in school. I went by what he taught me, then I was just hoping my children would teach their kids what I taught them.

In spite of the complexities of power relations among adult men and women in this culture, historically (and now) the Bloods highly value babies regardless of gender. Women think it was natural for men to want boys and women to want girls, because the teaching role flowed from father to son, mother to daughter. Today, Genevieve, who is thirty-two, admits, "In our race or anywhere, it's always the male baby that people want. The first baby you want a boy. That's how I felt too, but then your firstborn, whether it's a boy or a girl, you still love them."

Growing up now is complicated for both males and females, because men have been separated from their traditional provider role and women often work outside the home. Nonetheless, the lessons resemble the old ways cast in a modern framework, as Norma, a mother of five, emphasizes: "I raised my kids to learn their own culture as soon as they can [about seven years old]. I make sure they learn to cook, how to clean up the place, everything." Boys learn these chores to some extent, but as in the old days, they gravitate to work outdoors, she says:

> Our fifth child was our first boy. He used to help his dad. He was driving the tractor one time. You could hardly see him! Every time his

dad stops for dinner, he gets on that tractor, makes two or three rounds. He always likes to see his face with dirt on it to show that he is working. He started working really young. I did the same thing with my girls; I taught them to use their manners and to be friendly with everybody.

Norma also takes her children to the Ninastako Cultural Center and talks to them about the displays of traditional life there. She does not speak Blackfoot, but stresses that she teaches "all my kids to respect the elders and their dad."

CONTEMPORARY POWERS: "SHE'S STILL POWERFUL"

Which gender is stronger? Most Bloods argue that emotionally, socially, and psychologically, it is the woman. Blood women describe themselves as being tougher and having more persistence and adaptability than men in the face of change. This is not to deny that many men adapt well, and that many women suffer from problems similar to those of the men, but most perceive men as stronger only in the physical sense.

Flora, a Blood homemaker who has remarried after a bitter divorce, expresses the feeling pervasive in her community: "It is always the woman's responsibility." By "it" she means that even today people expect the woman to be responsible for food, her children, and spiritual life. Usually when a family separates, the children go with the mother; fathers seldom take them because of the substance abuse that may have shattered the family in the first place.[38] People perceive the father as less capable of taking care of the family, observes Flora, "so the women are more aggressive. They are not too proud to go to welfare, where a man won't." She explains this through the example of her brother, who does seasonal construction work. During the winter, when his income dries up, he refuses to go to the welfare office ("He is too proud"); his wife will go, however, because the family must eat. She makes contacts through the social service agencies and might find a job: "That's why the woman is more aggressive than the Indian man."

"I haven't seen anyone die from swallowing his pride," laughs Joe, a Blood elder in his seventies, admitting that his wife's influence has helped him become a fairly successful man. He ties the shifting roles of men and women to changes in power relations. Joe agrees that women have held on to their traditional role and powers more than the men have been able to do, a situation that ultimately compromises the next generation.

"You've got to listen to your wife . . ."
See, the role of the man has changed completely. In the old days, the woman was powerful, and she's still powerful. In a way, she's more powerful than the man, and this is why we take the woman as a sacred thing—she's the life giver and the teacher. Today, the man—he's supposed to be the provider and the protector, but too many times he's not. When you lose that to the woman, you become weak.

In the old days, the woman walks behind the man for a reason. Not that she is inferior, no! Today the woman walks in front of the man, because she wants to be a feminist like the white society. They ask, "Why do the men walk in front of the women?" To protect the life giver and the children behind her!

I tell my wife, "Go ahead to the welfare first." That's what a lot of men say. They don't want to get rejected, it's too painful; so they tell the woman to do it. Or you do it over the phone so you don't have to see the person. Instead of the men doing it, the roles have switched.

Well, with me, the wife has more power. I was henpecked. In order to get along in life, you've got to listen to your wife. All the ones that are well-to-do on the reserve, it's their wives that got them going. Take my old lady, she got me to where I'm at. She always tells me, "Come on, get up. The early bird gets the worm." That was one of her main expressions. But I worry about the little ones. How many women are the teachers now? They put their kids in day care, and the child isn't learning anything.

Women say Blood men realize that women are outpacing them and becoming more aggressive. Women are not sitting back anymore and letting men dominate in class; they are speaking up for themselves. As Donna, a twenty-one-year-old university student, points out, "We are letting the men and the teachers know that we are aware of the issues involved in politics and economics. Women are just stronger and more resilient." James, an addictions counselor, understands why women resist giving up any of their power to men:

A man lost his role when he became an alcoholic. He becomes sober, and he wants to take that role back. Will the woman relinquish that? No way. That's why it's so important to have counseling. She has done the banks, the business, taken care of the kids, all of this for ten years, and now this crazy guy wants to be her boss! That's where you start to compromise. Understanding her role and his role, and your responsibility to your children, that's the main thing. Native people always gear their prayers to the children—they are your future! If you treat them good, you're going to be a beautiful old man. You're not going to end up in an old people's home.

In the spiritual realm, women still own the bundles, which typically consist of a buckskin dress, a feather headdress, paints, and other religious items for ceremonies. Jackie Red Crow writes that the Okan Society of the Blood Reserve honors the holy woman every year with a special ceremony for "the goddess of life":

> During the four day ceremony the participants present bundles of goods. These goods represent the four animals, the four birds and the four plants mentioned in the sacred myth. The importance of this ceremony is the hauntingly beautiful and sacred way in which language, symbol and object are fully integrated. The items the women . . . keep in their bundles are real particles of soil, skins of animals and plant life. They are natural objects, tangible items which create immediate images in the mind.[39]

Beverly Hungry Wolf's description of the bundle evokes powerful images of life along the Belly River: badger, weasel, squirrel, and gopher skins, rawhide rattles, an elk-hide robe, feathers, and natural sacred paints.[40] Medicine women pray for people in time of need and bring fried bread and Saskatoon berry soup every evening during the two weeks of Sun Dance.

Sometimes keeping the bundle weighs heavily. Sandra Bear ("Sally"), at thirty-nine, approaches the role cautiously, a "reluctant" medicine woman. Sally is the third oldest of six children. A few years ago her father became very ill, and Sally's mother grew weak from caring for him. As one of the women in the band who own a bundle, she asked her daughter to take responsibility for it until she felt stronger. (Sally thinks the bundle, which one can either inherit or purchase, was passed down through her family. Anthropologist Esther Goldfrank says that originally people paid for the bundles in blankets or horses, an observation that Sally confirms.)

When Sally's father died, her mother went into a decline, so Sally had to keep the bundle. She does not understand why her mother chose her over two older sisters. At first she didn't want it; she accepted responsibility for a year, but she was afraid of it: "It means you have to be more of a lady, and I'm no kind of a lady." When Sally appeared at Sun Dance in blue jeans one night, other women reprimanded her because jeans were inappropriate for the occasion: "I could wear them anywhere else, but not there. That was not fitting for my role as a holy woman."

Although Sally felt very dubious about this "honor," when it was obvious that her mother would not be able to take the bundle back and people started coming to Sally for prayers, she decided she had better find out more about her culture and native religion and "do right by it." After asking other medicine women to teach her, Sally traveled to Ottawa, where she spent hours in the library researching the Horn society and the bundle. Sally stills feels nervous but is slowing growing into her role as holy woman, as I personally observed:

"Sun Dance"

Sally has invited me to join her at Sun Dance. Since I am to sleep in her tipi, I have to buy a sleeping bag in Cardston. Today, I'm the one in jeans; she has donned her Sun Dance dress—a peasant-style flowered shirt with short sleeves, flowing skirt, and wide leather belt with brass decoration around the waist. Like the other medicine women, she wears a flowered, gypsy-style head scarf and a colorful shawl pinned around her midriff like an apron. We load the truck with our gear and the Saskatoon berry soup and head for Standoff, about eighteen miles from the edge of the reserve. We pass the entrance to Standoff village and follow a dirt road about two miles up to Sun Dance.

Dozens of old-fashioned tipis huddle in a loose circle in a vast open field, surrounded by an assortment of vans, pickup trucks, jeeps, and horses. Sally warns that I must not take pictures, because Sun Dance takes place on holy ground (although she lets me take one from the access road, from a distance). Sally worries that we are late and feels embarrassed because for the second night in a row she has almost missed the ceremony. She hurriedly throws her shawl around her shoulders, grabs the pot of berry soup and the fried bread, and plunges into the crowds sitting around the inner circle, distributing her offerings. With this simple act, Sally bridges the woman's role from out of the nineteenth century, and earlier, into the twentieth century.

Role reversal complicates male-female relationships and dramatically affects the balance of power between the sexes. While women achieving more power and rediscovering old powers is positive in some ways, if men do not secure power commensurate with their own self-image, the result can be extremely dangerous for women. Blood women speak of the loss of balance between the genders as a critical source of frustration that contributes to domestic violence. They believe that role reversal makes men feel angry and insecure. Now schools are training men as electricians, plumbers, welders, and bricklayers so they can compete more effectively. Nonetheless, economic development and job training staff point to a high population of unemployed males and search for better ways to make them employable. Until they regain the pride and esteem that comes from helping provide for their families, men will continue to seek the escape routes of alcohol, drugs, and suicide—and the explosive release of violence.

Love, Marriage, and Divorce: The Woman's Responsibility

Even traditionally, the bond between husband and wife was tenuous. In the old days, rich women could leave their husbands if the husbands did not treat them properly. Since the parents chose the husband, they were very protective of their daughter if he beat her; the parents simply came and took their daughter back home. Poor women sometimes left because they wanted a better husband who could give them wealth. Now, if a battered woman returns to her parents, they often send her back to her husband. Sally explains: "You made the choice of husband and the parents didn't, so you have to take responsibility for the consequences." Arranged marriages were common in the old days, recalls Esther, an elder woman:

"I paid for him and he paid for me . . ."

I was sixteen in 1938. Them days we don't have much education—our parents didn't care about it then. As soon as you reached sixteen, you leave school. Our folks just think before we start running around we have to get married, and there is nothing we can argue about. Just follow their orders. My parents picked my husband because they know him well, that he was a hard-working boy, and they know that he can support me with my children. We was blessed with nine kids; me and my husband have been together for forty-eight years. It was during a Sun Dance that I married my husband. That was the year I left school. I didn't "go out" with him, what these young kids do now nowadays. You have to get married as soon as you reach sixteen, and there is nothing a girl can do but follow her parents, what they want her to do.

We used to plant way on the east side of the camps. Then my mother, my auntie, my brother, they brought me across to this place here. That's where my husband's parents were. He had to wait for me here, and then my parents brought me across with a whole bunch of blankets and horses and gave them to his parents. My mother had all this stuff. We exchanged gifts, and that's the Indian way of marriage in them days: I paid for him and he paid for me, and so that is when I married my husband. Our Indian marriage.

After we had our first child a couple of years later, we got married by the church, legally married. I have been happy with my family. Imagine, married at sixteen; I had my first child when I was nineteen years old, and they were close up, too.

Connie, now in her fifties, also married at sixteen. Her story illustrates the complex admixture of luck, distorted relationships, and persistence that often converges to create a woman's life in a changing society. In contrast to Esther, Connie was of the generation that could choose her husband, whom she loved very much. For the first few years they lived out on the edge of the reserve raising cattle; he worked in the barn, and she worked in the house except to water the horses. They were very happy, but when they moved closer to Standoff, he began to drink. It was liquor that ruined their marriage, Connie relates, because he would stay out all night and become violent when he returned. Although he was a good provider and she loved him very much, she could not stand the beatings, so she asked the Royal Canadian Mounted Police (RCMP) to pick him up and pressed charges against him for assault. After his sentence was suspended, Connie's husband beat her again. This time, although Connie recalls hating to take him back to court, her husband received a six-month jail sentence.

"I thought he would kill me . . ."
He would go out on a binge every few weeks; the binges got closer and closer together, and he would be away longer and longer each time. When he finally came home, he would beat me. I did not want my children to grow up seeing this. I didn't grow up like that; my father was always very kind to my mom.

In the middle of his prison term, his grandmother died. I thought he would kill me . . . if I kept him from being there when his grandmother died. So I arranged a pre-release for him so he could attend his grandmother's funeral. He came home for a week, but I was so afraid of him that I couldn't let myself get close to him anymore. It was over. He went away.

My oldest son hates his father. He is old enough to remember what it was like. The two younger boys tolerate him—if they bump into him on the reserve, fine, but they don't go out of their way to see him. My daughter loves her father, is close to him, and visits him all the time.

Two years later I took a training course up at the university in Calgary. A psychology professor noticed that I was shaking every time we talked about battered wives. He said I should go to a psychiatrist and see a lawyer about a divorce. I did. I asked for nothing; I gave him everything. I just asked for custody of the kids, but I gave him visiting rights. In the fifteen years since our divorce, he never came to see the children, he never recognized their birthdays, he never saw them for Christmas. I found out he married a young woman later and had four kids by her. To tell you the truth, I was so jealous that I wanted to scratch the woman's eyes out. I wanted to scratch the baby's eyes out when I heard about that first pregnancy.

Then I felt sorry for her—he left her, too. They divorced, and he married a third time, had another child, and divorced again. It's the drinking. Now he's living with a white woman. I like her because for the first time in all these years, he sent his children Christmas gifts. I'm still single, though. Sometimes I feel lonely and maybe wish I got married again, but I still have my children and my brothers and friends. They're all very important to me.

A young Blood woman, dismayed by the effects of alcohol on her marriage, seriously contemplates divorce as the only method of stopping the downward cycle of their relationship. When asked about the most significant person in her life, Cheryl replies, "I guess my son, considering right now there are problems with my husband. Right now he is on my blacklist. I see him as an alcoholic; I don't know if I can live with it. It seems like every forty days he will go out on a real good binge, and each time it's getting longer and longer. It's not my problem, and it's not my fault." After hearing too many broken promises from her husband that he will stop drinking, Cheryl is ready to be on her own: "I feel like I could take care of myself and my son. I have been doing it the past two years anyway, supporting my own family."

Mary is a senior holy woman who sees families reeling from the ravages of alcohol. Other medicine women address her as "Ma," explaining that "she is the mother of us all." She travels to the reserve schools to teach the children traditional crafts, and at the age of seventy-five has more work than she can handle. After a wedding ceremony, she delivers a long, melodious prayer in Blackfoot, then adds in perfect English, "I wish I knew better English, because then I could have translated what I said into English and everybody who didn't know Blackfoot would understand the happy things that I said for the couple." Mary believes that children learn about family life, and despair, from their parents:

> A teenager may come home and see both of them flaked out from alcohol, day after day. They feel that there is no hope for their own future, so they take their own life. We had a twenty-four-year-old man who recently committed suicide. His younger brother committed suicide the year before. In that case, both parents drink a lot and the house is always a mess, and it didn't seem that there was much hope for them.

If children learn more about their culture, she stresses, they will recapture the sense of purpose and pride that makes them strong enough as individuals to contribute to a strong family.

Challenges Confronting Women

Closely interconnected challenges face Blood women today: the devastation of alcohol abuse among their partners and themselves, having to raise families alone, and discrimination and restricted opportunities. Blows to male pride and self-esteem spur alcohol and drug abuse, which in turn depress male pride and self-esteem. Blood women agree that the trio of alcohol abuse, role reversal, and broken marriages often results directly in domestic violence and, in turn, can propel women into the primary breadwinning role as single parent.

VIOLENCE, LIBERATION, AND ALCOHOL

A Blood social worker describes an all-too-familiar situation: "Husbands beat up their wives because the wives seem to have gained the higher position—she is the working person, and he probably can't find a job." A mental health worker observes the connection between alcohol and assault: "There is a real bad alcoholic problem on the reserve. I think it is due mainly to lack of employment for the male, so they are idle. That is the main problem."[41] And an alcoholism counselor theorizes that now some people on the reserve have skills and are becoming competitive "like white people now, instead of that sharing part." Two or three hundred years ago the Blood Indians survived without technology, he says: "They had a beautiful way of life. Everything was provided for them by the Creator and Mother Earth and the sources around them. Today some of us don't know how to survive. Some of us can't even start a fire. They don't even know what the meaning of fire is, meaning of a rock, meaning of a plant, meaning of a bird. We have become blind to that, we become weak. The women we work with can't stand pain, either. This world is a drug world. It hits women hard." Rosetta, age thirty-nine, talks about how hard it is to cope:

"I would be afraid of his anger . . ."
My oldest child is a male, and my youngest is a female. I've probably been harder on her over the years than I was on my son, because he would get angry and I would be afraid of his anger. I would back off from him, whereas I always knew that no matter how angry my daughter and I got with each other, we would always make up and hug, say I love you—and it would be okay, you know, we'd cry a little bit. I never had that feeling of security with my son, that if I really got angry with him and held my ground, he would still be there. I thought he'd get so mad he'd leave. I'm talking about the teenage years. Maybe that's

something we need to look at, too. If people get into enabling behavior, the whole community has to try to break that behavior before you can say you're dealing with the disease of alcoholism.

I fell into it without even realizing what I was doing, and I think that's why it was hard for me to get out of that. When I first got married, when my husband would go off and get drunk, my mother-in-law would expect me to go look for him—if I didn't go look for him, I didn't love him. I got into that for a long time. I don't know how I finally realized it. I guess when my children got older. Before that, if he called, I would get up at two o'clock in the morning and go get him. Really stupid things like that. I was made to feel guilty if you didn't do these things for him. I realized when he finally left that our whole life revolved around what he wanted to do.

Rosetta asked her husband to leave in order to restore peace to her life and stop supporting his drinking. She works two jobs and is trying hard to keep her young family together. She hopes her husband can find his own spiritual rebirth by shaking off the poisonous shackles of alcohol.

RAISING CHILDREN ALONE

The challenge of raising children as a single parent faces some women in all cultures. For Blood women, it happens all too often. The high rate of family breakdown and illegitimate births starkly contrasts to an earlier time when Blood women were known as "modest," married very young, and came from stronger families, as elder Annie recalls:

In them days when a girl gets herself in trouble, like carrying a baby, the whole reserve will be talking about her and against the family— "Why didn't they discipline the girl?"—but today there is no discipline. You don't know how many girls have illegitimate kids. Nobody cares. I don't feel right about it. It's the men that gets those girls in trouble, and they don't turn around to marry them and support the child. We just pity the girls. That's through drinking. The girl gets herself in trouble. Nobody bothers. It's just like—I don't know how to express this—it's just like being animals. That's how I think of it today.

Nonetheless, in a close community there is substantial support for women going it alone, and many women cite raising children alone as the most significant accomplishment of their lives. They express gratitude for being able to talk to other family members and other women raising children alone. Indeed, women cite their own mothers—many of whom were also single parents—as pillars of strength; they respect their mothers and want to be like them, as a Blood craftswoman whose father was a heavy drinker explains: "We went through a lot of hard times. She didn't break down, even when we all felt really upset. She could handle the situation, keep calm. That really helped a lot." Her mother always worked outside the home so her six children would not be sent to foster homes: "The authorities could have taken us away. She tried real hard when she was away from my dad, and she felt safe. That's what I think of her: She kept us all together and tried hard." Another woman adds: "I think my story is about the same as hers. My father was an alcoholic and my mother left him. She supported us until we got old enough to get our own jobs and support ourselves."

Confidence and strength reward these mothers and inspire their children, as a community college student in her late thirties proudly reports:

> My kids, before they didn't look up to me, but now they see me going back to school and they are trying a little harder to do better in school, too. They have a better view of what they want to do when they get older—teachers, nurses, or doctors. When I was that age, I didn't know what kind of career I was going toward.

Some women stubbornly hold on to relationships: "They'll get abused and abused and they won't do nothing about it," health worker Paula, age thirty-four, relates. When they finally make the break for freedom, pride in managing alone results:

> I was just sitting at home and being really miserable and a nag, being bored. Coming to school and meeting people was great; before, I didn't have very many friends because I was always at home. Raising a family as a single parent, I'm proud of that, bringing the kids up by myself.

The first year of separation was hard, until Paula decided that she wanted to raise her children without them seeing her depressed. Her goal was to "bring them up happy" by talking to them and helping them understand what had happened: "They seem to be getting along okay. They are happy, you know." Another health worker agrees that being a single parent has given her a sense of purpose, and education has given her the tool for achieving her goals:

> The most important thing was having a son. He really filled in my life. Before he was born I had no goal, and now I do. I have him. I just work and spend my money on him. The other significant thing would be this course I am taking to become a health assistant.

DISCRIMINATION

The third challenge is equally daunting. Historic discrimination against native people has placed Blood women in a politically and economically inferior position. Institutionalized racism and open discrimination still influence job opportunities in urban areas, contributing to a dilemma that results in the failure of many well-qualified people to reach their potential.

Contemporary discrimination that often cuts along gender lines mirrors male dominance in the old Blood social order. Paula believes that men have significant advantages over women: "We are discriminated against in the sense that we can't own land unless we are legally married to a man and he dies, then that is our land." Sometimes it seems exceptionally difficult to get a house on the reserve if you are a female head of household. For example, Melanie, age forty-four, has found it difficult to get a house on the reserve: "That's another thing where I think women are discriminated against, because they will listen to the man. If a man went in there and asked for a house or anything else, they will give it to him first before they'll acknowledge the woman's request." If she has "a fantastic idea to open up a business on the reserve," jealousy may play a part in turning down her request for economic development funds, she says: "If a man thinks you are going to get ahead with this—if you are doing it on your own and you want some help from them—they can just say no to you. They'll say, 'Well, she is a woman, and she may do better than I am doing.' That's jealousy and that's politics all together. It can do a lot of harm." Blood women are tackling these challenges head on.

Toward the Twenty-First Century

THE ROAD TO EQUALITY

Blood women acknowledge that their position as Indians within Canadian society results in marginality. An active native women's movement on the reserve creates pressure to achieve balanced power between males and females, but the legacy of the nineteenth-century Indian Act has left them with a built-in status inequality. As with other Indian women in Canada, the law has treated Blood women unequally in comparison to men. As discussed in the previous chapter, after the act passed, a woman who married a white man lost her status and rights as an Indian (becoming "nonstatus"). By contrast, a Blood man could marry a white woman without jeopardizing his traditional rights. Although this quirk of the Indian Act has recently been challenged, its resolution remains complex, determined by individual bands.

Shirley, who works in economic development and has her own coat-making business, is a nonstatus Indian who has been in the process of regaining her status since Canadians passed Bill C-31 in the late 1980s. The bill allows women who lost their status because they married white men to regain their status as Indians. As nonstatus Indians, they may come back and live on the reserve with family members, but they may not own a house, take property, or share in the band's distribution of its wealth. Mary says that native women should be able to take the best from both worlds: the native and the mainstream. That is not to be for nonstatus Indian women, who live between two fires, a dilemma Shirley describes with anger:

> They won't let me take the best from both worlds because I am a nonstatus Indian, and I can't participate in the economic benefits of being an Indian, a status Indian. It's difficult. They have to make me status. They have two years to do it. The band is supposed to come up with a membership list, and any woman who wants to reclaim her status for herself or for her children can simply approach the band. They must do it by the new agreement. They can't keep it away from me.

Many Blood women have completed degrees and have established themselves in professional positions both off and on the reserve. Blood women have always been hard workers: In the early twentieth century, they began to leave the home for seasonal wage-earning jobs like stooking hay and working in canneries (if their husbands approved). They have always had more consistent attendance and performance records in school, which pays off in greater employability. Most teachers in the reserve schools and health clinic workers are women; women also receive the vast majority of social work and clerical jobs, hold some administrative positions, and work in areas like economic and cultural development.[42] In some cases they are outstripping their male partners, creating an often-uncomfortable role reversal in which women are dominant as providers and decision makers.

Politically, some Blood women see changes occurring in gender inequality. "Before, it used to be just men as council members—you would never see a woman in there—but for the last fifteen, twenty years, women have been in the council," says Paula. "In the band [administration] office, the only women you would see were secretaries; all the men would have the high positions, the directorship. Not anymore." (Women have served as council members and directors of departments for about thirty years.) Others agree that the situation is changing: "It is not as bad as it used to be back in the old days." Now many women work and have career goals, "where before it was just all men." A social service department worker notes: "Our director is a woman; our computer trainer is a woman. The only thing we haven't had is a chief lady, and there is a lady who is willing to take it." Another woman is less optimistic: "They have changed quite a bit on the reserves, but I think in a sense we are still being discriminated against."

WOMEN'S EMPOWERMENT

Women in their late teens reflect the concern of their generation: Will they be able to arrange the kind of training, education, and job opportunities necessary for giving their own children a better life? This pressure, which historically has been on males, is shifting to the shoulders of women. Although women say they want equal relationships, when they look around them, they feel skeptical. Many of the women they know, including mothers and aunts, hold the key to economic security for their families.

There is some evidence that the younger generation is beginning to take steps to restore gender balance. Males seem to be showing more interest in post–high school training programs and in completing their diplomas. At the University of Calgary, where many Bloods attend, a Blood administrator observes that 1986 was the first year in which an equal number of males and females enrolled. In prior years only a "handful of males" ventured into these halls, she says. "Now we wonder if men realize that they need to get a higher education so that they can compete, because the women are coming back with master's degrees. A bachelor's degree no longer satisfies them; they are now reaching one step higher. For men to regain the prestige or power they once held, they have to get a degree of some kind." A university counselor points out that previously on the reserve jobs were open usually to men, because "men provided the income, provided the security." That is changing as women return with superior qualifications: "It just didn't seem right, because many single women who are raising their children couldn't get jobs."

Some older Blood women speak of the negative effects of Anglican or Catholic boarding schools built on or near the reserve. White teachers communicated that "being Indian was not a very nice thing to be; we should try to be as white as possible and speak English." Children met punishment for using their own language, Blackfoot. Kara, a social worker who specializes in helping children adjust to school, refers to "the boarding school syndrome," which produces children with low self-esteem and lack of confidence "because they were taught that they're no good." Kara wants to work on her master's degree or even a doctorate, but when she took university courses she kept hearing a voice saying to her, "You're stupid, you're dumb! What are you doing here—you don't belong here!" She realized it was the echo of what she heard as a child, so she left school to work through her feelings. Eventually Kara pursued a social work degree. She is good at what she does and wants to help other women feel better about themselves.

As women try to support their families, they perceive high school and university education as the best way for them to enter the job market and to make a substantial income. Once they reach a certain level of self-sufficiency, says a counselor, "They are less willing to put up with the drunkenness, beatings, and lack of affection dished out by unhappy men. They walk out." In order to improve their chances of securing employment on the reserve (with its limited number of positions), women travel to Calgary or Lethbridge.[43]

They know that if they go back home without sufficient education, they will land menial jobs or none at all. If they achieve a bachelor's degree in education or social welfare, they can compete more effectively. Several women named education as the most significant experience in their lives.

These dreams must be viewed in the context of past educational realities for Blood women. The Canadian Department of Indian Affairs passed a policy in 1938 that no Indian child in Canada should have an education beyond the eighth grade. Of course, that old rule has long since been lifted. Education paves the way out of unemployment and welfare dependency; as one Blood woman argues, "It's the only way out." If a native woman has a good high school record, the government pays her expenses for university and gives her an allowance for living expenses ("Everything is paid for—we are lucky that way!"). Going to university while raising a family still presents challenges, however, because "government allowances never make do." A professor praises an older Blood woman who struggled to stay in university during a difficult pregnancy: "She had four children and gave birth to a fifth during school. She still got her degree. I really admired her courage for sticking it out and going right to full term."

The female surge toward higher education is possible, of course, because of their higher rate of high school completion. In addition, Kara says women seem to see educational achievement as a challenge:

> One woman will see another woman going back to school and say, "If she can do it, I can do it. So I am going to give it a try and see what happens to me." The men may be just a little bit too proud to go back to school. They think it's just young kids, or they seek the labor jobs, but there is no employment here unless you have an education. Anything you apply for, even if it is dishwashing, they'll ask what grade you finished.

Blood women are seen as superior to men for trying to complete their education; this is a major source of respect, even from the men, says Jeannie, a management student in her thirties: "When I was at home I was just Jeannie. Now I am trying hard, and I get respect from everybody—my uncles, my grandmother, my family, my friends. Many of them are in the doldrums, because I am working and they are not. They just stay home all day."

The women's good fortune, however, does not necessarily extend to acquisition of a secure position. Many study teaching, social work, nursing, and counseling, but when graduates return to the reserve, they find few appropriate openings because isolated communities with small populations have a limited need for professional workers. Favoritism plays a role, too, Jeannie fears: "Probably you have to know the right people to get into places you want to go."

DREAMS FOR THEIR DAUGHTERS

When asked to describe their dreams for their daughters, Blood women invariably and first talk about a good education. Education will provide the daughters with independence; they will be able to support themselves and their families. Many also want their children to learn Blackfoot and the ways of the traditional culture. As a woman in her sixties says, "I want them to do everything together with their family. I raised my kids to learn their own culture. They should do this, too." They do not want their daughters to share the fate their generation experienced—married at sixteen or seventeen, often to abusive men whom they eventually left. As their children grew older, they decided to go back to finish high school, often going on to university and/or working. These women want their daughters to do it the other way around and perhaps avoid the pain and suffering of raising their children alone and without adequate skills, jobs, or income. A university counselor explains:

> Blood women who come back to university say that if they had the chance to do it over again, they would have completed school right away. That is the message we are trying to get across to young people: "Go to school now. You can always have fun later. You are not going to lose out on anything." They drop out at grade nine, then there is nothing for them. They waste five or six years, get married and have children, still going nowhere.

Younger women are especially likely to be the major provider for their families. Many men have lost their status—and therefore their power—in the community. Men search for new sources of self-esteem and pride through education and economic development. The future may include greater equality between women and men as Blood Indians move toward pride and self-sufficiency, balancing their traditions with contemporary opportunities.

Mary insists that as she grew up, she learned to respect her people and her culture. She understands the problems of her daughters and sons, granddaughters and grandsons as reflections of a trying time—a transition from freedom to dependency, from dignity to degradation, wrapped up inextricably in the power of alcohol and a loss of spirit. This requires the greatest battle of all to conquer, yet Mary believes that the dreams of education, equality, and harmony are possible for the generations to come:

"They look so beautiful . . ."

Girls drink around, get into accidents. That's liquor. It ruined our men, our people, and today there is just a few people that die of sickness. The rest is all accidents—killing, stabbing. It's getting worse on our reserve. I sure pity this young generation; hope and pray for them. Wise up and go back to school and be somebody! Make use of your education. Today you cannot just go and ask for a job. You have to be in grade twelve and higher to get a good job.

That's why the Sun Dance is really important to us. Some of the young boys, they all join in this Horn society, and now those guys are trying to be straight with drinking. Get back their culture, which is really nice. They look so beautiful—all young men dancing. I just admire them. Look at them dance; before it wasn't like that. But now all these young men look upon their own culture, which is really good.

They have their pride again to be an Indian, which I am really happy for, out there dancing and enjoying themselves. We really enjoy looking at our young people coming back to their own culture. They are learning to pray for other people, especially our elders. I wanted to be happy, not be a hermit and living by myself, but then you could get caught in tight spots getting married. That's why it's important that the young ladies—they look so beautiful—go to university now.

Mary dreams that all her children and grandchildren will ride the vehicle of education toward a brighter future. Above all, she hopes that families will teach their children about the beautiful culture she remembers from long ago, when the Blood lived closer to Mother Earth.

The Last Night

After Sun Dance, we sit in Sally's tipi. Although she had given me two pieces of fried bread and a cup of tea (made from fresh wild mint) before we left her house, I am famished. She offers me some cold Saskatoon berry soup, then roasts hot dogs over the fire inside the tipi. I say that we used to do that when I was a little girl living on Lake Erie, but we roasted marshmallows, too. Sally reaches into her cooler with a grin and pulls out marshmallows. As we hold them over the fire on slender sticks, it seems very strange and yet very natural that Sally and I are sharing this meal. I am thousands of miles from home, and she is crossing thousands of miles of culture between her roles as a traditional medicine woman and a provident modern woman with a cooler filled with hot dogs and marshmallows.

We sit near the fire, sipping tea, in a tipi that measures about fifteen feet across. With a few mattresses tucked around the sides, it is very comfortable. Old pieces of carpet lay around the center fire in a mosaic of faded colors. Several small round stones form the perimeter of the fire. Extending outward from the fire, wooden pegs pierce the ground, with a thin bed of marsh grass strewn among them. A smaller fire at the end of that area burns grass for religious purposes. Our eyes begin to smart, because Sally has used damp wood. She complains to herself: "The elders always say that you should use the old dry wood, it doesn't smoke. I knew that."

We talk about her life. Sally and her closest friend, Mady, were in an automobile accident a few years ago. Mady was driving one rainy night, ran off the road, and hit a grader. Sally had a badly smashed jaw and spent a month in North Carolina having it reconstructed. She felt very frightened by all the black people around her at the hospital, then suddenly realized, "Hey, this is just how a white person feels when he or she comes onto an Indian reserve, so just relax! These are good people and they are not going to hurt you." She talked herself into being comfortable, but said she hated being in an urban environment and could not wait to get home.

We talk late into the night about love and marriage, children and dreams, until Sally announces that it is finally time to "do our visiting." She had promised to arrange an interview with Donna, an elder in her early seventies, but I have despaired of meeting her at

*this late hour. To my surprise, however, at 11:30 we let the fire die
down and leave our tipi for Donna's.*

Donna motions for me to sit down near the potbelly stove that
dominates the center of her tipi. It is very warm, in spite of the cool
Alberta night. This energetic elder leads the interview herself and
seems happy to talk about her life. She names her children, her
grandchildren, and her great-grandchildren, listing them by age and
discussing how their lives are going. Tears spring to her eyes after the
long list as she goes back to add more names: "We've lost five. Two
of my own, three grandchildren. I don't want to put in any sad story
about the deaths of my kids, but I just wanted to mention it."
Donna's baby died in infancy, and her forty-five-year-old son was
killed last year in an alcohol-related car accident near the reserve.
Two teenage grandsons and a four-year-old great-grandson have
died in similar crashes, the toddler just a few weeks ago. Donna's
voice quivers with anger and grief as she remembers a young man
who was about to become the first Blood to receive his medical degree from the University of Calgary. He was killed on a mountain
road when he and his friends went out drinking to celebrate their
graduation.

Outside, singers and drummers pass from tipi to tipi, making
noise to keep evil spirits from harming the elders. The men, who
share responsibility for guarding the holy tent in the center of the
Sun Dance circle, take turns all night to ensure that no one touches
the sacred bundles. About fifteen men sit face-to-face in two horse-
shoe-shaped rows near the tipi. Kneeling, they play an old
handgame, beating boards with little sticks and passing an object
around the horseshoe. The steady beating and chanting provide a
rhythmic background to our interview. At 1:40 in the morning I reluctantly bring my talk with Donna to a close, fearful of exhausting
both of us.

I grope my way down to the outhouse in the pitch black, tripping
over tipi ropes and bumping into a couple taking advantage of the
night. The stars are absolutely brilliant, revealing the full spectacle
of the Milky Way. Lights flicker inside the tipis, like fireflies inside
folded moth wings. It is quiet, almost mystical out there on the
plains, with the Rockies asleep in the distance. Painted designs on
tipi walls dance across the night sky, thrown into relief by the dying
fires inside them. Sally and I whisper from under our blankets for a

few more minutes, watching the dying embers of her marsh grass fire; we finally fall asleep around two. Sisters.

The next morning, after putting three liters of oil in the pickup truck, I start the long, lonely stretch back to Calgary after another week on the Blood Reserve, guzzling a can of diet lemon-lime pop and wolfing down a bag of potato chips for my breakfast. It is hot, dusty, and peaceful. The Rockies peer across the foothills from the west. Tomorrow, I fly to the Arctic to interview Inuit women. It seems like a million miles away.

4

Daughters of Sedna

Inuit Women of Pangnirtung, Baffin Island, Northwest Territories

We're no longer married to hunters, most of us, but we're still following the pattern of grandmother who went before us to prepare us for the future, for making decisions. That is very important. That's always been passed on. It's not written, it's not a law, but it's here. Sometimes I wonder, my goodness, we're very busy people.

—Qaida

En Route to Pangnirtung

My daughter, Kyra, sits beside me as we fly north from Ottawa on a 737 jet. It is very expensive to buy food in the Arctic, so we strap provision boxes for a summer's stay into the seats up front. The one-dimensional map of Canada that I memorized as a little girl in a one-room schoolhouse in Ontario sprawls beneath us in three-dimensional reality: The eastern shoreline of Hudson Bay, the Great Whale River of northern Quebec, Ungava Bay, Hudson Strait, Frobisher Bay. Images of explorers and whalers rush through my mind. After three hours of flying over seemingly endless and uninhabited tundra, then snow and ice, we land in Iqaluit, Baffin Island—the first stop on our way north.

Ever since I read Farley Mowatt's People of the Deer *as a teenager, I wanted to meet the Inuit, who survive in the world's harshest climate and often starved to death when the caribou herds lost their way. Now virtually all Inuit live in settlements, and my daughter is the teenager. I feel strangely moved and connected to her as we climb into a much smaller Twin Otter plane, the "workhorse of the*

Arctic." As we begin the second leg of our journey, most of our fellow passengers are Inuit.

We sit inches behind the pilots and peer through cockpit windows as we fly across lower Baffin Island, over Cumberland Sound, and up the fjord toward our final destination: Pangnirtung, almost 2,500 kilometers (1,500 miles) north of Ottawa. The world floats below us in cold Arctic colors—white, silver, gray, icy blue. Trees disappeared hours ago. Bare, craggy mountains loom thousands of feet on either side of the plane. Suddenly we see a tiny gravel runway below, perched on the edge of the fjord and flanked by houses; the runway doubles as the hamlet's main street. The plane banks steeply and turns toward the village, like an Arctic tern diving for fish. We watch the tiny forms of people scattering from the runway as we make our precipitous approach. Through the cockpit I see only water, then gravel, then a chain-link fence dead in front of the plane. We have landed abruptly, but safely. My heart is beating wildly with fear and elation. This is the Arctic!

Dozens of Inuit villagers have come out to meet the plane and its twenty passengers, as is the custom in the North. When the propellers spin down, the pilots will allow us to scurry under the belly of the plane to retrieve our boxes. The local Secretary Manager, with whom I communicated many times by telephone and fax in the process of securing the council's permission to do research in "Pang," helps us into his van (one of the few vehicles in this pedestrian community). Tonight, he says, we will stay at the village's only inn. Tomorrow we will begin living with an Inuit family, then later we will stay in the Anglican mission with other researchers.

There are no docks at Pangnirtung. A thirty-foot tide alternately hides and reveals huge rocks that plague even the most competent boater. The water is so clear, it's like looking through a glass tabletop to the rocks below. I imagine glaciers surging through the pass millions of years ago, creating the tunnel effect at Pang, and shiver instinctively. At the mouth of the fjord, the mountains transform into low islands of water-worn rocks that look like whales and walruses and monsters from a distance. The fjord opens into Cumberland Sound to the south, and suddenly we can see shimmering water forever, broken only by Mother Nature's frozen sculpture, the giant icebergs that glow in brilliant blues and greens.

We fall asleep in our tiny room at the inn after a dinner of canned *ham, canned potatoes, and canned green beans. Later, out on the land with our Inuit hosts, we will be treated to meals of bannock, tea, blueberries, seal, and freshly caught Arctic char—"country food." Tomorrow morning we will meet the women of Pangnirtung.*

L ong ago, according to Inuit legend, the great goddess Sedna threw herself over the side of her father's canoe rather than marry a man her father chose and she despised. As she clung to the boat's side, he cut her fingers off, and she slipped into the black, icy waters forever. Her fingers became the whales, walrus, seals, and fish that fill the Arctic waters with life-giving bounty. Today the daughters of Sedna are still strong and givers of life. They are struggling to recover and preserve the best of traditional culture, recapture balance between male and female power, and to help their daughters find pride in being an Inuk.[1]

Dubbed Eskimos (from *wigas-ki-mowak*, "eaters of raw meat"[2]) by northern Indians, for thousands of years the Inuit ("the people"), as they call themselves, were scattered across the vast, icy reaches of Baffin Island in the Northwest Territories. Long before European exploration of this continent, the Inuit lived a nomadic existence in small bands, pursuing game and hovering in igloos, skin tents, or sod huts to survive the Arctic cold. Caribou thundered across the tundra and through the mountain passes, enticing the Inuit to follow for meat and fur. The hunt dictated when to move and where to live. Glaciers draped the mountains and fed the rivers and fjords. Life was lived in intimate harmony with the land and the sea.

Over the centuries the Inuit learned how to strike a balance with nature. The Arctic environment was both magnificent provider and formidable foe. Far from idealizing life "out on the land," contemporary Inuit are open about "the bad times." Periodically, sudden and inexplicable shifts in the regular path of caribou herds would cause starvation. The elders of the elders (long since dead) passed down stories about perseverance through such great climatic forces as the Little Ice Age and other warming or cooling trends that threatened their very existence. The people shared to the last fish and huddled around the last fire until nature reversed herself.

Contact with whites proved to be even more problematic. The collision of cultures that began with early explorers like Martin Frobisher in the sixteenth century and continues today through the invisible waves of television has resulted in both loss and hope. The physical and economic changes in Inuit lives are dramatic enough, but the transformation of culture dominates their conversations. The double-edged sword of opportunity has cut through traditional Inuit culture with cruel swiftness. The Inuit have been plunged into the value system of a culture light years away; soap operas and sitcoms compete with drum dancing and traditional games. They have been stripped of their identity as nomadic people of the land and brought into permanent settlements, like Pangnirtung, that boast prefabricated houses with indoor plumbing and electricity. The outside world has impinged on Inuit life in every conceivable way—from birth control to Nintendo—creating important changes in how women and men live, work, and relate to each other in the twentieth century.

Out of Tradition

TRADITIONAL ROLES: "LIFE WAS HARDER"

"My mother always looked after seal skins—scraping off the blubber, drying them, stretching them, and making them into things like *kamiks* [boots]," recalls an elder, "and my father was always hunting, bringing back the food. I was happy." In traditional Inuit culture, a clear division of labor existed side by side with flexibility and shared power. Male and female roles balanced on the fulcrum of daily subsistence. Although the Inuit sharply delineated men's skills and women's skills, the survival imperative ensured a fairly equal relationship grounded in reciprocity and mutual respect. Women's work was different, not inferior. Roles intermeshed as life revolved around the natural rhythms of the seasons: hunting, gathering, fishing, sewing—always preparing for the next long, deep winter. Men hunted for the food that women processed. Women helped prepare the caribou hides that kept men alive on the hunt. Women looked after the children, made clothing, cooked, and cared for the shelter. Men needed women's skills as processors of food and skin as much as women needed the raw materials from which they created nutritious meals and protective clothing.

Women worked hard to keep the family warm in a harsh, unforgiving climate where a human face can freeze in sixty seconds and the wind chill can drag temperatures down to eighty degrees below zero Fahrenheit; an exposed human can die within fifteen short, painful minutes. Men learned to make igloos in less than an hour as a blizzard approached. Women made and repaired the *kamiks* that kept men from losing toes to frostbite or freezing to death. The gender calculus was elegantly simple: If the woman was not skilled at making warm clothing, then the man would freeze to death on the hunt. If the man did not hunt, the woman could not make clothing to protect herself and her children from the elements. The roles were equally vital.

Men carved fishing and hunting tools and constructed *kamotiks* (sleds) out of hides and treasured bits of wood and metal from explorers and whalers, sometimes using frozen fish for runners. Boys accompanied their fathers when they took the dog teams and *kamotiks* out hunting. Women gathered berries in the summer and dried them to feed the men during the fall trips; they fished with sticks and occasionally killed a seal when the men were away. Women made tents from skins and helped build the *qammaqs*—sod and caribou-skin houses stretched across whale jaw skeletons set carefully into shallow pits. A young girl learned to sew by making clothes for tiny dolls fashioned by her mother. By the time she reached puberty, a girl understood the basics of clothing construction and how to prepare skins. Caribou-skin parkas, duffel socks (later with embroidered tops), and fur boots and mittens were her stock in trade. Generations of women taught each other these skills, mother to daughter. Qatsoo, who is ninety-eight, recalls her childhood in the whaling camp on nearby Kekerten Island during the late nineteenth century:

"We did a lot of hard work at that time . . ."
In the summertime, when the skins were dry enough, my mother gathered all the skins and sewed them together to make a tent. In the wintertime, when the men were hunting caribou, she dried more skins and made clothing out of them. She made *kamiks* and something that looked like pants—using the caribou leg skins—and she made mittens out of seal skin.

In early autumn the women started getting ready for the winter. We made tents and seal skin clothes for the men first, before the ladies' and the children's. When it was wintertime, we started the caribou skin for men before everybody, because we were so used to it. We did that every year, making the clothes for different seasons.

The men went hunting by foot on the flow edges; once it was all ice, they went by dog team. When the spring came around, in March or April, they went on the ice (where they could have an igloo) and hunted for baby seals. Anybody who went hunting didn't eat all day, but they brought a ring seal skin that you can blow up to use for water. We scraped the fur off the skin, and when we sewed it we always kept it wet so it would be easier to sew; we braided the thread before we started sewing it. Every time the thing got old, it would tinkle! Then we all went back to Kekerten and lived in our permanent houses, our *qammaqs*. Once we had the baby seal skins, we started making them into clothes for the summer. The meat is good, too. I love eating boiled seal meat!

In the springtime, men made *kamotiks* that just fit the boat so they could go hunting down by the flow edge. Every male went except for the elders and the children. When the men were out hunting, we women went hunting too, by dog sled, and we would catch some seals, but we didn't go very far.

When the men were to be back any day, we started boiling some seal meat with the *qulliq* [the woman's oil lamp and stove]. There weren't any camp stoves at that time; men didn't eat all day while they were out hunting—that's why women would get the meat ready. When we moved into Pangnirtung, that's when we started seeing camp stoves.

When we were getting ready to start the *qulliq*, we would hammer at the fat so it wasn't just one big blubber. We used Arctic willow to make sure the blubber was crushed so it was easy to burn. We set up metal legs so the lamp didn't touch the ground. We made tea and boiled seal meat, then put all the oil back in and started another fire.

After the men were at the flow edge trying to catch some whales, they went back to Kekerten and stayed for a few days and tried to get ready to go hunting again for walrus. When we got some walrus, we took the blubber to a big pot. After walrus hunting, we would say, that's the end of the hunting for the year.

By then we had enough food for the whole year. We would stay at the camp and take our time cleaning our stuff, and maybe get ready to go caribou hunting again. We wouldn't use the big boats that we used for whale hunting; we would go by different boats [*umiaks*—round boats made from animal skins, known as "the woman's boat"] and bring along a kayak. As you can see, we did a lot of hard work at that time.

Seal, caribou, fish, beluga, and berries formed the basic Inuit diet, supplemented occasionally by birds, ducks, and clams. The Hudson's Bay Company ship also brought tea and other staples; when they ran out of tea, the women used leaves from the land as a substitute. When it was time to move camp, women rowed the *umiaks* filled with people and gear, while the men steered.[3] Women played a central role in the culture, throat singing (a guttural, rhythmic vocalizing that persists today) and playing a popular sticks-and-spindle game. Importantly, women could be shamans; sometimes couples shared the shaman role in their camp.

Women created small associations (*Kitaqs*) when they lived in camps and, like the Iroquois and Blood women, "looked after everything" while the men were hunting. As in similar cultures, the man's frequent and often extended absence from home fortified the woman's position.[4] The Inuk woman made the day-to-day decisions while at the same time respecting her husband's authority. An elder explains: "Inuit women are the planners. They look after the future with their children and their grandchildren. All the men did was bring the food, most of the time, and the women planned everything for their life ahead."

TRADITIONAL POWERS: "HE HAD THE FINAL WORD"

Many outsider reports of traditional Inuit culture depict a highly male dominant household in which men make the decisions and women obey orders. Men hunted and women stayed close to the camp. Some argued that women were completely dependent on the men for survival. Men not only had the opportunity to build reputations as hunters, but also interacted with traders, explorers, and missionaries, establishing relationships with outsiders. Men could build social prominence and power in a realm from which women largely were excluded. Still, Inuit women enjoyed considerable influence based on their role in the domestic sphere.

Inuit women who remember their great-grandparents and grandparents paint a much more complex picture of female-male relations. Survival was a shared responsibility to which both genders contributed. The woman had certain tasks that she enjoyed and developed competence in; a man had other tasks that he knew best. Men realized that if women did not do all the sewing and cooking and taking care of children, their own lives would be in jeopardy. On the whole, men respected women and did not take their contributions for granted.

Elder Inuit women insist that in the traditional extended family, the mother and father shared authority ("They were equally respected and sometimes feared"). Parents raised children to respect their elders, male or female: "Whatever they say, it's the law." In the same breath, elder women say rather matter-of-factly that the man was the boss, although they agree that male and female jobs were equally important to the functioning of the community. In terms of the power distribution, the husband was clearly the head of the family: "He had the final word, and that's just the way it was." An elder woman (who agrees with modern-day women's liberation) says that "women should be respected for what they do and for being head of the house because they know more about the house—cleaning and all the other things they do, how they care for it and the people in the family. It should be equal, the man and the woman being bosses. I don't know why men are always being called the head." An Inuk minister, Iola, describes how men defined their power relationship with women:

> In the camp we usually had one leader, but everybody had a say, even the women. We never really ignored the women or left them out of the decision making. The man always goes to the woman to ask what size and shape hut she wants to make, how she wants to do it, where she would like it. That's women's decision making. The father and the mother would build the hut together.

As Inuk leader Ann Hansen points out, one key to this complexity lies in the Inuit language, Inuktitut: "The word for *man* means the one more manlike, and the word for *woman* really means the one more womanlike." Inuktitut thus contains the notion that manlike and womanlike characteristics exist in every person. A woman learns sewing, but if she wants to develop "man's skills" like hunting, then "that's identified as being a part of her character, not linked to her sex." Hansen believes that a strength of the culture is freedom to be an individual, even though the society clearly defines male and female roles. Whether a girl's interests lie in fixing ski-doos (like her father) or in sewing (like her mother), she will choose which path to pursue. Martha, an elder, supports this notion: "Men and women were equal because both the girl and the boy were taught by their parents through their childhood until they reached their teens. A girl learned the man's way and the boy learned the woman's way, so it was equal."

This definition of male and female spills over into power relations between the sexes. Although Inuit women may not have a precisely equal voice, their expertise in things female constitutes the basis for a certain indisputable authority. Like most other hunting and gathering cultures, the Inuit tended to accept the principle of ultimate male authority, but there is also an image of "boss women" in the Inuit tradition. Their oral history portrays women as competent not only across a wide range of domestic activities but also in fishing, helping with construction, hunting, and (more recently) sculpting and print-making.

According to some women, both members of a head couple shared traditional leadership of the camps. Qaida, age forty-two, remembers her grandfather as "captain of the community," a role he shared with her grandmother:

> They would look after the whole community together. My grandmother would be the person to deliver the babies. . . . Both men and women were the leaders, because men couldn't look after the women in those days, or still now. My grandfather couldn't deliver the babies or sew for his family or help other families who needed help. It was the woman who was looking after the women's side. She would teach us how to sew, how to make things, how to cook, how to survive, how to scrape the hides, to dry them the proper way. All those things a man couldn't do—he could, but in those days he didn't!

Qallunats (whites) used to go to the camps by small ship, and sometimes they brought their wives. Because of their ability to provide work, sustenance, and small luxuries for the Inuit, Qatsoo says "*qallunats* used to be the boss" of everything during the whaling days. They employed the Inuit as guides, whalers, and processors. Whaler's wives often became powerful leaders among the Inuit women. Qatsoo recalls that her father—the great Angmarlik, after whom the Pangnirtung cultural center is named—was the leader for men ("only for men"). At the whaling station, the boss for women was a *qallunat* wife of an American whaler. Qatsoo's mother worked for this woman, "for her place to be clean."

Among the Inuit themselves, however, Qatsoo remembers that the men seemed to be stronger than the women and told them what to do. She believes that women were stronger only as cleaners: "At that time we didn't have soap, so with an *ulu* [the woman's knife] we would scrape the dirty skins." The community's norms allowed men to expect women to take orders from them, but "the man was not commanding his wife all the time," recalls Iola. It depended on the couple: "If the man was really harsh on his wife, he would usually make a lot of commands, he was really the boss. But not all men did that, even in the old days." Rosie, age fifty, agrees that "the father was the boss" in the camps; the mother did the cooking and sewing. The men made decisions about when and where to move, probably because of their acknowledged expertise in game movements and climate changes. (In her own twentieth-century marriage, this pattern has persisted; Rosie's granddaughter does not want to get married, but believes that if she did marry, her husband would be the boss.) Women "always had to listen to the men," Lena recalls. The whole family had to go hunting if they were to survive. "They didn't complain." Jeannie agrees that men were more powerful because women usually went where the men wanted to go.

Martha's wedding ceremony included "words about the man being the leader." She adds, "Every time my husband went hunting or camping for the year, I would always go with him, because my husband was the boss of the house." Yet they were equal in their work; each had his or her own role, and sometimes they worked as a team. Rosie also makes this distinction: Men may have been the ultimate and legitimate authorities, but women were equal to men. Men may have had superior physical strength and musculature, but women were strong in other ways and balanced the male roles. Geela, a forty-year-old seamstress, remembers: Women seemed to know better than the men, even though men seemed to be the boss, but men had more control over everything." Kudloo recalls that the husband was boss in her family as well ("It's always like that"). Men respected women for their work, however, contributing to the balance of power: "Whenever I made something, I would tell my husband to be happy about it. When I was a young woman, people would talk about me—I was really good in sewing, I was a fast runner. I didn't want people talking about me, but I would talk about it to my husband. I would tell him to be happy about the things I made." The male took precedence in decision making within each couple. Would they sit down and discuss it? "It wasn't like that then, but the wife would have to agree." This was particularly important long ago regarding the Inuit custom of wife lending or "spouse exchange." Inuit seldom took this practice lightly, and it did not involve promiscuity, as some journalistic reports indicated. On the contrary, wife lending was always temporary, often involved Inuit men from other camps, and required the consent of all partners, including the wives. The purpose usually was to help forge kinship bonds between unrelated families, which in turn created cohesion among the network of camps in a region.

Beyond the power relationship between wife and husband was women's obedience to parental wishes. Depending upon circumstances, couples might live with her parents or with his, learning from both sets until they were ready to establish their own home. Jeannie was not very happy when her parents told her to live with her husband's parents, but she easily agreed because she was taught to respect her elders: "Then I was like a slave because my husband's mother always had something for me to do." She would never argue with her mother-in-law, because her own mother told her to listen to her in-laws: "It was like that. Once in a while my mother-in-law would look at me with a disagreeing face because I would do something that I didn't really know how to do. That made my mother-in-law unhappy."

What would happen to a woman if she disobeyed her husband? "Whenever we disagreed about something, either my parents or his parents would tell us not to talk back or shout at each other. They would tell us to think more about the life that's ahead of us." Jeannie tells her own daughters-in-law "to be good to their husbands and not argue about something that's not important. I'm following my mother's footsteps." Later Jeannie adds that when her husband shouts at her children, she interjects a few words to protect them, and "whenever I shout at the kids, my husband says something back to me."

The Turning Point: Leaving the Land

On the long time line of Inuit history, contact with whites occupies only a small period but has created the most monumental transformation of Inuit life and culture. Male explorers, whalers, missionaries, the Royal Canadian Mounted Police (RCMP), and Hudson's Bay Company personnel led the collision of cultures. Contact with *qallunat* changed the lives of Inuit women as they watched their men adopt increasingly patriarchal attitudes toward females. Nineteenth-century Scottish and American whalers hired the Inuit as cheap labor, which brought the Inuit a few luxuries and a way to increase their livelihood. The whalers benefited from aboriginal survival skills, but complicated race relations when they took sexual advantage of Inuit women. Serious problems also started when the whites introduced guns, alcohol, and then drugs to the North. Inuit are surprisingly willing to take equal responsibility for the human wreckage produced by the misuse of alcohol: "When white people came up here with all the booze, we used it. I don't blame only whites for it." As an RCMP officer points out, however, "booze and disease" were not the only intrusions: "The RCMP, the Hudson's Bay Company, and the government itself have imposed their ways on the Inuit people and destroyed their culture." Missionaries altered the culture when they defined Inuit religion as "bad," stressed formal marriage, and made divorce taboo. Life changed for Inuit men, too, as their ability to perform a central role as providers slipped away after the Canadian government moved the Inuit into settlements during the 1960s.[5]

By the middle of the twentieth century, illness and starvation among the Baffin Inuit reached proportions that no humanitarian government could ignore. The decision to resettle during the late 1950s and 1960s was anchored in many reasons that seemed valid at the time: the ravages of disease imported by whites into the fragile Arctic ecosystem, especially tuberculosis, polio, measles, and influenza; changes in fur trade economics; and Canadian government aspirations to secure Arctic sovereignty.[6] As the deadly combination of human disease and canine encephalitis swept through the camps, it became almost impossible for the Inuit to continue to live out on the land.[7]

For Inuit culture, the most critical turning point thus came with their largely involuntary resettlement from tiny nomadic bands into communities that now range from 250 to three thousand people. The Inuit suddenly found themselves living in what seemed to be very large groups. Each band came into regular contact with Inuit from other camps as well as with the growing number of *qallunat* who lived and worked in Pangnirtung. An Inuk elder recalls, "When we come together it suddenly becomes two hundred or one thousand people. Our cultures and the way of living started to change then." Alienation, marginality, and loss of culture begin when population density climbs above the point where "everyone knows everyone."[8] The sudden shift from a small band to a small town heralded the demise of traditional culture, says a mother of three teenagers. She is "not sure they did us a favor" by bringing the Inuit in off the land "because the Inuit, we lose our culture then. From the beginning of the white people way, we don't have any idea; it was very different."

The far-reaching impacts of resettlement have come into focus thirty years after the Inuit were moved in from the camps. We are only now beginning to appreciate the social repercussions that followed as their independence converted into welfare dependency overnight. As the population of the tiny community on Pangnirtung Fjord increased, traditional skills began to disappear, and dependency on government programs skyrocketed.[9] Use of the ancient language, Inuktitut, declined. Social bonds frayed as families felt the pressures of a larger community. Although the government eventually controlled widespread starvation and tuberculosis, few Inuit now live well by either their own standards or those of the southern Canadian provinces.

Today, Inuit communities generally face a kaleidoscope of frustrating social and mental health problems, including lack of jobs and high hunting costs. Good housing is "perennially short," infant mortality is five times the Canadian rate, the nearest doctor is (on average) hundreds of miles away, per capita income is one half the Canadian average, and the cost of living is astronomical.[10] About two-thirds of the population receive some sort of transfer payment from the government. Alcohol and drugs add to the recipe for disruptive change.

Especially in the North, social problems are symptoms of the rapid change that throws culture off balance and threatens identity.

Welfare dependency and geographic isolation contribute greatly to the confusion of gender roles and the struggle for a new definition of both ethnicity and gender. With the move to government-created settlements, the way of life and the roles of men and women also began to shift. Many Inuit men lost their train dogs to the ravages of canine encephalitis. During the resettlement process, they often were forced to leave their equipment behind at the camps, because harpoons and sleds were too large to fit into the small planes that lifted them into a new world. Few men now remember how to make the precontact tools. With the train dogs gone, the hunt has become an expensive mechanized endeavor that requires men to have jobs in order to pay for ammunition, rifles, and motorized canoes or all-terrain vehicles.[11] Consequently, Inuit men have undergone a form of economic emasculation. Women began to see alcohol abuse, family violence, welfare dependency, and unemployment—a concept that was virtually irrelevant in the camps. Women and children suffer from these modern ills, all too often victims of men who are themselves victims.

Other changes followed the Inuit into settlement life, especially television, the "magic in the sky" that since 1975 has beamed into Inuit homes intriguing images of *qallunats* living in beautiful warm homes, eating prepared foods, and driving luxury cars. Even before the advent of television, Inuit children spent a significant portion of their waking hours sitting in school. This experience opened up new worlds, but also served to distance them from their parents' world. In the old days, survival meant depending on one's family, communicating well with them, and helping each other. Now, says Rosie, "It's really different. It's sad for me, because I know that we're going to keep losing our culture because of all these things if we don't do anything about it."

Meeka believes that one of the primary markers of dramatic cultural change has been the decline in women's sewing: "In those days, they were always sewing clothes for the family. Now we can buy our clothes but I still sew caribou parkas and *kamiks*. I like to do it. I like to keep my culture. We can't do it without the men hunting." The significance of sewing goes far beyond its economic and physical advantages. The sewing group meets twice a month to stitch and talk about life. Weekly classes to teach the younger girls to prepare and sew skins are liberally sprinkled with gossip and commiseration. Is there anything women can to do alleviate the social problems facing Inuit today? Qatsoo replies, "Make *kamiks*—sew."

Into the Twentieth Century

CONTEMPORARY ROLES: "THE OTHER WAY AROUND NOW"

Today, the Inuit still fish with sticks—usually hockey sticks with bent nails in the ends—and make canvas tents with electric sewing machines for summer camping. They can still use local plants for tea now, "but all we can think is to go buy tea from the store," says Meena.

Both male and female roles have shifted dramatically with the decline of traditional culture. Since resettlement, clearly defined gender roles have faded. Moving from a hunting economy into the settlements jeopardized the male role. The Inuit increasingly depend not on what father can bring home from the hunt but on wage labor, Hudson's Bay Company food, canned food, and welfare. Inuit community health workers stress "country food" (fish, seal meat, caribou, berries, and other traditional Inuit foods) as still being the healthiest for their people. The need to provide at least some country food gives otherwise unemployed males a sense of worth and identity, as a woman leader explains: "Men are encouraged to hunt and fish; if they are not hunting, the food that they can get in the stores is very poor and very expensive."

The woman's role has diminished less dramatically. She is still cooking, cleaning, looking after the children, making the clothes, or doing the shopping; like Iroquois and Blood women, her role is largely intact. For example, one legacy of the nineteenth-century contact with whalers is the contemporary woman's custom of making bannock every day, cooking this tender bread on top of the stove in a heavy iron frying pan. Virtually every Inuk woman I visited—whether or not she worked outside the home—proudly served her version of this straightforward centerpiece of Inuit life. The Inuit carry bannock on all trips out on the land or in the boats, and consume it in great quantities (along with gallons of tea) at home as well. Baked slowly on the back burner, it provides the warmth and calories essential for survival in a frigid climate. Similarly, many Inuit women still sew, even though they use electric sewing machines and thread instead of thimbles, needles, and sinew.

Why has the male role not adjusted or expanded in parallel fashion? A teacher's aide thinks that we must reflect on the traditional ways: "If you go back to culture, maybe the previous role that the man played is breaking down, because out there at the camp the man is the boss. He calls the tune . . . what time you get up, when you go hunting, who brings the food. While the man's role is breaking down, the women are at home doing all the women's things." This is no longer true. Now, he has to depend on the twentieth-century means of earning a livelihood, a nine-to-five job ("It doesn't depend on brute strength anymore"). Because few of these jobs exist anyway, he is left empty handed.

In addition, many men are seasonal workers, so "they have to depend on a woman to bring in the dough," as long as she continues to work steadily. This gives her more power and authority because she earns some of the money; now she thinks she has the right to have her say. The trend toward role reversal generates both positive and negative consequences. A communal relationship to wages is harder to establish than one to food. Inuit are less likely to share something that money can buy, which also causes some problems. An Inuk seamstress in her forties argues that in the old days men controlled

> almost everything, but it's the other way around now. Women have more control over things. . . . At that time, usually a woman had to cook, but now even a man can cook for the family. It's better this way. Sometimes I would want to go back, but it's hard. At this new generation it is easier because everything seems to be going pretty well, because at that time their parents used to struggle to keep their families alive.

Women are more likely to complete high school, get a steady job, and (increasingly) to be the major provider for their families. This role reversal and other factors have resulted in frustration and a loss of self-esteem among Inuit men and contributed to higher rates of alcohol and drug abuse for males.[12] Wages give the native woman more power and authority, or so she believes. Yet because traditionally native peoples shared whatever wealth and resources fell to the bands and families, there is still an ethos that argues against increased power based on mere earnings: "If a woman brings the money, it still belongs to the whole house. Before, if one man in the camp brought seals, the whole camp shared them." One Inuk health worker in her late twenties, whose live-in boyfriend makes more than she does only because he works full time, believes that women currently bring in more money than men in most families, especially in her age group. She feels fortunate that her man has a full-time job.

Is there more pressure on Inuit women now? They are not sure, but, as in the past, women work hard. Leah, who is seventy-two, remembers: "We used to do everything, even sew. We made *kamiks* and *amoutiks* [jackets]. When the seal-skin boots wore out, we repaired them, but now I don't do it. I don't make *kamiks* anymore." Leah learned by watching her grandmother and sister. Now she makes dresses with a sewing machine—when she has time left after taking care of her grandchildren, while her daughter works outside the home. Ann's story suggests some of the radical redefinitions of men's and women's work that Inuit face today:

"There are many things to do . . ."
My cousin Leah hunts, she fishes, she traps in the winter to catch foxes; that's to help her husband to have more money, so they can have more to eat, clothing, and hunting equipment. She's not the only one. There are many women who try to help their husbands so they can live more comfortably. They do many, many things. They're involved. . . . some of them have jobs in the community, working for the government or the school, and at the same time they keep their children.

When they have a spare moment they sew seal-skin boots or *amoutiks*, so there are many things to do. They're very involved in community work or in the Anglican church. Most of my friends do many things for people. Their work involves helping women to deliver babies; when people are sick, they stay with the sick person and cook for their families. That's what most of the women I know are doing right now. My husband has a stronger role with the children than my brothers do with theirs. My husband is not one who helps with dishes and helps around the house, because he's not interested in those things, but he helps me with the big tasks, the big jobs.

Men and women have different jobs, though. Take hunting. Once he brings the game home, it's the woman's responsibility. When we were first together, my husband caught an animal and he brought it home, and I just left it on the counter. I was doing other things and he got quite upset with me. I didn't understand why he was getting upset. It was my responsibility, and I didn't understand that.

Now Inuit women attend meetings of the National Council of Women or the Inuit Council or get involved in administration in the hamlets, but historically men have been in the forefront. The role reversal implied by this shift takes on added poignancy when the *only* work men can do is domestic work. Some men embrace activities previously thought to be solely in the woman's domain; others feel somehow diminished by housekeeping, cooking, and child care. Some are resentful and engage in verbal or physical abuse to regain a semblance of power in the couple relationship. There are exceptions to this picture painted with broad strokes, but many believe that men are under more stress and pressure and are experiencing an identity crisis: "What am I going to do now, if I can't grow up to be a hunter?"

Eena, who works outside the home at a full-time job, has her largest meal of the day at noon. In her absence, Eena's husband does the cooking. The same situation holds for her friend Apea. More and more men, they say, are taking over the traditional domestic role of women. Most like it, they believe, but sometimes the men get tired of doing the cooking: "They say, 'I have to do this all the time, it's your turn.'" When their husbands are away hunting, these two modern Inuit women return to their traditional cooking duties. The men take construction or other seasonal jobs in order to bring cash into the household. Otherwise, they try to hunt to supplement the family's food stores: The char, seal, and caribou are stored in the community's free deep freeze, "so we can use it as we want."

This interchangeability of male and female roles is reflected in many facets of Inuit culture. While some worry that a woman who supports her family may act as though she is now "head of the family," many women speak of the deeply held respect they accord men when they are out on the land. The degree of role flexibility for both women and men varies greatly, but when a woman is working and her husband is not, problems can ensue, as a clerk suggests:

This is not part of our culture, because the man should be looking after the families. The woman's job is to look after the children and to help them grow. If the woman is working and the husband is baby-sitting, his self-esteem hits bottom. Maybe he feels that he's not a whole man, because he's not able to provide for his family.

The mother role is very important to families. "If the mother is not looking after them well, the children usually have a different attitude about life. Even though it's important for women to be able to have a job, in our culture it's really different."

WOMEN AS HUNTERS: "HER FIRST KILL"

Perhaps the most symbolic shift in traditional gender roles is women's expansion into hunting. For example, two young women in their thirties discuss the most important events in their lives. Their answers reflect the two worlds they inhabit on a daily basis, traditional and modern—and how the role of competent woman has brought them into formerly male domains. One claims that she enjoys going out seal hunting with her husband, "but I couldn't skin a seal. I learned how—I was so glad that I could do it!" Her husband made an *ulu*, the woman's traditional curved blade knife, out of an old saw. Similarly, Leah (like many other women) describes the happiest times of her life as boating and going inland for caribou hunting, camping, and fishing. Although Leah and others admit that very cold weather is hard, the joy of being out on the land shines through their stories.

Hunting remains an integral part of traveling around Cumberland Sound and Pangnirtung Fjord. When we went with Inuit families to visit a historical site, search for whales, or go camping, they inevitably had a rifle on the bow of the deck, ready for seal hunting. The custom of husbands taking their wives hunting persists into the late twentieth century. Jonah and his wife are in their thirties; like other couples their age, they enjoy "doing things together," especially hunting and fishing. Just as his father took Jonah out in the old days because Jonah was his son, he would not take his wife "because she's the woman." Jonah prefers to do things differently: "I take the whole family, and that's why it's different."

Males in the family support a woman's involvement in hunting from an early age. Ann's daughter, at the age of one, was visiting her grandfather out on the land when her older brother brought a small bird back to the house so she could kill her first animal: "He was very proud! Everyone was very proud that this small bird was her first kill." Killing the bird upset Ann, but the rest of the family was proud that the toddler had gained some identity as a hunter, as a person who has taken the spirit of an animal. Similar rituals exist for when a boy kills his first seal, caribou, or whale.

BECOMING A WOMAN, BECOMING A MAN

Gender still provides the major dividing line for chores. When parents "ask us to help, we do," says Eena; occasionally boys help in the kitchen, but "only once in a long while." Girls help with washing dishes and, when they get older, with cooking. Even in a household that includes young women, the mother is more likely to be the regular cook and seamstress. In the presettlement days, children learned the skills most appropriate for their gender through play and games, as an elder woman recalls:

> When I was growing up, we had homemade toys made out of seal flipper bones. We cooked them first and played "pretend house" with them. Our uncles, fathers, and brothers made wooden dolls for us—that's how we learned to sew. We made clothing for the dolls . . . parkas. We didn't know we were learning, but we learned to talk at the same time, with all these homemade toys. That has disappeared . . . most of them are museum pieces now.

The pride of conquering nature through time-honored skills shows through in Mary's story:

> *"The ladies were really proud of me . . ."*
> I made a caribou parka for my husband. That's my first time. I couldn't believe myself. I should have done it ten years before! My mom wanted to do it all. She thinks I won't do it as quick. She's been sewing all the time, but she wouldn't let me do it. I wasn't trying hard enough, I guess, because she kept telling me, you're going to spoil it. All the older women wouldn't let the young ones do it—we would spoil the skins or the material!
>
> I feel we shouldn't just leave sewing up to our mothers; we have to teach our kids. If I show my daughter how to make a *kamik*, if she

spoils it, it's okay. She can keep trying . . . that's the only way she's going to learn. I started making waterproof *kamiks* not long ago. My mother kept telling me I'd spoil it, but I was very eager, so I did it and they turned out well: They were waterproof! The ladies were really proud of me.

You take the seal skin and take the fur off first. You have to dry it, then you have to chew it with your teeth to make it really soft. I'm sewing it right now. I haven't finished this jacket yet, because I'm working on something else. The younger girls have to learn how to prepare the food, too, how to be a good mother. Men cut caribou up and put the meat inside the ground without the skin [to keep it from one year to the next].

Jeannie's mother taught her how to sew, and she improved through practice. Her daughter, Eena, does not sew: "I am interested; when I have the time I will learn." Lena, thirty-two, sews modern clothes as well as traditional boots, duffel socks, and mittens. She learned from what her mother told her, and "I learned from myself, too, by watching." Saila's mother died when she was young, so no one taught her how to sew. When she was a teenager, she used to look at clothing and admire the handiwork of other women; through trial and error, she taught herself.

Sewing and working with skins and furs are indigenous to women's culture in the Baffin region "as far back as you can go." Preserving this part of Inuit culture, though, runs counter to many realities of their contemporary life. In fact, the Inuit could survive without their traditional skills; those who do not engage in winter hunting (to obtain caribou skins and meat) can survive with southern factory-made clothing. Ironically, just as it was a hundred or a thousand years ago, the hunt necessitates having the fruits of the hunt: warm skins.

Apea says that the children enjoy learning traditional sewing in school as part of the cultural inclusion program ("They think it's great"). It is not too late, she hopes, for the young girls to learn the old skills that so critically defined the woman's role. For her generation, the learning has not been so easy:

Even when we wanted to learn, sometimes our mothers looked like they were lazy to teach us how to do it, and they would refuse: "You're going to waste that material," they would say. Maybe if they had taught us we could do some traditional sewing. We know how to do duffel socks and parkas and stuff like that, but not the traditional clothing. We can do the skinning and tanning, but we can't make a pattern.

Jukeepa derives deep pride from cutting her own patterns for boots, mittens, parkas, and leggings; however, few other women do so: "We can only sew it if somebody cuts it into patterns." Her friend, Peona, agrees: "We don't know how to sew traditional clothes. We're the generation that missed out. We can't make *kamiks*, either. We didn't learn how to do it. Nobody showed us how."

The older women know how to sew, of course, and are increasingly becoming aware that they must find ways to pass on their skills to their daughters. A women's sewing group meets every Thursday and Saturday, and "anybody who wants to come here and sew" can join the group. Some women buy homemade clothing from other women. They try to welcome young people; for those with little children, attendance is more problematic and often undermines the intention to develop new skills ("You work all day, and there is no time. I want to stay home."). Jukeepa and Peona laughingly add that when things get bad, their mother makes traditional clothing for them: "That's the bad part, I guess. She just provides us with them . . . they're cheaper and warmer."

If there were some seed money to support the fledgling but high-quality Pangnirtung sewing business, more women could work at producing *amoutiks* and *kamiks* for marketing throughout the North. They could easily compete with the garments sold through stores and outfitters. The recently built Weave Shop expands women's opportunities in this realm.

Beyond the power that emanates from wage production, in many native communities women are taking on major responsibilities in "high places." One woman, Lucie, is an adult educator; one sister is a council member; another sister is a health worker. Her brothers have not "come out very much. . . . They're fishermen, practically illiterate, but very capable. They are of the old school. They can survive out on the land." One is an excellent hunter who supplies the settlement's stores. "It's like night and day," says Lena of her brothers and sisters. "It's unbelievable that the girls are doing very well and the boys seem quite happy to be hunters."

CONTEMPORARY POWERS: "IT'S GETTING CLOSER TOGETHER"

Traditionally, an Inuk woman had substantial control over her house and children; a man was powerful because he was a strong hunter. Since he was away for extended trips, the woman became accustomed to running things by herself. Women now in their forties, fifties, and older generally accept that the man is ultimate boss, but those in their twenties and thirties want to be equal.

Although many women cite lack of good jobs as a major problem, those who are under thirty-five may work more consistently for wages, so they have access to cash. Even when women bring in the paycheck, however, many men still view them as somewhat lower in status than men, which causes friction in the family.

It is difficult for men to see women fitting into the employment picture more readily than they do themselves. They grew up seeing their mothers being treated like servants by their fathers.[13] The woman was there to nurture; now she leaves the house to earn cash while her partner tends to the home and children, as a settlement employee, Davidee, relates: "I expect my wife to be the boss in the house. There's nothing wrong with that. But I don't expect her to be the boss when I'm out on the land. We understand each other— it's going to be that way, and it's worked." They share in managing the money, but decisions to move from one community to another have been based on his career. She worked in Iqaluit as a correctional officer, but had to quit her job when he accepted a position in Pangnirtung.

Davidee suggests his view of female power while talking about his very bright and articulate teenage daughter. He is not sure how this young woman "is going to make out" in life: "She's different from my other daughter. She always talks back; never settles just to say yes. She always has something to say." Her style stands in contrast to the traditional Inuk woman, who would "go along with her husband even if she disagreed." Since "the guys are educated like that, too, they expect the woman to conform." He adds, "My father was the boss. We don't argue about it. We respected him more than anything else in running the family. It's not like that now."

The power differential comes out in self-perception. Older women, who were used to bending with the male-driven tide of daily affairs, are not likely to feel powerful. Some of the younger girls, women believe, are becoming more modernized. Because the older husbands hunt, they still feel that they are the bosses of the household, and that the wife is lower on the list. For many Inuit couples, children come before the wives do. For example, women agree that historically it was often the man who made the decision about adopting a child in or out of the family (a common practice); even if a woman did not want to give up her baby, she would bow to her husband's preference.[14] Though this is changing, men still exert considerable influence in this arena.

Sheila, age nineteen, believes that the man was usually the boss in the past and still is now, particularly when it comes to handling money and the house: "Maybe they would agree on some things, but from my point of view some men are very strict. Some men might say, 'We're moving to this house, but some would talk about it first.'" Sheila believes that she and her boyfriend would easily agree on such things.

Women feel that men are stronger physically and have more political power, but that women can be stronger emotionally. Men are also beginning to have more respect for women. Iola believes that the man is boss "everywhere in the world" except in the home:

> About the woman's work, I cannot be a boss. I can't really argue with my wife when she's making *kamiks*. I have to agree with what she has to say because she knows. For house building, she has to agree with what I've done. It's equal; it's always like that. We've heard many times that in the past the woman was the slave of the man, especially Inuit. You cook, you look after the house, you raise the kids. Yes, men were the boss, but women always have their own power.

The servant image of women is diminishing. Now couples in their thirties and forties jointly agree before marriage upon control over money. ("My wife and I have one account," says Iola. "We are equal in that respect.") They both can write checks and would discuss any major purchase. Meeka, who is in her forties, agrees that men and women of her generation often share power as a couple. If they have good personalities, can communicate well, look after their family, and are trustworthy, they should be able to construct a fairly equal relationship: "The woman's voice would be heard as much as the man's voice."

Most women of Meeka's generation reject male domination.

Though their mothers accepted a subordinate role, younger Inuit women do not, as Meeka relates:

> When I was growing up, I didn't always agree with my father's side. He sent me here when I didn't want to leave my parents. I was hurt; I never forgot. Myself, I don't want to control my family just from one side. I like to control my family from both sides, to talk about it and deal with it. My husband likes that.

The power differential shows up in the classroom, according to a white teacher who says that Inuit children listen to a male teacher: "You're heard, you're given attention. [But] even if you're a principal and you're a woman, the boys just ignore you. Nothing!" When female teachers go to a male teacher for help—"he walks in and the atmosphere changes." Resistance to female authority may actually help block the progress of young boys in terms of completing high school. At school the boys see girls as "more or less" their equals, except when it comes to sports: "Automatically the boys take over, and the girls are left to the last." This dominant mode is most obvious in the senior classes. Boys and girls are still equal in the junior classes "until the boys grow big and strong and tough and rough."

Eena and her mother illustrate the generational change in attitudes toward male domination. Eena's mother, who is in her fifties, says that for older women, the "men are a little higher." She is not sure why it worked out that way, but for their daughters, equality prevails, as Eena insists: "If it weren't equal for me, I don't know if I would still be with my man now. I believe men and women have to have equal rights. Nobody should be more powerful." Eena's mother defines women's power as "not having to agree, things like that." Disagreement frightens some women because "men have always been higher, but there are many things that women know, too." For example, sometimes women are more intelligent than men. Eena argues that men do not have to be more powerful, but try to be; she does not understand what engendered the difference between her mother's generation and her own.

Although women agree that in their mother's and grandmother's generations men had more say, men and women nevertheless were equal in some elusive way. Now women think they have more say. The youngest women—like their counterparts in many other cultures—prefer equal power in their relationships with men, although they admit that boys their age still want to be the boss. How could they resolve this discrepancy? Annie suggests talking it out: "I think talking is the best. If we had kids, the father would want to be the boss, but making it equal would be better for the children because then they don't have to figure out which parent is making the right decision."

Some middle-aged women believe that men still assume the right to the position of head of household, but compromise before they make a big decision. Others want that to be the case, but insist that it is not true among "the men around here." The traditional balance of roles and power extends into the late twentieth century. Most Inuit women believe that men are stronger, more powerful, and more likely to run their community than women are. The gap is closing a little, however: "Some have ladies on their committees. It's getting closer together."

Strength, though, is relative. When it comes to emotional strength, Inuit perceive women as being much stronger than men. As in many cultures, when Inuit women face a problem, they are willing to seek help; they talk to each other about their anger and disappointments. The mental health committee confirms this general impression. Accounts from both men and women in the Inuit community point to an equally clear pattern for men: They succumb to more emotional, lifestyle, or addictive problems but solicit help far less often than do women. Women's power links directly to their ability to be more open than men. Even so, although suicide rates remain relatively low in Pangnirtung, social service workers report more suicide attempts among women than men between the ages of fifteen and twenty-five:

"Women take the pills . . ."
The hangings and the shootings are more likely to be men, but women take pills. We see a lot of younger women that take a handful of pills, and maybe some antibiotics or something, and then they throw up. It's usually because they've had a fight with their boyfriend, and they usually come for help right away. They're sorry. It may have something to do with having relationships and problems, and not having any other ways to deal with things.

There are still women out there who are afraid of the man, and they don't get much support from their relatives. Some people seem to want to shut off what's happening. Even if someone tries to talk to them, they don't want to do anything about it. They just want to close their eyes to it. This is still an active hunting and fishing community, so there are more outlets for men. They all play floor hockey, volleyball, base-ball, or badminton. It's women who seem to get more depressed here.

Love, Marriage, and Divorce: From Arrangement to Choice

The tradition of arranged marriages functioned to ensure that all marriageable adults found partners during the child-bearing years—an important concern for small populations in a harsh environment. Arranged marriages also protected blood lines against intermarriage, linked bands with each other, and, according to some older women, served as a buffer against prostitution, promiscuity, or early pregnancy without the stability of a relationship. As an elder puts it, however, "that's the part where women seemed smaller than men"—in other words, they had less power.

Traditionally, marriage marked the passage from childhood into adulthood, usually around the age of fifteen or sixteen for both males and females. The onset of menses and an arranged relationship marked the female's transition into maturity; the male entered adulthood as soon as he married or lived with a woman. An elder male recalls that parents would tell a son, "Now you've got your own way and you can handle it—raise your family. No more dependence on your parents." They expected him to provide for his pregnant woman. Today, if a woman expects a child, she will often stay with her parents, relying on them instead of on the child's father, says the elder: "Before, when they started living together, they had to move from the parents' house. If they lived in their own place, the man had to provide everything . . . seal for clothing, things like that. That was his responsibility."

Traditionally, all the equipment of the father would go to the son. If there was more than one son, the young men would share it in order to set up their own households. Most young people married out of their camp, a common custom that decreased chances of mixing blood lines too closely (and a parallel to the Blood and

Iroquois marrying outside their own clan). Negotiations between two families would take place, says an elder, then "the parents would just give their daughter to the man for marriage." The men of the camp were instrumental in arranging marriages.

Neela, a seamstress now in her early fifties, relates how she was betrothed at sixteen years old: "At that time I had a boyfriend. My grandfather on my mother's side arranged a marriage for me. I didn't really want to marry this guy, but I had no choice." Mothers would write each other about a son's interest in the other woman's daughter: "If the son wants to be with her daughter, then the son would go to the camp and be with her." Jeannie, who is fifty, entered a marriage arranged by her future father-in-law: "I minded, but I was expected to go along with it." She likes that women today can choose their own husbands.

Usually the new couple would go to the camp of the woman's family, but they could move to the camp of whichever family needed them the most. For many elders, marriage followed a period of living together and the birth of the first child. Martha, age seventy-eight, recalls that she started living with a man when they moved up to another camp: "We got married in the settlement when we moved here. We had nine more children, but they all died, two only a few months apart. Some died in the ocean [in boating or fishing accidents]. I only have three left."

Lucy, a thirty-nine-year-old whose parents arranged her marriage, remembers this period clearly: "Even though couples would go through bad and good times, they knew they would always be together." Divorce was virtually unheard of during the presettlement period. After the missionaries began to filter into the region during the late 1800s, marriage in the Christian manner became commonplace. Ceremonies conducted by an Anglican minister at the old presettlement mission began to replace the older custom of the man simply joining his new wife in her tent or igloo. Leah, recalling her own experience at the tender age of sixteen, believes that arranged marriages were a "bad" custom:

"I was really unhappy that night . . ."
I remember one time we were at the church on Blacklead Island, there was a reverend baptizing the man who was to become my husband; that was before we even met. I was the only one there. When I was

home in bed, with everything on—clothes and blankets and everything—I heard the door open and close. I was hiding in the blankets. There stood a man with long hair, mustache, bearded. I was really scared! He was there to go to bed with me, but I was wearing my clothes and I put on my new *amoutik* [parka] that had beads on it. At the back there were some pennies that made noises like bells. When I sat down they made *so* many noises, but my mother never woke up or said anything, which made me hate my mother for ignoring it. I was really unhappy that night.

Anyway, he joined me in my bed. I just lay there, because I didn't know what to do. I was scared because I was always told that I wasn't supposed to hang around boys. When we were in bed I tried not to touch the guy, but I think that I touched him when we fell asleep. It was really creepy. I thought he was creepy. . . .

We started living together after that night. I was sixteen; a year later my first baby was born. He stayed with me until I was old enough [to live with him] because my mother thought that I had to learn some more; then we moved to my husband's camp, and we stayed there. We stayed with my mother-in-law until I knew how to sew a tent and get ready for the things that my husband needed.

My husband had some very big dogs that looked almost like wolves, so I would use a stick to scare the dogs away, because they always stayed at the porch of the *qammaq*. I had trouble going in there. After we became a couple, I was sad because whenever I went out visiting, my husband would go after me—he thought I would be with someone else. He was really jealous.

One choice that contemporary Inuit women can make for themselves is that of marriage partner. Women (now in their thirties and forties) who were born during the transitional era began to choose their own husbands. The younger women take it for granted that the choice of mate will be theirs alone. The guiding principles for choosing a mate have not changed much from traditional to contemporary times, although now there is less emphasis on male prowess at hunting. A "good Inuk woman" does not have too many children, works hard at sewing and cooking, is a good mother, and is faithful, kind, and honest. A "good Inuk man" should be a good hunter (which traditionally meant being able to make dog sleds, harnesses, and spears). He should care about his wife and family, provide traditional food for them and for his elders, stay away from alcohol or drugs, and be faithful to his wife. For contemporary women, paramount qualities in a man include having a good job, a pleasant personality, and a forward-looking attitude. A teenager describes her boyfriend: "He's well educated, and he's training to be a professional mechanic or something. I like many things about him I can't explain. Girls my age go for the looks and education, their kindness. All the good things."

Challenges Confronting Women

LIVING BETWEEN TWO CULTURES

"Today we are in shock from everything going so fast," Mona reflects. "When I talk to my youngest daughter, she won't know what I'm talking about. This depression comes up when we are in between [Inuit and mainstream cultures]. We ask ourselves, what's going on?" Life out on the land holds a certain fascination and purity for most Inuit women compared to life in the settlement, as Lucie, age forty-five, recollects:

> I think we were happier in the camps. We never considered ourselves poor. We were very rich in the heart because we had love and closeness. Here I am working, being a mother, but I am a mother in a very different way than my mother was. When I was a child—not too long ago, just over twenty years ago—I was a child in a real Inuit way, old traditional way. I was clothed in skins when I was a baby. So, in a very short time, my kids had no way of seeing what I went through.

"I will never forget the old times," says Rosie. "They were hard times, but life was better in many ways." She traded skins at the Hudson's Bay Company for "a lot of money." Says Meeka, "I can't live the *qallunat* way, because I remember living in the camp. I still like to keep my culture, but it's hard now because we can't do anything about it. I can move to the camp and try to use it, but it's no use." Rhoda expresses this dilemma well:

> *"I'm just living today . . ."*
> I won't be able to take care of my kids all the time. Today I'm living in a limbo. I'm not working; taking care of kids, I don't consider that work. I wanted to work with them and enjoy them, but I found out it's

not going to be so right now. They're growing up in front of my eyes, and I'm not doing anything. I'm not enjoying it. I'm not part of it.

I'm the example of most of today's women. I don't know how to do the work that the old people did, yet I haven't found new meaningful work. I know how to make *kamiks*, but I'm not making them every day. I'm not really learning how to make caribou-skin parkas. When I was younger, I knew how to make traditional clothing, but I've forgotten how to even start sewing now. I don't have a career, not even a job. So I guess I'm sort of in the middle, eh? I'm not really up to either one of them, and I don't know how to move toward either one of them. My mother's life was much harder than my own life now. I'm just living today. With their life they had to work hard. I just do a little teaching.

Many Inuit women point to "losing our culture" as one of the most important problems they face. "The new generation has a lack of learning," middle-aged Meeka says, referring to what she and other women of her generation took for granted as skills central to their role: working with skins, sewing, and preparing food the traditional way. Although some women teach their children the old skills, not all do. The post-relocation period was a relative vacuum culturally. Recently it became apparent that the culture would die out completely if the schools did not teach traditional skills and knowledge.[15]

The Inuit have not completely lost their culture, but it certainly has changed in confusing and dramatic ways. Many families try to spend time out on the land, hunting and fishing or clam digging and berry picking, as the seasons dictate. This is out of necessity, for few families can afford to feed themselves solely through wage employment and buying from the Northern stores. But it is also for pleasure; for regaining a diminishing sense of family unity and harmony between Inuk and nature; and for remembering a time when male and female roles were more clearly delineated and parents had more control over their children.

VIOLENCE, LIBERATION, AND ALCOHOL

Another challenge Inuit women identify is what they call "spousal assault" and men leaving their wives or not taking responsibility for children. They use the term *spousal assault* to describe violence between couples, regardless of formal marriage status or whether they are living together. The fact that younger women are more likely to be the major provider for their families may constitute the central, underlying reason for the alarming rates of spousal assault that plague Northern communities. Men feel threatened by their loss of status and identity and by women's increased power. Unfortunately, as in other communities, spousal assault often represents a desperate attempt to rebalance power relations between males and females. As Rachel, a housing officer who has separated from her husband, explains, "That was the case in my relationship: I was working and he was not. I think that's another reason the relationship didn't work out. Seemed like he was threatened about anything." The marriage rate has plummeted as women try to avoid the violence that comes with frustration and substance abuse. Many Inuit women now resist commitment to men and worry about their likely role as principal providers for their children. This creates both confidence and uncertainty.

A minister in his thirties explains how a man's self-esteem might diminish when his partner takes on the provider role: "Maybe he feels that he's not a whole man, because he's not able to provide for his family." He adds that some people may think, "This is not part of our culture, because the man should be looking after the families, not the woman. The woman's job is to look after the children and to help them to grow." Of course, if she is working outside the home, the mother cannot fully carry out her traditional role. If the father baby-sits, resentment builds, the minister says: "The mother is really important to the families. If she is not looking after them well, the children have a different attitude about life."

A woman who is trying to reconstruct traditional mechanisms for coping with domestic violence observes that Inuit men have been relegated to a nonessential role, or "hung out to dry":

> Many people nowadays still don't want to work because they know they can get welfare, which is wrong. The government makes you totally a wimp: "You should be hanging on a clothesline. You can't do anything, might as well dry out." That's the image we were given; we didn't ask for it. The men say, "I've been hanging on a clothesline too long."

Some Inuit women say they think alcohol is the major culprit behind violence against women, but others believe assault comes when the man holds in his feelings and grows angry or jealous.

Shelters for battered women may or may not be useful in a village of only one thousand people. "Here in town, we have to get a shelter. . . . Some people say they think it won't help, but many say it will. They need a place to talk privately, the men and women. That's one of the goals of our mental health committee." Says elder Martha, in comparing life in the camps to life in the settlements: "I don't really know why men beat up their wives now, but in the old days men used to go hunting every day if it was good weather. If the weather was bad for a few days and they had to stay home, I noticed that they became irritable and angry. More men are staying home nowadays, and some even baby-sit; maybe it makes them feel weak." She adds that she learned that if a man is angry with you or hits you, "As a woman you don't hit back or talk back, because you know the man is stronger than you."

Rhoda remembers one case in her camp of "a lady being hit," but has not seen or heard of another case besides that couple. If there was spousal assault out on the land, the trend is much more alarming now, she adds. The rates of domestic violence vary from community to community, depending on its size, relative economic prosperity, and the availability of alcohol. The larger communities with high levels of unemployment and ready access to liquor suffer from higher rates of spousal assault. Smaller, tighter communities, especially those that prohibit the sale and/or consumption of alcohol, have fewer severe problems in this area. Employment is not an antidote to assault (many cases involve employed males), nor is being an officially dry town, as a nurse explains: "The rates of spousal assault go in spurts, related to how much alcohol is in town. If someone gets a shipment in we may see two or three people in a weekend, and then we won't see anyone for another month."

In "wet" towns, women and men are much more likely to cite drinking as the major cause of spousal assault. An RCMP officer comments that in Iqaluit, "they usually get more family violence calls. Here we get very few, and only involving younger families; we used to get more. It's getting better, or maybe the mental health committee hears about it." He characterizes this community as relatively quiet: "Break-ins and drunks; very few family problems. Disturbing the peace. Those are the main calls. I don't think the women really have a problem. If you look at the majority, maybe there's a few who get beat up by their husbands." He does not see bruises or black eyes that would give away unreported assaults.

LACK OF DAY CARE

A third major problem for Inuit women centers on lack of day care. Although there are "some very progressive families in this town"— couples who have a good education and jobs—chauvinism abounds, says Lena: "If they've got kids at home, the man wouldn't go and baby-sit. He wouldn't change a diaper. That's women's work. Do the dishes? You've got to be kidding. The woman cooks, does the dishes. He doesn't care if there's ten kids and one on the way. That's her job. She deals with that." This creates a tension for both men and women. No wonder that so many women name lack of day care as one of their most pressing problems, as Lena explains:

> I think the biggest problem for women is no baby-sitter, because many women here who have a baby still want to work. Even teenagers keep their own kid and attend high school, so they have a problem. There's no baby-sitting house, no building.

Fortunately, a community day care center building recently floated up Pangnirtung Fjord on the summer sealift ship. Although it is not a solution to the tug-of-war between couples, it helps provide a communal solution to a problem that faces women everywhere.

Toward the Twenty-First Century

THE ROAD TO EQUALITY

For the most part, Inuit women believe that a woman should earn the same as a man for a particular job and that, on the whole, women should be able to enter the same occupations as men. They believe in the fundamental equality of women and men, the right of young girls and women to be educated to the extent of their desires and abilities, and the propriety of women to work outside the home as long as someone responsible cares for the children. As in many other communities, women over thirty seem to have heard more often than younger women of the 1982 clause entrenched in the Charter of Rights and Freedoms of the Canadian Constitution that prohibits discrimination on the basis of gender. Women in their late teens and early twenties seem almost oblivious to the women's movement, the 1982 legislation, or the key issues that absorbed their mothers and aunts—yet they take for granted many of the movement's principles and vaguely believe in women's equality. The older women say things have "improved here and it's going to get better," but they also seem more acutely aware than younger women of the magnitude of their struggle.

The exact language of the constitutional clause may not be so important to women as the fact that it acknowledges women's rights. Inuit women agree that the details may not be so important: "I haven't really heard that much about it, but from what I understand it says that men and women could have better relations and better communication. I think it was a good idea." Of course, the constitution does not refer to improved communication between men and women; it simply proscribes gender discrimination. That some women interpret this to mean "better relations" between the sexes is an unintended by-product.

The concept of women's rights, though sometimes blurry, has spread mostly through radio and television, which are important sources of information and opinion for women in isolated communities. Women speak of a growing consciousness of their rights: "In many ways the relationship between men and women is still good, but right now I think many people have started to realize that women have rights, especially with the Charter of Rights. We start talking about women's rules and this sort of thing." For example, Geela, a seamstress, hears about women's liberation through friends in other parts of the Northwest Territories. A single mother of three young children who sustains herself by making coats for tourists, she likes the idea of equal opportunity and equal pay: "I don't want to go *over* men. I want to be equal." Her friends agree.

Women in Pangnirtung have not infiltrated hamlet governance to the extent that men have, although women serve on the council. Meeka thinks there will be a woman mayor someday soon. Importantly, she can identify a woman she thinks would be interested, capable, and electable: "There's one I know who can do it. She used to be a deputy mayor."

Meanwhile, women are gaining ground as workers in the public sphere. The strengths engendered by generations out on the land play out in a different arena today. Within the context of the family, the Inuk woman still plays the central role of domestic organizer, planner, processor of food and skins, teacher of children, and helpmate. In many cases, she brings her management skills, ingenuity, and persistence into the world of work beyond her front door. Whereas her work encompasses two roles, the man's contribution is compromised: His traditional role as provider and hunter diminishes within the contemporary settlement context, and he encounters serious difficulties in obtaining stable employment. The woman has a tighter hold on both traditional and contemporary work roles.

WOMEN'S EMPOWERMENT

One source of power for women, ironically, can be found in their relative conformity. Like women in many communities, Inuit women tend to perform better in elementary and secondary school than boys do; this improves their chances of doing well occupationally. Employers view Inuit women as reliable, dependable, and persistent workers, which means that they have a better chance than men of building seniority and stability. An Inuk woman who works in a social service agency adds that women who support their families also define themselves as head of the family. If they have a problem with their husband, they go to the social worker or bring charges against him with the RCMP: "The women seem to go too fast, they reverse [the traditional roles]." Furthermore, when a woman works outside the home and the man goes out on the land to hunt, "they have to hire a baby-sitter or send the parents to look after the children. That might also cause a problem for them."

Young Inuit females are keenly aware of the connection between paying jobs and education. In fact, says a high school teacher, some "feel they will have to support their families, so they're getting the education. Employers perceive them as more reliable, so they're getting the jobs." Ironically, this places pressure on younger women, who face the likelihood of becoming the major provider for their families. Sheila says her friends often talk about the inevitable link between their education and their future:

"I'll end up being a bum or being a housewife . . ."

My girlfriends ask, "If I don't have any education, what am I going to do?" That's their main concern. I often think about it, because I'm really concerned about my future. It sometimes scares me. If I don't have enough education I won't be able to get a job. If I can't get a job, I'll end up being a bum or being a housewife—or not even a housewife, just a bum. Some of the guys worry about it, too. They are all in school and haven't graduated yet. Comparing them to my girlfriends, their thoughts are almost the same. They say, "I have to finish grade twelve or even further, even if I don't like school or getting up in the mornings." They're really pushing themselves to have a good education.

Even if you find the right man—and he is working very hard, making good money, and you are working—I think it would still be the same. Mostly women are supporting their families. Women have rights, too, so why can't we do what we want to do? I want to keep on learning something new.

Young women in high school, according to a teacher, have clear ideas of what they want for themselves, what kind of lives they want to lead, and what kind of homes they want:

I'm a bit disheartened, because it's all southern values and goals they aspire to . . . very secular, southern, and materialistic. They say, "Oh, yes, we like our culture," but they don't want to go on the land, and if their parents go, they'd rather be here with a summer job.

They might contemplate suicide because their dreams overshoot the realities of opportunities in the North. ("Bright young girls, smart young people. They don't know what to do with their lives.") They fall prey to young men who abuse them or are threatened by their aspirations for more training or their intention to leave the community to find work.

Although on the surface it may appear that men have better jobs and wider opportunities, the reality is quite different. Women may earn less and have lower status positions, on average, than men, but they work more consistently in the wage economy,[16] primarily in health, education, and clerical jobs. Expanded opportunities await both women and men under the self-determination represented by Nunavut, the newly-created Inuit territory carved out of the current Northwest Territories.

DREAMS FOR THEIR DAUGHTERS

Geela's dream is simple: "I hope that my children will see our life, follow what we do. I hope I teach them by my own action, but I'm sure they'll have a different life from us." Apea and Eena have one dream for their daughters: "Finish their education and try to convince them that education is important to get a good job." Indeed, among the younger generation of Inuit women, dreams of being "a scientist, a cop, a nurse, or a doctor" are not uncommon. Some teenage girls say they will go south to find a better job.

For others, thinking about the future is too threatening. As one woman says, "I go day by day." Fourteen-year-old Jenny clearly feels torn between southern and Inuit ways. Her Aunt Mona knows the pain of being caught between two worlds, but tries not to stop her children from learning southern ways and being a part of both worlds: "I cannot make my child a white person. I can't make her Inuk totally. She is part of both. I want her to be part of both, so I have to do things that allow her to do that. That's hard sometimes." Mona feels caught "in between, because we don't know this culture that we're trying to get on to, and we can't go there because of our culture and our food [which is unavailable in southern Canada]." She believes things might improve a little for the next generation "because my daughter is going to know more than I—the good way from your people, and the good way from my culture."

Many women agree that some members of the younger generation seem lost, as they do not have the skills of either culture. Some women are frustrated by their behavior. In talking about the crime and problems with alcohol, one says that she has "very little respect for the younger ones." In the next breath, she adds, "It's probably not their fault. They're caught between two civilizations." She would like to see them do more to help themselves. Saila wants her daughter to "have a good life" and does not pressure her to be perfect. Will her dream of a good life for her daughter come true? "I don't know the future; I can't predict it. But I know if they are like me, they are not going to have a good life."

Reepa has brought her children "down south" to Toronto twice, and her oldest girl wants to go to school there: "She's always dreamt of being a dentist. . . . If I keep doing what I'm doing today, talking to them whenever I can, understanding them when they're going through a tough time, I think their lives will be okay. They're all very good children." Iola believes that new technology will change his children's lives for the better: "Myself, I catch part of hard time and easy time. I'm in the middle." And in a community that has faced its share of family violence, Apea adds, "If my daughter's husband started treating her like dirt, I would knock him out. I wouldn't see him hitting my kids. I don't really like that situation, and I don't get treated that way." A middle-aged woman says of her daughter: "If she was starting to live with a guy who gets mad and gets outrageous, I would get mad at him and start hitting him. I would for sure. I wouldn't stand up for a person who gets mad at people who don't get mad at him."

Beyond these dreams of opportunity, education, and harmony, what will the future hold in reality? The predictions range from pessimism to guarded optimism. "I think our traditions—as long as we keep our language and our hunting—will be alive," Meeka hopes. What will life be like in Inuit communities twenty years from now? Jukeepa responds, "It's hard to say, but I think my culture will die mostly." She acknowledges that the opposite could occur if her age group works hard to teach children their culture. Women say that they will need to embark on a self-conscious and deliberate campaign to protect, preserve, and pass on Inuit culture. This will be a formidable task, though.

Men also fight to keep their culture alive, Lena believes: "They still go hunting. They don't want to lose their tradition. They're concerned." Inuit are quick to add that the problems they face are not especially unique; other communities share these dilemmas.

Collective efforts across generations have fired the aboriginal rights initiatives of the 1980s and 1990s. Enlightened consciousness stemming from higher rates of university education and southern experience combined with the radicalizing process of trying to get native rights entrenched in Canada's Constitution during the early 1980s. For the Inuit, these efforts crystallized in one overarching dream: the creation of Nunavut, proposed since 1974 and approved by native constituents in 1979. Nunavut divides the Northwest Territories along the tree line, roughly along the lines of traditional Inuit and Dene Indian usage. The people of the Northwest Territories, native groups, and the Canadian government ratified the agreement in late 1992. This accomplishment reflects the strength of such native organizations as the Inuit Tapirisat, Inuit

Committee on National Issues, Inuit Women's Association, Council of Yukon Indians, Native Women's Association of Canada, Metis Association of the NWT, Metis National Council, and Native Council of Canada.

While Inuit women look to Nunavut as a doorway into a prosperous and more autonomous future, the legacy of political dependency parallels the legacy of welfare dependency: Those who grew up in the settlements have known life only as an administered people.[17] Many critics of the agreement wonder whether the Inuit will be able to resolve intergroup conflicts and constructively administer the resources at their disposal.

The move to autonomy will be difficult to effect after lifetimes of government control, but as a program director points out: "We should stand up and use our own policies and decisions. If we know what we're doing, Inuit will realize we're running it the way they want. I like the government policies; they work. But I think we should have more of our own." Increased political power, if it is shared equitably between men and women, should herald positive gains for Inuit women on economic, educational, and cultural fronts as well.

As Chinese women say, "In every crisis there is an opportunity." For the Inuit, the crisis of resettlement has created opportunities for a lifestyle and riches totally unheard of out on the land. In every opportunity, however, there is also a crisis. Threats to Inuit culture and self-esteem, family strain, and social problems give credence to that proposition as well. The major challenge facing the Inuit as they approach the twenty-first century is to craft a new, vital culture that is truly theirs, not just an amalgam of traditional Inuit ways and contemporary southern ways. The gift of the elders is their keen memory and old skills; the gift of the middle-aged is their frustration and pain, which have sounded the alarm; the gift of the young is their ability to work creatively across the generations toward a new culture that is uniquely Inuit.

Leaving the Arctic

Weeks of interviewing are over, so Kyra and I hike up into Auyuittuq National Park (just twenty miles north of Pangnirtung) with my husband, Norm. We cover ten miles a day for four days in total, un-

developed, uninhabited wilderness. Everything we need for survival is on our backs in thirty-five-pound packs. Inuit wardens hike the pass, covering an astonishing twenty miles a day along the treacherous Weasel River Valley and keeping an eye on the almost four hundred hikers who attempt the park each summer. Every eight miles a tiny hut awaits the weary hiker—not to sleep in (except in dire emergencies), but to record names, weather conditions, and wildlife sightings in the log book.

The river twists and turns through the Arctic desert, embraced by craggy mountains on either side that thrust sparkling white glacial "tongues" into the valley. We camp near huge rocks in an effort to break the wind that seems an almost constant companion. It is August and the temperature hovers around forty degrees, while the worst heat wave in decades flattens southern Canada and the northeastern United States. The sun shines all but two or three hours a day. One night, at Windy Lake, our tent is the only one left standing. Kyra and a few other campers huddle in the hut while the wind grabs and twists our small dome tent in a thousand directions.

Morning comes and we begin the long trek back to base camp Overlord, where we will sleep overnight prior to being picked up by an Inuk outfitter. The journey proves to be a near disaster. The last two sunny days have begun to melt the glaciers; what had been a half dozen side streams to ford on our way out have now multiplied to forty or fifty, fed by a wide mother stream that cuts down a mountain into the Weasel River. We must ford the streams, taking our boots off and putting them back on after each crossing so that our sneakers, not our boots, get soaked. We pick our way gingerly through rocks, sand, gravel, and more rocks, slipping and leaping, trying to stay dry enough to survive. It hits all of us that we could die here in this unforgivingly harsh and isolated landscape, whose beauty lets you forget how delicate the balance is between humans and nature. Suddenly I realize what the Inuit women and men were talking about when they insisted that each one's role is crucial to survival.

We plod on and on, now hours past our expected arrival time at Overlord. Norm is imagining the pebbles to be rubies and emeralds and sapphires. None of us speaks. Exhausted, I am using two walking sticks, mine and Kyra's. Finally we make Overlord, where hikers sit around a campfire sharing stories of their journeys into Auyuittuq.

They have saved us soup, which after our ordeal seems more like filet mignon. At eleven o'clock at night, fourteen hours after we started walking, we climb into our sleeping bags; I keep my sweater and jogging suit on because I can't seem to warm up. Within two hours, having defeated the reflective nature of the sleeping bag's inner lining, I wake up shaking violently. My head feels like ice, my legs are numb. I slip in and out of sleep for a few minutes, each time dreaming of the Inuit in People of the Deer *who froze to death. I awake knowing that I must call for help or die, but, like in a bad dream, my voice will not work. At last, in an effort that feels like heaving a giant rock from my chest, I call Norm's name. Another hiker wakes up and shouts that I have hypothermia.*

Suddenly I am outside under the stars with Kyra and Norm on either side of me, trying to walk around to warm up. It is too late: My speech is slurred, my legs are like jelly, and I cannot think. Some instinct takes over and I blurt out, "Take me to the wardens' cabin." They drag me up the slope and pound on the door. It is after one in the morning, but the two Inuit wardens are playing cards. They take one look at my white face and swing into action. They sit me on the edge of a bed, throw an old army blanket over me like a tent, place warm plastic gel packs under my arms and on my stomach, and bring the camp stove near me. After a few minutes they make me sip hot Tang. Slowly, the color starts to come back into my face, and they let me go to sleep in their bed. One turns to Norm and asks, "You her man?" He nods, and they order him to get in bed next to me and motion Kyra to lie on my other side. This is the best antidote to hypothermia: the warmth of other people. The wardens sit up all night, waking me every hour to count to ten and say my name.

The next day I am evacuated by a special Parks Canada boat back to Pangnirtung, where a van waits at the harbor to take me to the nurse's station. My vital signs are fine, but I suffer from chest pains for several days. The wardens say I was lucky to have made it through the night without a heart attack. I say I am lucky that they know the arts of survival.

5

Standing Alone, Together

Jamaican Women of Toronto

Although many women try to hold on to the traditional role, sometimes circumstances—the realities of North American life—do not allow us to do that. Sometimes there are many conflicts trying to stay in that role. Hey, you have to have two jobs to pay the rent, because maybe he's out of a job. It's difficult to play that role of housewife, nurturing the children and the husband.

—Elma

En Route to Toronto

After a few days of rest at my parents' home in London, Ontario, I swing onto the 401 toward Toronto. The timing is perfect—the city is throwing its annual Caribbean celebration, a fitting beginning to my interviews with Jamaican women.

The sun casts a warm blanket across the crowds lining the sidewalks and catches sequins and bits of mirror sewn into the brilliant costumes floating along University Avenue. It is the parade for Caribana, the annual weeklong festival that draws West Indians from all over North America. Huge feathered wings in every color of the rainbow symbolize the joy of this celebration; the males sport the most spectacular plumage. Steel drum bands, dancing, and laughter permeate the streets of Canada's largest city. Toronto is a patchwork quilt of ethnic neighborhoods, but this week belongs to those who have come from "the islands"—Jamaica, Trinidad, Tobago, Grenada, Barbados, and more. Yet the crowds are also full of people from other heritages who have come to share the excitement that echoes through the concrete canyons of the city's financial district.

After the parade I walk along Eglinton Street, the heart of the

137

West Indian neighborhood. Though many people with West Indian roots live in other sections as well, this part of the city clearly marks the commercial and cultural center of island tradition. In the cafés, I find Jamaican chicken, goat stew, and other delicacies. Bushels of sugar cane, bins of fresh shellfish, and mountains of tropical fruits mark the specialty food shops. Beauty salons offer braiding and hair weaving.

Later in the evening, after the crowds have dissipated and the air cools, I make my way to the Caribana Ball, where "Miss Caribana" is chosen amid cheers and popping flashbulbs. More sequins, more dancing to an irresistible reggae beat until the small hours of the morning. Tomorrow I will take the ferry to another island—in Lake Ontario, just off the downtown shoreline—where the steel drum bands will compete across the velvet grass of a pristine city park; then I go back to Eglinton Street to begin the interviews.

I t is 1966, and times are hard in Jamaica. Delia's lover, the father of her three young children, has not been home for more than a month. She knows he is staying with his other woman only a few miles away, and that he will be back one of these days with a grin and some presents for the kids. Delia sweeps and washes, just like she does every day, making the small house sparkle. But today is different. She steps out onto the porch in the hot noonday sun, clutching a letter from her best friend, Florine, who has gone to Toronto on a domestic-worker visa. "I'm so lonely up here," Florine writes, "but I keep telling myself that maybe by the end of my year I can find some other kind of work and stay on. Then I can bring my kids up and we can have a better life. Other women do it. Why don't you join me, Delia? It wouldn't be so bad if you were here!"

Delia sits down in an old rocker that she has strategically placed to catch the only shade on the front porch. She reads the letter again and again. Memories of her man's last visit flow through her mind: the loving, the laughing—and the beating he gave her when he mistakenly thought she had been "fooling around" with another man. She hears echoes of her own sobbing, then suddenly feels a rush of anger and courage mixed into a single stream of determination to make a better life for herself, too.

Delia leaves the children with her mother and heads for the immigration office for one of those interviews she has heard about. She will go to Toronto alone, she will put on the maid's uniform for a year . . . just a year. She will start a new life and send for her children later. For the next few months, when the prospect of emigrating seems all too terrifying, Delia tells herself over and over that she can do it—she can leave her children and she can make it in Canada. Finally, her papers in order and a ticket in her purse, Delia heads for the airport. She has never flown before; she has never left the island for any reason. Tears spring to her eyes and her heart almost breaks as she flies north, away from her family, her friends, her lover, and what Columbus in 1494 called "the fairest isle that eyes have beheld."[1]

The large and lush island of Jamaica lies ninety miles south of Cuba between Haiti and Nicaragua. Like the other islands in the Greater and Lesser Antilles, which swing in a giant arc through the Caribbean, Jamaican history saw European conquest and settlers who first drove out the native inhabitants (Arawaks and Caribs) and later orchestrated the mass importation of African slaves to work sugar plantations that still blanket the island. Jamaica was under British rule from 1655 to 1962, when the drive for independence finally succeeded.

Jamaicans wear the cultural insignia of a people who have lived under the yoke of servitude. "More than in any other New World region, slaves dominated the West Indian population numerically,"[2] a condition that stands in contrast to the African experience in the United States, where slaves were always an embattled minority. Emancipation came in 1834, but according to Walker the legacy of slavery permeates the social arrangements of Jamaican culture:

> Although they came from a variety of African backgrounds, languages and cultures, slavery imposed a new social order. Uprooted from the conditions and institutional forms which made them relevant, African traditions were modified by attitudes and behaviour developed to cope with slavery. Beyond the plantation, as well as within it, slavery produced a highly stratified society with divisions based on colour and oc-

cupation. White skin was associated with the power of the masters, black skin with servitude. The absence of sufficient white women encouraged mating between white men and female slaves, whose mixed offspring became a caste situated hierarchically between free white and slave black.[3]

Family structures in Jamaica reflect the history of slavery and shape women's lives. The lighter-skinned middle and upper classes followed the European pattern of marriage, monogamy, and male-as-provider roles. The darker-skinned lower-status (and lower-income) groups, descended from African slaves, followed a pattern of matrifocal households connected by loose commitments rather than marriage. These arrangements, chiseled out of the rules of plantation slavery and the economic demands of emancipation, continue to influence gender relations and family patterns, Walker notes:

> In freedom as in slavery the black family required the support of both parents, an economic reality which gave a high degree of self-reliance to women. Since formal, legal marriage was disallowed under slavery and remained outside the free black tradition, a series of common-law unions became usual and, as the male partner moved into a new relationship, the children would stay with their mother. Few West Indian children would spend their entire childhood with the same adult partners, or share paternity with all their siblings. A distinction had to be made between the biological and the functioning family, the latter assuming primary importance and including a variety of blood relatives.[4]

Jamaican women can trace their cultural roots back to the Ashanti-Fanti peoples of Ghana (the primary source of Jamaican slaves) and an African tradition of female independence and matrilineality supported by an elaborate extended family system and a prominent role played by the mother's brother.[5] Slavery shattered the extended family in Jamaica, however, as it did in the United States, often isolating women and their children in female-headed households that lack consistent support from the men who are supposed to provide for them. Furthermore, as Carole Yawney points out, a mother-centered household does not necessarily mean that women hold power in society as a whole. A third of Jamaica's adult women are listed as head of their household (and almost half in the lowest-income areas), yet in terms of outside employment or political power, women lag behind men.[6]

Patterns of marriage, extraresidential relationships, and consensual cohabitation that prevailed in Jamaica have carried over to the Canadian context, but without the economic and family supports typical of island life. A shortage of men and the devaluing of domestic work, both of which place women in a vulnerable position, exacerbate these patterns. Many women raise children alone while they struggle in unstable relationships with males who rotate among several short-term or intermittent liaisons.[7] Although many Jamaican women now live in the affluent comfort of Toronto's suburbs and enjoy professional careers, most agree that issues of commitment and respect still plague their relationships with men.

Like many other Jamaican women of her generation, decades later Delia has established herself in a professional position with a large company in downtown Toronto. Her children have long since joined her and graduated from high school. Delia's mother has died, her old lover does not write anymore asking her to sponsor his immigration to Canada, and Florine lives nearby. Although Delia's dreams have come true, as a Jamaican woman she is part of a racial minority in Toronto and suffers the double challenge of being a woman of color in a predominantly white culture. "Women have more pressures living in a Western culture," Delia muses. "West Indian men have just one strike against them, whereas we have two: being black and being female. It's twice as hard to get to the level you should be on, whereas the only strike against a man is that he's black. We have to deal with all that, and then we have to come home and still carry the load of the household as well."

Out of Tradition

TRADITIONAL ROLES: "YOU CATER TO HIM"

A good Jamaican woman has many virtues to attain. People expect her to be a good mother, have the meals prepared, keep the home clean, provide emotional support for the children, and cater to her husband's needs for sexual fulfillment. Monica, who came to Toronto as a domestic in the mid-1960s and is now a social worker, puts it in a nutshell: "You're gonna take care of your husband." She recites a poem she heard on the radio. "It went something like this: 'With your eyes you worship him / with your fingertips you clean the house / with your arms you embrace him at night to give him security / and if you do all these things you'll find that you get back just as much in return.' You have to give first, though, don't you?"

In Jamaica, both girls and boys were taught to do household chores, including cooking. Girls might do a little gardening if they were inclined, but there was pressure on males to learn farming. Says Trevor, a writer in his forties who grew up in Jamaica:

> I've always liked cooking and cleaning, so it wasn't really hard. My mother taught me to cook, bake, wash—I did everything, also the outside part. The girls wouldn't do the outside. They stayed in because outside is more physical, and most Jamaican parents try to protect the girl. Very rarely would you see a Jamaican woman on a ladder painting a house. The way she was brought up, that was her daddy's or brother's job; but you will see her inside doing well in the kitchen.

In adulthood, however, the division of labor was stricter, with few men contributing to domestic work. "Looking back to my mother's days in Jamaica," muses sixty-five-year-old Myrtle, "I would see the role of the woman as a partner in the relationship, in terms of the household chores and the funds being shared, each person contributing equally to the upkeep of the home and the children, and also being able to get some emotional support from the spouse, so the woman is not the sole supporter in that area." That was the ideal.

When males were the primary breadwinners, a man with money and good looks made a good catch. If he had money he could fulfill his traditional role of husband, and if he was good looking, "that was nice, too." The woman's role centered on making day-to-day decisions about cooking, cleaning, decorating, and raising the children. If she worked outside the home, she chose activities that preserved her ability to run the house as well, perhaps craft work that she could sell from her home, or day work for other families. Hattie, fifty-seven, remembers that "most women in Jamaica who have jobs work to get extra money by dressmaking or sewing. Maybe they sell cosmetics or go to the market. They find ways of making a little money, but mostly it's the guy who provides."

At sixty-nine, Mavis remembers well the lessons she learned as a young girl in Jamaica: "You grow up, you get married, you look after the family, putting yourself last, because this is what you saw your mothers doing. Absolute fidelity—whereas the men are allowed to have many relationships outside." The woman should be "like a grandmother or a mother. He works and brings the paycheck home. You are just obedient, cater to him," Myrtle adds. That was considered the fair exchange, even if a woman saw little of her husband. Monica remembers indignantly, "One West Indian man said to me a woman's place is in the house, the kitchen, and the bedroom—and she's so quiet!" Women also worked hard to keep their children in clean clothes, as Mavis describes:

> If it was one suit on the back, it was washed and ironed every night. In those days, most Catholic schools required white uniforms, and they were supposed to be spotless every day. The lower-class people could not afford to have two or three changes of uniforms, so the mothers would wash this uniform every day and iron it and starch it so their children would be spic-and-span the next day. No one wanted her child to feel out of place, even though economically they were different. When you lined them all up you couldn't tell.

Trevor parallels the women's view of their island role. He says his ideal woman reflects traditional standards: "She is a homey kind who doesn't talk too much about money. She looks after her kids, looks after me, and we have a pretty decent life together. Cook and clean and keep the place nice, keep the children clean—a woman like that, she's got me." Trevor likes a wife who can pass on good manners to the children. He goes on to say that Jamaican men have been socialized into being partyers and womanizers, which leads to the double standard of "good" and "loose" women that exists in many other cultures. Womanizing men exploit the "loose" women, who are not marriageable material. Trevor tells his son that if he ever brings a woman home,

> make sure she's a girl of good character—that's very important with me—and then I'll tell him to be nice and be honest. But I'll tell him the truth, if she doesn't have very good character: "Once your dad winks his eye, don't bring her back, please." I want him to look for a girl who didn't run around too much. One boyfriend before him is acceptable.

In my time, it wasn't, but here in Canada I guess it is. More than that, keep looking.

Reba, who is thirty-eight, comes from the old school where "you never have sex until you're married—that's strongly ingrained in my head." She agrees with the traditional role of women and will try to pass that on to her daughter. Other women question this obvious double standard.

Cyrene, a cosmetologist in her forties, points out that long before the mass migrations to Canada, there were women in the West Indies who broke out of the traditional mold: "We had women school principals, librarians, community workers who have been doing marvelous things." Sometimes they were married and had a home helper to reduce their work load; more often they carried both roles. The model of the two-career family was familiar because in the islands, "he had to have a job, too." The man retained his role as primary breadwinner ("preserving his status, his prestige, and his ego") and was considered head of household even if his wife worked outside the home. Cherrie, who is forty-five and came to Canada in 1967, remembers the plight of poor women who were forced to help support their families:

> Poor women were breadwinners as well. They *had* to contribute to the income, because the man's was never enough. They *had* to maintain those jobs, often as servants for well-off families. Some of the women would do two or three jobs. They would do your housework, take the neighbor's laundry home, and bring your clean laundry the next day. They worked nonstop.

Lower-income women aspired to give their children advantages they never had themselves, so poverty did not necessarily bar upward mobility: "Children from those poor families became teachers or doctors or nurses. That's one of the things West Indians have in common. You may be high up there, but when you get together to talk you remember where you came from—you never forget your home."

In Jamaica, says Monica, "some families emphasize education, whether you were a boy or a girl. My mother stayed at home and took care of the children, but she instilled in us that we should have education and a career." Marriage and having children were to come after schooling. Girls, especially, were encouraged to get an education because "our mothers stayed at home and they thought they missed something."

"A good education . . ."
My mother told us she wanted to go on and have a career, but because of her seven children, which came very fast, there was no time for that. She instilled in us the need for good marks by telling us:

Labor for learning before you grow old,
For learning is better than silver and gold;
Silver and gold may vanish away;
But a good education can never decay.

She never nagged, but she kept repeating those lines.

We all had to pay for college education in Jamaica, and it was one behind the other. We were all expected to be a teacher or a nurse or a civil servant. I let my parents down and they never forgave me, because I never wanted to be a teacher, and my aunts were teachers and we were always given that model to follow.

As middle child, I found it quite difficult because there were three before me, and they were going straight through, no turning back. As soon as you pass to the next grade, the other one takes your place, and whoever didn't make it would suffer because you'd be thrown out: "You've been given your opportunity, you didn't take it, now there's another one we have to look after." When I went to England, I couldn't stand the pressure of having to make it. They wanted me to become a nurse but I didn't, and every time I'd go to my parents they'd talk about my sisters—"Oh, my daughter the nurse, and my daughter the teacher"—and I knew they regretted that I didn't become a nurse. I said, "I'm a medical secretary." That wasn't satisfactory. "I'm a social worker." What's that? Now I'm an immigration officer; they don't want to talk about that.

Glenda's father wanted her to become a public health nurse: "There was something special about that, the brown uniform, driving in a car—it looked very glamorous, there was respect. My mother wanted me to have the best education, the best clothes, the best of everything, but no defined career." Glenda grew up in rural Jamaica. Her father was a sheriff who supervised several districts ("People looked up to him, and that's the environment . . . instill higher values, because the class thing was very rampant in Jamaica"). He had a large farm and employed several helpers; Glenda's mother did not work outside the home: "We had people clean and help with the washing, which is the norm in Jamaica." Even though Glenda's family might have been considered "lower middle class by West Indian standards," they had upper middle class values toward behavior, morality, and education.

For most women, however, a professional career was secondary—a woman might be intelligent, "nice, but that's about it." In spite of the reality that her income could enhance her family's lifestyle, a true career typically was not in the cards: "She is displaced," says Monica. "Misplaced!" counters another. Only a few men believe that women should be career-oriented. Although these assumptions are changing in Jamaica as women and men finish higher education and travel to other parts of the world, the traditional homebound woman's role until recently was as clear as the turquoise water that connects the islands.

TRADITIONAL POWERS: "WOMEN WERE DEPENDENT ON MEN"

In traditional Jamaican culture, it was perfectly acceptable—even desirable—for the husband to hit his wife if she failed to obey. Even beyond that, women tolerated some abuse because they had few options. As Hattie recalls, "If your husband beat you a couple of times, you don't divorce him for it. Women were dependent on men. Even if your husband beat you twenty times, you have ten kids—where would you go?" Says Jamaican educator, Brenda, who is thirty-nine, "We are used to being nurtured within the family context. We are dependent and interdependent. We're not 100 percent independent people, which is true of traditional families in most cultures." Consequently, although many Jamaican women found sources of extra money, they derived their primary sense of identity and their power from being caring, nurturing, and competent homemakers. And, like Chinese women (Chapter 7), they were expected to obey.

Gender and power intertwine in traditional Jamaican culture. Because men were brought up to feel that women were placed on earth to cater to them, a trend that goes back to parents and grandparents, they naturally expect that their wives should cater to them. The gender-power link is also reflected in the enduring importance of having a male child. In part, this related to keeping the family name. Oliver, a musician in his sixties, recalls that men were taught that "if you don't make a boy, you're not strong enough. To be a real macho man, you have to produce a boy, so you try hard. I've outgrown that, but when my wife was making the first kid, I was looking forward to it being a boy, and it happened anyway, so I was happy." A woman may in her heart want a girl, "because then you can dress them up and put braids in their hair, and women go for that," but because of the male predilection for a male child, women also want to have a son "to keep the man happy and keep him home."

"There are two kinds of West Indian men: the intellectuals and the scalawags, with very little in between," says Oliver. How would a father teach his daughter to distinguish between the good men and the scalawags? "I'll tell her that, as a father, I know how a man can build up his ego and pride and feeling good about himself by playing that role of the Romeo, the lover." He can feel successful and validated even if he cannot perform the role of breadwinner: "That big ego part with the West Indian—where he really has to be the person who is looking after the home—if he's not doing that, then he's had it."

Jamaican women clearly remember a key distinction between male and female roles, as Erroll, a retired mechanic, elaborates: "Jamaican women would hardly ever hang out at bars or taverns, but men would. You'd be sure to see the men every Saturday night in different bars—their wives always stay home. Saturday night or the weekends is a big time for the father, so he's free to go alone. If he takes his wife to a nice dance or a dinner, that's an exception to the rule." Women were left behind partly because "they'll have a half dozen kids and there were never any baby-sitters," but the powerful male culture also shaped a couple's social life. The assumption was that the man had the right to play (and to play around), Erroll adds: "Traditionally the woman always stays home to look after the children and clean house while daddy is wandering all over."

The Turning Point: Coming to a Cold Country

"Toronto is a cruel place," laments Estelle in Austin Clarke's novel *Storm of Fortune*.[8] Her friend Bernice, also a domestic worker from the islands, agrees. In her mind, Bernice has killed her employer seven times in the few months she has been in her service:

> No woman should have to leave the West Indies to come up here in this prejudiced, unfair, two-mouth, cold country to work as a servant for Jews and Anglo-Saxons or whatever the hell they call them, wasps? . . . No black woman should work in a serving job for [a] white man, in a white country, and in the same country these f—ing white people don't want to rent you a room, or give you a job.[9]

The first West Indians arrived in Toronto to attend the university during the 1850s. After World War I, many who had worked in Nova Scotia came to find jobs as porters, bellhops, and maids, having been "restricted by prevailing stereotypes to service positions."[10] Blacks were labeled lazy, sexually overactive, criminally inclined, and genetically inferior.[11] Immigration ceased until after World War II. The immigration flow picked up again in the 1950s, 1960s, and especially the 1970s. Men outnumbered women until 1961, when females began to outstrip males; by 1981, the ratio was 96,000 males to 115,000 females.[12]

Jamaican women tend to marry within their own group and to rely on social networks within the West Indian community. Walker reports that "as with all immigrants, West Indians experience insecurity and disorientation on first arriving in Canada, and they require understanding and support. The pace and size of the Canadian urban centre is overwhelming, apartment living is confining, even the climate offers a rude shock."[13] In typical "chain migration" fashion, one adult immigrates first, sending later for his or her spouse and children. In this case, the woman often tests the Canadian waters first (as more recently also with Chinese women):

> Between 1955 and the later 1970s female immigrants consistently outnumbered males from the Caribbean region. The period required to save enough money to bring the family could extend into many years for the West Indian woman. Meanwhile her children might be in the care of their grandmother, and by the time they came to Canada their mother would be a stranger. Sometimes a new step-parent would have been added to the family, and new siblings. Although economic circumstances continue to require the mother to work outside the home,

Caribbean men tend not to share in household chores and the mother is left with double duty to perform. The resulting family frustrations produce personal anxieties which add immeasurably to the usual stresses of the migratory experience.[14]

Naturally, cultural differences begin to appear between those who immigrated one or two generations ago, as they begin to assimilate, and recent immigrants who reflect cultural changes in the islands during the past twenty-five to fifty years.

Before 1967, professional women—especially principals, teachers, bankers, and nurses—came into Canada as domestic servants under the old immigration laws in order to take advantage of a young nation's opportunities. They entered through the West Indian Domestic Scheme, which allowed entry to single women between the ages of eighteen and thirty-five who were in good health and held a minimum eighth-grade education. After one year as a domestic, women could be granted "landed immigrant" status. "Most of them, in fact were not servants before applying: secretaries and clerks, teachers and nurses, as well as the unskilled, took advantage of this opportunity to gain a foothold in Canada."[15]

Monica, now fifty-five, looks back to when she was a young woman. Although she had been immersed in the traditional mandate of catering to her man, "some kind of yearning, a longing for independence" gripped her and other women of her generation: "We desperately wanted some opportunity to get away, and once the opportunity arose, we took it. This is why we immigrated to Canada as domestics in those days," to escape the narrow definition of womanhood. Others fled bad relationships: "Women can make the ultimate threat. She can just take off and leave the man, sometimes the kids, and run for her life, hurling 'I'm going to New York! I'm going to Canada!' over her shoulder."

After 1967, when Canada opened its doors to a wider range of immigrants, many professional women entered without having to call themselves domestics. Then more couples arrived together, as Cyrene explains: "For instance, I came as a registered nurse, and my husband came as a professional engineer. Not only did we come from England like this, there were many people coming from the West Indies as professional couples." Cheryl arrived in 1969; her daughter followed later with her mother-in-law.

The majority of West Indian families came to Toronto when we did, in the late 1960s, early 1970s. To be allowed into Canada, you had to be going to university or be well educated and financially secure. Now we have a cross-section coming in for different reasons.

Many upper-class people left because the islands have changed, and many lower-class families left to seek broader opportunities, in either case always more women than men.

The first settlement centered around Bloor and Bathurst Streets in central Toronto, up to Eglinton Avenue and Oakwood. Over time the more affluent have moved into the suburban areas, creating an amorphous feeling to the West Indian community. It is not as tightly knit and geographically focused as it was in the past, and some of the women who live toward the edge of the city talk about feeling isolated. Their neighbors are pleasant and friendly, but all they do is chat over the fence. The lively urban-Caribbean street culture is hard to transplant to sprawling suburbs.

Life in Canada has not been easy for domestic workers, as Makeda Silvera documents. Women who found themselves in intolerable working conditions faced a cruel jeopardy: If they complained to the immigration department and lost their job, they immediately became "illegals" and could be sent back home within minutes. Icy, a woman who left her own children in Jamaica and became attached to her employer's child, illustrates this common trap:

When I just start working there I couldn't understand why they hire me, for the lady of the house was home all day not doing nothing. Then I find out the lady is an alcoholic . . . it is the lady that I end up baby-sitting. She use to drink from morning till night. Her husband use to hide the keys for the bar, but that didn't stop her, for I end up going to the liquor store every day. If I didn't go she would threaten to fire me, and God know, I couldn't let that happen, for I know they would send me right back home.

Well it went on like that for a long time until her husband start quarreling with me. Imagine, innocent me! Some evening he would come home and I still cooking. He use to quarrel that I spend all day watching TV. Every night I use to cry. For I know it wasn't true, because a lot of days I have to clean up his wife's vomit and put her to bed before he come home. And then he pretend that he don't know what going on. Pretend he don't know she get drunk every day.

I like the little boy very much and didn't really want to leave him, but I couldn't take it no more. I went down to Immigration and I start to cry, real loud, and when I remember my children I cry even louder. I got back the same officer who say this was the last chance he was giving me.[16]

Domestic workers became "invisible" women in families where they were expected to be silent servers without personalities or opinions. Although many Jamaican women came to Canada later without the guise of a domestic worker visa, the nature of their experience is mentioned often as a bellwether of West Indian life in Toronto.[17]

Into the Twentieth Century

CONTEMPORARY ROLES: "WE'RE MORE INDEPENDENT HERE"

Life has changed dramatically for Jamaican women in Canada, many of whom now play the primary breadwinner role. Women from the islands bring in substantial salaries in order to help their families thrive economically in Canada, often supporting them completely. This role shift threatens some men, because women have a newfound economic independence that arms them with considerable power. Jamaican women in Toronto see themselves as strong, independent, and unique. The matrifocal culture of traditional Jamaican society has been translated into the Canadian setting. Although the stereotypical image of the domestic worker persists, many West Indian immigrants are white collar and professional women. As in Jamaica, many are heads of household. Many women raise their children alone, with the multiple burdens that implies in modern, urban settings: "Whether we are single or married, many of us feel single, because we don't get help from the men. Our men don't care too much, to be honest."

Jamaican women find themselves juggling the dual streams of daily activities—provider and parent/homemaker—in a double role that affords little relief. Some women take great pride in holding down multiple responsibilities. As Velma, who is thirty-six, says: "I work in a doctor's office, I do my kids' school, I'm involved in [a] parent-teacher group. I'm involved in community groups, chairperson of the membership committee. I'm involved in another community center. I don't know where I get the time, but I'm there. I sing in the choir. Too much! I'll take up all the tapes!"

Reba believes a good man should be able to show love and "appreciation of you as a person and as a woman." He should be kind, gentle, and a good father; support his wife and children; and ensure "that we have enough to eat and drink and have a decent life—generally sticking around the home and caring for his family." Reba feels that "most West Indian men are not supportive. They are always out partying and womanizing—and I don't mean just going out with the boys once in a while." Some men will work very hard, but on weekends (as in the islands) they like to party. The difference is, they fail to support their families as men did in Jamaica, which sometimes leads to family conflict.

A good man should also be "someone you can laugh with, communicate with, and always be there when you need him," says Velma. Brenda adds the traits of honesty and being supportive of anything a woman does (and "not chauvinistic"). He should respect a woman's beliefs and support her decisions: "Those characteristics are lacking in some men, no matter what color they are."

Jamaican women are more likely to have jobs outside the home when they move to Canada. "We're more independent here," claims Reba. "We have to be, because we can't depend on the men here. They're unreliable." In fact, some women see the pattern as a vicious circle: Women who immigrated as domestics had to learn to be independent in a hurry; when their husbands came to Canada the men were forced (and able) to depend on the women, at least initially; this allowed them to be "less reliable"; the women learned not to depend on them; and so forth. "Coming here, women are more independent, so the men draw back; because the women have more jobs here, it's easier for the men to be dependent on them," Reba explains. "West Indian men don't do their part here—very few of them do—[so] the woman sometimes gets stuck with the responsibilities of the home and the children. A very low percentage of men show interest in their families."

The Jamaican man "comes in if he feels like it," Velma laments. She has two daughters by one man and a son by another; neither man agreed to marriage: "If he doesn't come home tonight or for a few weeks, so what? If you're not the kind of girl who allows this, forget it." Women complain that "black men are very immature. They're not free, they don't tend to say how they feel. They can't show affection." Bernadine reflects, "I don't know what it is. They can't even say 'I love you.' It's very hard for them." They are also in a hurry and either don't know what they want or want too much, says Julie: "Everything has to be there for them at the same time. They're not patient about taking it step by step. Obviously it's going to cause problems."

Even worse, the "West Indian men in Canada don't show much respect," Reba adds. "There's something in the air here." Others agree: "Even the same people change. To me, men or women, West Indians come here to Canada, and we're just not the same. Wherever you go, men on the whole are immature."

In Canada, economic power helps some women avoid violence and emotional abuse. Most women work in order to survive; if the husband abuses them for a continuous period of time, they can always pick up and leave. "They're feeling a little more like they are somebody," Monica observes. They are proud of their contributions to family and society—"they're not a tool at home to work on when he is ready. The whole role has shifted . . . role reversal . . . so men compete with you." If a woman has a better-paying job than her partner, he interprets that as a threat rather than as two mature people trying to work together to provide for the family, and this leads to marital breakdown. "As a woman, you might make ten or twenty thousand dollars more than your husband, and he can't live with that," says Brenda. Having been conditioned into the concept that their wife should not work, the reality of coming to a "capitalist society dominated by white men" has made the men impotent in many ways, she believes. Women see that Jamaican men have a hard time in Toronto, where white males hold sway: "Men who were big shots in Jamaica come here and feel like second class citizens, and they withdraw."

A counselor sees more depression in men than in women, because the former do not seem to be able to reach their potential in Toronto. Discrimination and lack of fit with the job market may cause a man to take his frustration out on his family in physical, but especially emotional abuse: "It's neglecting the family, having an 'outside interest' . . . not being supportive . . . not fulfilling those duties they agreed to. Most of the time there is a vacuum in those relationships, and the women are left on their own." Since they cannot take it out on their bosses, when they come home they take out their frustration on women: "The wife is not going to throw you out, but the boss can take away your job. She has to be obedient and subservient. We are also aware that working white women find the same thing."

Velma knows what her ideal partner would be like. Her standard has gone far beyond mere economic support: "Someone I could relate to and really talk to, because if you can't hold a good conversation, there's no way you can get to know them. Most black men you can't do that with, because they won't open up to you, even if they're feeling it, they just don't know how to say it. They're concentrating on one thing only [sex]." She wishes men could open up and show respect: "They just haven't got that anymore. Once they're here, it's gone."

Women also seek a man who is supportive, a good father, and helpful around the house. For women in their forties or fifties, that kind of man is difficult to find, says Andria. She approaches her middle years with a sense of loneliness and loss "because in our age group, most of them would be married or going through a divorce or separation." Does hope figure in this landscape of dissatisfaction and anger? Even for younger women, the ideal man who "provides for the family" and "takes care of his woman" may be hard to tie down, Cherrie admits:

> We would love to find that. It's a hope, it's like a dream. When you come across two or three who have those characteristics, it's wonderful, because they're very far and few between. However, in the Caribbean I grew up in, that characteristic was there. It was lost somewhere along the way between leaving the Caribbean and coming here.

The Jamaican woman in Toronto takes on a necessary and desirable quality: strength. As Elma explains angrily:

> She has to be the head of the house, more or less, taking care of the children, paying the bills, taking care of him. So if you have three children, make it four, because you have to be mother, wife, friend, everything to him. You name it, you are that woman. If the house needs building, you call the carpenter and build the house. Possibly you ask

him for money, or else you go ahead and do everything and he just lives like a king, and you're just there looking like the dog's leftover supper and he becomes interested in other women.

Robert, a cultural worker, confirms this view as he talks about the dilemmas faced by his mother:

> When I look back at the model set by my old man, it was provider and worker, but he has the freedom to pick up the car and go out whenever he wants and leave my mom at home. She started yelling about it, so he started fixing the car all the time. She says one day, "He always fixes the car on Saturday mornings, he never stays around the house. I'm going to get myself a car, too!" Now my mom has become very independent. She's broken out of the housewife role—she's put so many plants around the house now, it's like a jungle. She expresses her creativity that could not get expressed because of my father. I can be beaten into place because the wrong example was set for me. My girlfriend is a violent feminist and very original and intelligent. I like her to express these things.

Brenda also resents having to coddle her husband into responsibility: "I've got him well trained now. We share housework and he's good with the kids. When I'm out working third shift, he'll stay and look after the kids and cook and clean. He's right in there with me, so that works out fine for us. He wasn't very good with them when they were little, he was still a little nervous. Once they were one or two years old, he would take over."

Some men hold unrealistic expectations for women who work full-time jobs outside the home but still look after the family: "This is where life becomes difficult for a West Indian woman in this culture, and even at home, because the men still expect the old-time traits. There's no way you can do three or four jobs. He comes home and expects to find the dishes done, the house clean, the kids clean, and forgets that you were out there working eight hours just like he was." Professional women struggle to divide the household labor equally with spouse and children so as to escape the double burden that always dogs their heels. The escape seldom succeeds. Hyacinth, a twenty-seven-year-old married mother of four children, describes her life:

"It's still my job . . ."

I've certainly gone through changes myself in my role as a woman, as a wife, as a mother. I grew up in Jamaica with my husband, and I decided I wasn't going to get caught in that trap. [My] mother-in-law lived with me for about twenty years, and she did all the household chores. I did nothing because if she was there, fine, she liked doing it. About two years ago she started to live with my sister-in-law, and I made the decision that I was not going to do household chores: I never did, and I'm not going to start now. So I called the cleaning service and I said to my family, "This is what we're going to have. The extra duties will be divided among the four of us, and everyone is going to pull their weight. I am not going to pick up the slack." And that's the way it's been working.

Tonight my husband cooked supper. Now, women have everything organized in their minds: It's your night to cook, so before you go to work in the morning you take the meat out of the freezer. As we left this morning I said, "What are you going to cook for supper?" He's resentful—they don't plan like we do—so it still falls on your shoulders.

Sometimes women slip back into the old caretaking role. If the place starts to look like a mess, it's really easy to say, "I can't stand how that looks anymore" and just do it. We divvied up all the cleaning jobs to do on the weekend; all of a sudden, people don't want to do the toilet, which is the norm, really. I totally ignore it, but there comes a point when I can't ignore it anymore, so I clean it. It's still my job. Eventually.

BECOMING A WOMAN, BECOMING A MAN

Fathers like to see their sons play soccer and sports, says Olive, but "that's true of all nations. I don't think that's specific just to West Indians." The girls are decked out in dresses, with ribbons in their hair: "Be pretty. Look like a girl." Boys are dressed "like a boy," she adds: "If the father sees him not looking like a boy, or if he's not active in sports, the father worries that the boy will turn out to be a homosexual. Once the boy is playing soccer and doing these things, he's okay. If the father sees him staying out in the kitchen with his mother and not getting out to play with the other boys, he starts to get worried."

Trevor contrasts male and female socialization: "Growing up as a boy, you were told not to cry. You're not supposed to express your feelings, but a woman can cry as much as she wants. I grew up knowing that I always have to act as a macho man, even if I hurt." Monica adds, "Boys are given many affections. They're pampered. That's the traditional way of sending them off into the world as a man. Here, the whole cultural thing is changing." Women in Canada are more likely to teach their sons to verbalize their feelings. Says Delia:

> I am trying to raise my son to be the type of man that I hoped to have for myself; he's picking up the values I'd like him to have. He's considerate, he doesn't think there's a distinction between men's work and women's work. If something has to be done, it doesn't matter who does it—unless it's the garden and the lawn. There are limits to every principle, right? And the dog poo—I refuse to do that!

"West Indian males seem to lack that sense of responsibility because as boys in the home, they might have learned things, but they had no responsibility," declares Cherrie. "The girls have to do everything. The boys do nothing, so they do not learn responsibility. They get into marriage and they still expect not to have that responsibility." Some women believe West Indian families in Toronto unwittingly continue to teach children sexist values that were relevant in the islands but are no longer useful in the Canadian context. For example, Velma feels critical of a friend who treats her daughters and sons differently:

> The oldest is a girl who will start university this year. My friend would allow her fourteen-year-old boy to go to a party and get home by himself, but this girl would have problems getting permission to go out at all. The girls are always sheltered. You are chaperoned everywhere you go. This sheltering affects a woman because you're afraid to make certain decisions—they were always made for you! In relationships, you look toward the man to govern your life, because the boys were always given that freedom to explore, whereas the girls were kept back. The boys were allowed to become more confident and adventurous.

Jamaican women struggle to bring their sons and daughters to a new definition of male-female relationships. Velma tries to teach her son domestic skills so that he will be able to fend for himself as a man: "He's rejecting all these things and saying that's a woman's job. I work and I come home and do everything. He will get up from the table and leave his dish there. I have to raise hell, fight to get him to wash it." Andria's story indicates a glimmer of hope for the future:

"This is what I would like from my man . . ."

My son sees how hard I work to make a good life for him. He's only thirteen years old, and already he's got his life mapped out. He's going to be married, he knows how many kids he's going to have, what he would like his wife to do, how he would treat her. He would like an educated woman, not necessarily beautiful, but a woman who is kind and with whom he shares interests. He wants them both to work before they have kids so they'll want the same thing.

He's very considerate toward me. He went to the Caribana parade by himself, with only a few dollars, but he brought home a pink rose for me. It was all wilted, but he said he protected it, that it was important—that's the attitude he's going to have.

We have many talks. I do role modeling for him and tell him, "This is what I would like from my man—I like loving and I like being pampered and those little things. This is how you should treat your woman. When you're dating, you should give her flowers and perfume." I also talk to him about the dangers of the drug scene, the impact on his future in terms of having a career and a profession. I always try to get him to aspire to good grades in school, and to make sure he knows education is very important so he can provide for his family some day.

Andria has taught her son to cook and do his own laundry: "He always says that when he gets married he will treat his wife differently. It's because he's heard me complain about my husband so many times, and he just sits there like a sponge and absorbs it." In response to the skepticism of other women, she admits that peer pressure may deter her son from being different with his wife than his father was. A woman in her forties expresses below the dismay many feel in trying to raise their children in a nonsexist manner. The traditional mold seems almost unbreakable:

I brought up my daughter to believe that a woman's role is just as important as a man's and that there were no defining rules where the woman should cook or wash or clean, or be a teacher or a secretary. You could be an astronaut or whatever you wanted to be. And that men are not the most important thing in your life. Yet, when she was fourteen and started socializing more with other girls, her values started changing. She would speak to me from a different perspective than how I taught her. The peer pressure is great out there.

CONTEMPORARY POWERS: "YOU REALLY FEEL LOST HERE"

Because of their unique immigration history, the position of Jamaican women in Canadian society generally differs from that of Jamaican men, who are often less educated and less well-employed. Some Jamaican women see Canadian society as more "male dominated" than the islands culture they came from (in which men were dominant, but women played legitimately strong roles). "Male power was not as blatant or cold as in this society. You really feel lost here, and you feel helpless." At home, the man "appears to be the boss, everybody respects him, and the woman is respected because she is married to him—here it's not like that," says Elma. She explains that since women came to Toronto earlier than most men, they may be further along in their careers, which creates another discrepancy.

"It's a woman's world, Canada is . . ."
I wouldn't marry a man who's coming from Jamaica, because he can't fit in with me here. That's one of my problems. I'm a well-established woman, and it doesn't matter how established he is down there, he'll never come here and match me. It's a struggle. Even if he is educated, I am head to head with him.

I see that in the government where I work. Women are paid the same, we compete the same. It's a woman's world, Canada is. Men would say, "They have changed. . . . They are no longer the women they used to be." Perhaps we're more like the new Caribbean woman—liberated, very liberated women, not the traditional women they know from the West Indies. This means standing up to the man, which makes it very hard for all of us. Men have a more fragile ego and are more sensitive about many issues than women are. Women tend to adjust better.

Some women say they strike a balance with their husbands or partners, especially if both are professionals. Cyrene and her husband, an engineer, work together on making decisions: "My husband is an intellectual, so he'll make decisions about the kids' schooling and what subjects they should do and why and when."

They pool their financial resources together; she manages the home, while he manages mortgages and "bigger things":

> I make good money. He makes good money, too, but he knows where there's a better buy, what will happen down the road. He's a Ph.D., so I credit him with having a bit more knowledge regarding finances, but I decide on the colors and what to do where. He wants to do tiling, I decide the color. In disciplining the children, he is most embarrassed if he puts his foot down about something and then I butt in. I can't do that, and I don't like it when he does it to me. We have to present a united front to the kids. I'm with them a bit more, so I would be guiding them more often, but we do it together as best we can.

Other relationships lack such balance. Velma describes her boyfriend's punitive reaction to her attempts to be assertive: "'If every woman was the way you are, Velma,' he said, 'women would be running the country. I don't like the way you talk.' They don't like you to be too strong or independent. So I said, 'Go to hell, I don't need this.' They really look at you when you talk back to them." Velma's colleague at work, James, told her that a married man had advised him, "When you finish school, you'll be getting married soon. When you find your woman make sure you wear the pants. Don't get a woman who can rule your head."

That attitude is typical of the Jamaica in which Velma grew up. An outreach worker, Valerie, age fifty, believes that sexist attitudes, although rampant in the Caribbean cultures, are perpetuated by European culture as well:

> We've been talking about Canadian and West Indian, but European culture plays a great part in West Indian culture. European women are very weak, too, the husband is the boss. European women constantly portray their lives [to their domestic help] in terms of "my husband" this and "my husband" that. . . . As West Indians, we get caught right in the middle of the sexist attitudes from both cultures.

Now, as women earn a living and in some cases experience elevated economic power, they feel less and less sympathetic toward "this sexist nonsense," as Valerie relates:

> *"You have to play the game . . ."*
> I've found as a black woman that I've had to learn to play games and how to manipulate a man. You actually have to become manipulated

yourself throughout the whole relationship. Let's face it, if you decide you want someone in your life, you have to play the game. My boyfriend is from Trinidad, and if it means allowing him sometimes to think he is making the decision, I have to do that.

If you want to do something on your own, you have to choose your words carefully, not just say, "Today I want to do this." You've got to say, "It doesn't mean I don't want to be with you, I just want to do something different or with someone else." I have to choose so carefully, and be very diplomatic. Many women do this.

I can already see that he tends to patronize me when it comes to decision making. He says he wants to be there all the time: "Don't worry about it, I'll take care of it." He says, "You know what you're doing, you can make the decision," but he always has something to say about it, even if it's exactly what I'm saying.

We met in my first year of university. I'd go study with my girlfriend, and he'd call me and say, "What are you doing there? I'm your boyfriend, I need all your attention." He was very jealous of my friends. He would get very angry and upset. You don't have the freedom to be your own person, your individuality. I'm getting sick of it. When women get economic power, the men are going to feel threatened, they really are!

In contrast, Cyrene sees herself as "one of the exceptions" because she is not willing to play these power games between man and woman:

"I won't have any part in it . . ."
Knowing what women have gone through, and what my mother has said—"Don't let this happen to you, make sure you have a career"— I'm just not willing to play the game. My individuality was instilled in me very early. I knew that I would have to find a mate, but that I wouldn't play any manipulating games: Just accept me as I am. Sometimes I'm flabbergasted. I'll expect my husband to take something badly and I'll give him time to come around, and I'm amazed at how quickly he says, "Oh honey, if you think that's a good thing . . . ." He'll go with it, without having to research it himself. He feels that I have the ability to make that good judgment and he'll support me.

He came here as a little boy, so he was brought up in this system. It's different, but I'm still amazed by it because he's a man and he's West Indian. I feel I'm very fortunate, he's been conditioned that way. I have no patience. My girlfriends say I'm so lucky and I say, "Why do you put up with that?" They play the manipulation game, but for me, I won't have any part in it.

Other women feel this path is easier if a woman supports herself: "You're free to work. You can wake up at six o'clock in the morning and go to the grocery store and leave him sleeping, no argument. You can go to work from ten at night until whenever, no argument from him, as long as he knows you're working. You're independent then, you're a feminist then. But the minute you take the feminist thinking into social life, that's when it stops."

Traditionally, as noted earlier, the man could play around, socialize with his male friends, and disappear for the weekend while the woman stayed home. The same pattern holds for some couples in Toronto, but the power relationship has become more complicated, as Velma relates:

> Man tells you he loves a woman who's a feminist. You know why? He has to make no decisions. If I want to buy a bedroom set, I buy a bedroom set. It's my money, and I'm that kind of person. I don't have to say, "Honey, what do you think if we buy a bedroom set? You come with me to this store and we choose one together." I need a bedroom set, I go out and I buy it. When he sees it, he says, "Oh! You buy a bedroom set and you don't tell me anything!" I say, "It's my money, and I don't need your permission."

Other women feel that once you are in a partnership, certain things should be discussed. Hattie would review the need for a bedroom set with her husband: "As a woman, I don't think I lose my independence by consulting." Another puts it this way:

> If my husband wants all these nice things, he has to give me a little more privilege. Don't expect me to be a little goody-two-shoes behind you when the only thing I am allowed to do is work, and everything else I have to discuss with you. I call them fringe benefits: "Oh darling, would you wear your brown dress today?" or "Would you put on your black negligee?" And if I tell you, "Don't go out to your friends," and you go anyway, those benefits won't be yours. So anytime you want to have that nice relationship, we have to meet each other halfway, or else I'm going to go ahead and do whatever I want.

The anger of many women who shoulder the double burden by taking on a major providing role for their family comes through in Bernardine's complaint:

> I end up saying to my husband, "The only thing I am allowed to do on my own is work, go to the grocery store, and dig up the whole garden, so that when it's done you bring your friend around and say, 'Oh, see our lovely garden!'" But if I decide I want to go downtown, I have to say, "Henry, what do you think if I go buy myself some lovely earrings?" He says, "No, you are not buying those earrings!"—which I'll buy anyway.

Valerie says her husband accepts her working and might even help with cooking the evening meal, but if she decides to go out with her friends, "that is a no-no." She must ask his permission: "Is it okay if I go hang out with girls from the office?" If she accepts a friend's offer to stop for a drink on the way home, he might be waiting at the door with "one of these [a fist], and we'll get into a big fight." If a friend drops by and invites her to a show downtown, he may try to stop Valerie dead in her tracks:

> He's not there, so you get all dressed, maybe planning to leave a note. As you're about to leave, he appears. You can't just continue; my husband threatens to come to where I am. A simple thing such as coming to church! Ninety-five percent of West Indian men don't allow their wife to come to church: "How could you leave me on a Sunday to go to church? It's the one day we have to spend together!" So you end up not going to church, and ten minutes after you decide to stay home, a friend calls him up, and he's gone.

Women cannot pinpoint ways in which they are considered superior to men, but they believe many men think they are superior to women. The "attitude is, I'm the man and I'm the boss." Because it has been that way "from way back when," the controlling attitude is very hard to break. If women refuse to submit to that control, family breakdown likely ensues. The choice becomes devastatingly hard: loneliness and independence, or commitment and loss of autonomy.

The choice is even more poignant because most Jamaican women frown upon divorce. ("They weren't brought up that way.")

Women characterize themselves as "forgiving and always giving in" to avoid divorce or separation. A woman will try to alter her ways to suit her man. "She knows that most Jamaican men who leave the house will not continue to help support the woman and children, so to avoid that she gives in." As soon as she tries to assert herself, he will stifle her by saying, "You shouldn't talk. I am the man, and what I say goes." She finds it hard to bring her point across, even when she knows she is right, because "men always feel they have the last word. Even if it means they have to give you a punch or two, they will do it to shut you up."

Since females are taught that male authority is paramount, breaking out of old molds is excruciatingly difficult. Says Reba, "You've seen your father being the voice. Your mother couldn't say too much—some women did, you always have that minority—but the majority of men have the control, and most West Indian women and men grow up seeing that, so it's very hard. If you go to a West Indian home and the wife is in control, the boys would say, 'Hey, he's the woman in the house.' That's an insult, that does something to their pride, so they always have to be in control." Reba puts up with her husband's need to control (which he says is part of his cultural upbringing) most of the time, but "once in a blue moon" she'll stick to her guns and disagree with him. This leads to an argument that may never be resolved:

"We have very good balance . . ."
If it's not that important we just drop it, and if it is important, nine out of ten times I'll end up giving in to him, but we have very good balance. Something else might come up that I'll get my way. When we were going to buy this house, I didn't really agree. We were in a fairly good neighborhood in a big house, and I didn't want to move. It was a real issue, but then after he showed me everything, why we should move, the neighborhood, I finally gave in to him. At the same time, I picked the house, and he said okay—and I'm happy we moved. In another situation he might give in to me, so we give and take. Somehow it works out.

He's not very good with money, so I try to hold the purse strings. He doesn't mind, but that's not a normal thing for West Indian men. They work, they get their paychecks, they cash it on Friday evenings. Half the time the wife doesn't even know how much he's bringing home. He does what he wants with it, maybe gives her some money to run the house. Half the time it may not be enough, but as long as his wallet's full and he can go partying with the boys, wear nice clothes, that's fine for him.

I look after all the finances. He knows for a fact that he spends too much money. I compromise with him; I'm reasonable. In regard to the kids and their education, we talk about it. He's good with things like politics—he's up on what's happening in the world, and I'm not, so I listen to him; if it makes sense, I say okay. With that kind of compromise, we seem to work out. The things he's good at he will do, and the things I'm good at I will do, and we keep a happy balance. We don't seem to run into too many problems.

We both discipline the children, but he's stronger than I am. They will get away with things with me, whereas they know they can't with him. They've got great respect for their father that way. Some mothers can be pretty heavy-handed, and some men can be pretty soft. It depends. I find some West Indian men, they don't care too much.

Audrey, who is twenty-five and works as a television model, describes her unhappy marital situation:

"It's my way and I'm sticking to it . . ."
We're separated now. We were married seven years; five years was too much. We had an understanding that he would pay the rent and buy the food, but oh no, he wouldn't give me his paycheck. No, that's asking for too much. We each paid half and put it together, but I always have the tendency to have things of my own. If it's my bedroom set, I say, "You can't sleep on this bed, it's my bed." He can't come home and sleep on it because he didn't put any money into it. If he put money into it, it would be his bed, too. I like buying things on my own. Maybe I have a hang-up about that, but it's my way, and I'm sticking to it.

I can remember my parents sitting down at the table and working out the budget for groceries, so when I got married, I viewed it as a partnership. We pooled everything in a joint account. I know from talking to other black West Indian women, what they would tell you and the advice they give to me—and advice I would give to black women, or any woman, for that matter—is it's okay to pool your resources, but you still have to have something for yourself that he doesn't know about. Many *men* are keeping quite a bit of it back for themselves. Every woman across the board has done that. It's a way back thing.

Some men just come in and hand the woman the paycheck, especially in the older age range, say forty and up. Sometimes they have a problem when they gamble and don't think of their responsibilities first. They own a house, but she carries the mortgage. She ends up doing everything, because this month she can't guarantee that he'll bring his money home. Sometimes when it gets out of hand, he'll pay the mortgage for a month to simmer things down, but regularly much of the financial burden falls on the woman. If the kid needs something, she's the one who buys it.

This is why I say women are stronger. Most of us are. Men are stronger in terms of position, but women are really the stronger ones. We're here with our kids alone, and we grow them up. I don't think men could do that at all . . . get themselves going and a job going and the house. Very few can. Very few.

The Jamaican woman in Canada has been forced to develop an array of strengths in order to cope with these battles, large and small. They feel they have emerged stronger than ever. Rather than becoming dependent on their men, they have become unique persons, says Audrey:

We plan, we make decisions for ourselves, we move forward in spite of the ifs and the buts. We go along and if there are problems, we turn to our friends and hash things over, but I don't think we necessarily turn to our spouse anymore to get support. What we do is we present them with the facts and say this is what we intend to do, or this is what has happened. It's not to get their support, it's to update them on what is going on.

One propellant behind this shift is that Jamaican women in Toronto have taken advantage of extra courses and special training, an edge which makes them eminently more employable and earns them higher salaries. One woman observes that women have grown but the men either have not or have grown in only one direction: "We seem to grow as a well-rounded person. I will do academic courses and personal development courses and specialty courses. We take everything under the sun to be well rounded. Whereas with the men, they will only do academic classes. They're growing in their work related field, but they're not growing in a humanistic way." Only whole people can be full partners, Elma declares:

"We should be sharing the work equally . . ."
We've talked about the one thing that West Indian women at home were doing all the time—making sure everybody was looking nice, always washing and ironing every minute of the day to make sure there were no wrinkles here or there, which is crazy when you have polyesters, you know. As a result men have become used to that. It's our fault! We've all referred to the mother's role, that they spoil the men, you'll hear many say that. Put them in this North American city away from Mommy and they have difficulty sharing the household tasks, or if they do they say, "I'm helping you." They don't say, "We're sharing the work." You shouldn't be helping me; we should be sharing the work equally!

They still look at the house as the woman's role, even if you have a career outside and you're working eight hours the way they are. They still expect you to come home and do another eight hours. There's total disregard for you as a woman, as a human being, as someone who lives and breathes. You know, this man is doing the same amount of work—probably you're working even harder. You have to because you have two strikes against you, they have just one. Yet you're supposed to come home and have a second and a third job, which is incredible. When it comes to decision making, they're so apathetic and very depressed—they can't go outside themselves to have an insight as to what the next move should be. The role becomes yours, and it's really tremendous.

Initiating social activities also marks women's strength: "The men become totally dependent on you; it becomes too much. You wonder why you have to do that all the time." Whether it's planning brunch or making reservations for the theater, women say they take the lead. Last year Florine deliberately refused to invite anyone over for six months, just to see what her husband would do:

I was rebelling! I love to have people over and cook and make them happy, but for six months, no brunches, no suppers, no saying "Let's go to the movies," nothing. But I went out on my own, right? I phoned my friends and invited them out, or I drove back to my office and read a book with the radio on and came back when it suited me. It worked perfectly for me! But it didn't work for the household. He sat, read his paper, watched his TV, until I finally hinted that it had been a long time since we had been out. I had to bring it up—it didn't work! He changed for a short while, but it didn't last.

Women complain that as in Jamaica, men are always ready to party with their friends but show an inexplicable apathy toward socializing with their wives: "They will pull up their boot strings for a month or two, and then they slip right back into the old groove again," says Vanessa, a waitress who lived for a while in New York City before coming to Toronto. She has Jamaican friends in the United States who complain about the same pattern: "They have a perfectly beautiful marriage on the outside but they have to make all the decisions; it's all on their shoulders." These women see the uncanny resemblance to their mothers' traditional lives. "Basically we end up carrying through the roles our mothers had, where they took charge of everything. Even though in North America we may have a career and education and all the other things our mothers didn't have, we're still doing the same basic thing at home."

Other complicated sources of male power exist. Women report that it is far easier for West Indian men to cross the racial line in Canada than it is for women. "We tend to put up with the black man's lack of sensitivity," Vanessa observes, "because if he meets a black woman who won't cater to his needs, he says, 'Fine, I can go to a white woman quite easily.' He's in demand in that sense, whereas a black woman rarely will go with a white man. That women outnumber men contributes to male power."

Brenda believes lowered self-esteem comes with the loss of power men knew in the West Indies. Jamaican men define themselves as very strong and self-sufficient, "but down in their soul they know they're not, they protect that image," says a counselor. "They'll do anything in the world to show 'I am the man, I am secure,' but they're very insecure, very fragile." This places an even greater burden on the women who are left to pick up the pieces. Men lose their dignity because in Canada, the women must work in order to survive. Men cannot provide for the woman and children, "so they have lost their strength. They can't control her, that's it. They have given up. All the positive things they had, they're not using those positives anymore." Brenda adds: "They keep looking back, reminiscing. . . . 'When I was home I was this, I had this, and nobody treated me this way.' It's dehumanizing. They feel they're no longer men. Then they take it out on the woman. You're not only discriminated against by society, as woman and as black, but by your husband or boyfriend again at home."

Love, Marriage, and Divorce: Island Patterns Transplanted

Many Jamaican women express anger with the state of male-female relationships in Toronto. They dislike the "circuit rider" approach to intimacy that some males take; it makes women feel used and degraded, and it does not work in the Canadian economic environment. Why do they put up with it? Velma hypothesizes that some women have been brainwashed into thinking they must have a man in their life, which prevents them from being strong in the larger sense: "When I say strong woman, I'm not talking about the kind of strength from raising a family on your own. I'm talking about emotional strength. It's one thing dealing with your son and doing everything with him and holding two jobs. But emotional strength—being able to stand on your own, not needing emotional support from a man—the woman who can do this and say, 'Tough,' has my respect." Velma pauses, then adds, "But that is very hard to find."

The source of the present pattern of relationships can be found in long-standing traditions in the islands, according to many women. In Jamaica, mating relations generally follow three distinct patterns, each with its own set of informal rules: marriage, extraresidential mating, and consensual cohabitation.[18] Marriages, associated primarily with the upper class, are considered indissoluble. All men should marry; a woman must be strictly faithful to her husband, and a man (although he may have affairs) may not live with two mates under a single roof. In this arrangement the wife is responsible for children with her husband; lineages are known as "bloods" and are taken from the father's side (patrilineal). The father has ultimate authority over and custody of children. As a husband, he is obliged to take in children from his wife's previous unions, and he is expected to provide for some of his wife's kin, if necessary. Informal separation dissolves the union, and bigamy is rare.

The second arrangement, extraresidential mating, is also publicly recognized but prevails among lower-income families. In this arrangement, the man has exclusive rights of sexual access to the woman, which allows him to know that any offspring are his.[19] The man may have two or more extraresidential mates, even if he is married; the woman must remain faithful to her partner for as long as the relationship endures; her fidelity is often achieved by living in the home of her mother or oldest female kin, which also adds stability and supervision; and senior kin serve as witnesses in paternity disputes. Children born out of wedlock live with the mother; such children are often placed in the home of the mother's mother, creating many three-generation female homes. A child born out of marriage or before marriage, however, is socially equivalent to a child born in marriage, and the "male has to fulfill his parental roles in order to maintain his relation with his mate."[20]

Consensual cohabitation may be a transitional stage between extraresidential mating and marriage, but usually not the reverse; it tends to be an unstable and ambiguous arrangement unless it serves clearly as such a transition. In this "normal course of development," the man has primary responsibility for the elementary family and for his mate's kin and her issue by former unions. No legal or religious sanctions are required, and informal separation can dissolve the relationship. Either party may be the "head" of the relationship, and if children arrive, man and woman may share responsibility equally although a high incidence of childlessness exists. If the relationship is dissolved, custom and law leave the children in the woman's care and "redefine the couple's parental roles exactly like those of separated extraresidential mates."[21]

In consensual cohabitation, a high degree of structural indeterminacy exists. Known as "keeping," common-law marriage, or (legally) as having a paramour or consort, consensual cohabitation is a frequent arrangement among Jamaican families in Toronto. Historically, the mix of these three forms has led to "scattered elementary families" and "grandmother families,"[22] as well as the oft-mentioned Romeo or "scalawag" male image.

Certainly religion and social class affect issues such as fidelity and pre- or extramarital intercourse, and not all women accept the more loosely constructed arrangements that leave them insecure and sometimes very frustrated. Olive relates the story of two friends who broke off destructive relationships because they were tired of the abuse and the man's failure to provide. They were also angry with many other women who tolerate abusive relationships, as in the case of Florine's fifty-year-old sister: "The husband has also been living with another girlfriend for ten years, and he comes home and he beats my sister. I'm really furious with her. I ask her why she puts up with that—she's the one who earns the money, and she stays there!"

Among middle-income couples, a husband may occasionally stray, but he does not have affairs openly. He operates in a more discreet manner that helps preserve his marriage and family. Middle-class women "can always get out because they have a job, they can look after themselves," says a computer programmer. Lower-income women and those with several children need the support of a second wage earner; they cannot manage on their own. Florine thinks this may be changing because support systems exist for women who are physically abused.

A Jamaican sociologist in New York studied Jamaican families there, reports Vanessa, focusing on how much the women had changed since coming to New York:

> They move out and leave their husbands behind, they tell their husbands to get out, and they take over and take care of their children. He was biased, he was really on the man's side. He was saying, "These women in Jamaica, they were happy, they were middle class, they had cars and everything, and the man worked hard to take care of them. Once these women came to the United States and they got a job, they no longer need this man."

Another woman objects that marriage does not break down overnight; it takes a long time before a woman finally decides to give up everything. She admits, however, that the time may come when a woman rejects the doormat role: "She no longer feels that she needs to cook his dinner or wash his clothes to be a woman. And men know this. They know that once that desire and need is no longer there, it's a losing battle for them. It's like a mental shift, isn't it?" The emotions that support the role dissipate, and "the man feels like he's no longer a millionaire—this woman is gone, she's leaving."

Cornelia's story illustrates the conflict women in this culture feel when confronted with feelings of loyalty and feelings of despair about their relationship. A nurse who promises herself and her husband that she will leave if she cannot take it anymore, Cornelia wants her marriage to work, but not at any price:

"I can't leave him because I'm loyal . . ."

Nothing is forever; there are no guarantees. There is only so much of that silence I can take. I would rather be on my own, but West Indian women have always felt very committed to their children. In spite of the abuse and in spite of what is lacking, you'll hang in there for the children no matter what. You develop strategies to cope, because first and foremost are my two kids. I would never, ever abandon them.

Now many women separate and go their own way rather than divorce, because it's a different culture and if you've been here twenty years, obviously you're picking up some of it. Many of my friends are planning separation, and they talk about it in terms of years: "It's three years to go." I have also made reference to that, but then I look back and I feel sorry for the man. If I leave, he's going to vegetate, totally disintegrate. Another human being down the drain. If I stayed, maybe I could help in some way, so I develop strategies to cope. Do I still love him? I really don't know.

I see it as a partnership. Loyalty. Maybe friends. That's what my girlfriend at work said: It's loyalty; it's not a question of love. She has the same sort of little problems, and she says, "I can't leave him, because I'm loyal." I would go tomorrow if it weren't for the kids. But then, after the kids have grown up, you're too tired to fight.

Going it alone can leave much to be desired, however, says Velma.

Many married women think it must be great to be single. I'm single, I'm out there doing everything. I own the house, the car, the job; my child goes to soccer; and I'm doing it single-handedly. The women who are married, they're doing it too, but they always have someone to turn to. I don't even have anyone that I can say, "Could you screw that in for me?" When I come home at night I put on my music and talk to my radio, but I know no one is there. When you see that you're on your own and it's not easy to turn to someone, you would freak out. So to save your marriage and hold it together, you pick up the slack.

A married woman retorts, "But you end up doing it yourself any-way. Sometimes the aggravation of waiting for him to fix something isn't worth it. I would be there myself with the hammer and the nails. You should have seen me on Friday, waiting for this guy to help put the curtains up. I said to heck with this apathy, let me do it myself." If you are going to live alone while living with a man, why continue? Says Cyrene, who thinks of leaving but holds on: "My situation isn't to the extreme where I would leave. If it got to the stage where there is too much aggravation—I can't sleep, I can't function, and I'm preoccupied with the marriage—I would have to leave. I guess I would survive, because I'm doing it all myself now anyway."

Challenges Confronting Women

MARGINALITY AND RACE

In addition to gender-based differences, Jamaican women also struggle with issues of ethnic stratification and racial identity. Phrases they use to describe themselves include "a black woman first," "a black person living in Canada," "a black Canadian," "a Ja-maican Canadian," "a West Indian Canadian," and "a black woman who is Jamaican Canadian." For virtually all these women, whether or not they have become Canadian citizens, they feel at least some identification with West Indian culture in addition to race and na-tionality. Cherrie considers herself a black Canadian, and then a West Indian Canadian: "I identify strongly with my West Indian heritage." Since so many women lived in England prior to coming to Canada, they "don't have any hang-ups about being black or West Indian living in a white culture."

Glenda identifies herself as a black woman first and a West Indi-an second, "because if you ask what country I'm from, I would say Jamaica—but to me, being from Jamaica and being a West Indian are one and the same." Others also refer to themselves as "black women" but sometimes identify themselves as West Indian. They build strong ties to the West Indian community through participa-tion in groups such as Tropicana, Harambee, and the Congress of Black Women. Says Cyrene, "I am a black woman with other black women, but it doesn't make me feel any different from any other woman. I think of myself as a person." Olive echoes these sentiments: "I consider myself a woman, just like everybody else—the thing is, just a different nationality." As an expression of their bond as black women, many participate in informal groups to exchange anecdotes about the problems they encounter everyday "as a result of pigmentation" or geographic origin: "Discrimination and frustration have caused us to come closer together, so we cry on each other's shoulders and give each other enthusiasm to go on."

Some Jamaican women stress the strengths of a multifaceted identity, as expressed by this social worker (and reminiscent of the comments by some Chinese women): "I have the best of both worlds. This sounds kind of flowery . . . but to be a part of the Canadian mosaic, I can offer something other than just being Canadian; I feel very good about it." She feels proud of "being black" and of her West Indian roots. Others emphasize that being a black woman in Canada means they have to work harder than whites and harder than men in order to achieve even close to the same levels. "It's frustrating sometimes," says Vanessa. "The reality is that you're in both categories at the same time, females and minorities."

Interlocking oppression means that discrimination and restricted opportunities visit Jamaican women twice, a situation that parallels that of African-American women. A government official relates that "I am aware of discrimination. I know that I am a black person, and being a woman at times is very difficult to cope with. I know there were many opportunities for me to advance—the reason that I didn't was because I was black and because I was a woman. However, I have not let that keep me back in what I have tried to achieve. I know that I have to work three times harder because I am black and a woman, therefore I always do my best to excel in whatever I do." In Michele Wallace's words, West Indian women "have no choice but to fight the world . . . because they struggle daily against the racist, sexist, classist power of white men, against the racist, classist power of white women, and against the sexist power of powerless Black men."[23]

A community activist who defines herself as a "black person living in Canada" says this affects her job opportunities. The most serious problem facing Jamaican women is that they are treated differently because they are "people of color," she says: "You have to instill this in children, which is sad. I have to tell my son, 'Don't use your blackness as a crutch, but at the same time remember that because you're black, more is expected of you and you have to give more of yourself.'"

In the West Indies, race did not define a person's identity as clearly as it does in predominantly white Toronto. Although many distinctions in terms of class, color shading, and racial background exist in Jamaica, says Brenda, "I was a teenager when I came to Canada—being black and a woman never occurred to me! I was just a person, a human being. In Canada, they always remind you that you are different. I know I'm different and I'm not ashamed of it. I am very proud that I'm a black woman and that I've contributed to the community."

Others agree that from birth or initial immigration into the country, "People just look at you as black. . . . They see your color first." A medical secretary is grateful that she is a "very strong person" like her mother, because warnings of racism slapped her in the face before she even made it through the immigration process:

"What you think is home is not home anymore . . ."
Before I came to this country, when I went to be interviewed at Canadian immigration, this man said to me, "Aren't you worried to be going to Canada—you're black—with all the racial problems and everything?" I said, "No, I'm not scared, because they've got racial problems everywhere, and let us not kid ourselves into believing that Canada is going to be any worse than any other place." The difference is, you have your people to support you in the country you come from, compared to here, where everyone is to themselves.

When I went to look for work, the first thing a neighbor said to me was, "It's fifty-two dollars a week, but compared to your country, that's many money." I said, "Yes, compared to my country it's many money, but compared to my country living here is very different." So I went to work in a fur company, cutting all the fur and putting it together, and I noticed that what you think is home is not home anymore.

It's different here. You have to work twice as hard, you have to be more on time. My last job I quit because of that, because I am a worker and this guy will walk around all day and do nothing; if I go to the washroom, he complains to the boss. One day I said, "What's going on here?" He says, "You're always in the washroom." I said, "What's wrong with that? I have to work eight hours and if I have to go to the washroom, is that a crime or something? I don't care about you! My daily bread was not promised to me by you, so if I am working eight hours and you're not satisfied, I'll quit."

Similarly, when Vanessa started her first job in a Toronto restaurant, she was excited about it, then noticed a racial bias: "I would be the only black person working there on the weekends, and they would make me clean the washrooms, do the toilet, do the floors, and I said to myself, 'That's not fair,' so I quit. I was very upset." Vanessa did not complain about this treatment, but other women insist that a black woman has to learn how to speak up for herself when she is bombarded by racial slurs: "Don't insult my mother. Insult me, but don't let me ever believe that you think that my mother was a fool! That gets me because my mother sent me to school and she taught me many things, and when you pass her and come to me, I have to defend my mother."

Those who come to Canada straight from the West Indies with no job skills and poor language skills face enormous challenges. Some get by through physically working hard in factories. Jamaican women say they are not ashamed to take even the lowest, most menial jobs, "because you want to get ahead, and you're going to push and fight." Once they land a secure position, they may feel locked in, as Reba explains:

> Being black, it doesn't matter whether you are male or female—you're usually more afraid, as opposed to white Canadians, to risk going out to explore other avenues. You think, "Well, I've put in this service, I'd better stay with it because I don't know what else I will get." It's not that someone is saying you're not allowed to apply for that job, it's just an internal barrier that you've created, unless you're a very big risk taker.[24]

"The positive side of being a black woman is the fact that I'm conscious of it and I use that consciousness in positive ways as much as possible," Elma states: "I cannot be born a white person. I have no control over that, but I try to be as equal as possible . . . go back to school, educate myself, try to be a decent citizen, and follow the rules." The support of other black women helps give her the strength to go on. Similarly, Monica talks about how being black adds strength to her as a woman, "because you have all the support out there from other women that you need to go through life." She adds that she has white women friends who also form part of her support network:

"We end up in pockets . . ."
I can see that women are women, no matter what color you are. Many times if there were not women, I don't know what would happen to us. . . . We are the greatest supporters for each other. I can say that loud and clear anywhere I go, regardless of race. Discrimination against women doesn't happen just in Canada, but you don't have to deal with racism in the West Indies. Not to that degree. There I had black teachers, black doctors, a black prime minister.[25] There, you have the class struggle.

I have friends who are in mixed marriages, and I associate in a circle where people like that will feel uncomfortable. I don't want somebody telling me, "Oh, you have a white friend." I have friends who strictly keep just black friends, period. They see me as a no-no. So we end up in pockets. I don't want to be someplace where I have to be defending myself: "You're not really black." That happens. . . . I don't want to have to say, "My white friend is coming over," or have someone say, "Why didn't you tell me that person was white?" I don't associate with certain types of blacks who feel like that.

Isn't it from their negative experience with whites? Sure. I was surprised that I was able to work my way up at my job with all the human rights complaints I filed, yeah. But we've got to get beyond that. I say to myself, "Look, you are living here, so you have to try and change, give them the benefit of the doubt, say good morning. When I walked in and you looked down on me because I was black, I was looking down on you because I was raised in a black middle-class culture. Who the heck do you think you are? You don't know the type of lifestyle that I had."

Do you know why it's even harder in Toronto? It's because the prejudice is so subtle. They'll smile at you, yet behind your back, they're trying to get you out of your job or something. They know that they're only going to let you go so far, even in school. It's a vicious circle. You tell your kids, "You have to be twice as good if you're going to succeed." That puts an inferiority complex on the kids, and that's why it keeps going and going. The kids think that they can't just be ordinary.

There are many problems being black. Adults should do more to help the kids with this, because I find younger people are more sociable. They don't really look at color as much as the older folks do. I went to school in England when I was younger, and I didn't think of black or white; we were just kids. We used to play, we drank from the same bottle, we would bite from the same candy, and it was okay. Then suddenly I became a mature woman, I came back to Canada, and everything was different with adults. They would see color. Still, it's difficult to know what to say, because being black and a woman is a double barrier. Oh, yes!

Being defined as different leads some women to reaffirm their pride as women of color. Many are deeply involved in the West Indian community and speak of the support they find there in facing the complexities of marginal status. As the generations in Canada mature, some are shifting away from the earlier concerns about assimilation, notes a teacher: "I find myself wanting more to identify not with Canadian culture, but with the West Indian culture." She does not necessarily mean preserving the culture, "because sometimes we have a tendency to isolate ourselves from the rest of the community, which I don't always agree with," but to spend time nurturing West Indian groups: "I still think it is important for a black person to have that niche."

Other immigrants, such as the Chinese, Indian, and Pakistani women who make up a large share of Canada's new population, share this dilemma. The Immigrant Women's Editorial Collective fears that reports on immigrant women do not allow women to speak for themselves: "Researchers are concerned to discover their 'objective' conditions in the labour market, to reformulate their concerns into issues which can be fed into the policy development apparatuses or which can be packaged into discrete programs."[26] Even the term *immigrant women*, the collective feels, is loaded with racist and classist undertones. The term is used primarily to describe working-class, nonwhite women from Third World and southern European countries. White, middle-class women from Great Britain or the United States are not usually referred to as immigrant women, nor do they typically see themselves as such. Thus even the act of naming them helps to render immigrant women marginal within the society that has offered them residency and citizenship.

RAISING CHILDREN ALONE

Velma, now thirty-six, was sixteen when her mother in Jamaica married her off without any choice in the matter. She had three children and six years later was divorced; she has never remarried. Bonita, also thirty-six, had her first pregnancy at seventeen, but never married and had two more children by the same man. These women are still seeking a committed relationship and companionship, maybe even marriage. For now, they are more interested in supporting their children and leading a good life. As I speak with them, they are on their way to a movie audition in downtown Toronto. One has dyed her hair auburn and combed it into ringlets; the other sports an Afro, with a scarf tied around her head in a twisted style. Says Bonita with a grin, "Nothing ventured, nothing gained. You have to try! Who knows what will come out of it?"

Having children outside of marriage is not unusual in this culture. In Jamaica, Velma recalls, "They have kids—it's nothing for fourteen- and fifteen-year-olds to have babies. Everybody accepts it. But in Trinidad, no way. They'll think you're a social outcast. You have to go and hide until the baby is born." Although these attitudes are softening, says Florine, "When I was growing up, a pregnant girl would have to hide, maybe with family in the country or out of the area, to avoid the shame. After the baby is born, everybody likes a baby, so it becomes accepted."

Teenage pregnancy is common in Toronto, as Hyacinth notes: "We have a high percentage of pregnant teenagers who are black. Teens have different kinds of problems—they don't want to live at home, so they can go to Humewood House, sort themselves out, and then go into the community again to live with mom or whatever." Abortion and contraception are not widely acceptable, says Nettie, a school nurse: "That's why you see so many single West Indian women with a kid. Contraception has been here since the 1970s, but I don't think too many women use it." For some women, lack of education holds them back, she explains: "You see one woman, she's so poor, but she has about ten kids, she can't even feed them. But if you offer her the Pill she'll say, 'No, I can't take it, it'll make me sick.' That's because nobody's ever told them why they should be using it." If their mothers "were not brought up that way and didn't believe in these things," the daughters will likely shun birth control.

Nettie dreads telling her own daughter about contraception, even though she knows the girl's first period is not many years off: "Her father will wring her neck. He'll wring mine, too. We've never even discussed where babies come from, to tell you the truth. That's one thing with West Indian people, we don't discuss these things at an early age. I see here in Canada they do, but that's still a no-no with us, telling these kids so early." Sixteen would be a good age to sit down and discuss the realities of womanhood, Nettie believes, although she guesses that her daughter would already have learned some of it from school long before then. Ironically, as a school nurse, she educates young white girls in a way that helps them avoid teen pregnancies:

"My mother will kill me, my father will kill me . . ."

One of my beefs, when I'm at the high school working, the white kids will come to me and say they suspect they're going to be sexually active, so I should give them advice about how to go about getting some prevention, and I'll tell them exactly how to do it. But you see a black teenager cuddling with her boyfriend, walking arm in arm, and you know the next move. You call them to your office and give them advice, and they will not follow through on it at all. The next thing you know, this girl is pregnant.

They always say they're not going to do anything. You tell them, "Okay, you're not going to do anything, but this is information that you will probably need." Maybe the kids are afraid to go to a doctor and say, "I need contraception." In a community where people know each other, then mother or daddy might find out. They say, "My mother will kill me, my father will kill me." We have quite a few teenagers who are moms at the school now. The school board has decided to accept the kids and try to educate them, because it's better than having them on the street.

We have family planning clinics in the neighborhood, run by doctors and public health nurses, and everything is absolutely anonymous, but you can't convince the girls of that. In the high schools, the kids know that I'm not hired by the board of education and I don't share anything with the teachers. The other public health nurses in the family planning clinic keep everything absolutely anonymous as well. The students don't believe it, though. If they see you talking to the teachers, they suspect you're talking about them.

It's also a macho thing on the guys' part to see how many they can father. I remember when a boy stopped one family planning class to say, "You people don't know what you're talking about. When you want to get it on, you just don't have any time to stop to use anything, you know?" He was just being a showoff in class, to show how wonderful and macho he was. The kids shot him down and said, "Hey, you have to control yourself no matter what." He felt a little bit humiliated.

Teenage boys feel grossly embarrassed to go to the drugstore for a packet of condoms. They will buy toilet paper and toothpaste and everything else, then just slip the condoms in the bag. They'll pay for it, but they have to make sure who the other customers are in the store at the time. I tell the girls, "*You* are the one who will be pregnant; *you* get the condoms at the family planning clinic." I'm encouraging them to take responsibility for it themselves: "Keep it in your purse, and you'll be safe."

I am a religious person, and this is sometimes difficult for me because I don't advocate premarital sex. But because I work in this area, I see the kids when they've had one or two babies, and they're stuck in that basement apartment where it's damp and this kid goes to Sick Kids [Toronto Children's Hospital] every so often because he's got pneumonia and there's no food. . . . I say to myself that it's best they avoid having children. I feel very comfortable talking to kids I know are sexually involved.

Velma agrees that young girls today can control their lives in terms of pregnancy, if they so desire. When she was a young woman in Jamaica, she knew nothing about birth control. Her mother knew that she was sleeping with a man but gave her no advice: "That's normal. There was no birth control, so you took your chances. You'd be so scared to pick up a condom at the drugstore, especially in the West Indies." Because so many young women were getting pregnant without being married, little stigma was attached to being a single mother. "Marriage is not that important," theorizes Velma, "because half of them end up being unhappy in the marriage anyway." Now in the West Indies, contraception is widely available and "practically free."

How would Cherrie feel if her daughters got pregnant at sixteen, as she did? "I talk to them about that. The youngest one is sixteen now, and there's no way I would like that to happen to her. I would protect them, give them the Pill or something. Then again, they're going to do what they want." The key issue for young women now is choice: "If you get pregnant, it's because you want to get pregnant. You can wait, you can finish school, you can have a boyfriend, you can have all the sex you need if that's what you want, and you can still have a career as long as the ambition is there. That's why I don't worry about the kids today so much, because if they do something it's because they want to do it. There's so many choices today."

VIOLENCE, LIBERATION, AND ALCOHOL

Violence against women has many sources, as in any community. Here, women hypothesize, men face problems of discrimination and prejudice in the work force, the frustration wells up, and they take it out on those closest to them. They blame the woman and children for everything. "Abuse is high," says Monica, "but many black men are afraid to go to prison and they know what the penalties are for violence, so they're very particular. Even if it does exist, some of the women don't report it. It's not up front, they keep it under cover."

Unlike in some other cultures, Monica reports that in this community battering women is not usually associated with drinking:

> If a guy is drunk, he'll go to sleep or whatever. He's not the kind to get drunk and go beat people. It's just their temper. You let them get away with it once, and that's it. Black women aren't firm here. If a guy beats up on you once, you make up, you say, "Okay, nobody's perfect, but if you ever do that again I'm gone." He does it a second time, but all you do is shoot off your mouth. You stay with him, and then ten years later you're still staying with him. Who's sick, you or him?

Monica speculates that men will do whatever they have to in order to be in control. The man beats a woman because she disobeys: "What they call disobedience is you trying to speak your rights. You disagree with them, and that's disobedience." Therefore the woman has asked for it; if she wants to avoid violence, "then shut up," Monica adds wryly. She would rather be alone. Cherrie feels outraged by the situation she sees one of her friends accepting:

"She's living in hell . . ."

Now, if I had a husband, why should I go bankrupt, have to leave my apartment, go live in public housing, and still have him live with me, beating me? And at the same time he has another girlfriend on the side. It's weird! Why would he be living under my roof? Is it sex she wants so bad?

He broke her finger, and she's still with him! He beats her not just once or twice, we're talking about a ten-year period. She has three kids. He has this other girlfriend who takes care of his financial needs—she signs for his loans to get cars. Whatever he needs! The wife knows it, and the girlfriend, well, I can't even blame her if this woman is going to be so stupid. I don't even want to think about the girlfriend anyway, just the wife. She's taking it all. Why?

If they want their way and you're saying no, they'll just do whatever they can to get their way. This is how these men work. What makes the difference between a woman like that and a woman like me, who won't take it? I'll tell you. I see other women and I sit back and think, "Gee, how could she let that happen?" It really bothers me, because I'm thinking very constructively about life, and I learn a lot from all these other people. There's no way now I would let a thing like that happen to me.

If my friend comes to me, cries on my shoulder, I'll try to give her advice, but she never listens. She'll never do anything about it! She's living in hell, and she wants to live in hell, because all you have to do is cut him off. She threatened to throw him out if he didn't find a job, and he was so nervous, he went out and found one. The only reason he did is because he didn't have money to get a place of his own, so he's dependent on her, really. He'll keep that job for maybe three months, then he'll quit and be right back at home again. He has power over her. They get physical because they they're male and they think they're stronger.

Some women said after our discussions that it might help if they talked about these issues with each other in small groups. Andria believes that "we should have more clubs and things to do together, but it's so hard to get a bunch of women out. Many are set in their ways, they don't want to pick up and make another start." In other words, raising consciousness and developing the power of sisterhood might bring a woman to the point where she could no longer tolerate abuse and neglect, which itself would be intolerable. "My sister's like that," says Andria:

> She's forty, divorced, and met someone who wasn't very constructive. I said, "You're not going anyplace with this man, forget him!" She wouldn't. She said, "I'm too old to start again." She had a little dry cleaning business of her own but went bankrupt because he wouldn't put in any hours. When he was supposed to make deliveries, he would get his newspaper and go to the racetrack. She sees this happening! I'm saying, "Get rid of the man now!" It's been five months since we've spoken. She lost her beautiful furniture, everything. She's staying with friends and the man is still there, so I know what I'm talking about. It's us! We're doing it to ourselves, because we're too scared to be strong.

Andria does not believe that "there's a black man out there who'll hold a position and be strong enough to run a household." The anger wells up inside her when she realizes that she should not have to feel that way. She rants and raves and tells her man not to talk to her: "Don't even bother to open your mouth and talk, because I ain't gonna listen. You gotta look at a man and tell him that's bullshit." Andria says women hang onto a bad relationship because "I've got a man" sounds like security. Other kinds of security are more important to her now, like her own job and feeling good about herself.

> What is it that keeps a woman holding on to that fantasy? It certainly isn't love. Is sex so important that they put up with that shit when they can survive on their own, financially? It must be sex, with some people. It's not hope! Not when it gets worse and worse, when people get physical. I feel terrible when I see this. And I feel even worse when I see my own teenage son starting to treat women the way he sees grown males treat us. No one wants to see their child like that, but they don't listen. It's something in them. It's a part of their life. Some of us smarten up sooner than others.

Some women feel that physical violence is horrible, but emotional abuse and refusal to communicate feel even worse. Women complain about men who deal with their anger by not dealing with it, sitting in silence day after day. Cyrene describes a friend who was married for twenty years to the "most perfect husband—

adorable, gorgeous, everything." Yet he complained about every-thing, even that the chicken was not cooked properly so that he could crack the bones. She would withdraw, refuse to cook, bring home take-in food, so he would have nothing to complain about. He would not accompany her to social events and never initiated companionate activities: "He was just the perfect man and it killed her. She says her marriage didn't fail, her husband just didn't grow, he did nothing. A perfect husband just sitting there, doing noth-ing." Her friend was the "go-getter, going here, going there, doing things. He's dead!" It is almost as if some men revert to being chil-dren once they enter a relationship with a woman. Those women who see the light get on with their lives and refuse to let a man hold them back; the others fall victim to abuse.

ADAPTING TO A NEW COUNTRY

"We migrate to a new country, change all our principles," Elma says in describing how it feels to land at Toronto airport and be absorbed into a city of three million people. "The style of living is different here—it really is hard for people from other countries to adjust." The typical channels toward opportunity—education and work—present the most challenging hurdles for any immigrant. Coupled with race and gender, landing in a strange country pro-duces the need for double doses of determination, says Reba:

> You have to be strong and aggressive. You wouldn't know, being white—you wouldn't have to go through all these changes every day that black people go through. Every time you make a step, it's a change. You have to ask for strength every day.

Gwendolyn is an immigration worker who thinks women have a slight edge in adjusting to Canadian life. When the husband and children arrive, "There's some conflict, and he's already one step behind because she's been working and has her Canadian experi-ence." When women cope better in the new country, it is doubly hard for males, she believes, "because at home the man's ego was up there—he's the breadwinner, and that sort of thing." Unlike the Chinese and East Indians who came to Canada in family units, West Indians immigrated alone and only in a few cases with their hus-bands, Monica points out:

You don't have the support that the Chinese or the Indian would have. West Indian people often are here alone. It takes a long time for the others to join, even the children. By the time they get here you've gone through a change process; you have no choice. It's a new country, you go through the whole culture-shock syndrome. You have to change, then they have to change, then you're trying to change them. They find it drastic, so conflicts develop. It's usually hard on both sides.

Differences in adapting to change also result from age at immigration. For example, Elma and her friends came to Canada in their early twenties; their children were born and raised in Toronto. Women who immigrated after their families had been raised in Jamaica experienced greater culture shock and conflict when their children became attracted to Canadian culture: "When they try to teach traditional morals and values to their kids, it creates conflict, because the kids are seeing something totally different." Younger women praise their mothers for easing this cultural tug of war for them, as Elma says: "My mother took the better half of being West Indian and whatever is beneficial from the Canadian lifestyle, and put them both together." Elma's mother was steeped in West Indian traditions, but she realized that some of them would not work in Toronto. "Now I'm a mother," Elma reflects, "and it's easier for me, because my mom already made that transition. She helped me, so I hope not to have that conflict with my own child."

Toward the Twenty-First Century

THE ROAD TO EQUALITY

When a Jamaican woman says she would not talk to other women about her experience of being hit or abandoned, when she talks about why black women do not turn out in droves for women's liberation meetings, she reflects the impress of a cultural tradition that says the woman will keep her place, sacrifice, put up with all kinds of behavior—including abusive behavior—on the part of her man, and keep her mouth shut about it. And she will survive.

Some African-American women came to Canada during the Loyalist period of 1783 to 1870, and others arrived through the underground railroad system after the American Civil War.[27] Monica says West Indian women are aware of these early sisters who "were low-key, but came with a certain amount of political consciousness carried over from the United States. They started some kind of movement here." Now, however, black women express dismay at how difficult it is to get their peers out to association meetings, although it depends on the focus: "If it's too political, we tend to draw back, we don't want to get involved. But if it's a social or family event, they will come out for that."

Even small support groups are rare, although Monica believes that may be changing: "Ten years ago it would be very difficult to get women to a support group, but the consciousness is there now and you find women are becoming very supportive—you have the network, groups getting together to help one another. They realize that they all have a common concern, so it's easier to get them together now than previously." Velma believes that "black women are just too laid back, they're too much homebodies, and maybe this is why we have so many problems. We need to go out and do different things—sports, politics, whatever! It's not just cooking, cleaning, and waiting for your man to call or come home." The road to liberation and equality is neither straight nor free of potholes.

WOMEN'S EMPOWERMENT

Two Jamaican women, asked to talk about the most significant event in their lives, reply without hesitating, "raising my children by myself . . . and doing a good job of it." One adds: "I used to think that I was wasting my life, up until this point. But now I realize that I wasn't; it was okay for that to happen. Now this time is for me." They will capitalize on strengths developed through adversity. Perhaps they could have accomplished more if it were not for the children, for whom they have sacrificed much, Olive says: "I made sure they were happy—I didn't really care about me." As children grow up, women turn their thoughts to building a more secure and adventuresome future for themselves. "What am I going to do in the next three years?" Velma asks herself. "I look back and I ask, wow, is this me, this little kid? Where am I going to go? Where to start? Am I too late to pick up and start with me?" She wonders whether when she was putting her children first she should have been thinking about empowering herself as well.

This would be a tall order for many women, who say their children are the most important people in their lives. Some add mothers, husbands, and friends to the list, but children hold the center of concern. Gwendolyn's story illustrates well the progression she made in her own self-esteem:

> *"This is what I had to learn as a black woman . . ."*
> Originally when I was married, I thought my husband was the most important person in my life. Then I had a son and he was important, and more or less I put them both first. After I was divorced, my son was most important to me. You've been in relationships, and you tend to— I don't know if this is as a woman or as a black woman—but you tend to always think in terms of pleasing the one you're with, and that's why most relationships don't work out. I just finally realized that like the song by Whitney Houston—"The Greatest Love of All"—you have to love yourself.
>
> I was just doing everything everyone else wanted. I was really unhappy, and I realized it, so I'm taking steps to feel better about myself. You have to be a little selfish. Or maybe it is perceived as selfishness by others, but it's just taking care of yourself. It's hard when you've been brought up in one culture that tells you to always think of others, and then coming to North America, where self comes first. This is what I had to learn as a black woman. I had to come first.

Olive has learned this lesson the hard way. She always put her children first, but now they have lives of their own and never call to see how she is doing. Their detachment has turned Olive around: "The number one in my life right now is first my job and second my children. If it weren't for my job, there'd be no way out of anything at all. My two older ones are gone. They couldn't give a heck what I do, how I live." Of utmost importance to Olive is knowing that she has a job that gives her independence. "I'm not going to sit there worrying about my kids anymore. If something happens, I'm there to guide and to protect, but my job is more important. Without it, you feel like you're not alive."

Some women rethink their mothers' lives in order to achieve a better grasp on how a woman can be personally powerful. They realize that their mothers were strong women, as Cyrene suggests:

> We were looking at our mother in the wrong way. We thought she was weak when she was not. A mother would have been at home and taking

crap from the husband, but what she went through made her very strong, and if he left her she would be able to take care of herself. Even if there were fifteen children in one place, she brought them up in the right way. That made her a stronger woman. Even if her husband left for Europe, the kids were not left astray, your mother didn't fall apart. She took care of those children alone and brought them up to be men and women, sent you to school. Don't forget that. Hold onto it and be strong. At home, there were men who died suddenly and men who had gone to America and never came back. You never saw your mother walking in the road begging. When you grow up, you wonder how she managed.

Ironically, that strength relates back to putting children first and self last, Florine argues:

What were their values? She wasn't living her life for herself. This is the whole problem. She was strong, yes, but then we ask, should we have to constantly live our lives for our children? This is what as black women we're trying to get away from—this is when I say *I* am the most important person. In the West Indies, although she was strong, she really wasn't doing it on her own. She had the support of her West Indian family.

Hattie concurs: "West Indians come from a very nurturing society, both men and women, because of the extended family system, and that is a major factor in breaking up relationships among West Indi- ans . . . the absence of the extended family."

Others see clearly through this dilemma, which like the prover- bial double-edged sword, cuts through their lives. You cannot live for yourself alone, but you cannot afford *not* to live for yourself at all. "Anytime you start being your own person, what are you show- ing your children?" asks Myrtle. "You're showing them that they can be their own person." That is a positive act, but there have to be guidelines and responsibilities. One solution is to help children see their mother as a human being with rights and desires, one woman offers:

You know you have to cook dinner for your children, so you think it's your duty that you cook every day. Why not get the children involved in it so that one day when you want to go get your hair done, you say,

"Joe, cook the dinner tonight—you know what I showed you." That's living for yourself but you're not getting away from your responsibilities. That's guidelines. That frees you up while still being responsible.

For Jamaican women, resolving this dilemma is key to their empowerment. Instead of insisting that her son respect her because she is an elder or his mother, Gwen tells him to respect her because she is a human being: "As black women in Canada, we hold onto all these values from the West Indies that are relevant in that culture—and even there they are dying out—but you're no longer living in that culture, and you have to change." The other dilemma stems, paradoxically, from women's success, for which they are penalized, but which at the same time represents their empowerment. Bernadine explains:

"The strength we black women have . . ."
There's a big resentment from the men towards us for our success. I pick it up all the time. I hate to admit that it exists in a relationship, because then I become very bitter and angry. If I'm contributing to make you feel comfortable within the confines of the home and the relationship, why are you resenting me?

Again, it goes back to the growth and the strength that we black women have, that we soar forward regardless of what or who's in the way. Our skin color doesn't matter. Whatever we want, we're going after it, and we're going to get it. Whereas with the men, they say something has happened in the process of getting what I want, so I'm not going to try again. They look at you and say, "It's okay for you, because you can go out there and get whatever you want." Well, why don't you get off your butt and move the same way we're moving? It creates a bitterness, and it doesn't come out in a very open way. It's very subtle, it's very locked in, and then suddenly—bingo!—it explodes!

Women bounce back much faster from the tribulations of being in the minority in a new country, Bernadine adds. She also notes that men more readily succumb to the pressures of not getting a promotion they had hoped for. ("They would go into a shell and lock their family out, just sit there and not discuss it.") A woman would talk about it, though, especially by using her support network of other women.

DREAMS FOR THEIR DAUGHTERS

Clearly island family patterns constitute a central element of Jamaican culture that has not transplanted especially well in Canadian soil. Patterns rooted in chauvinism and lack of commitment have produced both strong women and frustrated women. Yet Jamaican women speak of other elements of traditional culture that support family and reflect the colorful West Indian life—parades, festivals, food, humor, dancing, and dialects. These, they feel, are worth passing on from one generation to the next. "We try to instill a little bit of the West Indian culture in our children, because some of it is very good," Reba insists. "I hope they pick it up. If they integrate it with Canadian culture, they will do very well."

What dreams do Jamaicans hold for their daughters? Cyrene acknowledges that "it's very difficult for the men, and I feel sorry for them sometimes," but she would like her daughters to learn how to keep the men from hurting them:

> They will do terrible things to hurt us, to belittle us. For example, I am a black woman, and if I go to a gathering and I see a black man who is equal to me, he will ignore me completely, and he will go to a lesser person and cater to her or him. He's only doing it to exclude me. That's the same thing that's happening in relationships.

Olive wants "everything that's good" for her daughter. When she was growing up in Jamaica, her mother wanted her daughters only to marry and have children. In contrast, Olive is raising her daughter to think about the opportunities that await her "with a good education in a country like this." Although her daughter wanted to go to university when she was a little girl, now (at thirteen) she is not mature enough, Olive thinks, to say, "Okay, I want to finish high school and go on." Olive hopes this shift toward achievement will happen eventually, but for now she does not force the issue: "What's the use? She's really not listening."

Other women stress education and choosing a career path that fits one's personality and values. As Velma notes, "The most important thing is education, because once you have that, even if you mess up when you're young, you can go back if you're ambitious enough." Reba wants her daughters "to be happy, first and foremost." Education and not feeling restricted to remain in Canada are both important, says another: "Wherever success can take them, they should go for it, and it doesn't matter where." Most women express the hope that their daughters (and their sons) will become professionals, reflecting the old class distinctions brought from the islands and reinforced by Canadian and U.S. mainstream cultures. Being a professional, they say, means working in a setting in which "you work for yourself, or you're calling the shots and someone isn't making decisions for you." Doreen emphasizes that "women have it a little bit different. It's not easier, but they seem more resilient, so I'm not as worried about my daughter as I am about my son."

Women also want their children to be more disciplined and less selfish, more forgiving and understanding, and, ironically, less "out for number one." Their dreams for their daughters are intimately connected with those for their sons. If males grow up lacking self-confidence and self-respect, these women feel, they will take it out on the next generation of females. Brenda wants her son to be independent and to respect himself as well as women: "I would love to see him grow up and be a good contributor to society. I want him to have a very good education, because to me that is the most important thing. This way he will be independent and not rely on anyone. He has to learn to be honest, and always think about his family."

Jamaican women speak about their daughters' futures with the same sense of resiliency they demonstrate in their own lives. Olive refuses to let lack of education and low income stop her from becoming the person she dreams of becoming herself: "Do I have any plans for the future? Lord! Many plans! I'm always thinking it's too late to pick up and start, but then, no, it's never too late. There's always something to do and get me going. I like my new job, and maybe I want to move on further."

Velma also holds dreams for her future close to her heart, echoing the sentiments of many women in this community who are beginning to celebrate their multiple strengths:

> Plans? Oh, tons and tons. I would like to own my own salon someday. I started to write a book, putting things together—it's been a year now. My daughters see my life and they say, "Gee, Mom, you could write a book." My son showed me an article about relationships between black men and women; he said, "Mom, you're always interested in things

like that." I said, "Yeah, I *could* do that." Since last year I've been
putting notes together from the struggling times at [age] seventeen to
now. It's so much.

By communicating to her daughter and the daughters of other West
Indian women in Canada about the promise and pitfalls of her own
life, Velma hopes, "Maybe our children will have a better future."

The Last Day

*My last interviews take place in "Melody Acres," a distinctly upper-
middle-class enclave a few miles west of downtown Toronto. The
large Georgian-style houses boast luxurious touches—red brick exte-
riors, graceful bay windows, hardwood floors, and Jacuzzis. Broad
winding roads and cul-de-sacs suggest affluent comfort.*

*Florine, a professional woman in her forties, greets me at the
front door. Inside, a dramatic staircase winds its way from the center hall up to the private bedrooms of four teenagers; paintings by a
local artist brighten the hall and living room. Florine leads me into
a plant-filled sun room and introduces me to three other Jamaican
women who live in the same neighborhood and follow professional
careers in government, education, and medicine. Florine and her
husband were childhood sweethearts in Jamaica. Over coffee and
cookies, the four talk openly about how their husbands see other
women on the side, as was accepted in Jamaica, but keep their affairs discreetly hidden from public view. The women express rage
one moment, apologies for the men the next. They wish this part of
their heritage would quietly go away.*

*I leave this idyllic suburban haven and journey through rush-hour
traffic to the other side of the city, searching for "Briarwood Park"
and the home of Glenda, a single parent in her thirties. Here, narrow streets follow an unimaginative grid; the townhouses are connected and compact, built cheaply twenty or thirty years ago. Small
windows look onto a dark courtyard and alley.*

*Glenda opens the door, and I walk into a cool living room lined
with mirrored tiles and velvety furniture. Faded wall-to-wall carpet-
ing leads up a tight staircase to the two small bedrooms shared by
Glenda and her preteen daughters. The small kitchen in the back of
the house has no table, and there is no dining room, so I interview*

Glenda and her three friends on the living room floor around a coffee table. Like her, Glenda's friends raise their children alone and work in low-paid service jobs. All married in Jamaica, and all divorced after a few years. They complain about their boyfriends, who circulate among two, three, or four women, visiting each for a few weeks or months at a time. Glenda and her friends rely on themselves and each other, not the men.

I am reminded that social class plays an enormous role in how women respond to their men, how they feel about themselves, and how men provide for their families. Women understand that the "playboys" they simultaneously love and hate sleep around and freeload on women because they often have no other source of income.

I am also struck by the fact that women in these communities at opposite ends of the class spectrum share common disappointments. Ironically, the women of Briarwood Park, after stressing their strengths as independent, single women, admit they still search for "the ideal"—a committed relationship that provides companionship and perhaps leads to marriage. They want the lives of the women of Melody Acres. The anger of the women in Melody Acres echoes that of the women in Briarwood Park. They, too, rely on themselves and each other. They, too, want commitment and companionship, and sometimes they dream of being single again.

The city lights burn with an eerie yellow-green glow as I find my way back through the neighborhood toward downtown and the freeway west. I think about family and the meaning of commitment. Next I will drive into Mennonite country.

6

God, Man, and the Godly Woman

Mennonite Women of Elmira and St. Jacobs, Ontario

Being a Mennonite woman is not much different from other Christian women if you are married to a Christian husband. A Christian woman doesn't have to feel oppressed if her husband is in his rightful place. There is a sharing together; it's not one down here and the other up here. We wear our prayer covering and teach it to our daughters not only for prayer, but as a sign of submission to a man. I feel comfortable with that. I don't have a really strong character. I shudder at being a widow and having to lead out, because I need leadership and I enjoy that aspect of our relationship.

—Rebecca

En Route to St. Jacob's and Elmira

I am awakened by birds testing their voices with first light. I've been sleeping on the floor of an old Mennonite farmhouse that my cousin Richard Billson, his wife, Janet, and their ten children live in near Elmira. They have welcomed me into their home and routine while I interview Mennonite families throughout the district. After a quick breakfast of homemade muffins and tea, I jump into my car and head toward the small village of St. Jacob's. It is Saturday, which is market day. The Southern Ontario countryside spreads out in front of me, gently rolling hills dotted with neat, prosperous-looking farms. I am in Waterloo County, about forty miles west of Hamilton and Hagersville (where I spent the first thirteen years of my life)

195

and thirty miles east of London (where my parents reside). Most of my relatives live within a fifty-mile radius. This is familiar territory, yet I have never met a Mennonite woman.

As I sail past another red barn I notice the family name written in bold white letters: "Lisa Shuh and Husband." Underneath, in smaller letters, the sign reads, "Joseph Shuh and Sons." A few yards down the road the potential meaning of this hits me, and I throw the car into reverse. This is women's liberation "writ large"! My mind concocts a vision of Lisa Shuh grabbing a bucket of paint and a brush one morning and asserting her place as a farmer, not just a farmer's wife or a mother of sons. I wish I could meet her, but I am too shy to knock on the door of the house unannounced.

I resume the trip toward St. Jacob's, a typical Ontario town with an old stone mill, a library, picture-postcard stone houses, and a few neat shops and cafés. Beautifully penned signs in German, a Mennonite cultural center, and a Mennonite bank mark this as Mennonite country. A stalled truck with its hood up sits next to a Mennonite horse and buggy; the horse nonchalantly munches straw, waiting for its owner to return. I park next to the horse and make my way toward the market. By ten o'clock it is almost ninety-six degrees, but in spite of the blistering heat I feel self-conscious in my sleeveless shirt and shorts. Old Order Mennonite and Amish women look cool and placid in their long-sleeved, long-skirted dresses, dark stockings, and bonnets. Old and new, traditional and contemporary are juxtaposed in a multitude of ways: vehicles, clothing, language, values, and lifestyles.

I seek shelter from the sun inside the market building, where it is mercifully cool. Intricately designed quilts line the walls, and Mennonite dolls and country crafts grace the tables. Women artfully display homemade treasures from their kitchens—fancy pastries, breads, tarts, relishes, cheese, pickles, and preserves. Men show cherry wood rolling pins, medicine cabinets, spoon holders, and ax handles. They help with sausage and cheese making, but this truly is a woman's market, named in honor of Leah Scheffelmeyer, its founder. Leah died a few years ago; now Marie, her daughter, runs the market with her husband.

The market, which spreads outside the building as well, bustles with diligent farm women who take pride in their wares. A dazzling array of fresh produce glistens with morning dew. One woman tells me that every Friday she and her mother, her sister, and her aunt spend all day producing hundreds of Chelsea buns, raspberry buns, and fancy breads. They are reluctant to talk to me because they don't want their little family business to become commercialized, but they offer delicious samples. An Old Order Mennonite woman proudly tells me that she has brought her jams and jellies here every Saturday since the market opened in 1973, and every Wednesday in the summertime.

Another woman is selling "cook cheese." One gallon of skim milk makes one quart of this runny cheese, for which the woman charges two dollars. She makes the cheese all day Friday, then lets it set for the next week's market. On an average Friday, by herself, she processes four hundred gallons of milk. A Mennonite man proudly tells me that his wife bakes dozens of white currant pies all Friday and Saturday to sell from their home. He brings several pies and fresh currants to market for her every week. Optimistically, I buy a Mennonite cookbook and remember when I used to have time to make my own jams and pickles. As I return to the car, the horse inches toward the shade, watching curiously as the disabled truck is towed away.

The year is 1573; the place is Rotterdam, Holland. Maeyken van Deventer carefully composes a note from prison to her young son. It will be the last time he hears from her, for today Maeyken will be led through the village square amid shouts of "Heretic, heretic!" to a ghastly death. Her mouth will be screwed shut, and she will be burned at the stake. She prays for her children, for her husband and parents, for herself, and for those who light the kindling wood beneath her.[1] Maeyken is a godly woman, a pioneer, and (with countless other women and men) a cofounder of a religion known then as the Anabaptists or simply Brethren, which later split off into Mennonites, Amish, and Hutterites.[2] She is the ancestor of the Mennonite women who follow her beliefs and many of her ways four hundred years later.

During the sixteenth century, more than nine hundred Anabaptists—about one-third of them women—were burned at the stake or drowned for their radical belief that it is senseless to baptize an infant or young child, who cannot possess the maturity and adult consciousness necessary to making such an important spiritual choice.[3] Mennonites historically rebaptized those who committed to the faith at a much riper age (in the teens or later). Because the ancient Justinian Code defined adult rebaptism as a crime punishable by death, Maeyken perished.[4] Other women were chained inside their homes to prevent them from spreading their faith to peasants or city dwellers during the turbulent Protestant Reformation.[5]

The Mennonites took their name from one of their more prominent leaders, Menno Simons, a Catholic priest from Holland who joined the movement in 1536.[6] At the core of Mennonite religion lies a set of principles articulated by women and men of sixteenth-century Switzerland and Holland who fled into Germany and France, and later to the American colonies and Russia: The church should be a group of voluntary adults (baptized upon confession of faith) and separated from the world and the state.[7] Believers adhered strictly to pacifism and nonviolence, refusing to bear arms, serve in the military, or take oaths. Like the Jews, they were hunted down, imprisoned, ridiculed, and killed. It is this history of persecution and escape that led the Mennonites to form tightly knit communities marked by a strong commitment to God, each other, their families, and the land that gave them sustenance. By the twentieth century, Mennonites had scattered throughout the world, creating prosperous farming communities wherever they settled.

The Mennonites of Ontario's Waterloo County (which includes the small towns of Elmira and St. Jacobs) share close historical ties with major communities in Pennsylvania. Their ancestors immigrated to Pennsylvania from Switzerland and southern Germany in the first half of the eighteenth century in search of religious freedom and fertile land. The American Revolution was an extremely painful time for Mennonites in Pennsylvania who, because they were pacifists, refused to join the revolution and were then accused of being "loyalists" to the British Crown. American soldiers entered their farmhouses, plundered their food, and stayed as uninvited guests. After the Revolution, a few Mennonite families walked behind their Conestoga wagons from Bucks County, Pennsylvania, into Southern Ontario.[8] Like the Six Nations Iroquois, many of whom also were loyal to the British Crown, these early Mennonite settlers were given free homesteading land. The first settlements, in Vineland and Twenty-Mile Creek along the shores of Lake Ontario, were established in 1786 and served as way stations for later pioneers.[9]

More than two thousand Mennonite pioneers from Lancaster County, Pennsylvania, followed the same route between 1800 and 1835 but settled along the Grand River further west. Ironically, they bought land from the Six Nations Iroquois, who sold off half of their original reserve.[10] This Swiss-German group (who spoke "Pennsylvania Deutsch") "brought to Waterloo in their well-filled Conestoga wagons much more than household goods and farm tools."[11] They brought "the invisible heritage" of religious faith expressed in small wooden meeting houses not unlike the Longhouses of the Iroquois. And they brought women's commitment to "keeping the network" of family and friends, as Kreider writes about his mother, Stella: "She was keeper of the memory: names, birthdates, family connections, bits of information from the church papers. She was a keeper of the Mennonite peoplehood, that intangible sense of belonging to a larger Mennonite community."[12]

For some groups religion forms an integral part of ethnicity, but the nature of their belief system does not induce them to form separate communities. For the Mennonites, the history of persecution and the nature of their religious precepts converged to dictate a unique lifestyle that is more easily preserved away from the mainstream of society. In Waterloo and nearby counties, Mennonites live in villages and towns with names like Punkeydoodles Corners, New Prussia, Heidelberg, and Rummelhardt. Part and parcel of their traditional ethnic identity has been the strict division of labor by gender. Although that division is softening today, being a Mennonite woman links inherently and explicitly to a distinctive identity that reaches beyond faith into all corners of her life: values, dress, transportation, education, and occupation. Figuratively, if not literally, she lives in a community apart from the tumultuousness of mainstream culture.

Out of Tradition

THE POWER OF RELIGIOUS BELIEF

Traditionally, Mennonites adhered to a simple, uncluttered lifestyle of humility and peace, based on their interpretation of the Bible and early Christian lifestyles. Women were to be nurturant, submissive, and godly; men were to be leaders and providers. A woman's place was strictly and respectfully in the home. Her access to a broad range of opportunities and resources was denied or discouraged, and men enjoyed clear hegemony within the family structure.

The traditional pattern appears relatively clear-cut, but trying to identify patterns among contemporary Mennonites is like trying to unlock a complex puzzle. They are no longer (if they ever were) a homogeneous group. Although strong and closely linked communities thrive in the early North American settlement areas of Pennsylvania, Ohio, and Ontario, Mennonites can be found all over the world. Although the historical image of superb farmers dedicated to living on and with the land is accurate, at least half of the Mennonites in North America now earn their livelihoods in businesses and professions. And although Old Order Mennonites (and Amish) conjure up a picture of somber clothes, rejection of technology, nonconformity, and a "simple and peaceful life," the vast majority of Mennonites now belong to less conservative churches that accept the trappings of modern life and no longer require women or men to dress in the old manner.[13]

In 1972 only 35 percent of North American Mennonites lived in cities or towns of 2,500 or larger (the standard measure of an "urban place"). As of 1989, almost half (48 percent) lived in such areas.[14] With increasing urbanization and liberalization, most dress and work in ways that would not allow them to be readily identifiable as Mennonites.[15]

Waterloo County, however, is home to one of the most cohesive Mennonite communities in North America. Here only 39 percent live in urban areas; of those who live in rural areas, more than 80 percent make their living by farming.[16] In 1861 Mennonites comprised 11 percent of the county's residents. Although that proportion has dropped to about 5 percent, it is because of population growth among other groups.[17] Out of Canada's 168,000 Mennonites, more than 13,000 of them live in Waterloo County alone.[18] Most Old Order and Conservative families in this area trace their heritage (via Pennsylvania) back to Switzerland or Germany many generations ago; other, more recent and urban Mennonite immigrants are of Russian ancestry.[19]

Beyond the complexity of residence, ethnicity, and occupation, countless subtle variations in religious conviction affect lifestyles.

In Ontario alone, more than thirty different types of Mennonites exist.[20] Obviously a single chapter cannot capture the richness and breadth of the Mennonite experience. By focusing on three types that range from one end of the spectrum to the other, however, we can see how the role of women is changing. In this chapter, women who are members of the conservative Old Order Mennonite Church, the moderate Conservative Church, and the liberal General Conference Church talk about their lives. As a contrast, two former Markham Mennonite women talk about why they moved toward the more liberal General Conference Church.[21]

TRADITIONAL ROLES: "IT'S HARD WORK"

At one end of the spectrum, Old Order Mennonites engage in agricultural work; eschew electricity, cars, and modern technologies; and seldom take education beyond the point at which their own schools cease to operate (tenth grade). Women wear long, dark dresses and bonnets and reject jewelry. Their traditional—and only—accepted role lies in the domestic sphere as homemaker and mother, although they may sell their home-grown vegetables, canning, baked goods, or quilts at the local market. A rural, religiously orthodox lifestyle prevails and segregation of the sexes in church is common.

Conservative Mennonites are more liberal than those of the Old Order. They use technology, including cars if they so desire. Women dress in less severe but characteristically simple pastel dresses with tiny flowers woven through them. The dresses follow the same style: long or three-quarter-length sleeves, a slightly flared skirt, and a double layer of cloth across the bosom (appropriately called a "modesty panel" or "cape"). Young daughters often wear dresses cut from the same cloth as mother's dress, reflecting both practicality and the symbolism of growing up to be like their mothers. Older teens and women who have been baptized wear their hair pulled back into a bun or simple knot, covered with a "prayer veil" (a small piece of sheer netting or tulle) that signals their faith and humility before God. They wear no jewelry, not even a wedding band. Most are homemakers and live on farms or in small villages, but a few have become teachers or social workers. As among the Old Order Mennonites, gender segregation governs seating arrangements in church.

Further toward the liberalized end of the spectrum, General Conference Mennonite women often pursue a university education and professional careers. Many live in small cities like Kitchener-Waterloo, or large cities like Toronto. They dress modestly, but in the full range of mainstream clothing. Couples seek egalitarian marriages, although traditional values still heavily influence their choices. They do not accept the Bible entirely as given, which allows them to lift some of the stricter rules, especially those regarding submission of women and dress codes. Melinda, age twenty-eight, is an elementary school teacher who articulates this differentiation: "We don't live by every precept. None of us do. The Bible says women shouldn't braid their hair and wear jewelry, but we don't consider that to be the essential point of the Bible." She compares the urban lifestyle and values of General Conference members to those of churches surrounding the Waterloo area, noting that the latter exist in "a much more rural setting, with many farm families. They don't have the university experience, or the experience of dealing with other people. I think that has an effect on how people live and think."

Sprinkled in between these end points on the continuum lie literally dozens of other variations of Mennonite faith, including the Markham or "Black Bumper" Mennonites (who believe that black cars are acceptable) and the Mennonite Brethren (who stress the conversion experience to Christianity). These gradations of orthodoxy make it possible for someone to remain in the Mennonite fold while moving toward a more mainstream lifestyle if he or she prefers.

In spite of this diversity, Mennonites across the spectrum hold fast to core values. Today, for example, Mennonites oppose both abortion and guns because they believe humans have a right to live and to live a good life: "That's why we're committed to missions and helping poverty," says a Conservative Church mother, Mary. A poster in the Mennonite Cultural Center in Elmira proclaims, "Let every Christian agree not to kill another human being," echoing the faith's long-standing commitment to pacifism. It is in the role of women that the greatest diversity appears.

The traditional roles in rural areas physically tax both women and men. For men, farming or related agricultural work have been the typical occupations. For women, days are filled with sewing for all members of a large family, cooking three meals a day, baking, canning, pickling, gardening, and helping with men's work when necessary. "It's hard work from morning until night six days a week," says a former Markham Mennonite woman. She admires the fact that Old Order women do all this without modern conveniences: "They're expected to entertain after church on Sunday, with the table stretched out for fifteen or twenty people for lunch. Next morning, early, back to the laundry. They have my respect, because it's not an easy thing to work like that for forty years."

Salome, in her sixties with three daughters who also embrace the Old Order faith, represents the typical traditional woman. First she worked for another family as a teenager, learning how to be a wife and mother by helping a married couple. Then she established her own family at twenty, which she remembers as the most significant event in her life:

> When my first baby was born, I thought it was the most wonderful thing there ever was. It almost seemed impossible that she was my own child. I worked for a couple who had a baby almost every year and a half, but this was my own. Maybe that was the most unbelievable thing. Our first baby, a boy, was lost. I thought that was about the saddest thing I ever experienced. We would have had four children if they were all living.

Now, as an older woman who has devoted her life to family and faith, Salome takes pleasure in bringing homemade preserves to sell at the market. She talks about the rhythm of her life:

"We don't live that way . . ."
Years ago I made everything myself, but I'm getting older and I haven't got the help now. Mostly I'm selling other people's things. Earlier I did all that canning myself, so I was really busy, but my girls married and I couldn't do it any more. I'm doing it more or less for a hobby, coming to market and selling for other people. My married daughter makes the relishes now. I still have one at home, but she goes teaching at school, so I'm alone most of the time.

We don't have electricity in our house, but about three-quarters of our people have it. For lights we have gas lanterns. In the wintertime we have a wood stove and a propane heater in our bedroom. We cook with the propane stove and have a propane fridge that we use just in the summer. We have a horse and buggy, but no car.

All the years we were farming, I went out to feed the hens and milk the cow. That's about all outside, unless my husband was very busy in the harvest time, or if he was away for a short time. I had a hired girl or my own daughter, so we did the whole chore—the inside work, the housekeeping, the cooking, and raising the children. We had a big garden; I took care of that. We were always busy canning. We made dill pickles and mustard pickles and mustard beans, everything. He'd come home late in the evening, and he'd be tired. He'd go for a swim in the pond, then to bed. Early in the morning he went to work again out in the fields.

I did a lot of baking—bread baking, pies, bran muffins, cakes, cookies. I didn't think of buying anything like that. Now I'm too busy; I can buy my goods here at the market. I still do my own sewing on a treadle machine. We have to buy material and make our own dresses and aprons, because the factories don't make them. People with hydro[electric power] have electric machines, but I've never sewn on one. They do it with their knee, don't they? Underwear, stockings, and shoes we buy.

My husband and I are getting to the age where we can't farm anymore. We're selling our land gradually; then we'll have the buildings and the pond and the pasture and just one little field that we work. He was planning on stopping farming, so he sold his tractor and uses horses instead. We raise lambs and sell the lambs and the wool; one of the lambs is sick. We have two hundred hens and one cow. He sold all the pigs just on Thursday. Now we have one big sow, and she's getting piggies again in two months. We have five cats and one dog, and she has pups twice a year. We've got twelve pups to sell right now.

We go on trips—not every year, but we have people in Pennsylvania of the same faith, right in Lancaster, so we go back and forth all the time. It is very quiet here. We don't get the daily paper. They say there is crime in Kitchener, just down the road a few miles. Maybe not as bad as in bigger cities; I don't know. It does happen around here, but it seems impossible to us, because we don't see it and we don't hear it. We have nothing to do with it. We don't have that thing where couples move apart—what do you call it?—divorce, I think. We don't live that way.

Lovina, an Old Order woman in her late fifties and mother of eight, describes her life as "extremely happy and completely fulfilled." She would be lost without the routine and sense of contribution she derives from being a wife and mother. A key part of her role lies in instilling a strong sense of family, faith, and community in her children. Reportedly a fine housekeeper in the best Old Order tradition, Lovina grew up watching her mother and dreamed of being just like her: organized, competent, and highly skilled in the domestic arts. Her life centers on church and family. She loves nature and follows the dictates of each season to determine the flow of housework and garden work:

> It's a beautiful, simple life. You raise your family, you do your house-cleaning at certain months of the year, you plant, you harvest. Summer months there's always lots to do: Garden work, outside work, flowers. I do all my own sewing, for the children and myself and my husband. I have the summer sewing done in the winter, and in fall I have my winter sewing done for the girls. Of course, as the girls get older, they gradually start making their own things. I really enjoy baking and trying new recipes. In the winter I enjoy quilting.

Indeed, housekeeping standards are very high and especially challenging with large families. Children help as they are able from an early age, which is again part of the woman's responsibility toward organizing the household chores. Erla, age forty-five, a General Conference woman who was raised in the Old Order tradition, remembers her mother's routine: "Sunday comes quickly if you have bushels and bushels of garden produce all week, and everyday cooking and mending that goes with a big family, and you've got all this preparing to do for a big meal on Sunday." Old Order Mennonite women would not put it quite this way, because they are modest about their achievements. Usually, when asked how they spend their time, they smile at each other and reply simply, "Working."

A woman's role is similar in other conferences as well, although in the more liberal groups many women work outside the home either full- or part-time. For traditional Mennonite women, few options exist; the domestic role is clearly mandated. As with Ukrainian farm families, male and female roles balance fairly well in order to ensure economic security.

"Visiting"—a major Mennonite custom, especially in the rural conferences—interconnects all the families in a district and may be a vestige of historical persecution and group migration, when sticking together was key for survival. This custom symbolizes women's traditional role of keeping the community and the culture together. Visiting ensures that Mennonites build social and spiritual bonds across rural distances. Children attend services from infancy and grow up with boys and girls from other villages, which often leads to life-long friendships, sometimes to courtship, and later to marriage. Each week a different church holds the service for the entire district, which might include eight or ten small churches. After the service, women of the host church greet strangers and guests from other churches; shaking hands means an invitation to share Sunday lunch with their families. The following week, another church in the district will hold the service.

Women prepare large meals on Saturday in anticipation of an unknown number of Sunday guests. Diane, a mother of seven who also helps do the books for her husband's business, describes this unique custom: "Our particular church often has services two Sundays in a row. Sometimes we have twenty people for dinner [the midday meal] and maybe ten for supper. It's a real breach of etiquette to shake hands with someone and not invite them to come. You really have to be prepared; that means cooking and cleaning the entire place the day before."

According to the Bible, a good woman possesses a meek and quiet spirit. "That's a definite sign of a good quality in a woman," observes Aaron, an Old Order elder. She respects man as the leader, and, through submission, she "has a new birth experience with the Lord, a change of heart." She will stand by her husband even if she does not agree with his decisions or if his choices have negative consequences for the family. By traditional Old Order standards, she should be humble, gentle, hardworking, and frugal. These words are not mentioned by younger, more liberal Mennonite women or men. For all groups, however, she must be an understanding and caring mother who has an abiding interest in her children, although she will not care so much that she fails to discipline. "Generally, if you respect your mother, you look for a girl who has the same characteristics," one man observes.

A good woman should also take good care of herself and her home. Peter, a General Conference husband in his late twenties, explains: "You do look at a woman's beauty, too. Not necessarily how pretty she is, but how she takes care of herself. You don't want someone that's going to appear sloppy, because that's probably how your home's going to look." Being a good cook, seamstress, and craftswoman adds to a woman's qualities.

Most of all, a Mennonite woman is a good Christian who takes on the "role as a strong partner, an equal partner in marriage." Early in a relationship, couples discuss the importance and nature of their faith, looking for common ground and shared beliefs upon which they can build a commitment. Progressive Mennonite men search for a woman who sees herself as "an equalist, not necessarily a women's libber." This means that the modern-day Mennonite woman should be able to hold up her end of the responsibility and share in decision making. Because of the significance of community involvement and visiting, she should also be able to get along with people.

A good Mennonite man should be strong, responsible, and—in this community—interested in farming and farm-related businesses. "If a man is a very gentle person who doesn't fit into the typical macho image, he has a pretty rough time of it," says one woman. "I feel sorry for little Mennonite boys who don't like shooting birds and who are afraid to be thrown in the swimming hole to see how they can cope. I think it's a tough thing." Another disagrees: "I feel, and so do my friends, that a 'real' man tempers strength with gentleness." Strong spiritual leadership tops the list of priorities for most women. Old Order wife Ella describes a good man as: "someone to lean on spiritually. . . . The Bible speaks of man's first responsibility in the home as providing for the needs of the family. It's necessary that a man is a good businessman, a good provider, and a good worker." Like the traditional Iroquois, he should be able to see beyond his family's needs to the needs of those in the surrounding community.

TRADITIONAL POWERS: "BELIEVING IN HEADSHIP"

This culture highly values women's unique qualities and contributions. Although in terms of gender stratification women clearly rank below God and men, the religious principle of "headship" that defines a hierarchical order of God-Christ-man-woman also mandates men to consult their wives on important decisions.[22] The justification for headship and for women's head coverings is rooted in 1 Corinthians 11:7–9, 11, and 12:

> A man ought not to cover his head, since he is the image and glory of God; but the woman is the glory of man. For man did not come from woman, but woman from man; neither was man created for woman, but woman for man.
>
> In the Lord, however, woman is not independent of man, nor is man independent of woman. For as woman came from man so also man is born of woman. But everything comes from God.

"Sisters" in the faith are responsible for displaying the sign of obedience to God's law upon their heads, an act symbolizing submission.[23] However, the saying that "a man who doesn't consult a godly woman is a fool" helps to ensure that women receive serious consultative status, claims a Conservative Mennonite.

In exchange for the man's place as leader, he is supposed to love his wife as he loves God. If he does that, a Mennonite woman is guaranteed her own special place: being treated with kindness, affection, loving respect; protection, shelter, and security will be hers. Mennonite women consider this a very even trade-off. When the balance does not work, a couple can separate, though this is an extremely rare event. During weddings, says Alta, an Old Order woman in her eighties, ministers employ the imagery of a triangle to describe headship: "God at the top, and man and woman at the bottom. The closer you are to God, the closer you are to each other." A middle-aged wife says she is, in fact, consulted and her opinions valued: "I wouldn't trade it for anything in this world. I don't feel that there are things that I can or can't do that I would be able to do as a Mennonite male." Another confirms this view: "I find myself believing in headship 100 percent."

Alta explains: "I guess that's what our coverings are all about. Our veils are a sign that we believe in headship—first God, then man, then woman. Headship does not involve superiority. It's a line of authority that God has established for order in his family. You have to have some sort of a line." An Old Order male church leader explains that Mennonites perceive men as having more strength and authority than women: "We find with Adam and Eve, there the

The Mennonite Concept of Headship

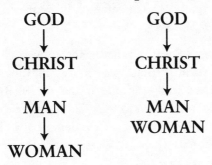

woman fell first. God in his infinite knowledge ordained it so that man would have the leadership; and when it comes to labor, the scripture says the woman is the weaker vessel. I think it's man's duty. . . . Sure, we are possibly a little bit stronger leader, but that gives us absolutely no right to abuse women."

In spite of this line of authority, with husband as leader and wife as submissive, they do not think in terms of a superior person and an inferior person. According to Mennonite women, relationships balance out more than these terms imply. Both men and women dislike the word *superior* because it "sounds a little bit domineering." Are men "better" than women? Not in any meaningful ways, according to Aaron:

> If you take that approach, you're wrong. We're all human beings, we're all living souls. To say that one is better than the other wouldn't be right. Women are *better* in their God-given position—whereas society now is giving them all an equal place, and I don't believe in that. Men working on construction crews and doing heavy work is right and sensible, but women who want the same jobs have to take all kinds of muscle-building classes first because they haven't got the strength. Man naturally has the strength, and I believe God has given man a leadership there.

By the same token, he argues, women can do other things better than men can, so that relationships balance out again: "Changing dirty diapers—women are just better fitted for that. I always feel so clumsy on a job like that. I don't do it that often, you know."

Mennonite women perceive their power as deriving from the role of mother. Rebecca, a fifty-eight-year-old housewife and cheese producer explains:

> As a young teenager I realized that headship was what God command-ed, but the older I'm getting, I see more and more the *value* of that order. I think if we really dig into it and see what God intended for women to be, it comes down to this: We can have more influence over the oncoming generation than the president of any big nation can have. He is for his time, and it's gone. We influence the next generation, and that's what carries on.

In this sense, the woman's role as homemaker/mother is just as im-portant as the man's, and maybe even a little more so in the long run. She just does not get top billing. Conservative Mennonite Dar-lene, who is forty-five, met an old friend at a high school reunion. The woman, who left the Mennonite fold, asked what Darlene does for a living. Darlene replied that she is "just a housewife." The friend chastised her for putting it that way, as Darlene comments:

> I was surprised to hear that coming from her. Sometimes even we think of it as not being very much, and we shouldn't feel that way because it's a God-ordained position. If we do that cheerfully and the way we're supposed to, then we'll enjoy it and it won't be a burden to us. Isn't there a quote, "The hand that rocks the cradle is the hand that rules the world"? In cases of the great men of the world, often it's a mother's in-fluence that made that man. If there's a good mother's influence, there's usually a good husband-wife relationship. And so it goes.

Rebecca says Mennonite women understand (as do women in other cultures) that formal authority may rest with the man of the house, but influence goes a long way toward balancing power. She remembers reading "that wise is the woman that rules her man but doesn't let him know it. Often what it boils down to is that you have a lot of influence, but you're not telling him what to do. Yet how you use that influence will definitely affect his decision."

Some Mennonite women exert more obvious power. "My par-ents had a business; I don't know who made which decisions, but my mom was very strong, a dominant person," says a woman in her forties. "My father would agree with her because he wouldn't want to talk about it." More typical probably is Crissie's recollection of her grandparents' relationship: "My grandpa had the final say. My grandmother had input and she made some decisions on her own, but major decisions that involved both of them he would make." Joanna agrees:

> In my parents' relationship, they try to consult and reach an agreement, but if an agreement can't be reached, it comes down to my father. My husband's parents consult very much on everything. Mom would rather stay out of the money thing. She appreciates it if my dad is willing to do that. Beyond that, they try to discuss every major thing.

The Turning Point: The Baptismal Commitment

For individual Mennonite women, the most significant turning point in their lives is the day they decide to commit to the faith through baptism. This act opens the door both to womanhood and to full identification with a religion and a unique lifestyle. The age at baptism and the conscious choice it reflects takes on particular importance when we try to understand the lives of Mennonite women. Although they are raised "in the church" from birth forward, and in many cases are educated in Mennonite schools, it is not assumed that they will necessarily continue as Mennonites into adulthood. Naturally, parents hope that their children will follow their ways—even in the same type of Mennonite congregation—but the point of conscious choice must be confronted. Each young woman, when she feels ready, requests baptism into the faith. For some this point of commitment never arrives, and they leave the religion. For others, commitment to a less restrictive type of Mennonite church resolves an inner conflict. For still others, peace and comfort come from being baptized into their mother's church, as often happens.

Regardless of conference, baptism means that Mennonite women choose to devote their lives to family, community, and church. That devotion is highly regarded, emphasizes Deborah, a forty-one-year-old Conservative mother of four: "God created us all as unique people. We have to find out who we are and shine in the little corner where he's put us. I don't care what anybody else does, my corner is here. I think it's great to have the freedom to choose that." The choice comes typically between the ages of fourteen and eighteen for Mennonite girls, although some commit as early as twelve and as late as twenty-one. After growing up in their church and observing the marital relationships of the adults around them, they choose either to join the church or not. Baptism into the faith does not take place in the unconsciousness of infancy, but in the awareness of early womanhood, but do young women really understand headship and male–female power relations at the age of fourteen or seventeen? For the most part they believe they do, although it is in some ways a leap of faith, as Sarah, who is nineteen, points out:

> There's an instruction class that we go through before we're baptized, but the initial conversion and acceptance of Christ would come first. That's why you're baptized. There's things that you start to understand and learn after that. You don't understand near everything when you're baptized.

Some women convert to the Mennonite faith after being baptized into another religion. Usually they are not required to go through rebaptism; their statement of faith is sufficient testimony for conversion. A Conservative woman explains:

> We hesitate to baptize younger than twelve, and we haven't done it recently. But any time after that when somebody requests it, and we feel after instruction that they are ready for it—mature enough to choose— we baptize them. We don't baptize a second time, unless they were previously baptized in another faith as an infant, but we still carry the name [Anabaptists] because they did a long time ago.

Mennonite women provide a challenging example of how observers outside a culture may superimpose their biases. Especially when they are younger, women may struggle with the principles of their religious community. "Some don't fit the mold. . . . It can be painful," admits an Old Order elder woman, Susannah. Yet most Mennonite women contend that they are happy and resent the judgment of outsiders who insist on defining them as oppressed women. The church and the community work to support a balance achieved through faith and personal commitment. Boundaries "are simply there"—reinforced by friends and family members who dress the same, share a basic lifestyle, and believe in the same core teachings of the Bible. "It's easier to be a parent with those boundaries," remarks Deborah. "The children question you, but they're not questioning you as an individual; it's the whole church."

Marie, a Conservative woman who has raised five children and helps with her husband's farm feed business, counters the perceptions of outsiders: "They seem to think that I live a very restrictive life. I don't feel that way about it. I have a lot to do. I don't find myself wishing that I could do other things, because they're against my beliefs and convictions. Although there might be some things that I would enjoy doing if I were not Mennonite, I don't regret that I can't do them." Although sex segregation in church is common, and gender roles are highly differentiated—with men clearly occupying the dominant position of head of household—most Mennonite women say they find security and sanity in this arrangement, as Marie articulates:

> I find myself happy in my place. I don't wish that I would not be a Mennonite. I'm happy in my role as a wife and a woman. I enjoy being submissive to my husband. I've never been able to relate to people that thrash at that: "why" this, "why" that? I guess I don't have as many "whys" as some people do.

Another woman remembers going through a period of questioning during her teens, "way back in the dim past, but it sure doesn't matter anymore." Eventually most accept the faith in their own way, she believes. Darlene, in her late thirties and the mother of two teenagers, feels content with her homemaking lifestyle. She sees herself following in her mother's footsteps:

> I find it interesting because my mother was very much a homebody, too. She still doesn't like to go shopping. I'm one of a very few Mennonite women who doesn't drive, and people ask me how I survive. I *enjoy* being at home. I also know that it can be very dangerous, because you can become so involved in your own thing that your mind isn't open to outside needs. I'm perfectly happy just working on the farm, in the garden, sewing, doing crafts. There are women who wouldn't be happy if they couldn't go out. My neighbor goes to the same Conservative church as we do, but she does all the secretarial work for her husband's business. She enjoys that much more than gardening or sewing. It seems to work for them; it wouldn't work here. Joe doesn't want me to be involved in the business at all, and I'm perfectly happy not doing that.

"There was a time that I had some struggles with some of these principles," admits a young Conservative mother, Angela. "I had to think it through and get to the root of things." Now that she observes some of her non-Mennonite neighbors having problems raising teenagers, things are falling into perspective: "To see how God's order is upheld and some of the problems that can be avoided has been a blessing to me." Says another, "I'm very happy. I wouldn't trade being Mennonite for anything in this world. I feel quite strongly that a home and harmony is the closest thing to heaven that you can find on this earth. There's disagreements and there's times you wonder, but those disagreements can be worked out so that you can peaceably go on."

A thirty-five-year-old General Conference wife, Jeanette, feels no particular pressure in being a Mennonite woman: "I never really think of them together. I don't see things that I can't do that I would be able to do as a Mennonite male. In that way, I don't feel a lot of distinction. In the roles between Mennonite men and Mennonite women, it's more of a personality thing. The fact that I'm a Mennonite female is just the way it is, I guess." Why are males and females segregated in church? "That's a good question," says Rachel, member of a Conservative congregation. "We've talked about that among us. Not that we have any strong objections to sitting together as families—we do it when we have special meetings, weddings, funerals. I guess it's a tradition that we've kept up. Maybe one of the reasons was to keep the young boys and the young girls from sitting together. I don't think anybody has a big problem with it."

Clara is forty, the mother of three young teens and foster mother for a succession of children. She accepts the prayer veil as part of being a Mennonite woman and cannot recall any serious rebellion toward it: "Basically, the sisters agree that it's a teaching from the Bible—First Corinthians 11—and they have a desire to wear it." Darlene, also in her forties, likes wearing the prayer veil:

> I dress the way I do and wear the prayer veil because it's part of what I believe. It's what God wants me to do. If you depend on tradition alone it's easier to leave behind your Mennonite heritage, but if you behave the way you do because it's basic to your belief and you are doing it because God wants you to, you will hold your practices longer.

The prayer veil and the plain apron dress are more than symbols of commitment to the church; they also serve as signals to outsiders that Mennonite girls and women are to be respected. Adolescent girls speak of the relief they feel in wearing the prayer veil, because non-Mennonite teenagers will not approach them with drugs and alcohol or make sexual advances.

Into the Twentieth Century

CONTEMPORARY ROLES: "OUR OWN STRENGTHS AND GIFTS"

"The only thing we'll be able to take with us to heaven is our children," remarks Clara, "and that's a sobering thought for each family—the fact that we are responsible for the children, for their outcome and their future." Because baptism is a choice during the teen years, parents cannot make the decision to become Mennonite for their children: "We can't have them saved, but we can plant a seed there that makes it easy for them to choose." Women take "very much to heart" this responsibility to provide leadership and homes that are conducive to following the Mennonite path.

Most Mennonite women seem relatively content with the typical role of homemaker and mother. Deborah acknowledges that her day-to-day routine with four children and a big house to manage involves "limitations." For example, budgetary restrictions result from her not holding a part-time job outside the home, and she spends much of her time doing repetitive tasks (such as housework) that "have to be done" regardless of whether she feels like doing them. She philosophizes that this can be the case in anyone's life:

> I could have the most fantastic career going outside the home, and I'm sure there would be parts of that career that I wouldn't feel like doing. I have a garden; I do a lot of canning. I was taught to do that, and we need it. I don't get a tremendous satisfaction out of housework, but I do it because it's necessary. I *do* get tremendous satisfaction out of being a mother.

In the past, a predictable division existed in most homes; if women worked outside, it was in volunteer roles. A woman who works part-time now might still carry full responsibility for the home, but many younger couples are carving out new roles. This translates into greater acceptance for women working outside the home, as well as sharing of child care, homemaking, and household chores. It might even extend to the woman taking on the role of primary provider while the man works as full-time homemaker, as a teenager, Peggy points out:

> I don't recognize my father sometimes! He's changed. My mother told him she wanted to go back to work and that he'd have to do some things around the house. Now he gets up every Saturday, hauls out the vacuum cleaner, and away he goes. When I was living at home, that just didn't happen. Even though my mother was teaching full-time, she was still expected to come home and cook all the meals. Now Dad helps out.

The woman's role in this culture still connects closely with the power structure that governs male-female relationships. Women have fewer legitimate options than men in terms of careers and education, but younger, professional men do not echo the traditional premium on wifely meekness and submissiveness. They seek companionship and an equal partnership marriage, says Paul, age thirty-two: "In particular, I was looking for someone that I could get along with most of the time. Not just someone that I could come home to, but someone that I could spend the day with." A Conservative Church husband explains that he wants to be there for his wife, because he understands the pressures she faces as a mother of three little children:

> *"It brings out the jewels in her . . ."*
> I married Deborah as a housekeeper, and because I love her. I don't want to go in the house in the evening and see her with a five-hour workload ahead of her, and I sit down and I'm done for the day. Why not help her along? If you lay your own wishes aside and help your wife finish up in the evening, it brings out the jewels within her that normally you can't get. That's where a big fault comes—a man says, "It's your work, you look after it, and when you're done we'll go to bed." She does not feel toward him the way she should, and things go downhill. Tenderness and open communication have to be the number one things. If you just take time to sit down and talk in the evening about the day's activities, women appreciate that about as much as anything.
> I must admit, I wish I did more. It's an area where I'm trying to im-

prove. Sometimes if I'm really bushed I'll lie down, or if she's still not ready I'll just sit there and talk. That helps, just being there. It's partly the man's fault, that they leave too much to the woman. The father has to take his responsibility, too, and sometimes that means helping in the house. I think if the man has time to help with the dishes, it's only right that he does.

Some of the chores around the house I like to help with—dishes, cleaning up a bit, putting the children to bed, and changing them. Yard work, watering the garden. I feel that those times together can actually be an inspiration to a husband and wife. It can be a time of closeness, even though it involves work. I'm sure every wife would be able to say they appreciate a helping hand.

I don't do the laundry, but I enjoy doing something bigger than just helping along here and there a little. If she's off at some women's meeting, I'll go and do something that she hasn't expected at all. I kind of enjoy surprising her that way: clean up the garage, chores that she wishes were done. But she knows how to sew—I hardly know how to thread a needle; it would be a major effort for me. We both know that she can do it in two minutes, and it would take me an hour to do one button. That holds true not just for sewing but for all the skills that her mother was sure to teach her.

This liberalizing effect goes even further in some contemporary Mennonite marriages. In some cases women earn more than men, as Paul observes:

For myself, trying to be a Mennonite male and thinking about traditional sex roles, I could get in real trouble. Crissie makes over ten thousand dollars more a year than I do. I try very hard not to assume that she is going to cook tonight. We want to avoid those roles. I'm a little bit stronger than she is, so when we built the deck out back I was the one who picked up the hammer, but when we clean the house, we do it fifty-fifty. As a Mennonite you feel certain restrictions, but that holds true for men *and* women.

These younger, more liberal couples tend to think about each person's talents and experiences, and they apply a kind of "household logic" to the division of labor. For example, Crissie stresses that "we have our own strengths and gifts, so we tend to divide the 'woman's' or 'man's' responsibilities as we are gifted or as we enjoy." Couples talk about sex roles before they marry and observe their parents, who in turn often find it difficult to understand how the younger couples run their homes. Says Crissie, "Parents want to keep those traditional ties going and, truthfully, it's hard for us to break out of their patterns. It's hard for me to say, 'I can help you build the deck. I know how to hammer some nails.'" Crissie and Paul do not see themselves as unique; many others are moving toward a more equal distribution of household labor in their marriages. "They basically work it the same way we do," Crissie adds. "They strive towards equality and working together instead of a strict division between the roles." Yet, says another young professional:

> I'm constantly frustrated to learn that there are many people our age that don't think this way. Because we went to university, there's probably a little bit of a difference there. Even some of the people our age at work follow very traditional roles. They both work full-time, and yet she's the one who's responsible for making sure that grocery shopping gets done, and so on.

One of the major changes for younger Mennonite women is learning to drive. Some help their husbands in farming and business in a way that their mothers could not, as Alma points out, almost apologizing for her newfound freedom: "A lot of it is going for things for my husband. I drive a van, and just this summer we discovered that ten bags of feed fit in the back, so I've been doing that. It's not like I'm going out to a ladies' party, or bowling, or a coffee shop."

Equalization can be a relief and a threat. Making these shifts from centuries of clearly and separately defined roles is not easy. Mennonite women talk of growing up in homes where it was considered normal for wives to cook, pick up after their husbands, clean, and do all the child care. Major adjustments are required to overcome these stereotypes. Some men find it a great effort to cook a meal, even though they believe in egalitarian arrangements and they recognize that their wives have numerous skills and abilities in other areas.

Beyond the household, some Mennonite women serve as lay ministers and deacons of their churches. Thinking about women differently is still a very new idea, however, as General Conference member James admits:

I'm not saying that it has totally taken hold in my actions, but my thinking certainly has changed in recent years. It's mostly just from looking around, and seeing what attitudes others have, and realizing that I fit into this mold of putting females into a box. Personally, it was enlightening to go through that kind of a change. You see so much potential in women. It seems a shame that so much talent is being wasted or not developed. The fact that Roz has gifts in areas of worship-leading and speaking, and I have similar ones—that we can both do an equivalent job—for her not to be able to do that is a real loss for the community.

James's wife works side by side with him in their missionary work abroad, in spite of resistance to her role from older Mennonites. Reading, education, and the media lead to "a different perspective," he adds.

Frank, a thirty-year-old General Conference Mennonite who spent two years serving as a missionary overseas with his wife, Estelle, came from a traditional home in which his father was clearly the leader. Yet he believes in greater equality for women in marriage and in the church: "I've seen what my older brothers have done in their marriages. They have made this shift toward a willingness to say *both* of us are going to do what we want. It seems fair and right to me." The trend toward greater equality fits well with the traditional Mennonite emphasis on mutual respect and consideration.

Eva, a seventy-year-old widow, confirms the significance of recent changes in the church: "In the setting I grew up in, there weren't the offices—like Sunday school teacher—that gave women an active role in the church. It was only the ministers' wives who had an active role, and that made it appear as if the men had it all and the women just learn. In many cases it wasn't like that." Now there are more places in the structure of the church for the women to play vital roles.

Two major factors are related to perceived legitimacy of female participation in church meetings and business: age and liberal posture. In General Conference and other more flexible Mennonite churches (many of them small and urban), women are allowed to play all the roles, albeit with occasional reluctance.[24] In some communities, ordination of women heralds changing attitudes. They redefine headship to imply God, Christ, then man/woman. Old attitudes are changing, but slowly, as is reported by a married woman in her twenties, who is part of the Mennonite community in Toronto:

> I was worship leader one Sunday, and I heard through the grapevine that somebody thought it was strange to see a woman up there. I don't think it's my place to go up to an older person who happens to be sensitive about certain issues and tell them they're wrong. I think that it is changing, and as it changes, I will fit in more and more. Most people here don't even think, when they're listening to the worship leader, "Is that a man or a woman?"

Working outside the home remains relatively untrodden ground for all but the General Conference women. "We have more conveniences than our mothers did," Crissie admits, "but I think our faith is holding more firmly to the traditional women's role. As mothers, we wouldn't encourage our daughters to go out and hold a career or another job. The most important thing that we can do is be at home and raise our children." As children grow up, some women might feel comfortable working outside the home, she adds, but "once you have children, then you should stay home unless there are very serious financial problems. If extra money is needed, then you can find part-time jobs."

Do women think deep down that men are superior, even though women are gaining more privileges and power in church life? Marilyn, in her fifties and famous for her quilts, thinks just the opposite. She sees a problem with women trying to fill the roles of men, because men and women are fundamentally different:

> They can't. It wasn't ordained to be that way. It just causes a lot of havoc. Even simple things like a woman wanting to be a police officer—she will build up enough strength to do that, but she has to work out every day to keep it up. Man was *born* with that body. Women can't fill that spot, and it doesn't really matter how hard they try.

This attitude swims against the tide of mainstream trends, but fits perfectly into traditional Mennonite values surrounding family and community. Making less money is not important, but being close to your children is, says Clara: "The way we were brought up, people would look at you and decide whether you *need* the money or whether you *want* it. If you can stay at home to do whatever you're doing, that's fine, but if you have to leave your home and get a baby-sitter, it wouldn't be accepted."

At one time in their lives, though, it is acceptable and even desirable for Mennonite females to work outside the home. When they are teenagers, many (especially Old Order women) work as "maids" for a small salary in another family's home. Because it takes families longer to accomplish the usual household and gardening chores without modern technology, it benefits both them and the young girls to create such arrangements for a couple of years. This enhances the girl's domestic skills, gives her experience outside her own family, and lightens the load of the host family.

BECOMING A WOMAN, BECOMING A MAN

The mothering role is a sacred trust that is defined as the highest career calling for a Mennonite woman, not a fallback position or something she can do in her spare time. Women do not plan on ten-year careers before they have children; typical families include several children. A woman embraces motherhood as a full-time occupation as soon as her first child is born. For younger and more liberal couples (who tend to have smaller families), some flexibility exists in which parent stays home, but one of them tries to do so. Socializing young children into the family and faith is a full-time job. It is also one that raises issues of child care in the event that both parents can work outside the home, as Crissie explains:

> We both very much enjoy the challenge of bringing up children. When we have children, it will be a tough decision who should stay home. Although we both enjoy our challenging jobs and being out in the workplace, we would also both enjoy staying home with the children. I don't necessarily know which one of us it would be.

Most families regard baby-sitters with skepticism. Says Erla, "We sometimes put them to the neighbors if we have to go someplace and we don't want to take them along. The older people, like the preachers and the bishop, don't really like it if you *don't* stay at home. We take them to church, though. The children are all in church from birth. It's our way of doing it." Deborah points out that even attending a domestic activity such as a church-sponsored sewing circle depends on the availability of family members to watch children: "I often can't be there because my husband can't be home in time to look after the children, so I either have to find another baby-sitter or forget about it. Many girls that do part-time work have relatives or grandmothers that they take the children to, instead of outside baby-sitters." This strikes to the very core of Mennonite values and priorities. It is better to economize than to give up a meaningful family life, Deborah argues:

> That's another thing we see against family life today. We probably have a habit of thinking we need to make extra money so both people need to work, and the children end up with baby-sitters most of the day, growing up in day care centers. Taking what the Bible teaches, we believe we are responsible to raise our children, to provide a home where they're nurtured and taught.

Children are valued regardless of gender. As Salome notes, "Of course, if a couple has half a dozen boys, they'd very much want a girl. On Wednesday my daughter had her first boy. She already has two girls, so she was kind of hoping for a boy, but she would never have been discouraged if it had been a girl. She'd have been happy." This inclusiveness extends to babies with mental or physical disabilities, and Mennonite families open their arms wide to adoptive and foster children who need a home. Children find love and discipline side by side; they are anchored in learning chores as soon as they reach eight or nine years of age. Salome describes the Old Order customs:

> The girls don't help in the barn as soon as the boys, but they help in the house. Eventually they will go and help in the barn, too. When my daughter was nine years old, she went out to the barn to watch the milk separator. She was too small to open that screw on top of the hole—it's on real tight—but she could wash the separator. That helped me quite a bit. Mostly the boys do the outside chores and the girls do the inside work.

A Conservative woman elaborates on this pattern of early training:

> My mom had a sewing circle at our house for a while, so she started me on an old sewing machine. My daughter uses the sewing machine, and she's ten years old—just straight sewing or patches. She's into baking

cookies, making Jello with pineapple rings. She's down my neck, asking, "What can I do?" She's out of that age group to play, play, play all the time. She wants to be helping.

Are boy babies and girl babies treated differently? Joy, a Conservative mother in her mid-thirties, speaks for younger women:

> I have three girls. When the first one was born, my husband said he didn't have to worry about getting a farm for a boy right away. There was no comment with the second, because we thought it was a nice playmate. But when the third one was born, people said we needed boys for our farm. I told them girls can drive tractors nowadays, too. You should see the girls out there! They sling hay bales faster than the hired men. That's a part of my childhood I enjoyed, too: I slung hay bales, I milked cows.

As far as educational expectations and household tasks, most of the younger, more liberal women try not to make distinctions between the sexes. In more liberal congregations, many seek "the right kind of books" to help them raise their children in the faith, but in a more egalitarian manner. Darlene imagines that she and her husband will "be looking for books that don't have those sex roles where Jack is doing his thing because he's a boy, and Jill is doing her thing because she's a girl. That also applies to how we're going to bring up our kids generally. We're going to let them know that they're equals."

Other women agree that it is crucial to work consciously away from gender-based expectations—a tricky maneuver if one was raised in a more traditional Mennonite environment. Admits one mother, "I know it would be very difficult for me to encourage my boy to enroll in a sewing class in junior high, if that's still not accepted. I don't want to push him into this." She will be sensitive to the prevailing expectations of their cultural environment, but "would like to give them the realization that they can do whatever they want regardless of being a boy or a girl. I want to help them become whatever they want."

Although the Old Order and Conservative churches are against the use of birth control, the less restrictive General Conference accepts it. Abortion is totally taboo in the Old Order and Conservative congregations and very much avoided in the newer factions.[25] A Conservative woman explains her position, reflecting the feelings of most women in her church:

"The importance of human life . . ."

People hear I'm against abortion, and they try to put me in a box with a whole bunch of other adjectives that must also describe me. I'm all in favor of women being in command of their own lives; they should have the ability to choose whether they want children or not. They've discovered all sorts of things about the fetus—then to think that those very much *human* beings' lives are suddenly being terminated, I have a problem accepting that. That's something that I feel very strongly about: the importance of a human life. I don't think we have the right to decide who should live and who should die, no matter what they believe or who they are. In Anabaptist theology, we believe that people have the freedom to live.

A long time ago in my church, a minister made the comment that contraceptives belong in the barn. Some people took exception to that; it was very crude. But you're really not supposed to use contraceptives, and I know that can cause a dilemma sometimes. When we got married and I had been commissioned to teach Mennonite school, this older bishop spoke to us; he speaks to all the married couples. He asked me how long I was commissioned to teach school. I said I hadn't committed myself. He told me he hoped I wasn't thinking of birth control. I don't think he usually says that, but I was so outspoken and we had discussed so many things, he thought he'd say that. If a couple has been married for a while and they haven't had children, the eyebrows raise. A big family is a good thing in a Mennonite church. They're so pleased with big families; they feel that women with nine and ten children are doing the right thing.

I'm not on the Pill; I just use natural birth control. We probably have our family. Our daughter wasn't really planned for, but she's been a joy. I would never have an abortion, but with four kids we're stretched a little bit emotionally. We try to spend time with each child every day, and we find as they get older it takes more. I just don't think I could ever give to eight kids or ten kids what they need.

Some mother's can handle having a baby year after year; others can't. . . . Maybe the pregnancies are difficult—they become frustrated because the babies keep coming, and they end up almost having nervous breakdowns. It's too bad, because God created them like that, and they're worthwhile people, too.

CONTEMPORARY POWERS: "IT'S A WORKING TOGETHER"

Younger, liberal Mennonite husbands uphold the traditional concept of headship, but they define it in terms of working together as a team. "As Mennonites, we don't want to hold the men up any higher than the women," Frank claims. "God gave that responsibility to man, and somebody has to have the leadership, just like in any business. But it's a working together." Mennonite women believe their place below men and God is simply God's plan for married life. Men are taught that headship, which gives them final decision-making authority in the family, must be approached with a heavy sense of responsibility and deep respect for their wives. Frank elaborates:

"Seek the counsel of a godly woman . . ."
Even though headship means that the man is in the leadership role, sometimes her ideas are better than his. We can accept that, too. Our way is not always the best way; it takes working together. We've never had a problem that we couldn't agree on somehow—meet each other halfway. My wife says, "If we can't agree on something, you're the one who makes the final decision, and I will support you." I appreciate that, but I'm still very cautious. If she doesn't agree, I will think it over several times because I love her, plus "seek the counsel of a godly woman"—there's a lot to that!

A minister once told me that his wife often disagreed with the decisions he was coming to, and he's learned to heed to her opinions. Oftentimes it kept him out of trouble! I believe that a woman has deeper insight than a man does. She can look into the future further than a man does. It varies greatly; in some cases, it's exactly the other way around. We need each other, and if God has put the couple together, they will balance: One is low on one, the other will be higher in the other.

My wife and I talk about guiding our children. If a child is asking whether he may do something, if the father isn't at hand the mother has to make the decision in light of what she thinks her husband feels to be right. If they're both at hand, in most cases the mother will tell the child to ask father. In little things like that, you are showing God's order of headship. What you have there is woman respecting her head, which is her husband; in turn she respects Christ and his word; and in turn she's taking God's plan in life, in the decisions that are made. Therefore wrong decisions are considered before they're made, so that things are directed and guided in the right way—then you don't have problems.

For contemporary women of faith, headship makes perfectly good sense. Says Darlene:

My husband basically runs the house. It's very much a combined thing, but if we had a major disagreement, I would leave it at what he felt. He's not a forceful person—it would be me giving in. I feel that as the head of the household, leadership is his responsibility. There have been times with the children that we've disagreed on how things should be handled, and I've gone his way, although I didn't really agree, but I felt that we had to put up a united front. I'd give up my argument if he felt differently.

On the other hand, Clara feels that she and her husband share authority regarding the children:

That's a combined thing. Because of my personality, I tend to do more disciplining than he does. He's very quiet and soft-spoken. I tend to take things quite seriously; he's a little more lenient. Sometimes he feels he shouldn't be quite as lenient, and I feel I shouldn't be quite as strict. I talk everything over with him. If there's a problem with the children or I've had a frustrating day, I go straight to him. He has a tremendous interest in the children.

Beyond headship, however, are Biblical passages that advocate the submissiveness of women. Since the liberal conferences approach the Bible less literally than the Old Order Mennonites (or any conference twenty or thirty years ago), such passages can be interpreted with more latitude. Judith, a thirty-five-year-old Conservative Mennonite and mother of four, says that the world is changing around her and that the church recognizes this:

It's a real struggle many times, when you read that and you view the Scriptures as the word of the Lord. We're supposed to follow this as truth. You basically have to put it on the shelf and say you don't know.

You can take encouragement from Jesus saying that "further truth you will learn than what I have told you." We are progressing; we have learnt more and better. Those passages had a certain relevance in their time, and they still hold some truth—we have to respect them for what they were—but we still have to keep our cultural situation in mind. You can't bury your head in the sand.

Young Nichola studies about marital relationships in high school:

> It depends on the abilities of the two people. If the woman is the natural decision maker, then she should make the decisions, and vice versa. If good communication exists between the partners in the marriage, although the husband has the final decision, he will take into serious consideration the opinions and convictions of his wife. If I ever get married I would be submissive to my husband, but I would want a great deal of communication in the marriage.

In terms of household decisions, in some homes the women make most decisions; in others, men take over on the major issues. Younger and more liberal conference women have more control, whereas older and more conservative (especially Old Order) wives frequently defer to their husbands. Even some Old Order women, however, take more liberties than they might have a generation ago. Lovina, who was brought up believing that men make the major decisions, describes the changes in her life:

> My parents were poor, so my mother was always scared to buy something without my father knowing. I was that way when we first married. I didn't like to spend anything without my husband's permission. . . . Well, maybe wee little things, but not anything over ten dollars. Now I go to the market and make almost as much money as he does. I kind of feel it's my own money. I *do* dare to buy—not real big things, but I'm much more liberal than I was twenty years ago. When I went to the store years ago, I never bought one thing that we didn't need; we had to pay for the farm. Now, if I see nice material, I'd grab it and that would be mine.

When a family business or big ticket items are involved, men still hold greater sway. A Conservative Mennonite woman understands that her husband and his partner should decide on business matters: "As wives we express our opinions, but they decide. If it's our private life, then John and I decide together. For cars we go out and look together, but he makes the final decision. For a house, he wouldn't want to make that decision by himself. He always asks me what I think." Around the home, many Mennonite women exert substantial control: paying bills, controlling the family checkbook, decorating, and routine child care. One woman sees an enormous difference between her marriage and her mother's: "If my parents were redecorating and my father told her to go out and buy a new Chesterfield [sofa], she'd refuse. She wouldn't dream of spending that much money by herself. He had to be along, even though he would trust her with every penny of it. *I* could make that kind of decision very easily." Another remembers her mother wanting to have the independence that comes from having her own finances: "I can remember my mother saying she didn't want to marry until she had a thousand or two in the bank, but it was hard to accumulate that much back then. By the time women had their homes it was all gone, so they had to lean on their husbands. We grew up handling a lot more money than our mothers did."

Over and over during these conversations about how power is distributed between a man and woman in a committed relationship, Mennonite women came back to the concept of mutual respect, trust, teamwork, and consultation. Symmetry marks these relationships in significant ways, Deborah explains: "I don't really think of it as being a power struggle. Love is the dominating factor. It's kind of a sharing thing. There's really no jealousy involved in the relationship."

Those who are exposed to mass media consider it unfortunate that men are portrayed as being more powerful than women and less able to express their feelings. Their preference clearly is for shared decisions based on communication, as Nancy, a young General Conference Mennonite, explains:

> Major things we talk about, weigh the pros and cons, forget about it for a week, then make a decision. With smaller things, it goes back and forth. In terms of major expenses, I might have more to say, but that might have to do with more experience or knowing more about the product. I'll do the bills one time, he'll do it another time—whoever happens to think of it. Teamwork.

Love, Marriage, and Divorce: Marriage Is for Life

To a significant extent, being a Mennonite entails an ethnic as well as a religious identity. A strong pattern of endogamy—marrying within one's own group—prevails, and Swiss, German, and Russian subgroups are still relatively distinguishable. Adeline reflects: "It was important to me to marry someone who shares my cultural heritage. Certainly I preferred to meet and fall in love with a man who was also Mennonite, because I thought that was the best way that I could live out my cultural *and* my faith heritage." She also wanted someone who was fun to be with, had a good personality, got along with other people, respected her, and enhanced her feelings of self-worth: "I guess it comes back to the equality thing. I don't think Mennonite women are looking for anything different than other women are looking for in a mate."

Marriage is central to the Mennonite woman's role, but a woman who remains single (sometimes called an "aunt") receives general acceptance. She may suffer from alienation and depression until she finds an approved alternative role such as teacher or missionary, says Lovina: "She is occupied in that way, still having all that contact with the children, and feels she's doing something useful for the community. We've had some others who are not quite as old, almost thirty, that have jobs in stores, and some in nursing homes." Nonetheless, marriage is the most integrated identity a Mennonite woman can achieve. For Old Order and Conservative Mennonites, the "marrying age" is twenty-one—a time when other young women might be pursuing a university education. Lovina would not suggest higher education for the young women in her Old Order congregation: "Once you're married and have children, your place is at home in your own house, in your own kitchen, raising your own children."

Nichola, whose mother married at twenty-one and gave birth to six children in eight years, has already chosen baptism at seventeen into a Conservative church. However, she sees herself veering from her mother's path:

"I will never be like my mother . . ."
I'm different from her, since I'm going to finish high school. I can see my friends planning marriage in the next couple of years and raising

families in the traditional role. That could be possible for what I plan, too, yet it could be more difficult. I will never be like my mother. I can drive, so I will be able to go away more than she can. I like sports and hiking, going out in the evening with my friends. That might cease, if I ever get married.

I have ideals. I'm not dating because I consider myself young and not quite ready for that stuff yet. Usually dating young leads to an early marriage, because you get to know the one that you're dating so well . . . and you usually don't date more than one or two men. We have a minimum recommended age of eighteen before we start dating. It's not enforced or anything, but up until that point you have your chance of observing young people of the opposite sex in the youth group. You know who you would be compatible with and could admire. Those are good years, because they prepare you for dating.

Nichola believes in the concept of romantic love, and she feels comfortable with the custom of men taking the lead in courtship by inviting women to a social or to spend an afternoon together. The length of courtship depends on when a couple begins to date. If a couple meets when they are nineteen or twenty, the courtship will probably last a year or so. Some find each other at fifteen; since no one wants them to be married at eighteen—they are not yet considered to be ready for children and married life—out of necessity theirs will be a five-year courtship. Otherwise, long courtships are not essential because "girls aren't into careers": They are ready to be wives and mothers.

Both men and women may pray about the relationship and watch carefully to see whether differences can be worked out before marriage; they assume that if the answer is no, the differences probably cannot be worked out after marriage. What happens if you believe a young man to be the person "the Lord intended for me," but discover after marriage that he has a problem with alcohol or becomes abusive? Nichola answers for her generation: "I wouldn't marry him unless I knew he was a true, sincere, fully believing Christian. If he were not, I would have detected that in other ways prior to marriage."

According to both men and women, adultery rarely occurs. As Old Order minister Jake warns, however, the Bible says that "to look on a woman and lust after her is adultery; therefore we need to be careful how we define that. What a man has in his heart, who knows. We teach to avoid that—it's wrong, it's sin. As far as committing the act of adultery, we don't hear of it much in our group. The penalty for sin is death, whether it's male or female. I don't think we can distinguish between the two." Ironically, the logic behind this equality of sin stems from the Mennonite belief that "a woman's soul means as much to God as a man's soul. If the woman sins and loses her soul, it's just as terrible as if a man loses his soul."

When a relationship fails to work, the church would not agree to a divorce, Jake continues: "That would not be acceptable. We prefer separation if things get that bad." What if a woman simply cannot go on with a bad marriage? No matter how hard she has prayed, no matter how much help she has sought, what if the man will not play the responsible, loving role expected of him? Salome replies for the Old Order Mennonites of her generation:

> She could live separate from him if he just wasn't livable, but we would not consent to a divorce. If she went ahead, she would lose her membership in our congregation. The liberal churches do allow it. We wouldn't, but we would still have a desire to help her see the error of her ways, and help her confess her sin and make amends. Then she could be brought back into the fold, but she could never remarry. We would rather see her come back to her former husband if reconciliation could be made. We feel that God doesn't recognize divorce. We've been taught that marriage is for life. In his eyes, that first marriage still stands; that's why we would not go along with a second marriage.

Apparently either relationships rarely deteriorate to an impossible level or the penalty for divorce is morally and socially too high, since the divorce rate among Mennonites is extremely low compared to the general population. (About 0.3 percent of the most progressive couples are separated and another 0.3 percent divorced; for moderate and conservative groups, the rate is virtually zero.[26]) For Mennonites, divorce represents the greatest contradiction of family and community values. A Conservative Mennonite mother of three small children tries to show them affection so they will feel secure:

> Nowadays, with divorce, one of the greatest fears of children is whether or not their parents are going to stick together. I think we

need to portray to them that they don't need to fear that. Marriage is a lifelong commitment. Not until God takes someone in death are we free to take on another partner. That's why the initial step is so important, to be sure it's the one that God has chosen for you.

Although more liberal conferences accept divorce and single status, "there's still a great emphasis placed on good, healthy family living," remarks a General Conference social worker. "It's important that the parents are home with the kids and that they do family things together. That's a big issue in our congregation and a big issue generally for the Mennonite church—importance of the family." Marriage is more than an intimate relationship between two people; it is "a witness" to how Mennonites conduct their lives and build their communities. In that sense, it is not surprising that the modern Mennonite marriage reflects the mainstream trend toward egalitarian relationships.

Challenges Confronting Women

Several Mennonite women caution against thinking that they have perfect lives and perfect families. They mention two main challenges: the emotional strain that sometimes results from living on the edge of society, and threats to integrity of the faith itself.

HOLDING FAST TO FAITH

Depression, "nervous breakdowns," and suicides (among men) are not unheard of, but the rates are very low, according to a Mennonite minister. Women attribute these low rates of social and emotional problems to their close community. With such a good support network, people feel that if they have a problem, they can turn to others who will care enough to help them through a difficult time. Therefore problems either get nipped in the bud or are not allowed to fester to the point where people murder, batter, commit suicide, or become alcoholic. These problematic behaviors fly in the face of the core principles of Mennonite faith: non-violence, peacefulness, and a simple life. In the Conservative Mennonite setting, smoking and drinking are not accepted. A few will try it, but if they are found out, it is a disgrace to the church and action is taken.

Yet Ingrid, age thirty-five, expresses concern that cracks are widening in the Mennonite shell: "I think our young people are exposed to a lot more than what we used to be, especially the girls." In the past, boys were exposed to more outside influences than were the girls. That is changing, says Ingrid, because girls are getting out of the home more: "I would like my boys to grow up on a farm *because of* all the things they can learn and the freedom that is on a farm." And, "outside" society holds competing values.

Among couples for whom the concept of headship is clearly spelled out, reversal of roles creates bewilderment and pain. Certainly the husband is supposed to play the spiritual leadership role, but sometimes it does not work out that way, and pressures result. Some men may not be able emotionally to handle leadership; conversely, some men may use "a little bit stronger leadership" than the delicate balance would imply. Either way threatens the fragile male–female equation.

If a man loses his job, becomes depressed, and cannot make decisions for the family, his wife could work outside the home to help. As a minister's wife explains, though, "We feel that it's better if the husband can work so that the woman is free to look after the children and be a homemaker." The church would step in to help during the crisis rather than see her leave the children: "We would hope she would come and tell the minister, but if she didn't we would probably find out in a roundabout way. Close friends and family would be ready to give advice." Women notice sometimes that a friend may find it very difficult to be submissive, because her husband will not make decisions or help with the children. This power vacuum "forces her to get out there and be aggressive, and it sort of gets reversed. I don't think it leads to a happy marriage. Some men aren't very capable leaders, and some women have very strong feelings about things." Adeline feels that she needs a strong man because she is not an outgoing person, but she knows women who are outgoing and married to more retiring men:

"She is still in submission . . ."
The decisions can be made privately, and the woman can fill in the weak areas in her husband's life without it becoming a real issue or conflict. A friend of mine is still in submission. She's still taking her rightful place, but her husband doesn't even sign checks. She takes care

of all the financial matters, he's the laborer. He brings home the meals to support the family, she does all the managing. She's being taught that you should be in submission, and she's wearing her head covering, but you can tell that she felt frustrated enough to the point that she's stepped out ahead. Then other women will say, "Well, he just doesn't do it, so I have to." They're not happy; they're frustrated to the point that they'll spill it out once in awhile, but they usually stick together.

I can see a direct relationship between marriage failures and women's liberation. Before they know it, the wife is coming home with a bigger paycheck. Anyone knows that the natural way is for the man to feel as though he is supporting his wife. It was meant to be that way. And then to feel as if he's down below her somewhere, it just doesn't work in the long run. It's not just pride, that's just the way it was intended . . . that men are above.[27]

THREATS AGAINST THE FAITH

In any community that attempts to draw social boundaries around itself, the flow of ideas through the floodgates can redefine the boundaries or weaken them. In the case of the Mennonites (with various degrees of permeability), education and the mass media represent the greatest threat because they are both pervasive and hard to control. The real issue facing Mennonite women is not how to stem the tide of technological and social change that has affected lives all over the globe, but how to redefine themselves in a turbulent world. Elmeda, an Old Order Mennonite woman in her late fifties, says her daughters are becoming more modern, even though they have stayed in the Old Order fold: "Not as fast as some are, but our whole church is moving that way. The old people don't like it. The middle-aged people are going more modern, too. It's been going that way for years already, and it seem the last few years much more so."

Schools always reflect the culture of those who support them. Mennonite communities have maintained their own school systems because they felt the public schools would infuse their children with alien and negative values. This is an expensive proposition, since they also continue to pay taxes, but it is one way the community can reinforce its boundaries. Teachers are trained in the summer by the Mennonites. Public education worries Old Order women like Salome and Elmeda: "You hear what goes on in the public schools, that they're being brought up differently than our children," says Salome. Elmeda asks innocently, "They don't teach the Bible in the public schools anymore, do they? I hear they don't want to. We want to protect our children from the ungodly ways and the unnecessary things, and we want them to know the Bible. That's why we have our own schools."

Education for Mennonite women therefore represents a quandary—both opportunity and threat of a weakened faith. Sara, age eighteen, who recently was baptized into a Conservative church and is one of the few Mennonite children to go through public high school, expresses her conflict:

> I'd like to have training, and my teachers definitely encourage me to attend university because my marks are acceptable, but there might be a danger in my losing my faith, so I've put that on a shelf for the time being. I might like to teach in our own Mennonite schools. I would certainly prefer it if *my* children would have qualified teachers. Even though I would feel limitations teaching with just a grade thirteen education, as far as teaching Old Order Mennonite children—whose teachers often only have grade eight—I would feel quite comfortable.

One Conservative mother says that she and her husband do not push their children to learn; most completed the tenth grade and then left school. Their sixteen-year-old daughter likes school and would like to finish at least grade twelve or thirteen, however, which means continuing her education either in a public high school or through correspondence courses. Most likely she will do the latter in order to avoid "the social involvement." This is a mutual choice between parents and child: "She doesn't have any desire to go to a public high school. And if she did, I suppose we would have likely somewhat advised against it, but I don't know if we would have opposed it entirely. At this stage she would probably be ready to hold her connections." In the more liberal churches, Mennonite women complete high school, earn bachelor's and master's degrees in a wide range of fields, and see the world as an open door occupationally.

Television is even more difficult to screen out. Even though it is permissible for Bethany, a General Conference Mennonite, to watch television, she avoids it:

We have no television in our house. I feel uncomfortable watching it even though there are many good programs, because I haven't been brought up to feel that it's necessary. I studied about television in school, and I still tend to think that the disadvantages outweigh the advantages. You can't get away from the outside influence we all must face. It depends on our own convictions and whether we're willing to live them.

Not all women who are raised in the Mennonite community *are* willing to live with its convictions or its restrictions. In fact, women who have gone to public schools are the most likely to reject their Mennonite upbringing. Ruth, raised as a Markham Mennonite, says that she and her husband felt constrained by the traditional way of life:

"We were never happy there within the boundaries . . ."
If we had attended a more liberal church, I don't think we would have felt the need to leave. I get very frustrated with the narrow-mindedness of people who are largely following traditions, who misinterpret the Bible. I think their concept of God is so wrong. The whole concept of things never changing, and being so fearful of change. It's almost as though tradition has become their God. They have big families, so of course the church is growing. For the most part they have solid home lives, and that's all great.

On the other hand, I do believe there are many unhappy people. To the ones who fit into that mold, it's a nice, safe, secure lifestyle. There are few decisions. You cook with everyone else; if there's a new recipe, you all take it home and you make it. It's great. You share the same house plant cuttings with each other, the same fabrics. But people are different. What about the ones who don't fit into that mold? What about the ones who are interested in more? If she's a questioning person, if she isn't able to sew, or lacks creativity in her kitchen, there's just no outlet: She's odd, she's different. I never fit in, either. I just didn't have the same interests that my friends had, and that's a horrible feeling—that you're different, when there's only one acceptable channel.

That becomes very frustrating and confining. You always feel like you're not "being content." Then, of course, because you're supposed to be content in all situations, you begin to feel that God's not pleased with you. Sometimes my husband and I think about going back, but we

Iroquois Women

Iroquois women of the Six Nations Reserve remember the strength of their mothers and grandmothers. They see themselves as powerful, assertive women who play a key role in keeping their culture—as in the doeskin wedding dress shown here—but who also take advantage of modern education to lift themselves and their families up to greater economic stability.

Blood Women
From the respected elder women who still serve as keepers of the faith to the younger ones who leave for higher education, Blood women insist that teaching children Blackfoot and traditional dances will help soften the blows of rapid social change.

Inuit Women
In a unique blend of old and new, this Inuk uses the traditional woman's knife, the ulu, to cut sealskin for a pair of warm winter boots—and an electric sewing machine for making her amoutiks or parkas. Like her friends and neighbors, she will teach her daughters sewing and fishing in both the traditional and the modern ways in order to cope with the collision of Inuit and white cultures.

Jamaican Women

For Jamaican Canadian women in Toronto, beauty is more than skin deep. Many women raise families alone or with only sporadic assistance from men. Keeping the home and hearth in spite of the double discriminations of being female and black in a predominantly white society presents a special challenge for these women who describe themselves as proud and strong.

Ukrainian Women

Ukrainian Canadian women stress the positive aspects of their relationships with men: supportiveness, mutual assistance, and respect. Central to keeping their culture, these women support education and the study of Ukrainian language. They see themselves as strong women who have a long history of hard work in the fields and the home, and who do "men's work" when necessary. Similarly, Ukrainian heritage men typically have engaged in "women's work" when the occasion called for it.

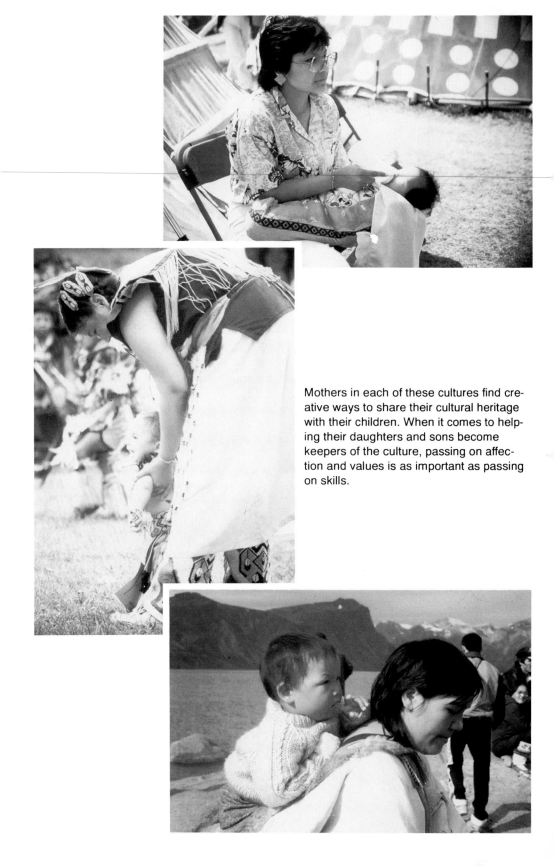

Mothers in each of these cultures find creative ways to share their cultural heritage with their children. When it comes to helping their daughters and sons become keepers of the culture, passing on affection and values is as important as passing on skills.

would have some frustrations if we did—there are lots of restrictions. Yet, there is safety in boundaries.

This is something I have been thrashing around personally, and my husband and I have talked it out. I think I could probably cope more with the restrictions right now than he could. He's very much an individual and resents any sort of restrictions, but the Mennonite church has a sentimental hold on me because of remembrances of a happy childhood. Certainly there were traditions that are good, solid, and nice to remember. I'm trying to create those traditions for my own family, but honestly, it's not the same. There isn't the same community spirit in any other church, and that's simply because everyone's lifestyle is so similar. It's a trade-off. In later years we tend to remember the happy things.

Barbara is also a "fallen-away" Mennonite, referred to me by many women as a symbol of social change. Although she has shifted away from the church, Barbara still leads a Mennonite life except for the garb, the prayer veil, and the strictness of the Markham group in which she was raised. She preserves a strong commitment to her marriage and children. She is a dedicated mother, a resolute Christian, and very active in her Bible chapel. She thus carries on key elements of Mennonite tradition outside the context of the Mennonite faith. Although the definition of women as submissive helped drive her away, Barbara's thinking has changed in her late thirties.

"I have really changed in my thinking . . ."
I have become as conservative as can be over the years. It's really funny because to all our Markham friends we left out of rebellion, yet I'm probably more submissive than they are. At the time I left, it bothered me very much; I was very influenced by people around me. I worked at a printer's office. I never attended university—I wanted to, but that door was definitely closed. I felt lucky just to graduate from high school. At this printing company we published the university's newspaper, however, so the students were there all the time, and I became very fascinated with their ideas. This was in the late sixties; this was a whole new world. I began to challenge things, and certainly the submission of women was one of them. When we were first married, I refused to use the word *Mrs.* Now I would say that was immaturity on my part. I latched onto the climate of the time.

I came to respect the concept of submissiveness again just through studying the Scriptures over the years and realizing that this is God's order for the home. I don't know what happened in your interviews with the other women, but for the most part I would probably agree with what they say, even though I don't wear the Mennonite garb. Our philosophy would be very much the same. I have come to a personal realization that some of the independence that I was seeking then would have been a very dangerous thing for me. I'm really glad that I came to that realization in time. Now I feel very fulfilled in being at home as a wife and a mother. I've worked part-time over the years at the newspaper, but I feel very strongly about being home with the children. I really am happy at home. It was like being in two worlds, and I felt like I really didn't belong there. I could have gotten interested in a career, but I know that I can only handle one major role, and being in the home is definitely it. I think it's a God-given opportunity to raise children, and for me it's a full-time job. I'm very satisfied in that.

Her parents and in-laws were very unhappy when Barbara and her husband left the church. The couple felt like outsiders at family reunions, even though some other cousins later left the church as well. Barbara tries to blend into the family woodwork by making sure her daughter wears a dress when she visits her grandmothers and by wearing modest clothing herself: "I anticipate some friction in the years ahead, as my daughter gets older. Her hair is very curly, that's going to be an issue. I'm glad we didn't have a daughter first, because it would have been harder. My son, at thirteen, is conscious of these rules. When he goes to see his cousins or their grandma, he wouldn't wear shorts." Even those who leave find it hard to leave completely.

Toward the Twenty-First Century

THE ROAD TO EQUALITY

Are Mennonite women oppressed? There is no such thing as an oppressed Christian woman, they insist. What about women's liberation? They say they are liberated. Are Mennonite men and women equal to each other? Lovina answers in the older language of conservative faith: "Before God we are, yet man is above us in that we

as their wives submit to them, obey them." A spiritual equality remains central to the male–female power relationship. Men and
women are equal in *different* ways. In God's sight, a woman's soul
means just as much as a man's soul. But when it comes to leadership—decision making for the family on major issues—the man is
to be in charge over the woman. Dorene speaks for Conservative
women, using the metaphor of the business world:

> We mentally put an employer above his employee on an imaginary
> scale and yet when it comes to the individual's character, we wouldn't
> say that the one is better or more worthwhile and important than the
> other. I think that's how God sees us as individuals. Although men are
> the God-ordained leaders in the family structure, that doesn't make
> them more important before God. God knew that, as in the business
> world, the best way for a family unit to function would be to have man
> as leader and his wife as "helpmeet."[28]

The language of the new egalitarianism among more liberal couples reflects a liberating tendency for both women and men. Under
the old concept of headship, the male who could not handle the
leadership role was placed under enormous pressure and experienced his lack of dominance as a personal and spiritual failure.
Now the team can function according to the personalities and
strengths of each partner, rather than a set model.

Usually we think of liberation in terms of someone being oppressed. Mennonite women do not typically see themselves as oppressed, though, and they feel liberated in the sense that they feel
comfortable with the choices that they have made for their lives.
Says Deborah, "The choices that I have made would probably make
me appear to not be liberated, but those are my choices, and I'm
very happy in them. I can honestly say that I've gone through the
whole process of wanting to be an individual, but it's much nicer to
be part of a unit. I feel I have tremendous freedom." Mennonites
historically have kept themselves from mainstream society in order
to protect their faith and integrity. Most conservative and moderate
Mennonite women see this as a very positive thing in their lives.
Their prayer veil, for example, defines them as women to be respected and to be handled with care—to be cherished and loved
and protected by men, rather than to be treated as playthings or
victims.

Outside the home, Mennonite women (who generally hold limited aspirations) report only minor discrimination because of gender in either education or work. Jeannie, a computer scientist, relates a seemingly innocuous incident that stuck in her mind:

> I was in the hardware store and I thought the man was very patronizing to me because I was a woman. He was just giving me a hard time. I went in to ask for nails, and he said that he wouldn't sell any nails today. Then I was asking for a particular size of nails, and he didn't have that size. He said if you're hammering through a four-inch board, you can't use a six-inch nail; you have to use a nail that's shorter than the board. I had the feeling that if my husband, Michael, had gone in for the nails, he wouldn't have had this reaction.

Ten years ago she might not have engaged in this type of analysis. Jeannie likes feeling good about who she is and only recently has taken for granted that women should have equal opportunity. Michael is in favor of these changes: "I'm glad that it can be taken for granted now, that Jeannie can go to IBM and have as good a shot at getting a job as a male computer scientist." This period of expanding opportunities in traditionally male-dominated fields has also left Jeannie isolated in education and in the workplace: "I've often been one female out of a class of thirty, but that's fine. I've had better summer jobs than most students have because of my field. People certainly have respected the field that I've chosen. I know that I could have a lot of jobs in that field and I wouldn't be discriminated against."

What, then, about the women's liberation movement? If you don't feel the need to be liberated, a movement will not draw you in immediately. Mennonite women are "liberated in Christ," as one woman puts it: "I think that's the only true liberation there really is. Many women talking about liberation know nothing about it, because they're in bondage. They're in this power struggle, striving to reach the top in a world that isn't meant for them, and they're not going to find happiness in that plan either." Bethany, age twenty-two, talks about her marriage in a way that illustrates how many younger Mennonite women see liberation:

> "*Wives, submit to your husbands . . .*"
> When people in this women's lib era look at the word *submissive*, they feel negative or "bad vibes," and I'm not sure that it was meant that

way. I'm not sure it was a "Submit and be stamped on" issue. I think it was "Wives submit to your husbands, and husbands love your wives." Perhaps it's two different ways of saying the same thing. I will submit to my husband, and I have no qualms about that. If he feels strongly on something, I'll back down and do it his way, because there's a reason he feels that way. But I know that he'll do the same for me, because he loves me. I see it as a very circular issue.

I read something recently, that women were made from the rib that was taken under the arm of man, so that we should be sheltered by him, not stomped on by him. And that she was made from his side, so that she should stand beside him, not behind him. I thought, women were made as a companion, a helper. I don't have problems with those passages in the Bible, because I've heard enough and seen it in that context so that I don't think it's a negative thing. I don't have trouble standing beside Steve and doing things with him, and making decisions with him.

Not surprisingly, some women feel the movement goes too far: "They have a bad reputation with many people, but most of their ideas are good ideas. They're a little bit too extreme for me. On issues such as abortion I don't usually agree with what the women's movement says. They go to extremes to shock people." Nonetheless, Mennonite women agree that generally feminists have done a good job of raising the consciousness of people about equal opportunity and issues like battering. Jeannie has never been involved in the movement in any way, though:

"I like being a woman . . ."
I like being a woman, and I don't think that I want to get anywhere and say, "I'm as good as you and I want to compete with you, because you're a man and I'm a woman." I have my talents, and I'll use them as best I can. If a man has different talents that are better for a certain job, then fine. I like the privileges we have as women. I like to get dressed up and wear dresses and look nice, not just be an office executive.

I agree with equal competitiveness. I would be more tempted to get more involved in the women's movement if I felt that at some point I was really hampered from doing something I really wanted to do because I'm a woman and it was the man's place. I believe in shared household responsibilities and team decisions and shared parenting if a woman does work for pay, and I don't like it when I hear that women shouldn't be up at the pulpit. In that sense, I guess I'm liberated from the traditional point of view. But it comes back to one thing: I enjoy being a woman! When we have children I intend to be the mother. I'm looking forward to being able to be at home and enjoy that privilege of being a female, rather than saying that "This is a burden and this is something that I don't want to do," or "I don't want to be held down because I have to bear the children." To me that's something that's positive, not negative.

When you asked what we think of the liberation movement, my immediate thought was those are the conventions where women get together and they don't wear their brassieres, and they scream at each other. That's the impression that I got from things that happened ten or fifteen years ago. It seems that what they did was discredited; many women at home didn't want to have anything to do with them. But I still think there's been an awful lot of benefit to people. Now we don't have to scream; quieter things are happening. Women are able to be themselves. If they want to wear pants they can, if they want to wear dresses they can, if they want to do a certain field they can, if they want to be home with children they can. You don't have to scream at us anymore. Especially in educated circles, that's largely where we have benefited from it.

WOMEN'S EMPOWERMENT

Although the Mennonite faith carries traditional messages that sometimes restrict women's freedom and opportunities, it also weaves a web of belonging and security that protects them from some of the more frightening problems that plague women in contemporary society. Spousal abuse and child abuse are not unheard of here, but they are rare. The love of God carries with it the responsibility to be kind and loving to one's neighbors, wife, and children, Mennonite women say: "If you've got a changed heart, hitting someone wouldn't be the natural thing to do. You're prone to anything before you have a changed heart." Men who hit their wives are definitely in the wrong, because the Bible "teaches very strongly for men to love their wives."

Commitment to the faith and to each other helps Mennonite couples smooth over the hard spots that arise in any marriage: "If we come to God and to His word, those differences can be resolved, and forgiveness can be granted to each other." Furthermore a minister says, a "Christian injunction says that the community can call on a person who is straying or having problems. They go to see their brethren and talk to them, so that they can bring the man back into the fold if he's drinking or has committed adultery or whatever." A few teenagers get into trouble ("They get into things and don't stay Mennonite"), he adds, but they rarely become criminals:

> In our Mennonite settings, life centers so much around our faith and our church, and the church tries to uphold the same ideals that we ourselves believe, so it adds another whole buffer to the family. You're trying to raise your family in a hostile world, so to speak. We're trying to raise our families in the broader church family before they reach out to some of those other hostile things. They will come in contact with them, and sometimes I think they should, but the church upholds the parent and the home upholds the church. This gives us an added strength to carry on.

DREAMS FOR THEIR DAUGHTERS

Lovina of the Old Order Mennonites simply wants her daughters to follow in the rural agricultural life she and her husband have known: "Farmer's wife is what we'd prefer, and that's what two of them are. One is at home, she's not married. She's starting to teach school. She's got a lot of nerve trouble; I don't know how she's going to get along with school teaching." The oldest one would like to work somewhere, but for now she is a mother's helper: "She'll be going on to a new case again; there's a little baby in their home. Most of us want to have some girl coming in. This particular one will want help for three months. Then she also part-time waitresses. She really enjoys that, working with a girl from our church who runs a catering business."

Myra of the Conservative group seems relatively laissez-faire in contrast: "The girls are the oldest; they're teenagers. They don't seem to have any real career goals, so none of us really circle around that idea. Although I think my second daughter has more aspirations that way in the future, she seems to be content and happy in her role as it is right now." One woman describes a daughter who is going to begin training at the local college to become a nursing assistant; she is happy, but hopes this does not deflect her daughter from marriage and family. Young Sara wants to teach before she gets married:

> I don't intend to get married as young as what some people might. I want the freedom of finding out who I am first, and helping others in a way other than bringing up my children. I'd also like to go into voluntary service, working with the missions. We feel it may be important to get out of school life, even for a year or two, just to get a little bit grounded. We can always go back to university if we want to later on.

Gender segregation among the more orthodox Mennonites is a symbol of symmetry and harmony. Of course, in relationships as in art, one achieves symmetry at the expense of fluidity, harmony at the expense of solo voices. A balanced family builds on clearly defined roles that leave little room for experimentation or freedom; a harmonious community builds on unswervingly committed individuals. Here the blueprints for being a woman or being a man are drafted by the faith, often in indelible lines. If both partners follow the teachings, they achieve balance and contribute to the harmonious community. If they rebel or fail, dissonance and discord result. One must then repent or leave.

The future of Mennonite women will depend on achieving a very delicate balance between symmetry and individual expression, preserving the faith and pursuing individual dreams that take them away from their small, protected communities. Living the utopian ideal is not easy in mainstream society. Like those who walked behind the Conestoga wagons almost two hundred years ago, young Mennonite women are pioneers, carving out new pathways toward being faithful and godly in a confusing and complex world.

The Last Sunday

An Old Order woman I met at the market invited me to attend services at her church, so I put on a modest shirt and skirt, then drive toward the famous covered bridge at West Montrose. Just beyond the bridge lies an old Mennonite church. I park across the road, trying to screw up the courage to go inside. I watch Mennonite families careen through the bridge, up the hill, and around the bend toward the church, racing their buggies and laughing. Men park the rigs at one end of the church grounds and chat with each other qui-

etly before entering the right-hand door. Women make their way to the left-hand door, gathering there for a few minutes before the service. Men and women will sit on opposite sides of the church: boys with their fathers, girls with their mothers. I sit in the car, transfixed, feeling like an intruder. Now everyone has gone inside, and I've missed the beginning of the service. It is too late to enter.

I open the windows and listen to the hymns, which, a woman tells me later, are sung while the men and the women do ritual foot washing in pairs—a sign of love and humility. The voices flow into each other, gently rolling like the countryside, blending into the warmth and harmony of a flawless summer morning. I cannot bring myself to break the serenity by starting the car engine, so I slip it into neutral, take off the brake, and silently roll down the hill. As I drive back to my cousin's home through serpentine back roads, I notice "No Sunday sales" signs near farmhouse stands—a reflection of this day's centrality in the Mennonite community.

7

Walking the Tightrope

Chinese Women of Vancouver,
British Columbia

This is a family society with strict rules. My grandparents say that a woman doesn't need that much education. They think that when you get married, your whole life will be your family. I think that should change. They always encourage boys to do more things. I remember when I was a kid I wanted to go out and play with my friends, but my mother would say, "Stay home and be a nice little girl."

—Pearl

En Route to Vancouver

As our plane circles over the city, a multicultural mosaic of three million people surrounded by mountains and sea, my heart skips a beat. This was the town of my adolescence, but its breathtaking beauty never fails to surprise me. After many years away, I am returning to talk with women in Vancouver's Chinatown, a thriving community perched on the edge of downtown, Gastown, skid row, and the waterfront.

This second largest Chinatown in North America is colorful and energetic.[1] It is a fringe area dotted with dilapidated buildings, but at its heart—where Hastings, Pender, and Main streets criss-cross the neighborhood—several refurbished nineteenth-century structures parade an oriental palette of dark reds for happiness and good luck and greens for prosperity. The sidewalks flow with immigrants and old-timers, residents and tourists, Chinese and Native Canadians. Tiny cafés press into the nooks and crannies of every block, their windows clouded with the steam of won ton soup. Sedate antique shops offer the treasures of a homeland very far away in miles and in culture.

Family-owned grocery stores spill their vegetables and fruits into sidewalk stalls, offering a dazzling array of choices. Ducks and chickens hang in butcher shop windows. Specialty shops, often run by women, proffer the ancient secrets of mysterious medicinal herbs and spices. Vibrant neon signs advertise dim sum and regional Chinese cooking, competing with the elaborate facades of old buildings that housed single men during the gold rush and railroad-building days. Chinatown's banquet restaurants, built in the early 1900s, still mark the primary attraction for outsiders. Women spend hours walking from shop to shop, looking for the highest quality at the lowest cost. Vietnamese and Cambodian cafés and markets punctuate the Chinese presence.

The elderly and children are everywhere. High-rise and garden apartments for seniors are sprinkled throughout the neighborhood. Mothers proudly parade their offspring in strollers, and toddlers ride high on fathers' shoulders through the crowded sidewalks. I make my way through the busy streets to the Chinese Cultural Center and stroll through the Sun Yat-sen gardens, which are meticulously laid out with sculptures and a temple brought, stone by stone, from mainland China. Pools and Oriental grasses add to the sense of peace and contemplation. I am ready.

Ying stands rigidly in her long red wedding dress. She dreads the examination about to come as her mother-in-law crosses the room, intent on lifting the hem of the young bride's skirt just high enough to check the size of her feet. Will they be small enough? Countless times since childhood, Ying has begged her mother to remove the bindings so her "three-inch golden lilies" could spring back into their normal shape and size.[2] Bitter images swim through her mind: the day her mother bent all her toes underneath the sole and crushed her tiny arch with a heavy stone; the daily routine of wrapping yards and yards of cloth around feet that never grew; the pain of hobbling in abbreviated steps that made it difficult to shop or even leave her garden; the warnings that if her feet grew "large" she would never find a husband. Today she sighs with relief that she has passed the ultimate test. Her mother-in-law is pleased. Her husband will find her miniature feet erotic.

Ying's wedding in the 1920s reflected the lowly status women held in feudal China, the cultural context from which early Chinese immigrants came to Vancouver. Foot binding (which started in the tenth century) had died out by 1917, but many women who immigrated to Canada endured its pain, as well as the trials of being sold into servitude by their own families for a few bags of rice. The modern Chinese Canadian woman struggles against the restrictive aspects of this historic image while preserving the keen sense of dedication to family that has been so closely woven through the Chinese value system for centuries. She walks a tightrope between obedience and assertiveness, between devotion and freedom from the constraints of family life in a new land thousands of miles from China.[3]

Chinese immigration to Canada dates back to 1858. First the men arrived via California, a phalanx of young money-wise peasants, landless hired hands, sharecroppers, small landholders, and a few merchants who left the Pearl River Delta of Guangdong province (on the southeast coast of China, near Hong Kong[4]) to work the gold mines in places like Barkerville, British Columbia. In the 1870s and 1880s more men ventured across the vast Pacific Ocean to build Prime Minister John A. MacDonald's dream, the cross-continental Canadian Pacific Railway. Thousands of Chinese men provided cheap labor for this massive endeavor, and many lost their lives in the treacherous passes of the Canadian Rockies.

Although these early laborers were valued for their dependability, many were met with hostile mobs who threatened them with harm if they did not return to their homeland—forewarning the volatile mixture of prejudice and discrimination that would greet Chinese until well after World War II.[5] Then, as now, newspapers warned that the Chinese presence would threaten property values, and after the Great Fire of June 1886 destroyed the infant Vancouver, an unsuccessful movement was launched to prevent Chinese merchants from reestablishing their businesses.[6] In 1887, "white workers from the Knights of Labor tied 40 Chinese laborers together by their pigtails and beat them, then burned Chinatown shacks before police moved in."[7]

Because the government levied a head tax against Chinese immigrants well into the twentieth century, very few men could afford to bring their wives to Canada.[8] Most of the handful of Chinese women who found their way into the mining or rail camps served as prostitutes, cooks, or laundrywomen. During this "bachelor phase," men outnumbered women and lived in *fang-k'ou*, formally organized associations or bachelor households designed to meet their needs; some still exist in Vancouver's Chinatown.[9] "Tongs" formed to provide fellowship, social services, and immigration assistance for the lonely and isolated men. Yee points out that "blatant anti-Chinese hostility was no encouragement to bring over a family. A man could send money and letters home, and then turn to prostitutes, gambling, and opium for solace."[10] Women were definitely on the periphery of his life.

Yee describes Vancouver's Chinese population in 1886: "114 souls, including 60 sawmill hands, 30 washermen/cooks, 10 store clerks [and] merchants, 5 children, 3 married women, and 1 prostitute."[11] Saltwater City, as the settlement around Burrard Inlet (now downtown Vancouver) was then known, grew to 120,000 by 1911 and boasted a Chinatown of 3,500 immigrants—with a sex ratio of twenty-eight males to one female.[12] (A similar pattern existed in Chinese communities in the United States.[13]) The almost total male dominance of cultural, political, and economic life during this early period forms an important backdrop for the position of women in today's Chinese community.[14]

It was only as men realized they might not return to China—and had been in Vancouver long enough to save the head tax—that they sent for their families. The severe gender imbalance began to diminish, hitting a ten-to-one ratio by 1921 during a heavy influx of immigrants. (The ratio shrank to three to one by the mid-1950s and is fairly even today.[15]) Along with their wives and daughters, wealthier merchants brought female maidservants to Vancouver. Sold by their parents as domestic help, these young women took on the status of secondary daughters who could marry into "freedom" by age nineteen. For many, the sojourn in Canada ended less fortunately: Rescue homes for runaway girls and prostitutes began to spring up in the late 1880s.

Between 1923 and 1947, discriminatory legislation virtually stopped the flow of Chinese into Canada. Women's organizations began to appear across Canada in the 1930s, a sign that more women were playing an active role outside the home. "The Women's Movement in China had an influence and so, in all probability, did the Women's Movement in North America" on the formation of these groups, according to Con and others, but still fewer women than men lived in Chinatown, and their presence was not well documented.[16]

A second surge of immigration began when some restrictions were lifted after World War II. These more recent Chinese immigrants from Hong Kong or Macao have tended to be educated professional, clerical, and skilled workers from urban areas. They have not required the same level of social services as the first wave, and the strength of the associations has weakened accordingly (although language classes and employment counseling flourish).

Now a third wave of Chinese immigrants floods Vancouver's shores. An extension of the second wave from Hong Kong, this group consists mainly of middle- and upper-income "satellite" or "astronaut" families fleeing the economic and political disruptions anticipated after Hong Kong reverts to the People's Republic of China in 1997. This time women (and children) acquire landed-immigrant status first, paving the way for husbands to join them later. The man stays behind to amass as much security and wealth as he can before 1997; once or twice a year he "commutes" by jet to join his family for holidays (hence the term *astronaut*).

New immigrants continue to arrive daily. Suburbs like Richmond have burgeoned with new development, including homes and hundreds of businesses that cater to the Hong Kong arrivals. Some older, well-established neighborhoods of Vancouver are being transformed as wealthy Hong Kong families buy up the small ranch-style houses built in the 1960s and 1970s, tear them down, and replace them with "monster houses" that take up the entire lot. While this causes resentment among whites and older Chinese alike, nonetheless the recent influx stimulates the city's economic base. Festivals, Chinese theater, dancing, food, and language link the cultural boundaries of the old Chinatown and this evolving suburban community, but the role of women has changed dramatically over the last century as Chinese immigration to Vancouver moved through these distinct stages.[17]

Out of Tradition

TRADITIONAL ROLES: "THE WOMAN WAS SERVANT TO THE MAN"

Today first-generation immigrants from Hong Kong live next to Chinese whose families go back five or six generations in Canada. Across all generations and time periods, however, Chinese women have lived under the same general prescription for womanhood: Confucianism. According to the precepts of this powerful philosophy, harmony springs from feudal loyalty, filial piety, and unquestioning obedience to elders, a pressure that continues into modern family life: "Should the ruler and the ruled, the superior and the inferior, male and female all know their places and act accordingly, then all would be in harmony. Just as the gentry was destined to rule and the common people were destined to be ruled, so were women destined to occupy a subordinate position to men in the Confucian social order."[18]

Veneration for males and the elderly permeated family life.[19] Families historically were patrilocal (when a man and woman married, they went to live with the husband's parents) and patrilineal (family name and wealth were inherited through the male side).[20] A woman's father-in-law commanded the highest authority and status in the household; her husband essentially was tied for second place with his mother; and the wife came third. This structure determined male and female roles and relied upon a woman's adherence to the Confucian principle of the "three obediences": to her father at home, her husband after marriage, and her eldest son in widowhood. Chastity, reticence, a pleasing manner, and domestic skills represented the "four virtues" against which her family would judge her.[21]

Reticence, the second virtue, meant that a woman played the docile role even when her own judgment dictated a different path. Fung tells the story of Boji, who lived around 580 B.C. Trapped in a raging house fire, Boji "chose not to flee, mindful of the moral code that woman should not leave the house unchaperoned."[22] By paying for her virtue with her life, she became immortalized.

"There definitely is a role for a Chinese man and a role for a Chinese woman, and they're very distinct from each other," offers a middle-aged woman. "The most important thing is for the man to go and find a job, bring home the money, and support his family.

The wife's responsibility is to train the children, bring them up to be responsible people, be a good housewife, and that's it." This portrait encapsulates the strict separation of traditional gender roles in China into public versus domestic spheres. Women's role was "always in the home and farming, and the men would help, but very little. After they finished the necessary work, they would just go off chit-chatting with friends and all that, but woman was in charge [of the household] twenty-four hours a day."

Elderly women capture the traditional role of women when they were young girls. Says an eighty-five-year-old widow, "The woman was the servant to the man—period." Women in their seventies and eighties remember the old days, sometimes with bitterness: "If a banquet was put on in a big hall, the women do not exist at the table at all. The men have to be first and after the men eat, they laugh, then the women sit down and eat. Now it makes no difference. You see many mothers taking their children out to restaurants for lunch or dinner, but in the old days you don't see that." Traditionally women were restricted to their own family compound. Those with bound feet had little choice; it was too painful to walk more than a few yards at a time.

An old Chinese saying declares that if you have a daughter it is a small happiness, but if you have a son it is a big happiness. "The man says that the house is dark and there is no light at all if there is no son," recalls an elder. Another proverb declares that "eighteen gifted daughters are not equal to one lame son."[23] At the heart of being a good Chinese woman, then, is the ability to bear sons; because sons carry on the family name, prestige falls to the woman who bears more sons than daughters. An old Chinese song celebrates the birth of a son with praise for his lusty howling and affirmation that he will "be lord and king of the house and home." A newborn daughter will be given no decorations, the song continues: "Her only care, the wine and food, and how to give no trouble to father and mother."[24] Sandra, age thirty-five, heard these songs as she grew up in a large family in Hong Kong, where her father was a worker and her mother a housewife: "We have seven children, because my mom had four girls first. My dad is the eldest son in his family, so my grandma said she still needed a grandson. The three boys were born last."

In pre-Communist China, because parents were dependent on

their children financially and sons had the responsibility to look after their parents, daughters were a dead loss to their families: "They would be married off, and once they were married, they were outside the family."[25] In contrast, sons grew up to marry a woman who would join the household to help take care of his aging parents. Also, because property inheritance flowed through the male, "once you give it to a girl, it will most likely belong to someone else after her. Parents doubly valued the baby boys; they were trying to protect the family name." Elderly women approve of the changes toward equality in this regard. The old ways made them angry, even though they were taught to accept them: "We had to follow the tradition and not complain about anything. If the wife gave birth to three girls and not one boy, she would have to cry. It's the tradition." During hard times, female infants were often drowned, abandoned, or sold.[26]

Even now conflicts occasionally emerge between a married woman and her in-laws because she has given birth to daughters and no sons. The in-laws assume it is the woman's fault if a son is not forthcoming. "In the eyes of the Chinese," says an elder, "the males are always the domineering sex. If a woman had two, three, four girls, the husband would find an excuse to have another wife, which we call concubine. Of course, he won't divorce the first woman, but he would have another woman come into the household who could produce a son to carry on the name of the family. But that was a long time ago." In a story that reflects the extreme value placed on males, one woman relates that her father was "kidnapped" in the north of China when he was seven years old:

> Someone used a toy to take him away from his family as he played in the street. Taizan people must have a son in the family to carry the last name, for security, so because a certain family did not have a son, they brought my dad from Canton to Taizan. That's how my dad partly grew up in that family.[27]

Women were very much a commodity in traditional Chinese culture. Ping, a sixty-eight-year-old, taps her cane on the floor to underscore her points. She vaguely remembers her parents, who sold her for ninety dollars when she was four years old. Being sold was almost like being an indentured servant; a contractual arrangement gave money to the parents and papers to the daughter. Ping insists that "it wasn't so bad," because the family who bought her was better able to suppport her—in fact, at age nineteen she turned down an opportunity to return to her natural family. Ping has never married and she says that her life has been happy even though Chinese culture defines the role of woman in terms of being a wife and mother.

TRADITIONAL POWERS: "THE WOMAN TRIES TO GET POWER"

Within this context of obedience and submission, where is the Chinese woman's power? An ancient legend, reminiscent of Eve and the apple, finds it in the moon:

> The extraordinary brightness and fullness of the moon during the festival (Mid-Autumn) has inspired many legends. One of the most famous involves Sheung Ngor of the Hsia Dynasty. She was the wife of How One, the famous archer. One day the archer secured the formula for immortality and youth from the Empress of the Western Paradise, but Sheung Ngor stole it and ate it. To evade the pursuit of her husband, she soared up to the moon with the power of the pill, where she remains to this day.[28]

For Chinese women, customs linked with age and sex dictate power, or power must be stolen, as with Sheung Ngor. Traditionally, women's power lay only within a family context characterized by extremes of hierarchy.

"Like fire and water," is how Choi, a woman in her seventies, characterizes the traditional relationship between daughter-in-law and mother-in-law. Choi says she was almost a nonperson in her husband's family. Inside the home she sometimes had the central power, especially over children and daughters-in-law, but with her husband or mother-in-law she was a second-class citizen, "a stranger in the house." Even if she abhorred the rules of the household or how they treated her, she had to quietly and cheerfully obey their wishes. Since the Chinese male's dominance over his wife was so entrenched, "The woman tries to get power from somewhere, so she dominated the daughter-in-law, who resented it." The older woman garnered power, albeit limited, for the first time in her life. She held a high position in the family essentially because she had raised a son. The daughter-in-law was like another child who had to accept her instruction, Selina explains: "Where there are traditional values, there is intergenerational conflict, but the younger woman must obey."

When in-laws moved in with the younger couple, any power not wielded by the husband shifted completely to his mother and father. That left the wife with no say and no position, Selina adds, except to live up to her household responsibilities without argument:

> A long time ago the man used to travel quite a bit, but if her husband was home, the daughter-in-law might ask him if she could go somewhere, like the opera. If the husband was more powerful than his mother, he would give permission. If the mother-in-law didn't like the idea, she would grumble and have lots to say, but if the husband is not around, then the young woman would ask the mother-in-law. If the mother-in-law loved opera, she would gladly give permission. She would go along with her! But if she didn't like those things, she would say no.

In the Chinese culture of her mother's age, says Annie (who is forty-six), "You know the woman is always subservient to the male. When you're a young girl, you obey your father; when you get married, you have to follow whatever the husband does. He has the last word." Much of the same sense of fatalism persists into the younger generation, she notes, "but with Western women it's totally different—they're equal. In Hong Kong it's the same thing because we're so Westernized."

Nine elderly women, all from mainland China and all in their seventies or eighties, sit around a table debating traditional male–female powers. A young Chinese Canadian university student interprets the session, commenting that she, too, has learned from listening to the older women. If they think about patterns of family power, the women come down on the female side: "The woman has the most power in the family, over the household and the children, and the man is only working to take money home and support them. *She* makes the most important decisions." When it comes to decisions such as buying land or major changes that affect the family, however, the man makes the final decision.

Two men in their eighties, who join the group late, offer an economic model: "The one who supports the family gets the most power." The women chime in: "It depends on the man. If the man is masterful, he makes the decisions. Otherwise, the woman takes responsibility. It used to be the man but now, in modern days, it's almost the same between the man and the woman. Before, the man had more power, the wife didn't have much. Now things are different, everybody's equal." The women giggle as they admit they like hearing about these changes from their granddaughters. The men shake their heads, laughing.

The contrast does not escape the older women. In their younger days, if they disobeyed, their husbands would bite them on the forearm. The architecture of Chinese culture is constructed around female obedience and male dominance. Yet, according to Jade, age forty-seven, who visited China and talked to her grandmother many years ago, women had some limited but very real power—over children, over daughters-in-law, and over grandchildren. "In olden days, men and women were equal in some ways. The man is always out there doing business, working, being the breadwinner. The woman is queen of the house—she has all the say in the house."

In traditional China or Hong Kong, if a woman felt frustrated about her lack of power, would she be likely to rebel or submit? Ah, age seventy-five, says she would "trick her way through," then seek appropriate outlets for her power:

> Very rich families had housekeepers and maids. The woman would exercise her power over domestic help and her childrens' spouses, especially the daughters-in-law. You can never get ahold of the son-in-law when the daughters marry. They would leave home—it's always the daughters-in-law that suffer. Now it's different. My own in-laws were very nice to me; I was just like another daughter, because we never lived together.

Faith, 43, recalls that her grandparents took for granted the man's right to bend a woman to his will: "Sometimes my grandfather would yell at my grandmother a little bit, and my grandmother would not answer back. It was nothing. They thought that was part of life. She didn't feel hurt—she understood that. Most women of that generation dared not talk back."

The Turning Point: Passage to Canada

For Chinese women in Canada, immigration clearly has been the turning point in gender relations, whether it was during the late

1800's to join their mates during the gold-mining and railroad-building eras, the early 1900s influx from Guangdong Province, or more recently from Hong Kong. Vancouver's economic expansion, natural harbor, and prominence on the Pacific Rim have always made it an attractive destination for Chinese immigrants. For men, immigration has represented a logical opportunity to carry out the male's role as provider to family and clan during hard times at home:

> As in other preindustrial societies, the Chinese family was an economic unit, keen to enrich itself, protect its interests, and enhance future prospects. In south China, family power was expressed through the lineage or clan, a network of families possessing a common surname and a common founding ancestor. . . . Overseas Chinese sent money home not only to feed their families but also to strengthen the lineage.[29]

For earlier generations of women, immigration meant a way to keep the family intact. Later, many women who were born in Hong Kong moved as children to England or Australia, then came to Canada to join other relatives. Now, in an ironic contrast with the railroad days (when almost all the immigrants were men), women lead their families to life in the New World. As with Jamaican families, often the woman acts as a migratory lever, later bringing her husband, children, and parents.

Older women from mainland China, younger women from Hong Kong, and Canadian-born women of mainland Chinese ancestry identify with traditional culture in China in different ways. Most older women come to Vancouver under the family reunion category, to join family members already in Canada. They often move out of their son's or daughter's houses because they want to be independent. This is a major divergence from the traditional matriarchal role of the elder woman in China, according to Sue, director of a senior citizens' apartment complex:

> They don't want to be the maid in the family. The daughter and the son go out to work. The grandmother is expected to take care of the grandchildren, serve them, and do all the housework. They're so tired of it and they don't want to do it anymore, so they get out of the family. Also, they are very good parents, thinking always of the best for the kids. They move out so there will be more space for the son's children,

or if they can't get along with the son-in-law or daughter-in-law. The children can't speak Chinese, they can't integrate together. For some of them, it's quite sad. They go on welfare from the government to get an apartment or move into seniors' housing.

Women from Hong Kong are more assertive, confident, and goal-oriented than women in earlier immigration waves; they come from an urban rather than a rural environment and a tradition of more freedom for women. Daisy, in her late thirties, explains why she and her husband came to Canada:

> We're worried about 1997. My husband was anxious to find a place where there is peace, where he can survive and work, and use all his potentials. He saw a notice that one of the companies was hiring a chief accountant, someone who could speak Cantonese and Mandarin. He wanted to leave Hong Kong so badly that he took the job even though it was a demotion. I miss my family very much; that's why I'm sponsoring my mother to come over. I want to look after her.

For younger women, adjusting to life in Vancouver carries different but equally trying burdens. Sylvia, age twenty-two, was born in Hong Kong:

> I finished high school in Hong Kong, where opportunities are not that great for further studies. I came here for the educational opportunity. My uncle, who came to Canada twenty years ago, sponsored me. I'm the eldest daughter in my family, and I have three younger sisters. The responsibility was placed on my shoulders to make sure my sisters were doing well. After I arrived in Canada, I applied for them to come over to school. Now most of my family is over here, but my parents are still working there to save money for 1997.

A young immigrant woman, Lee, tells a story of courage and loneliness:

> *"You have to help yourself . . ."*
> I left Hong Kong because I wanted to get away from my family. I chose to come to Canada to see if I can make it or not. I do have hard times in the beginning, because I haven't any friends. I just have my elder sister here. I live with her because my mom wouldn't allow me to live with others or alone; she wanted me to stay with somebody she trusts. I enjoy the life here. Sometimes I feel lonely, but I think I will over-

come that feeling as an independent adult. You can refuse anything that's out of control in your life. If some crisis comes up, you have to help yourself, so I want to train myself to become more independent that way. I don't mind the hard times.

I made some new friends here, even though I've just been here two years. The relationships are hard to compare with the ones I have in Hong Kong—the friends, schoolmates; we know each other for over fifteen years. You can't expect to have the same trust with new friends. That's what it's like for me here: You can't depend on your family and you can't depend on your friends, so everything is on your own. The English as a Second Language [ESL] training is hard, but I try to get through that.

I know when I am getting older in Hong Kong my work is quite stable. I know what I'm going to be: I am social worker, and then I become a mom later, and then years later I get that position, that salary, that kind of living standard. Everything is foreseeable, but I am not satisfied with that. Here, I think I can try something else other than social worker; maybe I have some hidden talent that I don't know.

At the end of this year I will go back and visit my parents. I haven't made the final decision yet about going back to stay. Hong Kong is changing; I think it will be a big shock. If my family moves here, they will need my help in setting up everything. The first few years they need to establish themselves—maybe I can't go back; I need to stay here with them.

My parents are planning to come here because they really worry about 1997. They know what the real picture is in China, and my grandparents had a hard time there, so they don't want it to happen to their kids. They think that life here maybe is not as good as they have in Hong Kong—they haven't any friends, but for the sake of my youngest brothers, they still want to move.

Another important immigration pattern that turns traditional family life upside down is that of the astronaut family, an arrangement that only the more affluent can afford. According to ESL teachers and social workers, about half of the Hong Kong families they see are living in this trans-Pacific commuting arrangement. Some well-qualified men, who cannot find a comparable position in Vancouver, choose to remain working in Hong Kong while their families establish residency in Canada. They are either overqualified or lack "Canadian experience." If these men take jobs that are below their training, stress results for the whole family: "It gets on their ego."

Often the wife gives up her career in the process of immigrating to Vancouver.[30] A woman explains why she and her husband decided to become an astronaut family after ten years of marriage and four children:[31]

"We had to try for the sake of our children . . ."
Life was so perfect and going smoothly until the agreement to return Hong Kong Island and part of Kowloon peninsula to China, which is a communist country. My relatives who stayed there had suffered under the communists' inhumane treatment. Ugly scars could be found all over their bodies. The most terrible thing is that people lost their personal freedom in choosing careers and religion, as well as freedom of thought and expression. There's a possibility that Hong Kong might adopt all those awful things after 1997, so we couldn't leave our children there to live without freedom of choice.

I had to give up my high-paying job and leave my beloved friends and relatives in order to start a new life someplace without communism. We felt so uncertain of the future, but we had to try for the sake of our children. I packed all we had and left Hong Kong just as my father left China 30 years ago. My husband stays with his family so he can keep working for a few more years. If my father was still alive today, he would probably be very pleased with what I did.

Ariana, a social worker, tells the story of her "astronaut wife" friend, who runs the Vancouver household in her husband's absence. It is not an easy life.

"Nobody to share decisions with . . ."
As a social worker I don't encourage that kind of separation. The early years of marriage are the best time to consolidate the relationship. Together you go through all the crises: how to raise the kids, how to start the business, how to do family planning. You develop the same objectives and direction. If you leave your wife and kids here, it's hard for the kids to recognize the father role and to build a balanced personality. It's no good for the wife—it's so stressful to handle this astronaut family with nobody to share decisions or good times or bad times with her.

The husband's in Hong Kong without the care of the wife and family. I don't think it's healthy for him to stay behind just for economic reasons. In Hong Kong women are very predatory: They see a wealthy man and ask, "Wife away?" Hong Kong has become a very hedonistic place; people will do anything to get out by 1997. That can also put the marriage in jeopardy, if the man is unfaithful. Of course she'd probably never know about it, so it works out for them.[32]

It may be easier for women to immigrate to Canada because they fill preferred occupational categories such as secretaries, nurses, teachers, and social workers—female-dominated professions. Even single women pioneer for their boyfriends, often at great cost to their own professional development and independence, as Faith explains:

"She's giving up a lot . . ."
My friend Ruby has no choice if she wants to get married and come to Vancouver. She'll come here first and apply for her boyfriend to join her. It causes many problems, because if she can't get a full-time job she's not qualified to sponsor her boyfriend. Ruby is alone here, and sometimes she wonders whether the relationship is strong enough for her to arrange everything for him to come over. They are apart for maybe years; they don't have a relationship. In the end, if the boy comes over and he doesn't enjoy life here or he can't find a job, he may blame her.

As long as the lady has a job here, then she should support the family and let the boyfriend stand on his own feet, take his time. If the burden of the family is bestowed on the female part instead of on the male part, it will cause anxiety and questions. My friend wants to get her doctorate, but she can't start anything until she goes through all this. Even when her boyfriend comes over, she can't go back to school, because in the beginning he will need time to find a job, settle in, and build a stable relationship. She thinks that she's giving up a lot, and that's the problem—she is!

A third pattern reflects the lives of women who were born and raised in Vancouver of Chinese immigrant parents from Guangdong Province. Joy, age thirty-six, talks of her parents' hard life. Her father came to Canada first in the early 1950s, and her mother joined him in 1956 in order to get married: "Mom's just the typical

Chinese mom who works in canneries and fisheries part-time and looks after us the rest of the time. My dad worked for Macmillan Blodell as a log feeder."

Jade's parents came from China to escape the poverty of their village. Her maternal grandfather had already come to Canada in the 1920s, beginning the chain migration. She describes a strange twist that suddenly made female children "valuable." When a female child was born in China, it was "useless" to register her as a girl: "If you register her as a boy, then that piece of paper is worth something to someone; a paper with a girl's name on it is useless because it can't take you anywhere." Wai, in her nineties, confirms that a family could then sell the paper: "When people came to Canada, they always had to answer the question, 'How many children do you have in China?' So some people were very smart. If they only had daughters, not sons, they used the daughter's name as a son. Later on, if another family had a son that is very close to their [fictional] son's name, they could sell the paper to the other family. My father did this. He had five girls, but he put them down as five boys." Kitty, age forty-two, tells how this ploy worked in her family:

"The women had to stay behind . . ."
The living standard was very low in China, especially in the village, so my grandma suggested to my grandpa, let's take our number three daughter to Canada to make a better living. They started to apply, and my dad left China before I was born in 1952. I never met my dad until I was twelve years old in Hong Kong; he was already making a living in Canada.

At that time, China was always having economic troubles. Ever since then my mom was left alone with the two of us. My dad was continuously sending back money to support us. My mom moved to Guangdong when I was four. When I was seven, China was having a big problem raising money to pay back what they had borrowed from other countries, so everything was very tight. No food, nothing. If you wanted to buy a pair of shoes, you had to line up for miles. My mother wanted to send me out of China, so she sent me away with her girlfriend from the same village, to Hong Kong.

I stayed there from 1959 until 1967. My grandmother stayed with me, and then in 1962 my mom and my sister applied from Guangdong to Hong Kong. They got there in late 1962. My dad suddenly decided to visit Hong Kong to meet all of us in 1964. He was a Canadian citizen already. That was the time when Prime Minister Diefenbaker realized the problem of Asian people—that the men only were allowed to stay in Canada, and the women had to stay behind.

Two ESL teachers work with immigrant women. They show a tough determination and resilience in learning the language that gives them freedom and employability—and sometimes threatens their husbands. Georgiana, a bilingual employment counselor who helps immigrants find jobs and plan careers, says her female clients lack education compared to the men. Those from villages cannot read or write Chinese, let alone English. They face language problems and marital difficulties. The husband will say, "You're so lazy, you don't want to go out to look for work." Some, Georgiana relates, are lucky enough to have in-laws or parents who "come in handy, to look after the young kids so the parents can work."

"Most immigrant women who are looking for work here are sewing machine operators, work in restaurants, or they work in food-processing factories making salads, Chinese sausage, and dough," reports Esther, who works with those immigrants from Hong Kong whose English skills and education are limited. She says that in spite of the image of Hong Kong immigrants as affluent and well-educated, many work in low paying jobs in restaurant kitchens, warehouses, or factories, earning the minimum wage. Those who have worked for a few years make a little more, she notes, but "if men have a mortgage to pay it's really difficult, so they want their wives to come out and work, too."

Into the Twentieth Century

CONTEMPORARY ROLES: "SORT OF A SPLIT PERSONALITY"

The notion of Yin and Yang symbolically captures the ideal Chinese woman of today, says Holly, a musician in her late twenties. Harmony and balance. Successful in her career and a good mother and wife. The good Chinese woman is confident, but she is also feminine and soft-spoken and knows her place. In the past, an eligible man would look for "a beautiful woman who comes from a good family with a good reputation," Ah recalls. "Even in those days, the girls were running around, you know, sneaking behind their parents' back. She would have to be gentle, and, of course, able to produce a son." Now younger Chinese women bristle at the old images and try to redefine themselves in a way that incorporates the best of the old and the new worlds. For most this means simultaneously working outside the home and trying to keep the family together.

Sometimes the emotion-laden values of the domestic sphere conflict with the opportunities of the public sphere, as Tina, who is twenty-seven, explains: "When she goes out, the Chinese Canadian woman has to be assertive enough, and when she's at home she has to be caring and pleasant. Sort of a split personality." On one side, people expect her to be competent, educated, efficient, and achievement-oriented enough to compete in the professional or business marketplace. On the other side, she must be soft, compliant, loving, and nurturant. These two sides not only cause painful internal conflict, they also compromise others' opinions of her. "Chinese cannot accept the fact that if a woman is very assertive, she might still be a good Chinese woman." Chinese women speak of treading a very fine line. Men, especially, may find her success in the public sphere threatening: "They always say, 'She's so bossy,' but we have to be like that to survive." Says Elena, a thirty-five-year-old librarian: "You have to be very careful that you know how to present yourself." Marketing director Pearl, who is forty-five, paints a picture of conflict:

> She should be soft-spoken, accommodating, friendly—but also assertive! The woman would go after things that she wants strongly. On the other hand, she would try to accommodate other people. A woman who was born in China or Hong Kong and has been influenced by the Chinese culture ever since she was born would be more submissive and would go along even if she doesn't agree.

Older women speak of the good Chinese man as a dependable provider who can establish a successful career. They want "someone who will look after the family—that's the number one thing in the Chinese culture." As head of the household, he must have strong leadership qualities tempered by a loving, generous nature. Younger women agree with these qualities, but also seek a man who is not chauvinistic, "yet who spoils you." They depart from the traditional pattern by seeking a relationship in which both parties contribute to the decision-making process. Reflecting the contradiction inherent in the female role in this culture, Pearl argues with herself:

> I like being female because sometimes you can get away with things. You get mistreated sometimes, though. I think it's very important to have the same directions, the same value system, but I want to be respected for my own opinion. I'm not hoping for someone very rich or very handsome. Most important, I want to share with him; I want him to know what I am thinking about and support me. On the other hand, I do want to support him in whatever he wants. But I want some independence.

Sharing household and child care responsibilities equally would help, insists Judy, an engineering graduate. Her grandmother and mother would not have dreamed of making her statement: "He has to be flexible. After we have kids, he has to do his part. When we both work, after five o'clock I want him to be a full-time parent—not just full-time mom and part-time dad. When I come home, I don't want to do everything, like cook and take care of the baby." Judy, who is in her twenties, sees her generation as "pretty much the same. We're not stupid girls—we're quite intelligent, and we're pretty much all good students, hardworking. We want somebody opposite, just to add some life. Someone different and unique. And I want someone who wants to be someone, I guess." Younger women prefer a man who will respect and appreciate them as professional, educated women but also be responsible, faithful, and loving, as the traditional Chinese husband should be. They express dissatisfaction with the ancient double standard. A wife should simply grin and bear it if her husband is unfaithful, but a Chinese woman would be "killed" if she were unfaithful to her husband. When it comes to decision making, they are more likely to put their foot down and say, "I want it done that way," rather than being inalterably deferential.

A shortage of Chinese men in Vancouver, though, narrows the choices for young women. "The Chinese boys seem very thin, very intellectual, with glasses—that's the stereotype," Judy observes. "There aren't very many around, it seems; maybe we're just not in the right city. They're not the sports-minded type, active and outgoing. They're usually the quiet, academic type." The field shrinks further because so many men are either married or engaged by twenty-five, says Virginia: "Tradition says they *must* have these symbols of stability." Others are "not in touch with their feelings," and some are gay. Many head for the opportunities in Toronto's business arena.

BECOMING A WOMAN, BECOMING A MAN

Chinese mothers traditionally dressed babies in red for the first few weeks, regardless of gender. Modern professional women agree that they will deck out their daughters in dresses and will try to instill in them the traditional feminine values of Chinese culture. A middle-aged woman now would buy light blue or white clothes for a baby boy, and pink, red, or peach for a baby girl: "More beautiful colors, or floral prints. The old folks make these little blankets out of floral prints for girls and solid colors for boys." "It's hard to say because I can't see myself as a mother right now," says Wendy, who is twenty-five, "but I think I would dress my little girl in dresses and frilly socks. It's nice to be a woman. I would encourage her to go out and try different things, though." At the same time, women say they would make sure their children were educated well and prepared for the career of their choice, rather than their parents' choice.

The primary distinctions come not in the way Chinese babies are dressed, however, but in how people treat them. As Jenny, age thirty-two, explains:

> I have a younger brother. I could feel the difference when my brother was first born and growing up. I'm the second girl, so people didn't pay too much attention to me. I never had any birthday presents until I was about eight, but he got presents when he was about three, very expensive presents. I could feel that difference.

Younger women agree on raising their children with a slightly different emphasis than their own parents displayed, as Lu-anne, a recreation worker, notes:

> *"Parents want to be controlling . . ."*
> Chinese parents live for their kids. That's the reason they come over here; that's why especially the mother sacrifices so much. She stays at home, she cooks the meals for the kids, she makes sure that everything's done for them, and she practically lives her whole life for the

kids. There's tremendous pressure on the kids to live up to her expectations.

Everybody is looking at you; they're comparing their kids to your kids. You have to make sure your kids conform, otherwise people will say you're not a good parent because the kids are doing this and that. Then they would lose face and see themselves as a failure—a rotten mother or a terrible father because they couldn't control their kids. That's why there are so many teenage-parent conflicts, because parents want to be controlling. They want their kids to live up to these expectations so they can brag over the phone with Auntie May and say, "My kids have straight A's on their report card," or "My kids are doing their Ph.D." That's all they live for; they talk about their kids because they have no other social life. I don't want to repeat that.

The pressure on the child does not always yield the desired results. When children balk at the discipline, parents become frustrated and take it out on each other (seldom on the child, in this culture).

Male children enjoy elevated status in the home, says Lu-anne. "We see it, not all the time, but it's something that's understood because we all come from more or less the same homes. We all grew up Chinese girls in a family where most of us have brothers." A woman with two brothers says she learned "that if you're a girl you have to do all the housework, while the guys can eat and leave everything. I had to do all the dirty jobs." Favoritism extends to priority being placed on education for males, Wendy adds:

> I wasn't encouraged to go out and try different things. I used to like drawing, but my aunts would say, "You can't make a living from drawing unless you get married." They don't encourage women to get an education, except that it will help you to have a home and a good husband. Chinese parents want the daughters to marry into good families. This is changing a little, but not fast enough for me.

A twenty-eight-year-old office worker says that Chinese families "expect too much from the male figure in the family. Even in the modern world, I have some friends who don't hesitate to get pregnant again if they already have two daughters. They think two is the maximum when it comes to educating and raising them, but they still need to take the risk and have another one, to have a boy in the family." Her friend points to the contrast between generations and the lingering preference for boys: "I'm sure if I got married, my in-laws would prefer a boy. I'm sure when my daughter gets married, we probably wouldn't care. Most of us are over that stage, but some of us are still like that. Men still do think that they would like to have at least one son to carry the last name."

The division of labor is clearly marked in some families, with girls doing all the household chores for their more privileged brothers. For daughters of Westernized parents, chores are fairly evenly divided from an early age. A few young Chinese women talk about being free to do more "male-oriented" things, and brothers who do more than their fair share of cooking. These are overshadowed, however, by the typical case described by Julie, age twenty:

> *"Mom favored him more . . ."*
> My brother got to take out the garbage because I was "too weak." We all tried to take turns doing the dishes. My brother got away with not doing other chores, because he was the only son. Mom favored him more because, of course, sons are so important in Chinese life. He's been away at university, and she misses him. When he comes home she'll cook breakfast, lunch, dinner. She'll do his laundry for him. She'll say, "Are you coming home for dinner? What would you like to eat?"
>
> I guess because the girls are not away, we can do the work, we can cook the meals. If she has plans for lunch, she'll say, "I'm gone for lunch," and that's fine. With my brother home, even if she is going out, she'll cook something first. If my sister and I confront our mother, she promises she won't favor him again, not even to do his laundry. Then what does she do? His laundry!

Even though she resents this blatant favoritism, Julie remains quiet and tries to get along with her brother and her parents.

To her litany of bitter memories, Julie adds that parents will say to daughters, "You shouldn't be climbing the walls or playing with guns; girls should be playing with dolls." In Hong Kong this attitude still prevails, but it is less evident in Canada unless a grandmother is raising children for working parents. ("She might reinforce that type of attitude.") In Hong Kong, parents would restrict their daughter from camping and other recreational activities that require an overnight stay: "The son can get that. The boys have more freedom. In some families, they save the resources for the boy's education first."

Many women speak positively of the enduring close-knit family structure that provides both a secure sense of belonging and an obligation that is sometimes hard to meet. Indeed, the Chinese family preserves a value system that allows parents to be protective and to set down a set of rules that children will either obey as a matter of respect or face searing shame:

> You must avoid anything that would shame the family. Living away from home would do that. Automatically it's assumed that you have a live-in boyfriend. Tongues will start wagging, old ladies will start talking—Chinese old ladies are very gossipy. My parents care about what's being said about the family.

Although males are important for carrying on the family name—thus making it hard for women to establish themselves as independent persons—females have an impact on the family name in terms of maintaining standards of morality and behavior. If she strays, a woman brings shame to the entire family and could be rejected by them: "You're no longer my daughter." Some young women believe that this is why they throw themselves into academic achievement; they seek the status traditionally accorded only to males. Will the next generation of males change their attitudes? As one woman says, "I don't know. My brother is the next generation of Chinese men, and if he keeps up this attitude, I don't think his wife will be very happy."

Even in Canada, young Chinese women report restrictions on their choice of activities. Mandy, age twenty-nine, describes how this affects her career path:

> A very good example is Toronto. We know that there are few jobs in Vancouver, and we know that in Toronto the streets are lined with jobs. But my parents won't let me go to Toronto because I am a girl, and it's not safe, and it's not good for my reputation if I leave home and go out on my own! They say I can't go to Toronto until my younger brother graduates from UBC [University of British Columbia] next year, and then I can go because then I would be living with my brother. My mother told me, "No, you can't move out on your own until you are married. You will go from this house to your husband's house!" I scorn at it, because I don't believe in it.

Mandy acknowledges that her "maverick" attitude causes problems, and that she may not act on her principles when the time comes. It is "just understood," she says, that young women will not move out on their own. Even living with other females would be seen as "being very loose unless you are in a boarding school."

Anita May's story illustrates the complexities of striving for balance between preserving the culture and becoming her own person. She deals with autonomy issues that every young woman faces; the difference is that she still struggles at twenty-nine to escape the secure web of her family:

> *"I would like to have my own world . . ."*
> My parents never treat me as an adult because I'm with the family. It's quite obvious if you're not married and you move away from your family—everybody asks, "Have you got a problem that you had to move out?" I have no problem with my family—I like my parents—but sometimes I want to have my own space and the feeling that I can do it for myself. If my emotions aren't stable and I'm not happy, then my mom asks, "What's going on? Are you okay? Do you want to eat?" I just want to be alone, but I can't say I don't want anything, so I will answer every question she asks.
>
> Maybe it's time for me to move out for better reasons, like migration to another place. I need some time to think about myself, what I'm going to do. As an adult I can do my own planning and find a job, be totally independent. I can start new work here, to see if I can do it or not, out from under the protection of my family. In the family, it's always, "Oh, I can't do anything; I'm their daughter."
>
> I don't want to make my mom or dad unhappy, but they just want an ordinary girl with a stable job—doesn't go out so frequently, spends more time with them. As an adult I would like to have my own world. I think it's hard to share with them. They think, "You eat well here, sleep well here, why do you expect more?"

Saying that the parental generation is chauvinistic might be too harsh, because they support their daughters' aspirations as long as they "don't go past a certain point" or become too aggressive: "Chinese girls do tend to rest upon stability, not wildness and craziness." Her boyfriend, Mandy says, is "afraid that I would become a different person from the way I am. That's what separates us from

Caucasian girls. We've been scared half to death for most of our lives of all the bad things that go on in the world."

The protectiveness works to a point, acknowledges Alicia, a university student whose parents have pounded into her a deep fear of being out alone at night. She calls it "brainwashing" and realizes that they care about her and want her to learn to care about and respect herself, which contributes to her positive self-image: "But with my Caucasian friends, it stops at a certain point. There's a time to be like that, and there's a time to let go. My parents don't seem to want to let go until it's time for the husband to pick up where they left off." Tradition renders the female a perpetual child, transferred from her father's protection to that of her husband.

By contrast, these young women swear they will raise their sons and daughters as equals: "My son can have a doll or stuffed animal as much as my daughter can," says Lena, a thirty-five-year-old born into a poor Chinatown family. "With Canadian-born Chinese, we all try to fight for being equal. We're in Canada now; it doesn't matter what sex you are. Males are not superior to us. They may try to be, but we try to match them."

Younger women of Chinese ancestry want the chance to take care of themselves, to be their own person, to make their own decisions, and to provide their own security and stability. Young women shoulder the responsibility (and opportunity) of making that cultural shift. The road is a long and twisted one.

CONTEMPORARY POWERS: "WE GET MORE FREEDOM"

Chinese Canadian women speak of the pervasive male domination among transitionally modern couples—those who are still very heavily influenced by the traditional culture and have not yet become fully assimilated into Western culture. "Chinese women nowadays don't necessarily listen to their husbands; there is discussion," says a teacher in her forties. "It's not just a male-dominant culture today." Before, the woman not only had to listen to her husband, she was housebound and isolated. ("You couldn't even see people.") A trend toward more equality marks many contemporary relationships.

Astronaut wives in their forties agree their lives surpass their grandmother's. "Yes! Yes! We like the freedom. We get more freedom!" They make all the household decisions, but discuss major issues with their husbands when the men visit once or twice a year. Women whose husbands live in Vancouver say the pattern often strikingly resembles traditional ways, though progress blows in the wind. One woman believes her husband has more consequential power than she does: "When it concerns business, the husband makes the decisions; when it's the family, the woman makes most of the decisions." If the couple disagrees, an argument leads to a compromise, rather than the male always winning. Says a woman in her thirties, "If it's social events that are happening at home, normally the woman makes that decision, but if it's major outings, like a trip to Disneyland, then the father would be the one to decide."

Another woman argues that wives give men power out of respect, not out of subordination: "Chinese ladies respect their husbands, so when it comes to important decisions, they let their husbands decide." In a few cases, "men are head of household only in name," May suspects. "Even in the more traditional homes the female still has the ruling power behind the scenes. It's just that in public everyone is led to believe, except for close friends, that the man is the head." Other women downplay that interpretation. Says a twenty-nine-year-old pharmacist: "I just look at my grandfather. He has control of everything. Whenever my grandmother says something, he says she's wrong."

The transitional generation sees contemporary Chinese Canadian women as "more courageous—there are many lady doctors and lawyers here. They have good careers. They're willing to have both family and career." Younger women aspire to equality in marital power, want their own checking accounts, and insist on joint control over major assets. They contribute money to the family but want to hold a certain amount aside under their control. Samantha, a thirty-five-year-old merchant, voices an attitude that could only come from the new generation of Chinese women: "Personally, I own my own properties, so I don't think I would like to share finances. In the long run, if anything breaks apart, the female is usually left destitute. I do advocate sharing, but I think females are left at a disadvantage and they should have a financial backup in case anything happens."

A few women in Hong Kong have made successful bids for political office; ironically, though, "people don't treat them as ladies anymore; they treat them just as individuals. They're not that common." In Vancouver, women have not yet figured significantly in the political arena. In the cultural center, women's portraits grace the halls: Were these important women who were instrumental in starting the cultural center? No, says a young volunteer:

> Well, they donate money. For $1,500 you get your picture put up there, so usually the husband pays for their part, as a couple. I guess power is the last thing that women would try for—money and prestige, yes, they might work hard on that—but power is something that solely belongs to members of the opposite sex.

Power in all its forms heads the agenda for younger women to change: "Things won't stay the same for a long time. After all, everyone is changing. The longer the Chinese community lives in Canada, the more they become Westernized or Canadianized, the more they will be powerful and in control. Maybe that will help to open a way out." Younger women see mothers and grandmothers who never had income, let alone a checking account; whose sole source of respect was their ability to raise children and maintain a household—neither of which generated spending money or independence; and who had to bend to their husband's will regardless of whether they agreed.

Even elderly couples who have lived in Vancouver for many years move toward more compromise and discussion, as a housing center counselor points out, but women still tend to defer to men:

> They do very well here and have good relationships. They maintain a fairer balance, not one over the other. I think they are quite Westernized and often talk about rights and fairness among themselves. Yet, in making decisions, the ladies always give up their rights—they never want to make a decision. They don't want to be involved. They just want to do what they're told. That's what they are used to, I guess.

Some Chinese Canadian women believe that Caucasian men, who also are power oriented, are more liberated "because they have been raised in Canada or America, where the feminist movement has been going on for a long time and women are becoming more assertive. The men are gradually coming to their senses." Chinese men, by contrast, are "set in their thinking" and have not yet absorbed the message of gender equality: "We're just starting at the very bottom and trying to work toward that." Two business owners suggest that Japanese women deal with an even larger difference between men and women in their culture: "The man is really dominant, and there's fewer women executives running big corporations. The Chinese tend to be more liberal in that sense."

The old customs and deference to males still shape intergenerational relationships, says Mandy, again reflecting the higher value placed on being male:

> When you're a daughter and you get married, you're considered a stranger in your own family. You're married off, you're no longer part of the family, you no longer have your own surname. All of a sudden the relationship between mother and daughter is totally different. I find it totally senseless. That happened to me and I was very, very angry. I said to my mom, "I'm your daughter, and I'll always be your daughter regardless of whether I'm a Wong or a Lowe or whatever: Stop treating me like this." When she'd come to my home she'd act like a stranger. It was useless, stupid. I said, "Why don't you just act like yourself as though this was your own home?" She said, "Well, this is not my home—it's your husband's home." So what?

More and more, Chinese Canadian women delay marriage and children until they fulfill their educational expectations and establish a career. As in the Blood, Inuit, and Iroquois cultures, women increasingly work outside the home to help support their families or to pursue their own initiatives. As with other groups, this tends to upset the balance established by patriarchal family arrangements: "Women are becoming more powerful. Even among my own family members the wife is more powerful than the husband," a middle-aged woman says with some surprise. Early signs of a shift toward equality and perhaps matriarchy are evident throughout the Chinese community. A social worker notices that "men don't bother with the minor details, and they think their wives can do everything. They let the wives do it, which gives the women more control."

Working women in their middle years often achieve a level of financial and professional security that allows them to establish equity in marriage, as Doris's story suggests:

"We'll see who's richer!"
We're kind of equal—not like before, when we didn't have a say in anything. I know many women who are really aggressive, and the hus-

band doesn't say much at home. They say the woman has the final word. I know many women who are more aggressive than before. It seems that they have all the say instead of their husbands. Now they are the breadwinner: "I bring in as much money as you do, so . . . ."

I make the decisions about the kids' education, because I was trained as a school teacher and I know better. He thinks he's superior about jobs, what kinds of careers the children should choose, et cetera. I'm very liberal. They're all at university level, so I say, "You study whatever subject you feel like studying; whatever field you go into is fine." My husband keeps on saying, "You have to go into economics or accounting." That's the field he was in, but my daughter wasn't cut out for that.

We have separate checking accounts. I look after the day-to-day things, such as going to the market. He looks after the mortgage, the electricity bills, heating bills, and so on. He pays for the children's tuition; I pay for the textbooks and clothing. We divide everything. I have control over the money I make. I never ask how much he makes or how much he has left, and he never asks about my salary. He likes to speculate in the stock market, and I'm the person who likes to play it safe, so I just put my savings in Canada savings bonds. We'll see who's richer!

Some women believe that men fear that if they once let their wives have a say in decision making, the men will lose power. Rose, a counselor who works with traditional families, tells them that "they can still make that final decision, but at least consider what their wife has to say because it represents how she feels. The whole thing is power." She observes the same pattern with children. Parents are reluctant to allow their children "any say in the family, because they feel that once kids start voicing their opinion, the parents will lose power." Rose tells parents that if they want their children to respect them, they will have to respect the children. This is a very hard concept for Chinese families to understand, "because everything is power oriented. There's a hierarchy: The in-laws on top, then the husband, then the wife, then the kids."

Among the newer immigrant families from the People's Republic of China, women see themselves as more equal with men. The majority of women have their own bank accounts. Men and women worked together in factories and on farms in mainland China and bring few stereotypes regarding work or educational opportunities with them to Canada, says Rose: "They see themselves as equal in that way, but when you come back into the family, there's that un-balance again." Couples discuss issues more and men give their wives "more leeway" than in previous generations, Lu-anne argues:

> The decisions are made between two people. Sometimes, when it has to do with things that she knows best, her husband will let her decide. Back then, even things that the woman knows best—like which pot to buy for the kitchen—he still had to have something to say. She still had to ask him, "Should I buy this pot? Is this the right one?" Of course, she had to ask for the money, too.

Now, if a woman puts her foot down, her husband will be more willing to relinquish his traditional hold on family authority: "You will be the one making the decision." Lu-anne thinks the reaction a woman receives depends on her attitude; a husband will more like-ly share power if the woman takes it. Before, she remembers, the man had to establish his own authority no matter what: "Even about buying a dress, which has nothing to do with him, he has to look at it. 'Should I buy it?' I still get some ladies like that at the store, older ladies. Every day. Younger ones, too! [They say,] 'I don't know, I don't know. I'll bring my husband in to look at it.'" Lu-anne and others of her generation feel that if a woman wants "to be a slave the rest of her life," she should think that way.

Love, Marriage, and Divorce: Commitment from Day One

Most women in traditional China married in their early or middle teens. Since the family was an economic unit historically, many women found themselves in marriages arranged when they were young children or even at birth. Although some couples met be-forehand, most met their grooms on their wedding night and grew to know each other after marriage. "A marriage is for your whole life, good or bad," which is why arranged or "blind" marriages sur-vived, remembers Yau, age seventy-two. The relationship begins from day one after the couple marries, she believes: "You just try to make it because the commitment has already started."

Men defined commitment broadly, however. The husband in tra-ditional Chinese culture could have more than one wife—which often was to the senior wife's liking, Yau recalls. Because co-wives or concubines helped distribute the weight of a woman's daily obligations (including sex), some of the older women said, "Look, I don't want to be bothered with you, go and get yourself another wife, don't bother me." If a woman did not want emotional or physical bonding with her husband, she could deflect him in this way. The first wife might even pay to have the second wife married into the home to ease her burdens and elevate her own status, Ping recalls:

> *"Having a mistress on the side . . ."*
> I heard my grandfather say that when he was a young man in China they had two, three, four wives, and in their eyes they were all legally married. It was all up front and socially acceptable; there was no disgrace. They all lived in the family compound—huge houses with many bedrooms around a courtyard. There would be a maid and butlers. Only the rich can afford that!
>
> The concubine was more than a mistress. She would have to come in and pay respect to the older wife, who sometimes was very kind to her. Sometimes, out of jealousy, the two would cause trouble. That's why there's a Chinese saying from my grandparent's generation. "If you want a day's trouble, put on a party. If you want a year's trouble, start to build a house. But if you want a lifetime's trouble, marry a second woman!"
>
> In my mother's time, it's different again. I heard my mother saying that her schoolmate's husband had another woman outside, so she was about to divorce him. In my mother's day it was more like having a mistress on the side, which is more like it is here, and it causes problems.

If the second wife was brought in to have a son, people might approve. But if the second wife produced one or two sons, and he still wanted a third wife as a status symbol to establish his wealth, "then it's not very nice in the eyes of relatives and friends." A man could divorce and remarry, but an unhappy wife could never divorce her husband. She could commit suicide, however, and hope that her miserable spirit would come back to haunt the husband and mother-in-law who upset her so.

Chinese men are not famous for being good communicators with women. Virtually all the women concurred that Chinese men guard their feelings. As a counselor says, "They'd rather shed blood than tears." Some women feel that inequality between the sexes throws up barriers to individual expression for both males and females, as a marriage counselor points out: "Sometimes men would like to show their feelings, really break down and have a good cry, but their status inhibits them from doing that." Of course, as with all gender inequities and imbalances, both males and females hurt. Men suffer from the expectation that they should hold their feelings in and be strong: "Sometimes that makes them feel very unhappy and upset, but they don't want to show it because of that role they're supposed to play." Women suffer behind the wall of silence.

Chinese women may also be slightly more reticent in expressing their feelings because they have been taught to hold their anger and disagreement in check. The more education you have, says a teacher, "the easier it is to express yourself and articulate your feelings, and to understand that there's nothing wrong with your emotions—you know, the Western influence. In the traditional way, you keep it to yourself or complain to a very close friend." Rather than say, "This is what I like and this is what I don't like," a Chinese woman would avoid direct confrontation and use facial expressions instead.

One counselor observes that although they avoid openly verbalizing feelings, some couples have solid, lasting marriages: "They never say 'I love you' and they never celebrate their marriage, anniversary, or birthdays, but they do have a good relationship." A quiet strength and deep respect flows between the best couples. Many men of the older generation are simply shy about their feelings: "They wouldn't kiss the wife in front of everybody. Their loving, tender side shows in private, so you think they're cold, but it's not true." Women are more openly affectionate with children, although men value their children and are attentive to them.

Spousal assault occurs when husbands and wives fail to communicate with each other. Showing feelings signifies weakness in a man, the counselor hypothesizes: "In that setting there's no communication in the home other than the basic 'Come and have dinner.' They don't really talk, misunderstanding breeds more misunderstanding, and pretty soon everybody gets frustrated and tempers flair." Says her colleague, Mandy: "Chinese families just don't see the importance of talking. When they finally do, it's out of anger,

and they start screaming at each other and nothing gets resolved."
Counselors tell husbands to realize that women have feelings. It is
difficult for these men to listen on an emotional level, having been
brought up in homes where their parents did not communicate
openly. Mandy adds that, as in most cultures, men do not come for
counseling as often as women do:

> That's frustrating, because you're not dealing with the problem. The
> husband has to do most of the changing. Of course, the wife has faults
> of her own that she needs to address, but the majority of the problem is
> with men. Some very traditional men feel that it's ridiculous for them
> to talk to a woman—especially having a woman tell them to respect
> their wives. That's the attitude. Often, if I know that a man is very tra-
> ditional, I will get a male staff member to talk to him. It's an uphill bat-
> tle all the way.

A guidance counselor sees some changes across generations: "I
think men are getting better. They're more emotional. I compare
teenage boys with men in their fifties, and I find them more in tune
with their emotions." The younger males are "not as stiff, not as
rigid in their ways."

Younger Chinese Canadian women still prize marriage, for the
most part, but on their terms. They will select their own mate and
many will delay marriage until they have achieved their highest educational dreams. Strong taboos against premarital sex prevail, accounting for very low rates of teenage pregnancy among Chinese
girls. Perhaps because of the historic significance of the father's
name being passed on to the son, it was and still is critical to ensure
paternity. Mandy believes that regardless of religion, Chinese girls
and young women understand from the "first day of teenage-hood
that we all have our moral standards." They should save sex for the
marriage bed, affirms Debby, who is twenty-one: "You see, Chinese
girls don't want to get that serious so soon. We've been brought up
with very strong moral values, and I think that reflects in our relationship with the opposite sex. Not many of my friends are going
out with guys. We always go out in a group. Safety in numbers, I
guess. It's understood."

Living together is not widely accepted, and in some cases it can
lead to being disowned. One woman notes that many parents will
say, "'Well, if you're on your own, okay, but don't come back to

us.' They don't recognize their own children as their daughters. It's a disgrace to have a daughter living with a guy without being married to him." Norms governing premarital intercourse and cohabitation are changing, but very slowly, Debby thinks: "Before, a woman cannot leave home and live with a man out of wedlock. You're considered to be a sinner or a great criminal or something. Nowadays, I hear about a few women living with men out of wedlock, so things are changing. The Chinese are taking it one step slower, but it's happening."

The trend toward grudging tolerance of premarital liaisons, delayed marriage, and divorce results in part from women's growing independence and self-sufficiency. The media also plays an important role in this transformation of long-held values, as Wendy suggests: "Many Chinese women think it's modern to do that; they think that it's the trend. At first it's the movie stars, the TV stars, who are doing it, and gradually all these fans, they're doing the same thing." Soap operas and sitcoms—the modern-day morality plays—depict a wider range of lifestyles than historically existed in the Chinese community, with its unyielding family imperative. These fictional lifestyles filter down into the daily lives of real women and girls.

Younger, university-educated women say they want more equality in their relationships with men; they expect their partners to contribute to child care and household chores. Some younger men "do a good job at home, cooking, vacuuming, everything, even dishwashing, because the wife is more domineering and more aggressive," says recently married Penny, who graduated with a degree in architecture. "Maybe the woman complained a lot; in order to avoid quarrels, he thought he'd better do it. My husband and I try to make the assumption that we share an equal responsibility. I shouldn't have to yell." The lives of the mothers provide lessons enough. A forty-five-year-old bookkeeper, Lana, describes her husband as a typical domineering male:

"The happy-go-lucky type . . ."
He doesn't do much. He'd never touch the babies, never change a diaper. They were wee little things, you know? When they could sit, sort of like a firm baby, then he would carry them. He enjoyed them, and in the evening he usually would take them out for walks, but I have to do

all the housekeeping work, cooking, everything. Right now I'm working Saturday, so I hired a woman to do the housecleaning for me. I prefer to do the cooking in the evening for the family. I try to make it as simple as possible.

What does he do to help me? We don't have a dryer at home, so he volunteers to take the big pieces of linen to the laundrette. He collects the garbage and puts it outside. He did the work of the chauffeur, driving the kids to their piano lessons and school when they were younger. Right now my boys are driving, so it's not necessary; the boys will take the girl with them.

He doesn't set the table while I'm cooking. Sometimes when the kids are free, they do it. I clean up after dinner. I do everything, even the ironing. Sometimes I get a little bored. Why should I have to do all that? I'm working outside the home, too, and I teach sewing on weekends, but in the course of life I'll take it easy. I take life as it comes. I'm the happy-go-lucky type. If I can't manage it, I say, "Okay, we'll just have a simple meal. Canned food and that's it." Usually by the time I get home it's six o'clock, and I start to do the cooking. If the children are good they have something prepared, have the rice rinsed or the vegetables cut up. If they're busy doing their essays for term end, I have to do everything. Tomorrow we're going to have a board meeting, and I won't be going home to cook, so he's going to buy takeout. Isn't that interesting? He wouldn't think of cooking: If I'm sick, takeout!

I don't have very much to complain about. As I said, I'm the happy-go-lucky type. One good thing about him, whatever food I make, he never complains.

Many parents insist that their daughters marry "a Chinese boy." Marrying a Caucasian is "a no-no," says Roberta, a nineteen-year-old whose parents do not care whom she marries as long as he is Chinese: "They keep saying, if you marry a Caucasian, don't come back." How does she feel about this restriction on her freedom of choice? "Right now it doesn't really matter. It's very hard to say, because if I fell in love with a Caucasian guy and my parents said no, I'd really be hurt and confused." Again, restrictions hit females differentially: "It would be worse if a Chinese woman marries a white man. Chinese like to pass on the heritage, and only a man could put their last name with the children."

Challenges Confronting Women

MARGINALITY, IDENTITY, AND EQUALITY

Chinese-ancestry women in Vancouver refer to themselves as Chinese Canadian, Canadian Chinese, Chinese living in Canada, and Canadians of Chinese background, depending on their time of immigration, level of assimilation, and degree of identification with the dominant culture. As Winnie, a business owner from Hong Kong, explains: "I'm grateful I can be here. I'm loyal to the country that has accepted me, and at the same time I don't want to lose my culture, my own roots. So I call myself a Chinese Canadian." Winnie is a classically marginal person who has not completely assimilated into Canadian culture:

> It's half and half, because I was born in China and I was brought up in a Western way, but I still have my Chinese tradition behind me. I say to myself, "You cannot mix and match. You have to accept the way it is now. Some way, somehow you have to compromise your position." You can't say, "Okay, I'm traditional and I'm just going to live the old way, like the old folks." We can't do that.

Chinese Canadian women talk about selecting the best parts of both cultures and attempting to strike a balance between traditional and modern values. Those who grew up in China or Hong Kong may see themselves more as Chinese because they are "products of the culture," still very closely connected to the homeland. Jade explains that nationality and race may not always overlap. Being Chinese is more identified with Eastern culture—China, Hong Kong, or Taiwan. Chinese Canadians born in Vancouver may have an identity problem because they feel Canadian ("Western") but look Chinese.

A subtle undercurrent of intimidation runs through their lives, says Faith: "In the beginning you feel off balance and suspect racism, but the people I've met in school and at work have been really great. Vancouver is a multicultural city with so many Chinese, people accept you the way you are." Determination intermingles with optimism. Amy enjoys being Chinese Canadian and feels lucky that she spent her first eighteen years in Hong Kong, where she learned about Chinese culture:

I can read, speak, and write Chinese fluently. I appreciate Chinese literature and art. When I came to Canada, I learned more about Western culture. Now I can enjoy the best of both worlds—good Chinese food and good Western food, good Chinese literature or English literature. I really like having the opportunity to explore both cultures.

A young medical student feels optimistic but suggests the tightrope she walks in trying to achieve balance:

We have two very respectable cultures. Canadian culture and Chinese culture make a very good mix. You learn how to be free-thinking as well as very controlled, very disciplined. Being Oriental is in, but you can't be too Oriental, because then you're stuck in those traditions that hold you back and you'll be envying women like Andrea Eng[33]—when you could have gone out and done the same thing. It's good to be an Oriental at this age.

A seamstress who was born in Hong Kong and came to Vancouver as a little girl finds herself "caught in two worlds." She was brought up in a very traditional Chinese home, with double standards for males and females ("I'm constantly aware of that"). She finds it helpful to recognize the balancing act she performs between Chinese and Western cultures. Reminiscent of an Inuit woman's "two big kids fighting inside her" all the time, Ethel, age forty, expresses the conflict within herself: "It's so difficult, because at times I think in terms of the traditional ways and at times I think in modern ways. Sometimes I have to struggle a little and ask, should I be following this route or should I be following that route?"

Chinese have their own patterns of life that are deep-rooted, according to Cathy, who is thirty-two: "The world is changing, but in a critical moment, will I give up the modern and follow the traditional way?" Says another woman in her thirties, "I'm very Chinese still; because I live in the Chinatown area, I can still speak the language. Some people in my office—who live in Burnaby instead of downtown, East End, or Chinatown—can't speak a word of Chinese and don't understand any of the customs. I'm caught in between being Chinese and yet Canadian." Women who live in the suburbs are more assimilated into the Canadian lifestyle "to the point of not even having their language anymore." Recently arrived immigrants hold more closely to the traditional lifestyle.

Being a "visible minority" female influences life chances. Historically, discrimination against Chinese women in Vancouver was rampant. Nursing schools, for example, refused to admit even Canadian-born Chinese women for many years, and women were restricted to waitressing or servant positions that often bordered on assumptions of their availability as prostitutes.[34] Nonetheless, Geschwender documents a clear success pattern among those who came to Canada in the 1960s and later, bearing testament to the fruits of their fierce determination: "Chinese Canadian husbands earn significantly less than their British-Canadian [Anglophone] counterparts. Chinese Canadian wives are still slightly better-educated, more active in the labor force, more likely to work full time, earn more, and their earnings constitute a higher proportion of the total family income."[35] This remarkable finding parallels the success of Jamaican women in Toronto, who have provided substantial support for their families in spite of racism, sexism, and discrimination.

Chinese Canadian women say they feel discrimination, but cannot tell whether it is because they are Chinese or because their English skills have not matured. Most feel that being a Chinese woman in Canada is "tough, especially when you deal with work relationships." Some sense discrimination because "people feel threatened" and blame the housing pressure and job shortage on the Hong Kong Chinese. A young business major has heard other women talk about discrimination, but has not felt it herself: "I haven't really gone out into the 'real world' yet. At university everyone is supposed to have an open mind. When I go out, it's usually to a Chinese restaurant or a movie, when almost everybody there is Chinese anyway."

Racial discrimination becomes confused with gender discrimination from both Caucasian and Chinese men, especially because women historically were defined as inferior to men. A university student majoring in social work explains her choice of major. She thought about going into law, but was told that it would be "really hard" to get business as a Chinese woman lawyer:

> First of all, Caucasians might not trust you. It doesn't matter whether you're a man or a woman, but because you're Chinese maybe you don't get the business. If you're a Chinese woman lawyer, it's even harder,

because the Chinese don't trust you—they don't trust women as much as men!

A pharmacy student explains that her parents prepared her for university by warning that she would have to work harder because she is Chinese and a female: "I would have to fight extra hard in order to get in, no matter what field—real estate, finance, or marketing. I would have to work harder than a man and be more assertive."

While parents now encourage their daughters to finish university, Abby (who is eighteen) says her parents warn her not to set her aspirations too high: "Don't go for doctor, lawyer, or engineer. Leave that for the guys, not for you. You have to be well educated, but not as good as the man, because it doesn't look good if you're bossy or if you go to the courthouse every day, or you work in the hospital twelve hours a day. It looks good if you can get a nice office job, so you can spend time at home with your kids." Not only are the male-dominated professions off-limits because they are seen as less feminine, her parents believe the old Chinese fear for their daughters: "You will never find a husband if you have too much education or (today) if you're too successful." If a wife's salary outstrips her husband's, "it looks funny." Abby adds, with a tinge of anger in her voice: "My brother is thinking about going into medicine. He has all the support. Everyone's saying, 'Study hard, don't worry about vacuuming or doing the housework.'" Regardless, Abby will pursue her goals. If she persists and does well in school, she says, her parents will come to accept her independence and achievement.

Similarly, the woman who works in an environment dominated by males—especially Chinese males—may find it hard to get her ideas across. According to a social worker, women are swimming against a centuries-old tide of male dominance in gender relations:

> It's in our upbringing: You're less important than your brother, Mom is less important than your father, grandmother is less important than grandfather. It's always female's less important than male, as simple as that. So of course you develop low self-esteem, because you see way back it's like that and it's all around you.

A silk merchant who runs a business owned by her father agrees that Chinese women face a double jeopardy in the work world:

"Not So Smooth as Silk . . ."

It's hard to say if people treat me differently because I'm a Chinese female or because I look young. People look at me and the first impression is, "You don't know what you're doing." When they get to know me better, then it's different. I went to a trade show in China for two years, so now people know I am the one to talk to, but the first time I went people didn't even think I existed. They thought I was just there with some man. Chinese in China are so used to dealing with middle-aged businessmen, to them it's funny—"I'm doing business with this young Chinese girl from Canada!"

As soon as I walked in, everyone looked at me. The attitude was immediate. I thought, am I welcome or not welcome here? Especially the Japanese do not accept the idea of a woman in business. I was making deals with people, and the Japanese talked behind my back: "What is that woman doing here? How come she's allowed into the trade shows?" They want to know why things are changing. It made me feel really strange. "Women should not have time for anything but doing housework and making babies and staying home, not outside running around to do business"—that's what they said! It didn't bother me at all. I feel proud.

Why should a woman have to stay at home? You have to try before you know whether you can do it or not. After the first time I dealt with those people, I had full confidence of being able to deal with them again; it's very easy after that. But they would be sure to pay the male-owned company first before the female-owned company. They'd be afraid of the male and think the female would not do anything—she can wait. The male can ask more than the female can, like special prices, special items. It's easier when they talk to each other. If you demand something from them and you're a female, like "I want you to pay this in thirty days," they will look at you and say, "No way." But if you're male, it's "Sure, okay, why not."

They have sales reps who take the orders. If you walk into a room in a silk fabrics department and a male walks in, they will ask him first if they can help him. They might think, "Oh she's here looking at the fabric because it's so pretty, or her husband is coming later." Men take advantage of businesswomen because we are young and female with a small company.

Cherry is a twenty-five-year-old travel agent for a Hong

Kong–based company that hires only Chinese men as managers, reflecting the gender bias that is embedded deep in British as well as Chinese culture. She elaborates:

> There is also the British influence. They still think women are inferior. You can see it in a meeting with head managers—they're all male. It's hard to get up the ladder being a female. There are more women than men in this office and in branches in other major world cities. More women go into the tourism industry. When I was in school, we had a choice of going into hospitality or tourism; in our tourism class of forty students, there were four guys. The women outnumbered the men incredibly, but all the managers are men.

In contrast, Cherry thinks that if she worked for a Canada-based company, being Chinese would be an asset; Chinese are reputed to be good workers, so being female would not be as much of a liability. Tess, a forty-seven-year-old employment agency worker, confirms that many employers seek out Chinese workers: "We don't have any seamstresses on hand. Everybody's working." Some employers are reluctant to hire young women because of the possibility of maternity leave, but factory managers try hard to find Chinese women. One manager protested when Tess could not send him a dozen workers: "When I told him of an organization that helps another minority group, he said, 'No, I prefer to hire Chinese women because they're hardworking.'" When she visited the factory, all the people in the production line were Chinese.

THE DOUBLE BURDEN

"The old Chinese don't like the way we go out to work," says a fifty-five-year-old grandmother who accompanied her daughter and grandchildren from Hong Kong. "They want to keep us at home, but now things are changing. Everything is so expensive, they don't mind. Before, if the wife goes out to work, it's no face!" Traditionally, a wife working outside the home would bring shame to her husband—indeed, to her whole family. It was hard for educated women to marry. "Your parents used to tell you, don't get educated, because you'll never find a husband," recalls a woman in her sixties.

Although most families are supported by males now, many Canadian-born Chinese men would be angry or puzzled if their wives wanted to stay home: "He needs her to help financially." Still, the majority prefer that their wives stay home and take care of the children. As in other cultures, when women do work outside the home, they generally make less than men and usually continue to take care of the home and children: "She's doing it all: home, domestic, and professional." This creates a double burden for women, as Faith explains:

> If the wife's job is really demanding, the man has to take up some of the responsibilities. He has to pick up the kids at four because he gets off then, whereas the woman comes home at seven and she still has to cook dinner. That's too tiring for her, so she asks the man to cook dinner—and at first the man is not too happy about it, but that's the way it is, so he has to do it. That creates problems, because the female is playing a dominant role and the man is doing all the supportive jobs. That's not the way it used to be.

As in the Blood culture, male friends might not accept a man taking care of children and home full-time: "He would be considered a very useless person. He has a wife to look after and a family to work for—why is he doing these household chores?"

Immigrant women may face a more difficult situation than Chinese women who were born and raised in Canada, according to Tess:

> It's very sad now, because with the economic situation in Canada, immigrants find it very difficult to find work. There aren't enough support services available to assist them with English training or job training. They find themselves in Chinatown in Chinese restaurants working for very little pay. Many male professionals lose their status, and that's very difficult for them; they're not able to retrain themselves to continue with their profession. They are unemployed, sitting at home looking after the kids, whereas their wives can work in restaurants and make a minimal living.

As in Inuit, Blood, or Iroquois communities, role reversal causes perplexing problems. Men feel frustrated by their lack of power and status, especially in a culture that has elevated males to such a clearly superior position. "He shows his frustration by scapegoating the wife," says an ESL teacher:

There's going to be hell. If the husband is considerate, he might lend a hand in the housework, look after the children, do his share in the home. Otherwise, he gets a bit cranky when the wife gets home: "This is not done. That is not ready. Food is no good." Keeps on complaining. Well, maybe that's out of frustration or out of pride. It causes divorce and battered women and chaotic situations.

Why would a professional woman from Hong Kong take a job that is beneath her training? Many immigrant women worked in lower-status jobs than their husbands held, which helps explain their willingness to work at any job in Vancouver. Furthermore, Tess theorizes, "to the man the job is the most important thing— that *is* his thing. To the woman, the job is not her thing; she can take any job. The family is her thing. She takes the job because the family would be better off, but the male thinks, 'My job is my job. If I'm a manager, I have to be a manager, I can't be a waiter!'" The "male ego" gets in the way; besides, "they wouldn't want to do housekeeping jobs. They don't know where to start. They've never done it before." Women who have recently immigrated and speak little or no English do not let these barriers stop them. They clean houses, work in factories and fisheries, work as chambermaids in hotels, and find other service or semiskilled jobs to keep the family afloat.

ROLE CONFLICT

Lee reflects on the challenges facing Chinese women: "Career and marriage. Career being because we still can't get as high. Marriage because it's a pressure, because Chinese parents expect you to marry early. You want to have your career as well as marriage." Most younger women will either delay marriage or work only part-time if they have children:

> My mom asked me what I would do. I told her she better stay close to me, so I can give the kids to her in the morning when I go to work. She said, "No way"—she wouldn't do that—so we came to the conclusion that I would have to quit work for at least ten years if I decide to have kids. I decided not to have kids and go for my career. I don't think there's a compromise. I might change my mind later if my partner would be able to take up part of the responsibility. I don't see how it could be done otherwise.

Lee's friend Anna agrees, but she recognizes also that it is difficult for a woman to return to work after taking time off for her family: "My sister graduated, then married and had to stay home. It's not as challenging as having a career. She wants to come out and work again, and she has to work doubly hard for it, updating and catching up."

Younger women try to find partners who will facilitate their balancing act between career and family. Cherry says that her husband would not prevent her from pursuing a career "because he's trying to be the modern supportive person." Yet, both he and her father would worry about her choices: "He'd say, 'Hmm, she didn't put me top on the list of priorities.' Being a good wife or girlfriend should come first." Cherry would insist on her right to set her own priorities—at least that's how she feels now, before the situation becomes more than hypothetical. Women whose mothers work outside the home are "not that old fashioned," although they still want their daughters to marry by thirty and express concern about the latter's morals.

The "modern thinking" Chinese Canadian woman in Vancouver faces an ironic situation, then, given these pressures and the dictates of tradition: She is expected to go out and work to help support her family's aspirations for upward mobility in Canadian society—but she cannot easily afford the nanny or the servant, nor does her value system include having her in-laws at home. She slips into the classic North American "superwoman" syndrome of being a full-time employee outside the home and a full-time domestic worker in the home. Many are not getting very much support with either household chores or child care from their husbands: "With young kids around and the baby-sitting fee so high, it's very difficult for women."

Some women disagree with the women's liberation movement because it has only released women into the labor force to supplement the family income: "We're just creating more responsibility for ourselves, because we have to take on the responsibility of a man as breadwinner—or part-time breadwinner—yet we have to keep the responsibility of household chores, child raising, and so on." The dilemma turns on the fact that women's role has expanded into the public sphere without parallel expansion of the man's role into the domestic sphere, as Cherry says: "He just goes to work and comes home. We call him 'the new man' if he does a little bit of diaper changing. I have a friend whose husband does the cooking while she goes shopping. Sometimes they reverse it; he cooks and she shops. Of course, they're young, in their early thirties."

Lena says the woman's expanded role puts more strain on the relationship. She feels angry and makes demands, while he "is still thinking like fifty years ago and says, 'Stay in your place, don't talk like that, and don't make demands.'" She refuses and asserts her rights, which he finds offensive. Alienation, separation, and divorce ensue: "Men are not adapting very well to the expansion of the woman's role, and the women are very tired," sighs Lana. Modernity clearly has its price.

Chinese women in Vancouver face a lack of adequate day care facilities, especially if they prefer a Chinese-speaking center. Those that exist are very expensive. Only women with a middle-class income can afford this luxury, reports a woman who is on the board of the Vancouver Society on Immigrant Women: "That's why we are always fighting for subsidized daycare for lower-income people. We need a day care center for young children in the factory area—say, around the garment factories near Chinatown—so women could leave the children off and go to work."

In China, many families could afford to have a nanny or servants who lived in the family home with many generations. This live-in role (utilized frequently also by the Mennonites) gave women an opportunity to live in a protected environment, earn their room and board, and learn important skills. For those who remained single, this was an acceptable lifelong role. For those without servants, the extended family assured that there would be child care: When the mother was sick, the grandparent would be able to take care of the children. Typically women of each generation had their own specialized sphere of duties—perhaps the garden (a senior position) for the grandmother and the kitchen for the mother/wife.

Today many women view living with nannies, servants, in-laws, and parents negatively, but considerable stability existed in these arrangements that actually may have lightened each woman's burden. Although housekeeping and cooking took more time without modern machines and technology, these social arrangements helped support the woman in handling her work. Communal organization of responsibilities was also less isolating. The downside of this ancient tradition is that it also created a history of male domination and female submission that persists into modern times.

Now, younger women think of staying home with their babies for a short period but returning to work as soon as possible, as Amy explains:

> My friend had a baby and stayed home for four months. She was thinking of a year, but she couldn't handle it. She's back to work now. I think his mom stays home during the day, but as soon as she's finished with her job, then she's a full-time mother and full-time worker. Many women stay home; there's nothing wrong with that. Maybe after I have the baby, I would change my mind—maybe I would say, "Oh, I want to stay home all the time and do everything for him or her." Right now I think I would want to come back to work.

Another woman agrees that going back to work would be ideal (especially if she did not want to jeopardize her career path), but she fears the consequences: "You see so many Caucasian kids with working mothers, most of them from broken homes and not very well adjusted. I'd try to do half and half—work part-time and stay home with the kids half the time—in order to avoid the problems." For some women of the younger generation, especially in immigrant families living under the same roof, "The old fogies look after the little ones so the couple can go out to work and the family will have two incomes," a counselor, Irene, says affectionately. In this case, the traditional family structure can be supportive in expanding women's professional opportunities. Although this can lead to family conflict if the mother-in-law becomes too "bossy," younger women are often able to set limits on the older woman's authority, Irene says: "My husband's mother has learned that if she tries to be traditional and step her feet into our family, she's not going to get anywhere. My husband believes that the family is him and myself and our children, and his mother has no say. That's really important." In some of the families Irene works with, though, the husband sides with his family, so the wife has to be submissive not only to the husband but to his parents as well. He demands it.

Toward the Twenty-First Century

THE ROAD TO EQUALITY

Chinese women in Canada seek power with balance. University-educated professional women feel liberated and say that being a feminist means "women fighting for their own rights," but few women in this community have been involved in any way in the women's liberation movement. Most insist that they are not feminists. Says one, reflecting the voice of many: "I'm not particularly against it, but I really don't understand much about it so I don't want to make a comment." Chinese women in Canada are not oppressed, they believe, "although in China there's more to be done." While they agree that traditional Chinese culture oppressed and restricted women, perhaps liberation is too strong a word to describe the changes that are occurring now: "If you give them the knowledge and let them go at their own pace," they suggest, women will find their own way to equality.

Chinese-ancestry women understand that their culture can empower them or restrict them. The younger generation is divided on how well it will pass on traditional ways. Some will preserve them; others will discard them as they discover how closely linked the cultural values are to the subordination of women. Says Debby, "If I have children, I would try to combine the best of the old Chinese values with the Western ones. I believe in family unity and stricter discipline than I see in Western culture. It's easier to teach children if you have strict discipline when they're young." They consider keeping the Chinese language and respect for parents: "It depends how much Chinese culture the parents have," Faith observes. "If we don't get much, then maybe things will be the Canadian way, which doesn't stress the difference between the boys and the girls."

To the extent that younger women move away from tradition, conflict can occur within a couple and between parents and children. "You have to understand the culture in order to understand why families interact in certain ways," says Cathy. For example, Chinese place a high premium on saving face. Everything has to be done in the most proper and efficient way possible, "so that you show everyone that you've accomplished something and that you're worthy." Marrying across races also means marrying across cultures, where some of these assumptions may not be shared. In addition, says Irene, couples wait a long time before seeking marital counseling because they do not want to admit they have problems caused by deep cultural differences: "There are certain expectations of a wife and certain expectations of a husband, and when there is a problem people are going to analyze it for you. Then there is that feeling of guilt and low self-image." Intergenerational conflicts are exacerbated when young women move too far from the traditional ways—striving for independence may alienate them from their parents.

In terms of discrimination, Chinese Canadian women agree that the wider Canadian society and the Chinese community are beginning to comprehend the devastating effects of both sexism and racism. Are things changing fast enough? The answer is not a simple one. One woman hints at the glass ceiling, saying that she is an editor, "certainly not a publisher." Another says, "I've had women tell me, 'Well, gee, we have a city councilor who's a woman, we have women lawyers, we have a composer and many musicians.'" Will more and more Chinese women reach the top of their professions, or are these just rare stars who have crashed through the barriers? "I'm willing to go all the way to the top, but you have to work very hard and be aggressive and assertive," Cathy responds.

Gains have been made in ethnic identity as well. Chinese women say their self-esteem is improving compared to white women: "Now it's almost pretty equal. It used to be that we would shrink back, but I think we're more brave because there are more of us now." Most see changes in the "new generation" of Chinese Canadian children, but believe their doubly subordinate ethnic and gender position will persist for some time. Women feel more impatient and angry about their lower status compared to men: "Even the older generation expresses it at female get-togethers. They're not rebelling, they're just complaining." Older women were taught to accept male dominance, but the lesson is beginning to wear thin. Although Canada offers protection against pay discrimination— "You can always take the case to the Board of Human Rights and complain about it"—some women do not appeal. "They accept it the way it is."

As one woman observes, though, the divorce rates are climbing. She says this indicates that Chinese women of all ages are insisting on equal treatment from men. Most women agree that inequality throws up barriers to individual freedom of choice for both males and females. The woman's life is more difficult because "women have more responsibilities than a man, and they are quite restricted in different areas—they have less power." Amy believes that men of her generation may be able to see "the other side of what a woman is facing. It makes a man's life fuller to understand more, as a human being, about what is expected of us."

A cultural center worker says that when they immigrate from the People's Republic of China to Canada, women begin to see that Western society treats women as equals. They can assert their rights more, even in the family, even if it upsets their husbands. Many men do not want their wives to go to English classes, ESL teacher Sylvia explains:

> It's a very small thing, but it causes a lot of problems in the family because he feels that if she starts to learn English, then she's going to learn more about the Canadian system and her rights and responsibilities. She's going to make friends, and there's more chances that she's going to get into the wrong crowd; they might influence her to rebel against her family and husband. Men are very controlling in that sense, because they don't want their wives to learn the Western way. They think that in Western society women do their own thing, are assertive, and rebel.

Chinese women need to be in touch with their rights, Jade argues, delineating what she defines as the bare minimum of liberation: "I'm not a feminist, but I feel that women should have a place in the home, that they should have a say, and that husbands should respect their wives as human beings with feelings."

Would Chinese women say they are oppressed? "They wouldn't say anything, because Chinese women *are* oppressed," retorts a homemaker: "Out of all my friends, there are three who would say something about that, but the others just shrink back and absorb it. They don't even realize they are being oppressed. Until the day they realize it, things won't change. It's not major today, compared to the past in China, though." A nineteen-year-old university student who is studying biology has a slightly different view. Her friends like women's liberation, at least in a limited version: "We're given equal opportunities and our parents push education, but that's as far as it goes. We want equal opportunity in the workplace because we all want to make money. We all want a job."

Other young women insist that liberation covers more than equal opportunities, as Debby argues: "Most of the responsibilities in the home are thrown upon the women. I only have to look at my mother. She works and she has to clean the house, do everything. If she doesn't clean the house, she has to hire a housekeeper, whom she pays. *She* pays, not my father, because she didn't do the house-work. You see?" She finds no reason to debate women's liberation and feminism:

> It should just be naturally assumed that there is equality. The day we dispense with all this terminology, it will be achieved. I heard Gloria Steinem say that will take eighty years. I guess I'm a bit of a black sheep in the group, when it comes to traditions. I don't believe in them. Morally, I think we all set our own standards, whether you are Chinese or Caucasian or any other nationality or race or religion. We all have what we think is right or wrong.

Young women buy into the notion that equality should be more broadly defined and include a restructuring of the male-female relationship. Males her age have not made the same shift, says Susie, but she is determined to change things:

"I have so-called feminist views . . ."
The turning point for me occurred when I was fourteen. I went to Hong Kong for a summer and saw the way my grandmother was treated by my grandfather: When he called, she came! She never had any financial security of her own. She came into the marriage a wealthy woman, but her money was automatically transferred to my grandfather. I saw this, and the way she was summoned. I just couldn't stand it. I saw my grand-mother weak and powerless. When I talked to her about it, she said, "Ooh, that's the way it is," and told me to be the same way.

My grandmother came in to talk to me one night with a worried look on her face and said, "You should always listen." She didn't say to whom, but I understood what she meant: Always listen to the superior one—brother, father, husband. Now in the family, I'm known as the person with wild thinking. The entire family thinks I have so-called feminist views. I don't think they're feminist; I just think they're normal—we're all equal. They think I'm a bit strange. My friends think I'm a very assertive person.

Another avowed feminist is Alexina, according to a cultural worker: "You should talk to her. She says she's not going to get married. She's going to have a career as a technical writer, she's going to make it big. She'll own a BMW, a beautiful condo, designer clothing. She's talking big. Wait till she's thirty and find out what's happened to her. She's still young, she's just twenty-one, and she thinks that life is full of roses and candies. I don't know."

Is Amy liberated? She says, "I think so. I prepare the dinners every evening, I do all the household chores, and so on, but I am free to say whatever I want to say. If we had a social gathering, once upon a time, women were just there—women and children were to be seen, not heard. Nowadays you can say whatever you want. You can be the star of the evening and talk your head off." She depicts her grandmother's generation as oppressed, although women had their own sphere of influence: "They have all the power at home because the men are seldom there, except in the evening; she's got a whole day to exercise her power over everybody in the house." Amy, though, would like some power outside the house as well.

WOMEN'S EMPOWERMENT

Increasingly, Chinese women see themselves as strong, competent, and self-sufficient. These feelings of personal empowerment are slowly surfacing. Women delay marriage and children until they have fulfilled their educational expectations and have established a career, but Mandy believes that limits to female power mean that true equality will be long in coming:

Chinese Canadian women are working their way up, trying to be on more of an equal level with men, but it will never be equal, whatever the nationality. It's difficult for women to be exactly equal with men. When you get up into high administrative positions, men will try their best to put you down because of their fears—there is still that stigma that men do not want to be overrun by women or be inferior to women. They believe the man is superior. Now that we are working our way up, they *have* to accept it to a certain extent, but they don't want to accept it fully—they'll get together and try to make you stay in your place.

It's difficult for men to accept it if the husband is lower than the wife. It's a loss of prestige or status because his wife is a professional and makes more money. That's why it will take a long time.

Anger with the ages-old imbalance of power is sublimated in conversations with friends, Mandy admits: "The more Western influence you get, the more apt you are to be frustrated and feel the inequality. It you don't have the Western influence, you accept whatever has been taught to you." Or, she says, women "try to go out into the men's world and prove they can do it." Younger women may have a greater chance of succeeding with the gangbusters approach at the expense of harmonious relations. Nora, a twenty-three-year-old office manager, describes conflict at home: "My mother just wants me to get married and be a good wife." She also mentions the simmering battle between the sexes at work:

> Whenever we see an article about equality or women being superior to men, we put it on the bulletin board. The males come around and rip it off and start arguments about it. We just do it for fun, but people really get caught up in it, and sometimes the discussion can get quite heated. A professor from the States wrote an article saying that women are superior to men. He said it was genetic and he talked about their work habits. That created discussion for almost a week!

Nora says that many women imagine what they could accomplish if things were different. Younger women are trying to burst through the barriers of racism and sexism—a formidable challenge, says Jo, a nineteen-year-old struggling through her first year of engineering studies:

> *"A woman is worth something . . ."*
> I want to show my family that a Chinese woman is worth every bit as much as a Caucasian woman, and every bit as good as a man. I want to show my grandmother, if she lives long enough, that I can succeed, that she could have done this, too—that a woman is not there to come running when her husband summons her. I want her to see that a woman is worth something, and is more than someone to bear children. She bore ten children . . . she has to know!

Right now I don't think she wants to see it. She dismisses me as a bit wacky. I wouldn't do this otherwise. I think half my determination came from this. I will be very disappointed if I don't succeed. I will be known forever as the wacky one of the family. Even the women in my family think I'm wacky, but it's worth trying to prove something.

DREAMS FOR THEIR DAUGHTERS

Women from Hong Kong who are struggling through their English classes have high aspirations for their daughters. How far do they want them to go in school? "As far as they can get" is the common answer. Historically, many Chinese daughters never learned to read and write: "Only the son was very important in the family. Now the thinking is that the girl and boy are the same." One thirty-five-year-old mother proudly announces: "When my daughter is only two and a half, I send her to school, and I plan for university for her already. I think the time has changed!" Her emphasis on education echoes in the words of Rosalyn, a forty-four-year-old whose three daughters are about to enter university: "I want them to be successful in the future, get into a career they really like, and, of course, be happily married."

Young Canadian-born Chinese women want their daughters to be bilingual and will start them on Chinese lessons at a tender age. They also have dreams of self-confidence and high self-esteem for their daughters. Says Cathy:

> I will be very careful with them in their childhood, because I strongly believe the first three to five years develop their personality, their temperament. Sure, peer pressure comes into it later, but the basics are there. Maybe with that foundation they will be able to communicate better. I want my children to be able to come to me with any type of problem.

Amy wants her daughter to "know about herself, to know about God, and if she wants a very high education, she will have it and all the things she wants to achieve in her life." Debby adds, "I just want her to grow up to be responsible. I never thought about whether I want her to be a traditional Chinese woman or adopt Western values. I think I want her to have the best of the two cultures, not to be overly one or the other."

Faith wants her daughter to have an "exciting, meaningful life, doing things that she thinks are worth fighting for; and if she doesn't get support from other people, she'll be able to get support from me, provided her motives are correct." All agree that following the traditional ways will be open to their daughter's creative interpretation. Most of all, they want their daughters to go as far as they can in school and to believe in gender equality, as a nurse in her thirties insists: "I would try to teach her from the time she is young that males and females are equal—although in terms of biological makeup they are different, and they carry different responsibilities and functions—in their approach to life, dealing with other people, and getting an education. We all start on an equal basis, and it's up to the individual to compete and make her way up and into life." This, of course, entails teaching sons to respect women as their equals.

Most insist that their expectations for their daughters parallel those for their sons. Lana, who describes herself as "very liberal," will treat her children the same, regardless of gender:

> I'm still a very traditional Chinese woman. As a Catholic, I want them to be legally and properly married. It doesn't matter whether it's a boy or girl, they should have respect for this. I know many Chinese parents want their children to marry Chinese only. I don't care whether they marry a Chinese, as long as they're happily married. It's their life.

Perhaps Nora, who sees herself moving up from office manager to a company director someday, epitomizes these dreams when she says that she wants to be successful not for the sake of making money, but to earn rewards that are congruent with her individual talents. Like many younger Chinese and Chinese Canadian women, Nora rejects the cultural cloth that bound their grandmothers into a life of pain and subservience. She wants to grow as a person, to be respected, and to keep in touch with the parts of her Chinese heritage that seem beautiful—the food, the clothing, the music and art. Nora, like other Chinese Canadian women, want to freely wander far beyond the garden.

On Galiano Island

A hot day means a blurry crossing to Sturdies Bay from the mainland ferry town of Tswassen. I am staying in a simple log cabin over-

looking firs, arbutus, and the mountain ridge along the back of Vancouver Island, all veiled in a steamy blue haze. I am writing field notes from my interviews with Chinese ancestry women in Vancouver. Wild flowers advance from the wood's edge toward the back door: poppies, sweet peas, clover, daisies, and many others.

I walk along the main road to North Galiano and swim alone in the icy inlet. I walk the beach, chilled but exhilarated by the quiet and chaotic beauty created by the collision of mountains and sea. Slipping on the kelp and seaweed, I struggle to find a footing among the stones and bleached logs and great hunks of driftwood. I write a poem about barnacles—"Stone Roses"—that deals with the fragility of life and love. Gulls, an occasional sea plane, and one solitary hawk circling in the thermals high above the craggy shoreline are my only companions. I like being alone. Suddenly I feel that the rocks and trees and birds know that I am here. I think about the Chinese women who are trying to find their footing in a new world that collides in so many ways with their ancient culture.

Captain Galiano, a great Spanish adventurer, must have surprised himself when he discovered this island paradise. How quiet and lovely it must have been then, a century and a half ago, untouched, unspoiled. The handful of Indians who lived here then must have had free run of the island and loved it. Now they huddle at the northern tip of the island on a "reserve." Boundaries again.

The T-shirts in the store say "Northern Galiano—Confiamos in Nostromos," meaning confidence in ourselves. We rely on ourselves. Do we? I wonder how women can find their path as separate human beings and develop confidence without discarding family and culture along the way. Confiamos. . . .

8

Three Corners of the House

Ukrainian Women of Saskatoon, Saskatchewan

Remember, our Ukrainian culture is about four thousand years old, the last thousand being Christian. Prior to that it was a matriarchal society. The concept of Mother Earth is very strong, rooted in the pre-Christian tradition. Most husbands today, if they know which side the bread's buttered on, they'll acknowledge it.

—Anna

En Route to Saskatoon

As I drive north from the Blood Reserve after a second round of interviews, a raging fever suddenly grips me. My vision blurs and I can't stay awake, although it is broad daylight. I stop to call my brother Robert in Calgary and wait for him to take a three-hour bus ride to drive me back to his home. For three days I slip in and out of delirium, coughing, aching, and shaking. The emergency room doctor says it's the worst case of flu he has ever seen. Comforting. I reluctantly delay the flight to Saskatoon and rest at my brother's, worrying about lost time.

Weak and wobbly, three days later I drag myself to the airport for the short flight to Regina, then to Saskatoon. At Regina my luggage never makes it off the plane. As the jet taxis down the runway toward Winnipeg I beg the agents to rescue my bags, mumbling through the weakness about tape recorders and field notes, cameras and contact names. Much to my amazement they radio the control tower, and the plane returns to the gate. The agents remove every

303

piece of luggage bound for Winnipeg and find my bags deep in the cargo bay. I am grateful for this professional kindness, since I have barely enough time now to complete the Ukrainian interviews.

As we fly over this bountiful prairie province, part of the bread-basket of the Great Plains, I watch the quilt-work farmlands spread out below as far as the eye can see. Different shades of green and gold suggest different crops: wheat, barley, rye, canola, soy, oats, al-falfa, and hay. It is flat, but as we near Saskatoon I notice the Saskatchewan River pressing its way across the prairielands, winding and twisting through some of the most productive soil in the world. Clumps of trees shelter farmhouses, serving as windbreaks against the ferocious "Alberta clipper" and other winter storms that sweep across the fields. More trees, more houses, and then suddenly a small city emerges beneath us: Saskatoon.

After a night in the luxurious old Canadian Pacific Railway hotel along the river in downtown (where I sleep for twenty hours straight fighting off the end of the virus), I make my way to Anna's home at the city's edge. I pass three Ukrainian churches, a Ukrainian school, a Ukrainian museum and cultural center, several Ukrainian specialty shops, a Ukrainian bookstore, and even a Ukrainian hot dog stand. The small city is quiet, with modest houses and tree-lined streets. The suburbs are more open, edging on the prairie and boasting larger lots.

Anna has offered to be my guide and to let me stay with her family. I awaken the next morning refreshed and ready to immerse myself in the Ukrainian community. Anna invites me into her garden, a quarter of an acre filled with luscious raspberries, green peas, squash, lettuce, and tomatoes. While she makes a welcome cup of coffee, I move swiftly along the raspberry bushes, plucking the ripest and largest for our breakfast. Later in the week we will make raspberry jam together.

Anna offers a crash course in Ukrainian cultural history from her living room. Her knowledge is overwhelming: She brings out books, papers, and photographs, and she points out proudly that it was a woman, Ol'ha, who was the most famous of all rulers in the old country. Her collection of Ukrainian art—all by women—could almost fill a small gallery. Paintings and braided bread, embroideries and tapestries grace virtually every wall in the house.

But it is the hand-painted Ukrainian Easter eggs (pysanky), each one unique and brilliantly executed, that symbolize most perfectly the colorful beauty of this culture. Anna gestures toward a large crystal punch bowl full of delicate eggs and invites me to choose one for my own collection. I select a geometric pattern in black, rust, and burnt orange, artfully designed and perfectly painted. The egg—symbol of life, symbol of woman, symbol of birth and renewal—sits next to me now as I write these memories.

P rincess Ol'ha walks slowly away from her husband's grave. Now she will be Queen of Rus, the ancient Ukraine—first widow of the kingdom. She weeps quietly for Prince Ihor, her beloved husband, who had tried valiantly but unsuccessfully to ward off an aggressive tribe of Derevlianians. There must be a better way than the slaughter and finality of combat, she muses to her grandson, Volodymyr. Rather than mount yet another war party, she vows to wage a woman's war of diplomacy to bring about peace and friendship between the two realms and to institute Christianity in Ukraine.

For the next fifteen years, from A.D. 945 to 960, Ol'ha rules with compassion and dignity, pressing for peace and the spiritual renewal of her troubled people. She succeeds on both counts, becoming the first Ukrainian ruler to accept Christianity. Chroniclers of the time describe her as the "wisest of all people," and women write songs for minstrels to sing in celebration of her bloodless victories.

Ol'ha died in 969 and was canonized into sainthood in the thirteenth century by the Ukrainian Orthodox Church.[1] Contemporary Ukrainian Canadian women in Saskatoon, Saskatchewan—a large enclave of Ukrainians transplanted from Europe since the end of the nineteenth century—still speak knowledgeably about the queen who proved to Ukrainian women that they could provide significant leadership for their people.[2] Her example has not been lost.

Women describe a period at the pinnacle of Ukrainian history when a matriarchal social system left its mark on the character of women and of family life. To this day, the stylized designs handed down for centuries for *pysanky* (painted Easter eggs) include a group known as "matriarchal": *Bohynja-Berehynja*, named after the Grand Goddess who appeared in the fifth and sixth centuries A.D., *Koroleva* (Queen), and *Knjahynja* (Princess). During the dynasty of kings, women were highly respected and powerful.[3] The *Koroleva* design depicts the greatest qualities of womanhood: "Queen is a symbol of the Earth Mother in all her splendor, arms raised in the act of creation, crowned . . . fertility, motherhood, warmth, wisdom and goodness."[4] From the ninth through the fourteenth centuries, Ukrainian women retained their father's surname and took part in receiving ambassadors and diplomats. Even after the fall of Kiev in 1240, women retained their right to own property and money, despite subsequent Tartar invasions and cataclysmic political changes throughout Eastern Europe. They could also sue, testify in court, administer local areas, and go to battle.[5]

> The upper Ukrainian classes as well as the common Cossacks led a warlike existence defending the frontiers against foreign invasion. Women were often obliged to follow their husbands in their expeditions, even to partake in the battles. Fighting at the side of the men for the defense of their country, the Ukrainian woman of this time displayed great energy and great strength of character. . . . [Women] took part in the political life, in the seatings of the Diets, and public assemblies.[6]

A Ukrainian Orthodox minister describes women as "prime movers":

> We were—I should bite my tongue; if my father heard me!—a matriarchal society, by and large. The first Ukrainian women's school was built in the year 1087. Women had the right to own property, and they had a voice in the legislative function of towns and villages. Later, in the fifteenth, sixteenth, and seventeenth centuries, when Ukraine was under the sphere of Lithuania and Poland, we had very powerful women who were members of brotherhoods—women who established the Foundation of Churches, Schools, and Monasteries.

A shadow passed over this ancient Ukrainian culture when the nation fell under political and social oppression. By the end of the eighteenth century Ukrainian lands had been incorporated into the Russian empire, and serfdom was reintroduced by Catherine II. Until 1861, Ukrainian peasant women fell subject to the highest mortality rates in Europe. Feudalism meant a miserable life for both women and men.

During the nineteenth century, Ukrainian women living under the thumb of Russia worked actively in the fight for Ukrainian nationalism, sometimes hiding pistols in their elaborate hairdos or inflammatory literature in baby cribs.[7] Women in towns and villages created extensive networks of activist organizations to establish libraries, day care centers, orphanages, summer camps, literacy programs, and food kitchens, and to sponsor concerts and plays. They worked not for women's rights (since "women were not only accepted as equals in these groups, but also elected officers") but to eliminate the subjugation of all Ukrainians.[8]

At the turn of the century, many of these women came to Canada, where their activism and courage created the context of womanhood for generations to come. The legacy of matriarchy and women's rights has followed them from the "old country" to their new homeland. Says Michaelina, who is eighty-two: "The woman holds three corners of the household." Traditionally, the man's power was coupled with his responsibility for protecting the family and ensuring the farm's prosperity. As Michaelina explains, however, "He comes home, everything is done. The garden is nicely hoed, bread is baked, animals are looked after. He wasn't the only one who had a say." For contemporary Ukrainian Canadian women, the context has changed to an urban environment, but the balance of power remains much the same.

Out of Tradition

JOURNEY TO CANADA: THE PIONEER YEARS

They came from the Austrian crownlands of Galicia and Bukovyna, counties such as Drobromyl, Tsishaniv, Vashkivtski, Zalishchyky, Sniatyn, and Sokal, usually from small villages sprinkled across the countryside.[9] Political oppression and relentless poverty caused by land shortages pushed families to seek a new life elsewhere; recruiters made Canada sound like the proverbial promised land, with streets paved with gold and plenty of land for everyone.[10]

Starting in 1891 thousands of peasants boarded the small ships that brought them to Canadian shores. The first wave (1891–1914) numbered more than 140,000. Most of these early pioneer men farmed,[11] but a few became blacksmiths or wheelwrights; some, like the Chinese men before them, helped build the vast network of railroads that connected the country during Canada's developmental phase. The second wave (1925–1930) of 68,000 hopeful immigrants gravitated toward urban centers. These two waves emanated from Galicia (Halychyna) in the Western Ukraine, which was under Austro-Hungarian rule. During the third wave, the flow came from Eastern Ukraine via the displaced-persons camps in Western Europe after World War II. Numbering more than 38,000, this group also flocked to urban areas.[12] Ukrainians in Canada assimilated more rapidly than any immigrant group, but those who came to Saskatchewan's open spaces spent at least a generation struggling on the land. This chapter focuses on women and descendants of the first two waves, especially those who began their lives in Canada as pioneers.

In the Western Ukraine, the native language was heavily influenced by German or Polish, reflecting the nearness of continental Europe; in Eastern Ukraine, the influence came from Russia. Because of the distinct nature of each immigration wave, women point out that Ukrainian communities in Canada vary greatly in their political and religious orientations. For example, members of the large third-wave Ukrainian community in Hamilton, Ontario, may hold different views compared to those of Ukrainian descent in Saskatchewan, who are third- and fourth-generation Canadians. In the struggle to establish their own independent church and resolve conflicts with the Catholic bishops, many congregations returned to the original Ukrainian Orthodox Church: "This is why we have the Ukrainian Independent and the Ukrainian Greek Orthodox Church in Canada. It was a revolt of the Ukrainian Catholic settlement going back to the original Ukrainian church."

Women of the older generation were born in Canada to first- and second-wave pioneers in places like Krydor, Hoodoo, Fish Creek, Brooksby-Enderby, Gronlid, Meacham, Melfort, Pelly, Match Lake, Swan Plain, Hubbard, Hudson Bay, Cudworth, and Canora, small rural villages that encircle Saskatoon and Yorkton, 30, 40, even 100 miles into the prairielands.[13] Most traveled to Canada with family members and friends, often from the same village.[14] In typical chain migration fashion, Mariia's grandfather entered Canada in 1914, just before World War I. He sent for his wife, son, and brother in 1922, having worked for eight years to earn money for their passage. As a child Martha, now sixty-six, heard stories about how her mother came from Ukraine "like a mail order bride," making the long ocean journey in 1928 to a strange land and a new husband. She worked, saved, and paid for her relatives to join her: "Our people came to this country for the freedom. You're looking at a group of people who came out of oppression."

Vladimir was not quite five years old when he first arrived in Canada early in the century, but he remembers how everything looked: "It was completely wild country. No road, no highways, no cars. Even no horses, just oxen." When the pioneers worked outdoors, they were surrounded by noisy clouds of mosquitoes that annoyed the ears and pierced the skin. People fanned the air with branches to keep the persistent insects away from their faces: "There was so much mosquitoes, they were just eating your eyes out. Everybody made a little smudge in a can. You couldn't go no place without smudge." Families planted themselves a few miles apart in the prairie brush, trying to establish a life against the odds, Vladimir recalls:

> Until 1906 nobody could raise any wheat. Short summer and the frost come in too soon. In 1918, we moved to a level place. My friend had to cut my wheat for feed, because the blossoms were all frozen in July. I walked a few miles west to St. Julian to see a pretty new lot with little hillies. I see the wells frozen completely. Worth nothing.

Some recruiters in Europe indicated that prosperity awaited all those who were willing to make the journey to North America: "The streets-were-paved-with-gold syndrome," Vladimir jokes. Ukrainians were "strange to the Anglo-Saxons," recalls Wasyl, who is eighty-two. "Nobody knew who we were. Strange language. More strange clothing. It took two generations at least to feel at home in Canada. No assistance of any kind. People come now, they have welfare; then, you were on your own. You were dumped on some acres and you looked out for yourself. No implements, no animals. We were survivors; we worked hard to prove that we could do it."

Mykhailo, born in 1906, came to Saskatchewan in 1928 through a labor organization that recruited him from a small Ukrainian village. ("Canada needs so many young workers.") He gave the agent three hundred dollars for his passage via ship to Quebec and train to Alberta, only to find a vast, undeveloped prairie and a little itinerant work that did not even cover the cost of work clothes:

"We had to survive . . ."

After all those miles, there was nothing there. The fellow that was guiding us left us on our own at a "town" that was just a grain elevator and a post office. All of a sudden we have to go for work, but there was no place to go. So we turn around and come to the post office and said, "Where's the work that the agent said there's gonna be?" And he says, "There's no work here. There's nothing we can do." We didn't know what to do, so we bought some bologna and bread and sat down. There were even gophers running around.

At last a bachelor guy came by and said we could come with him, but first we had to buy some coveralls, work shirts, and gloves. The fellow took us out to his farm and put us in a shack overnight. In the morning he'd come to give us cereal, bread, and milk. There was no table or anything. He just wanted us to cut a little surrounding bush to open up the land more. When we finished three days later, what he paid didn't even cover what we paid for our clothing. So one of the fellows wrote a letter back to the Ukraine and says to his wife, "Would you take me back, because there's nothing here. I'm gonna die here because there's no work." We walked toward Saskatchewan, taking small jobs along the way, making small bundles out of hay. We had to survive—we certainly didn't have enough money to go back to the old country.

Women speak affectionately of their "pioneer mothers." Vera, who was born in 1920 on a farm in northern Saskatchewan, says her parents lived from hand to mouth in Ukraine:

If they had an acre or two, they called themselves farmers. There was too much people for so little land. They lived off what they could grow. They came to this country and were faced again with crushing poverty because they had nothing, not even implements. They lived in sod and mud houses until they could get enough logs. I feel very emotional about that: When you get older, you appreciate this horrendous nothingness they faced out in the prairie. Yet their love of freedom and determination were always there.

The first homes were one-room underground "pit houses" (*burdeis*) that provided warmth against the prairie winters but little in the way of comfort. These primitive dwellings, used by virtually all Ukrainian immigrants for a few months or even years, measured approximately twelve by fifteen feet square: "The roof and gables consisted of poplar or aspen poles and tall prairie grass and were covered with prairie sod."[15] Sod was cut in a single strip from the unworked earth, using walking plows pulled by oxen. Similar to the early Inuit sod houses cut into the permafrost, the *burdeis* were windowless and dark; a tunnel led down a few steps or a ladder into the subterranean shelter. Tree stumps served as seats, Vera recalls: "That's how they started the first year. My mother's first baby was born there." Anna, now in her seventies, says her parents experienced a similar life:

> My mother was sixteen when she and my father came first to Manitoba in the 1890s. My oldest sister was already two years old. They hired out to an English-speaking farmer, where they learned to speak English and my mother learned how to make pickles. The Canadian government announced homesteading, and my parents thought it looked so good—all that land you got for ten dollars!—so they came to Saskatchewan. They really had hardships. They made a *burdei* and lived there until they could start building a house. They thought there were nice-looking animals around, so pretty, black and white. You know what that was—a skunk! One got into the hut. They didn't know that you should just be quiet and let it walk out, so dad shot it *inside* the hut. Ah, gollies!

Three years later Vera's father built a log house. For days the men filed the logs, notching them to fit tightly at the corners, which were held fast by wooden pegs. Slowly the modest cabin rose above the prairie grasses, affording a view as far as the eye could see. Vera's mother plastered the walls with clay and whitewashed them to a sparkling finish; she spread a glossy clay floor across the two interior rooms that would be home to a family of seven, as well as fowl or newborn calves in the dead of winter.[16] Windows let in the morning sunlight and the rosy glow of dusk. Doors with latches seemed an unspeakable luxury. The above-ground home was a divine sight to her mother's eyes.

Seventy-year-old Antonina tells the story of her mother, who came to Canada in 1908: "She and a friend built a log house with no doors. One night after they went to bed, a badger wandered in. They didn't know what a badger was, so finally they got up and left the house." The women shivered in the night air until the animal decided to let them have their cabin again. When Antonina's parents married, they homesteaded on a marginal piece of land that someone else had abandoned. The saving grace was a tiny house that protected the family for a few years, fashioned by skills that were transplanted from the old country:

> This little house was plastered with mud and straw clay. There were eight of us in two rooms! I'd mix that clay with my feet for my grandmother's outdoor *pich* [a clay oven[17]]. The bread out of that oven was delicious! We'd come home from school, cut a thick slice, put some butter on, bring the cows home, walk two miles, eat that bread. The husband and wife made ovens from steel, wood, and clay, that baked twelve loaves at a time.

Beds consisted of a few logs to raise the straw mattresses off the floor. Gunny sacks served as mattress covers: "We would wash the covers and put in fresh hay from the meadow," says Antonina. "Oh, it was so beautiful to sleep in! It was like sleeping with a touch of heaven—the smell of the grass, the fresh-mown hay. You just had to be careful not to put in any thistles, though." Antonina remembers that many years later she made her first infant daughter a hay mattress because she could not afford to buy one. ("Well, why not?")

Hanna was born in 1906, four years after her father's arrival in Canada. As her parents waited for Hanna's birth, they built a house of logs, plastered it with mud, and laid a straw roof. "It was just wonderful," she adds, "cool in the summer and warm in the winter. Ukrainians used solar energy long before people talked about it. Many of the houses faced south so that in winter, even when you didn't have many windows—you couldn't afford much glass—the sun would be low and shine inside to heat the homes. It sounds bad now, but it was good. We've all lived like that."

Life was not simple. The early pioneers had to walk ten miles or more to Yorkton, Saskatoon, Humboldt, or Prince Albert, the larger centers that offered sugar, flour, salt, and coal, the staples of prairie living.[18] They caught wild ducks if they were lucky; if not, they ate little but bread for long periods. Leon used to catch blackbirds for his mother:

> When we tell people that we used to eat blackbirds they don't believe it, but they were delicious because we were hungry. We used to get the

young blackbirds right out of the nest. They couldn't fly; they were nice and plump. Dad would open the door on each end of the granary, then we'd put a string on the handles. The blackbirds loved oats, so they'd fly in. Once we'd get about fifteen or twenty, we would pull the strings, close the doors, and take them home to my mother. We'd clean them, and Mother would fry them in cream. We used to catch young ducks, clean them; Mother would cook them, we ate them. No butcher shop. If you went to the store there was nothing there; we ate whatever the land gave us.

In the first years there were no roads. People followed cracks in the land or ravines or railway tracks to find the next scattering of settlers. When it rained it poured, flooding the fields and ditches and seeping into the underground homes. A few cows produced milk and cream for the pioneer families. Later, as villages grew into small towns, those lucky enough to have a surplus carried metal containers of cream on their backs to sell at the nearest rail-road station.

Irina, who is seventy-seven, had six sisters and one brother. She remembers the absence of paid labor: "We were so poor, I couldn't even tell you. I don't know how we lived. My dad rented a farm and cut twenty-five loads of wood for the owners so we lived for one year in their house. There was no welfare and no help in the 1930s. We dug Seneca roots; they were making something medicinal from it, something peppermint. If you washed them it was one dollar a pound, so we washed and dried them—but you need lots for one pound." The roots were tiny and delicate, like little strings.

One woman recalls that her father cleared a whole quarter of land (160 acres) with one ax. Pioneer farmers cultivated the land wherever it was easiest, guiding a walking plow with a wooden beam through the expectant earth. This was exhausting work. The plow was hitched to a team of two or four oxen; the beam loosened the dirt so the plow could turn the soil over into a rough furrow. Then the furrows had to be deepened and shaped with disc and harrow, acre after acre, day after day. Once the soil had been properly prepared, men (usually) cast the seed by hand, gleaner or peasant style, row by row. Without tractors, seed drills, or threshing machines, Ukrainians grew wheat and other grain crops by following the same methods used in the old country for centuries.

Planting began in April for an early September harvest. By late summer the sun forced miniature wheat berries into maturity, and the slightest breeze set the golden fields off in undulating splendor. Scythes and sickles, honed to razor sharpness, flashed from dawn to dusk as men swung their way through the fields cutting a bountiful harvest. Women stooked the grain and left it to dry.[19]

The first threshing machines, drawn by horses or oxen, were the miracle workers of the prairies. Like perpetual motion machines, they burned straw to produce steam. One year, eighty-year-old Orest recalls, the frost came drastically early: the first week of August. Fifty acres of his wheat were frozen, and the family suffered through a long winter without enough food or cash. Sometimes one bad year could send a family packing for the small towns that were slowly becoming cities as crops failed and the Great Depression took its relentless toll. Men remember worrying about whether they could support their families, as they were expected to do. Many sold wood to help keep city folk warm through a run of especially hard winters.

Harvest created great excitement and relentless cooking, serving, and cleaning. Women fed the ravenous threshing crews five hearty meals a day. Breakfast launched the crews around six o'clock; at nine o'clock they were ready for the first lunch; by twelve noon the crews were heading for the kitchen door for dinner; at three-thirty the women took lunch out to the fields again; then at seven or eight in the evening the exhausted crews ate supper at the house. Women would leave the kitchen to help with stooking until dark, then finish the last dishes at eleven, go to bed, and be up again at the crack of dawn. They carried lunches of sandwiches and coffee out into the fields to save the crews minutes of precious daylight. Hanna remembers the electric atmosphere of harvest time:

> Those threshing gangs were really exciting to me as a young girl! Everybody was dirty and sweaty. We were jumping with joy because parents would buy Corn Flakes for breakfast. All those sandwiches— store-bought instead of homemade bread! Some women worked on the threshing machines, too. My aunt did everything the men did. She had to haul grain. We *had* to stook.

Pioneer life exacted a heavy toll from everyone. Ukrainian women married younger than other women in Canada; they often died young in childbirth; and infant mortality rates were high.[20] Olga, eighty-two, remembers a story her mother told of having her fifth baby during harvest time: "They were making haystacks, and my mother started having pains and said, 'I'm going to have the baby.' Dad said, 'Well, let's finish the stack, then you can go back to the house and have the baby.' And that's how it was. She had to get up right away because we were too young to help her." Irina was eight years old when her sister was born during threshing time:

> My dad was hauling the sheaves when Mom went into labor. He ran to call the neighbor, who was a midwife. I was so excited! I waited outside the bedroom door, and I wanted to know what that midwife was doing here. She called me: "You have a baby sister." It was St. Michael's day, so she wanted me to call it Michaelina, a Ukrainian name. I didn't like that, so I gave the name, Nellie, and she christened her with water.

The next day the threshing crew arrived, oblivious to the fact that Irina's mother had just given birth: "Mom got up at 5 A.M. to cook for that crew. She was sitting on the bed, dressed up nice and clean with a little baby girl, and the men didn't even know! That was typical, yes, yes." Jean marvels at her mother's fortitude: "My mother was pregnant and had little children, and she still milked cows and stacked hay. My father wouldn't have done it if he was pregnant! She was tough. I don't know how she did it." Because of old stories like these, women and men both agree that while men may be physically stronger, women are tougher.

If the man was away when a child was born, the woman still had to do all the chores around the farm. Pregnant women often miscarried or delivered prematurely after riding in the horse-drawn wagons on "washboard" roads. They gave birth in the early fall when the house was chilled through with a surprise frost, or in the winter during blizzards. They went into convulsions or hemorrhaged to death from complications. Hospitals and doctors were few and far between, and rarely available in an emergency. Old cemeteries still tell the story of women's premature deaths.

Midwives helped enormously if they were close enough by, recalls Kateryna:

> I had four babies in hospitals. Four born at the farm. I had midwives for three; for one, my aunt helped. Luckily, I was fine, but my cousin,

who was seventeen with her first baby, hemorrhaged badly. It was wintertime, and she lived far from town. So what could they do? They sat with her until she passed away. Left a little baby.

That's what happened to my mom, too, when she was twenty-four. She was having a baby, and she lost it. It was blowing and snowing. She probably wouldn't have made it anyway, so far away to a hospital, so she just passed away at home. I had a younger sister, about two years old, and I was six. We looked after ourselves. We made it.

Somehow, with the kaleidoscope of women's and men's skills—some from the old country, some invented in the face of trying circumstances—the pioneers tamed the land. Gradually, onion-domed Ukrainian churches and one-room public schoolhouses sprang up against the prairie skyline, symbols of progress and hope for a people who had left centuries of cultural and educational tradition behind them.

TRADITIONAL ROLES: "OUR DARLING MOTHERS"

Sonia, a high school teacher in her late thirties, notes that in the old country, the exemplary Ukrainian woman was a hardworking wife and a devoted mother who formed the centerpiece of a "very matriarchal" family system.[21] A good woman was independent and "able to stand on her own feet," managing through very hard times to keep home and hearth intact, she adds: "These qualities of faith, family orientation, and diligence came down to us here in Canada. Women helped in the settlement of this country. We nurture these qualities and hope to pass them on to future generations."

"Women are women and they have their duty," says a man in his eighties. "Kitchen, housework, and bringing up children." The traditional division of labor clearly defined the Ukrainian man as provider and the woman as homemaker. "That's why men got married," seventy-seven-year-old Ivan adds, "because the lady's job is in the kitchen or in the house. If the man wants to help, he's welcome to help, but actually it's the woman's job!" Women's role and responsibility extended to the gardens, the children, the cooking, the sewing, the house, and the animals. "By the time women finished," says Mariia, "there wasn't much left except the fields and equipment, and that was the man's job." Later, when farms grew past the pioneer stage and small surpluses could be turned into farm implements to streamline the work, women sometimes helped run the threshing machine during harvest.

Men labored long and hard on the crops that meant feast or famine. William, now seventy-five, describes the typical division of labor: "I worked mostly in the fields. In the winter, I kept the horses and the cattle. In the summer, my wife kept the chickens and geese and ducks. She was all the time by the house, a housekeeper. When I bought a threshing outfit, I'd take it way out into the fields, so she was at home alone."

The woman's labor was critical to her family's survival. Women and men worked equally long hours at equally tedious and difficult chores. Farm life, like Inuit life out on the land, held an imperative that could be ignored only at one's peril. Most women describe the division of labor as "a great partnership." Their work included feeding pigs and milking cows: "Everything was the woman's work," Rose adds. Men were busy in the outer fields, chopping down trees, clearing away the bush, picking roots, plowing, planting: "They worked hard, too. No tractors, just a horse or oxen. Dragging the beam and plow, pulling the chains, dragging it some more. Everything by hand." Men took primary responsibility for calving. Maintenance on tractors and farm implements fell to the men, who were usually not expected to do much inside the house, but always there were exceptions.

Men did most of the outside labor, but if the men were away, the woman's "share" included both women's work and men's work. Ukrainian Canadian women speak with a hushed respect for their "darling mothers who did far more than their share from dawn to midnight." Says Olga, who grew up on a large farm: "I had to help my husband and—ah, I could write a book like this, what I used to do!" Other women chime in: "I guess we all could write a book." Mary Kinnear describes the typical routine:

> When she gets up she does the chores outside, feeds the cattle and milks the cows. She then prepares breakfast and washes the dishes, after which she follows the family to the field where she may hoe or drive a gang-plow, stook, etc. She comes in shortly before dinner, prepares it and cleans up, a matter of one and one half or two hours, then returns to the field until eight o'clock when she milks, after which she gets supper. This is a man's share in any other community.[22]

Kinnear could have added washing, ironing, churning butter, sewing, mending, and countless other domestic tasks that, along with child care, made up the Ukrainian woman's life.

As with so many women today, they zipped through housework at night. During daylight women worked around the farm in order to keep the place running smoothly. ("*Always* the ladies were outside!") Minnie's mother came to Canada in 1911; her story is a typical one of hardship and hard labor:

> Mother was pregnant when she come from the old country; she was very ill on the ship. They had to build a mud house; Dad had to go working. Mom raised a family of ten and had to work on the farm when they got their own land. She had to stack the hay. She was always out with my father, working side by side. Later on the older ones took care of the younger ones, then the wife could go out in the fields and work with her husband. Mom died very young, at fifty-seven; she had sugar diabetes, not looking after it like you should.

Rose, who is seventy-three, clearly remembers: "When I was six years old, my dad walked to Moose Jaw to work on the railroad.[23] When he came home, mother was up thatching the roof. I remember my dad cried when he saw my mother up on that roof." According to Jars Balan, pioneer life was even more grueling for women who stayed on the homesteads while men left in search of cash-paying jobs:

> Sometimes left along for months on end, they would be expected to play a major role in clearing the land, plastering the house, and planting and harvesting the crops. Far from their nearest neighbours and any medical help, many did not survive, and those that did were often prematurely aged, crippled, or spiritually broken by the arduous labour.[24]

Without automatic washers, dryers, or even running water, simply keeping a large family's clothes clean presented a major challenge. "My mother's life was miserable because she was the eldest," Klara says. "She had to stay home and help with the field work. She was just like a hired hand—that's what she says now—working with a team of horses and doing all the work that had to be done." Her mother always wanted to run away from her stepfather; at seventy-four she still feels bitter that she was not allowed to finish school.

"She was just a farmer's wife," says Rose of her mother, then adds: "She was a dressmaker, but she also worked in the fields with father. During harvest she'd put the children to sleep at dusk and go stook with my father until dark." A woman could do most of a man's job if she had to, according to Gail, a nurse in her early fifties: "My mother-in-law came from a family with no boys. She delivered more calves for the neighborhood farmers than anybody else did. To this day I have never, ever had any home baking in her place. She doesn't know how to bake!" Says Stefaniia, "My mother was a real hardworking woman." Her father died in 1947, so she and her mother ran the small farm until her mother fell ill:

> They're both sick, push me all the time, I working. After he died, my mom got hard time with two kids and homeless. My little brother said, "It's really over with us." She's sick, there is nothing to eat, nothing to wear—nothing!—just two kids.

In the 1930s Anna, the oldest of six children, helped with "male work." The law required children to attend school until age fifteen or the eighth grade, but Anna's father needed help so desperately that he met with the school to arrange for her early release from classes:

"I used to do everything . . ."
No protest helped me. I bawled day and night, and I still had to leave school. So I don't have any proper school finished, just to grade seven. I couldn't go until June to finish my grade eight. They let me out for the season in the beginning of May, and I worked along with father. There was a harrow without a seat—you had to run behind it. There was a seed drill and two horses; I walked behind that. You had to hold on and turn the thing over—that was a lot of weight for a young girl my age! I wasn't even fifteen!

I used to help with everything on the farm: milking the cows, chasing the cows, walking the cows. My mother and I tended the younger children, did the laundry, the cooking, the cleaning, the gardening; we tended the chickens and livestock. Couples shared responsibilities without "contract" marriages, saying, "This is your job, and this is my job." It all just got done. My younger brother helped father with the heavy labor in the fields. We did more of the yard work and housework. It seemed to me that women had to do everything. If they were fixing the pigs, she'd even have to be out there slaughtering or castrating them. If their husbands said, "Hey!" they were there.

Oh, I hated killing chickens! I'd starve before I could kill something, but you have to do it, because nobody else can. If my parents went into town, they'd say, "You make a meal." I'd have to catch that chicken. Cows calving—I'm the veterinarian! It always happened when I was home alone.

Aleksandra, age eighty-two, recalls that her parents sacrificed to enable her older brother to attend school: "I was one of the men-types, helping my parents on the farm." When she turned eighteen, they gave her permission to work for another farmer from May to October:

"It's heaven on earth for me . . ."

I had worked on a farm, so I was able to get better pay: $8 a month for seventeen hours a day, seven days a week! At 4:30 A.M. you're out two miles bringing the cows in to milk; then you have to bring the milk to the milk house, separate it from the cream; you feed the animals, all the cats, pigs, chickens—even before my breakfast sometimes. I help put breakfast on the table for the hired men, then I run back to the milk house and crank by hand that separator, one hour straight.

All this for twenty-five cents per day! I usually worked ten hours; that's an average of two and a half cents per hour. When I went to my father's funeral, I did morning chores for the lady and came back the next day to milk the cows, and she deducted me fifty cents that month! There was never any time off. In 1936 I got married. Out of my $48 earnings I bought a little summer coat for $12, some jars for my mom, and two or three pairs of running shoes because they were only 99 cents. I still needed a winter coat, and I found one for $19. Dad says, "When you get home, I'll get you that coat." I worked six months, and I didn't have enough for a $19 coat!

Yes, everything else has changed, and the cost of products has changed, but people want more now. Today we have buttons for every-thing in the house. Fridge! We had no fridge—that's why we had to kill a live chicken. We had no place to store it. I had all kinds of operations in my day, and a funeral—if you put all that in, you'd have a big book—but life now is very good. It's heaven on earth for me.

There was more respect then. My kids grew up in the land of plen-ty; they had everything that they want, though not to the point where they were spoiled. But do you know what my daughter says to me when I tell her about my growing up days? She says, "Mom, you had more fun than we did, even though we have cars and money." And I'm sure we did.

Ukrainian women held their families together through the miseries of immigration, war, the Depression, and countless personal tragedies, and they felt great pride in doing so. Rose, who is seventy-one, describes the very hard "dirty thirties":

"I don't know why people ask for liberation . . ."
Money was scarce. You didn't waste any time when you got home from school; you had chores to do. My grandpa used to go forty miles to seek work and carry one hundred pounds of flour on his back—on his back!—because his wife didn't have any bread for her children. It was easier for my parents, for me even easier, and much easier for our children.

In my day we had no preferences whether we worked with the men or not. We knew one thing: Once our parents said something had to be done, we always did it. The night before they'd say it, and the next day it was done. It was a completely different world. I don't know why people ask for liberation—we had that fifty years ago. We knew what equal work was, but there was no equal pay. These ladies knew they were to work for the home and never mind any pay. Children never had allowances. I wouldn't complain to my parents or anything, and I'm a better person for all of that. When I got married, I worked again on a farm. There was no difference between boys and girls. There was no choice—the girl had to do the man's job if she was the oldest.[25]

Still, I really like to see the man wear the pants. There's nothing I hate more than to see a man with no say in the house. We shared everything. I love it back then, it's great. On the other hand, when they moved into Saskatoon and Mom developed Parkinson's disease, Dad did everything. He waited hand and foot on her and vacuumed—the roles reversed at this point.

Even when money virtually disappeared in the 1930s, women managed to keep food on the table. If company came, the mother or grandmother would make her way into the cacophonous chicken yard to track down the plumpest chicken. She would grab the unsuspecting victim by the neck, fling it across an old tree stump, and swiftly bring down her sharp ax with the other hand. Blood would spurt from the arteries, and the headless hen would run a few steps around the barnyard in a bizarrely stubborn reflex dance.

After plucking the bird, the woman would roll up a small cone of newspaper, set fire to it, and carefully singe the remaining fluff and feathers. The glorious result would finally be stuffed with stale homemade bread and roasted to perfection or fried in cream. "Before you know it you've got a meal," says Eleonora. "We always caught about one hundred chickens a year, and I killed practically every one myself. I lived on a farm for forty years. You can imagine how many chickens I've killed—that's four thousand chickens!" Turkeys were similarly dispatched. Some women remember being afraid to kill poultry: "When I got married, I learned how to kill a chicken. When a man comes home from the field and he's hungry, you've got to kill the chicken or you're in trouble."

When the seasonal clock of farming allowed it, women spent their free hours embroidering, painting *pysanky* (Easter eggs), knitting, crocheting, making fancy Ukrainian breads such as *babka, kolach*, and *paska* (ritual breads), and sewing.[26] Sofia's mother made the family's clothing, a major economic contribution to their welfare:

> *"He realized what a good provider she was . . ."*
> My mother could sew without patterns. When the catalogues came, she would ask us which dress we wanted. You could get gingham or percale for twenty-five cents a yard. She'd order three yards for a dress, and cut it out and sew it by hand, very neatly. Sometimes she would sew all night. I sewed that way until my daughter went to 4-H when she was ten. That's when I learned to sew by pattern. Mother never had a machine. Dad realized what a good provider she was, because she saved him lots of money. He bought a machine for her for five dollars at an auction in Rosthern. That was big money at the time.
>
> Robin Hood flour bags or Windsor salt bags were pretty convenient. We didn't bleach them; we left the colors in and made little panties for the children with Robin Hood on them. They weren't rough once they were washed. Children weren't used to silks like they are nowadays. If a girl had to go to a dance and she didn't have the underthings she needed—flour sack! We made flour bags into pillowcases and dish tow-

els. In the 1940s they started putting linen dish towels in detergent boxes. My, my, weren't they lovely—we didn't have to use flour bags anymore!

We got married during the Depression. Our girls entered school during the bad years, so I made little blouses or dresses out of Bill's old shirts, and tunics out of old pants or suit coats. The girls looked so nice going to school in them.

Pioneer women spun their own wool for knitting on hand-hewn spinning wheels. In the old country, women *and* men made linen cloth for shirts, pants, and scarves; in Saskatchewan they recall old Ukrainian men who sheared sheep, spun wool, and knitted socks to sell to Native Canadians. As late as the 1940s, when manufactured spinning wheels became available, Ukrainian women used a board and stick to card wool before spinning it by hand.

TRADITIONAL POWERS: "LIKE A TEETER-TOTTER"

Were Ukrainian women oppressed traditionally? Most have difficulty relating to the concept. Poverty oppressed them, but the idea of being held down or kept in their place by men does not strike a responsive chord. Women in this culture seem to feel strong and in charge of their lives in significant ways. Always they come back to the fact that men sometimes help with cooking or sewing and women sometimes help with the heaviest farm work. This crossover of roles softened male power and buttressed female power.

Among the immigrants who crossed the ocean to Canada in the 1890s and early 1900s, necessity and the imperatives of eking out a living from the land tended to balance power between men and women: "It weighed and out-weighed. It was like a teeter-totter," recalls seventy-five-year-old Elzbieta. One day the husband might be the boss, the next day it could be the woman, depending on the nature of their work. The seesaw balance of power was anchored in deep trust and mutual respect. Even though occasional disputes arose, Elzbieta says "they never did anything to hurt the family or one another. Work had to be done for future living." Yet although women emphasize the balance of power or the matriarchal threads that weave through traditional Ukrainian society, patriarchy was far from dead. Older women remember being taught humility, which often involved domination as well, says Michaelina: "Parents dominated you, which as a young person you did not want to buy sometimes. But as you got a bit older and faced the world, you were thankful you were raised that way. You had to kneel down and say your prayers, surrendering to God. Knees meant surrender, so I follow that."

When women speak of mothers and grandmothers, they praise their strong organizational skills and ability to manage well in the face of enormous physical and financial obstacles. These tough, determined, and persistent women could hardly be described as subordinated by their men. Ukrainian women look to their pioneer mothers and those who followed them as positive role models whom they envy.

Women agree that in Ukraine, the man of the house essentially was "boss," but, as one woman suggests, "Maybe the women made them *feel* that way!" This story is told with relish:

> A general in the Ukraine was a big, big tall man; his wife was very small. At a convention he gave a dinner speech to the whole community, telling us anecdotes about how important he was, saying he was the head of the household. His wife gets up and says, "I am a very, very small woman, and my husband is a big person and a general in the army. You have a head, but you have a neck. In our household, my husband is the head, but I am the neck—whichever way I turn, he turns!" That's a lot in common with Ukrainian women!

This pithy story, without detracting from the Ukrainian man's position as head of household, underscores the woman's central place and power. Older women insist that a more equal relationship existed in the old country, that men and women worked cooperatively. There simply was no time to argue about who was in charge, Michaelina recalls:

> The family was very important to my grandfather. My grandmother worked hard and was a gem of a person, but grandfather was there to see that the family and farm were looked after. He was a very firm, stern, strong man, although grandmother ran the place, I'm sure. Women do that. It was her domain; he didn't know she ran it, but she did! If she had disappeared, grandfather would have been lost—he couldn't run the farm without her.

Men made the rules, yet seemed to realize that the best way to approach life was to work together. As Gail points out, her father "would peel potatoes for Mom, then lay the kindling to start the fire. He respected her." To some extent the man was considered to be the final arbitrator of decisions, but the woman held the corners of the house together when he was away.

"Men had more power," says Joseph, age eighty-eight, because their work was harder ("Down Europe, men go cut the harvest with the hand sickle, only a man could use it"). Peter, who is sixty-nine, says a cooperative enterprise between husband and wife led to shared power: "It didn't make any difference, because we didn't argue; work had to be done. Two minds work as one." While men were usually the family head, "in some cases, lady was boss, too. My wife's sister was boss because he was good for nothing. He knows just the bottle." Peter says women were equal because both sexes knew their jobs: "If I have to do something, I know what to do, I don't have to ask my wife if I could do it. She knows what to do, she does it. She doesn't ask my permission."

Perhaps the man's power stemmed from the deep respect he commanded by virtue of being grandfather, father, or husband. Although this sounds similar on the surface to the ritualized male dominance that Chinese women describe, in this case Ukrainian women were also revered and respected. Elderly women "took what they got and what they got they took. The man was the boss," insists Martha. "Today it's not like that. The young women won't take it! The older women were raised different; they knew the hard times. The young generation today doesn't want to stand for hard times." Women agree that peasant life in the old country or farming on the Canadian prairies did not lend itself to divorce. A woman alone would have had great difficulty raising children and keeping the farm going: "Before nobody get divorce. A different time, a different life."

Women had less freedom and their role was more circumscribed than men's, which contributed to the sense that men were the bosses, says Donna, age fifty-nine: "There was no women's lib at that time, yet my grandfather was the front person and my grandmother was boss in the house. Grandpa was allowed to do whatever he wanted, and Grandma couldn't. She had to toe the line and make everybody else toe the line." As with women in Jamaican and Chinese cultures, the woman circulated in her sphere, the man in his. Myrna, who is fifty-eight, has a slightly different version of male-female power relations in the early part of the century:

> In many families they shared power. At harvest they always worked together, which gave women strength and made the men look up to them. My mom is seventy-eight. She'll feel down and say, "Oh, I have to do everything for him! He wants tea, I have to jump up and get it." I'll say, "Mom, why don't you don't just say, 'Go get it yourself'?" Oh, heaven forbid! Daddy is still ruling. It isn't because he's the king and she's his servant, or because he's her man and she wants to make him happy. She was just brought up that way, and that's her job.

Power between men and women often centers on who has control over money. For pioneer women and throughout the Depression, "there wasn't any money to control," which might have helped equalize power differences. Wives and husbands usually went shopping together with whatever meager resources they had squirreled away, so a woman did not really need cash for herself. With so little to spend, couples used money cautiously and always for the bare necessities. Later, when families began to prosper, most women remember their husbands controlling the checkbook. As Olha says, however, "My husband controlled it, but I could ask for anything. He never asked me how I spent it." Some women say their husbands held the checkbook, but the women wrote the checks because they had more education. Though some had joint or separate accounts, all talk about proving that they could handle resources responsibly: "The more freedom you have, the more you pull back with spending. It was an absolute two-way street." Some families relied on the wife's financial prowess and literacy: "The Ukrainian woman . . . becomes the traditional stewardess of the house, including its income—which the husband hands over to her willingly and reliantly, having full confidence in its wise and optional utilization."[27]

As in every culture, women do not always agree about the question of power. Lidiia, who is eighty, laughs at her own bold joke: "Man is always on top!" Some complain that they do not have equal power simply because they "have to decide together"—in other words, they cannot make decisions without consulting their husbands. Many older women would not think of buying a car on their own, even if they had the funds. As with Mennonite marriages, in case of disagreement the man could make the decision, even though couples usually tried to ensure that both partners had their say. This holds true only "if they live the right life"; otherwise the husband would say, "I'm just the boss, I'm doing as I please." The major difference for Lidiia is that in younger families, "nowadays the ladies won't take as much as we took. If she hasn't got her way, the wife says, 'To hell with you, I divorce you, I'm gone. I don't want to suffer so many years, staying with you.'"

Minnie, age sixty-two, talks about her battles with her own sense of power in marriage: "Sometimes my husband could put his foot down. When the children wanted to take the car out, they'd come to me first. I called myself the in-between fool. They'd ask me, then I'd have to go to him and be very nice. I'd have to find the right time, when he was in a good mood, then I'd direct them to each other." Gail had the opposite experience. If she asked her father for something, he would reply, "What does mother say? If mother says okay, it's okay." That shows respect, Gail believes, "but sometimes I felt he was trying to save himself—if mother approved and something went wrong, then he would have mother to blame." Irina has mixed memories of how her parents and grandparents worked out the division of labor:

"I expected my husband to be the boss . . ."
Women were subservient. My grandmother on my father's side seemed very bitter. She felt she had to do more work than he should have expected of her, maybe because she had been bought—brought over from Ukraine—and owned. My grandfather was a carpenter, built churches. Religion was very important. It seems like he was easier, more fun and games. They came over, lived in the side of a hill. She had eighteen children; nine of them lived.

Boys could get off easier than girls. Grandmother was a little bit stingy as far as giving things, except where the boys were concerned. She liked to keep souvenirs from the Black Sea, like coral beads.[28] I keep those beads now. They're worth a lot of money, maybe two thousand dollars a string. She saved those and silver dollars, which she wore around her neck.

When I was first married, I expected my husband to be the boss, until I decided that I would speak out for myself. I was brave by then, but I still try to get him in a good mood just like anybody: manipulate him, let him think he's the boss. I made sure that the kids got their education. I had to discipline the children, because he was busy.

Alice, who is seventy, reports a more evenly balanced marriage:

"A fifty-fifty arrangement . . ."
Our marriage was not prearranged. We went together for nine years before we got married, but I started going out with him when I was only fourteen. I wanted to see a little bit of the world before we settled down. When we finally got married, it was a fifty-fifty arrangement. After the children came, we had a post office and ran a mixed farm. My husband was a mail carrier, so I took most of the burden of bringing up the children. I ran the farm and post office because he was away so much. He'd come home and say, "Okay Alice, what's happening today?" I always made sure that it was not too bad; I didn't want to shock him.

I guess a mother has a way of handling the children. They want to help because they love her. I told them to go to school and study—they all finished university.

In sum, for older generations of Ukrainian women, males often had "the last word," but as in Inuit families, because of a rigorous lifestyle that depended on both male and female skills, stamina, and cooperation, the power differential almost dissolved. Because necessity often required that women join in "man's work" and men often helped women with domestic chores, the extreme differentiation of roles that supports an extreme differentiation of power failed to materialize. Taboos against women performing male-defined labor, or the reverse, were relatively weak.

THE TURNING POINT: MOVING TO THE CITY

The long journey from rural Ukraine to rural Saskatchewan resulted in great hardship. Ukrainians were not immune to the frontier violence and social disorganization that characterize most groups that penetrate largely undeveloped territory. Nevertheless it was the migration from farm to urban centers that most profoundly shifted relations between men and women. As the primary unit of Ukrainian peasant society, the family withstood the stresses of immigration to Canada but began to feel the strains of urban migration. The move was equally dramatic: The proportion of Ukrainians living in rural areas dropped from 70 percent in 1931 to only 25 percent in 1971.[29]

"Nobody starved yet in Canada who went to work," explains Orest as he talks about why he and other Ukrainian farmers who had suffered through dead cold prairie winters finally made the decision to come into Saskatoon or other burgeoning towns. Many left farming on the heels of the Great Depression. On the farm, "love and joy were achieved through respect, deeds, and nature." People looked forward to the growth of whatever they planted. "As it was coming up, it was just like gold," Orest remembers. Money was scarce, but people did not worry because food would appear on the table as soon as the crops matured. Canning, preserving, and preparing vegetables and fruits for the root cellars would keep a family during the long winter ahead. When the crops failed and the cycle broke down, though, it was time for a change. Families gathered up what was left of their meager belongings, piled them on top of an old Model T truck or a horse-drawn wagon, and headed for dreams of prosperity in town.

Joseph made a living on four hundred acres of barely adequate land, but he decided to invest in better machinery in the mid-1920s. He went into debt, believing that this purchase would last his lifetime. Then the Depression hit, and year by year it grew more difficult to meet the payments. Finally, in 1948 he walked away from everything and came to Saskatoon. Without education, his only option was to work as a common laborer. Others worked as garage mechanics, plumbers, electricians, carpenters, and cooks; the women worked as cleaning women, waitresses, and seamstresses. The better-educated few were lucky enough to find jobs in offices or banks, and even fewer made it through university or normal school to become teachers.

With the move to town, as with the Inuit move from the land into settlements, basic social arrangements began to be transformed. Although men wanted to continue as major providers for their families, many women also had to work outside the home in order to help make ends meet. As Ukrainian Canadians began to assimilate into mainstream culture and to move into towns, a woman working outside the home raised suspicions that her husband was not a good provider. Economically, most families improved their lot, but some see a downside to the urban migration, as Orest points out: "People aren't as happy as they used to be. They drive nice cars now. You can buy a little truck. At least you can vote, but it's a different life altogether. They need all their amusement; they're living a different life now, a faster life." Central to this transformation are the changes in relationships between men and women. In the old days, the immediacy of physical labor that had to be done before nightfall helped couples avert or defuse arguments: "They might have a dispute in the evening, but come morning the chores had to be done." Now everyone wants their rights, and "there's a gap in between—all of a sudden, you can't please."

Everyone lived the same life on the farm, but urban life is different and more isolating, Milena observes:

> As far away from each other as we were on the farm, we knew each other better than we do now in the city, where we live house-to-house. We don't know our neighbors here. There we knew each other. Every quarter of land there was a farmer; if we hadn't seen someone in a week, we'd wonder what happened and visit them. Each neighbor knew about neighbors for miles around. We were concerned. Now people are physically much closer together but socially disconnected. There were no malls, we didn't get any news from radios, TVs. We worked on our own, but we visited with horses more than they do now with cars.[30]

On Saturdays, farm families journeyed into the nearest village not only to pick up supplies but, just as importantly, to socialize. "I look at the gap we have right now," Orest continues. "There is no more Sunday. It seems like people don't have time for each other. You get up in the morning, you go to church. Everybody's working on the outside, cutting the lawn, going shopping. In the old days, come Sunday, people would go visiting—now you just have no time for that." Every generation in town confronts the question of whether and when the church, another victim of urbanization and two-wage families, will fold. Some feel that as the Ukrainian language dies out, traditions, culture, and the church will also fade away: "Finished. Might as well close the doors and throw the keys away." Others see the realities of assimilation, especially as reflected in the climbing rate of mixed marriages. Some are very optimistic about the future, believing that education and economic opportunity go hand in hand.

Even for those whose education passed them by, working outside the home at low-status jobs represents a lesser burden than nonstop farm work, Gail observes:

> My mom worked very hard when I was little. My dad died, so I remember my mom struggling. She baby-sat for other kids and didn't have many luxuries. She had a wringer washer, a washboard, and an oak rain barrel for making sauerkraut. She still works hard, but things are a lot easier for her—she's gotten her reward now. She works for SASKPOWER as a cleaner, but she gets paid well. Eight hours and she can go home.

"It's a fast world" now, says Mariia, primarily because of modern technology. Women are delighted with the time-savers that ease their lives: "You don't use an oven anymore, you use a microwave. You don't wash dishes, you throw them in your dishwasher. You fly instead of taking the bus. The world is smaller." Life is a thousand times better for women now, most believe. "It's heaven on earth. Just go to the doctor, you get medicine. Long ago women suffered through childbirth and sometimes died—no hospital, no doctor. It's heaven now!"

Into the Twentieth Century

Women no longer have time to devote to community work as they once did in rural communities. For those who work outside the home and try to keep the household running as well, finding time to cook for church fund-raisers becomes a challenge. Antonina was married in the fall of 1943, when it was an "insult for a wife to go to work" because it meant that a man could not adequately provide for his family. The woman's role as homemaker was broadly defined to include overseeing the children, garden, and house. It also meant looking after her husband, and, for some, making sure that he went to university.

On the farm, parents hoped for a better life for their children. Later, as times improved economically, women began to realize that the new generation of urban children was not learning Ukrainian.

Ukrainian women ask whether a better life results if economic progress means leaving tradition behind. This double-edged sword cuts through contemporary lives.

CONTEMPORARY ROLES: "THEY'RE ALL GRAY AREAS"

Women sometimes hear their friends complain that their husbands should do more around the house. Says Khrystia, a secretary in her late forties, "A woman really has two jobs if she works full-time." When she comes home, the household chores remain unless her partner and children define the jobs as theirs as well. Some men, especially those who grew up on farms, take on their fair share of domestic tasks.

Younger women saw the "old-fashioned" way, and argue that elements of older patterns fit well with newer expectations toward egalitarian marriages. As Jean, a teacher in her early forties, notes:

> My mother did canning. I learned from her and from my husband's father, who taught me dill pickles and tomatoes. Alec was brought up old-fashioned, with homemade food. We both work and we both pitch in with housework, yet invisible lines still separate us. Baking is my job, and mowing the lawn is his job. He cleans the cucumbers and goes to pick the dill, but he doesn't get his hands wet.

Khrystia's husband helps whenever he can. He peels peaches and cooks the syrup while she slices the fruit for preserving. Her grandfather used to play a key role in making perogies. "I remember his job was to take them off the table, put them into the boiling water, and toss them around.

The division of labor, which always had great flexibility in Ukrainian marriages, shows even more elasticity now. In many homes, all family members pitch in with housecleaning in a relaxed, cooperative way that assumes tasks belong to everyone, not just to females. Anhelyna, age forty-eight, finds that even a part-time office job interferes with the way she likes to run the house: "My son will wash dishes and cook. My husband hates it, but eventually he'll do it!" Olenka, who is sixty-two, admits that her husband does not help routinely, yet in the wintertime he makes his own breakfast: "He's progressing!" Martha laughs: "My husband fixes himself a bowl of cereal. When I was teaching I often said, 'My husband never breaks anything, he never misplaces anything.

The way I leave it, that's the way I find it when I return.'" In terms
of financial power, Ukrainian women either have their own checkbooks or have equal access to a joint checking account. Sonia's
marriage divides equally in terms of responsibility and decision
making:

> We both handle the checkbooks, we both handle the bills. We discuss
> purchases and what we're going to do. We run the house together. I
> had strawberries to hull and dishes to wash the other night. I said, "You
> do the dishes, and I'll do the strawberries." No problem at all; he got
> up from his TV and started doing dishes.

Newly retired, Anna uses a push mower to cut the grass while
her husband drives the tractor mower. ("I prefer the exercise.")
Kateryna's husband helps her in the garden while she mows the
lawn: "I have a big garden with big weeds, so we do that together."
Adds Olha, "My husband won't use the dishwasher, because he
wants the exercise to wash dishes." She says the groundwork they
laid a long time ago is paying off later in life:

> I had to work so that my husband could finish school. He was a school-
> teacher and started taking law, but the war interrupted. He was ready
> to give up his education so that I wouldn't have to work. I wasn't afraid
> of work. We each had to take our turn selling gas, selling at the post of-
> fice, so that when my husband threatened to quit because he didn't
> want his wife to work, I told him I was prepared for any eventuality.

Men often hold the same values toward housekeeping as women
do, having been socialized into a flexible role as children. They prefer an immaculate house and contribute their energies to keep it
that way. Jean says she finds it hard to live with fastidious people:
"My husband's like that; everything's got to be done just right. The
housekeeping has to be just so, the cooking has to be just so. He's
got the touch test. That's the way he was brought up and it's in
him—very, very immaculate." And because men in the Ukrainian
community take care of children more than they used to and contribute heavily to the daily household operations, the burden is
somewhat lighter for women who work outside the home. As on
the farm, many couples tackle all the work to be done as a team—
as a well-oiled economic unit.

Eleonora reports that her husband and son vacuum and dust, although she may take the lead in noticing what needs to be done. In a typical division of labor, she plans meals and cooks; her husband shops and barbecues: "We don't think of chores as black and white areas. They're all gray areas. What needs to get done, gets done, like work on the farm." For those women who also work outside the home, the burden doubles unless all family members pull their weight with domestic work.

BECOMING A WOMAN, BECOMING A MAN

In Ukraine, traditionally, any color clothing could be prepared for a newborn's layette, regardless of gender. The early stereotyping of pink for girls (symbolic of sweetness) and blue for boys (symbolic of toughness) was absent. In Canada, though, Ukrainians have taken on North American customs that separate males and females at birth: "Here it's pink for girls and blue for boys, white for either. Never pink for a boy, of course. We are getting already this culture—if it was in Ukraine, boy, you wouldn't care! Girl is a girl and a boy is a boy. No difference."

Naturally, women say, fathers always wanted a son to carry on the name, but gender preference had more to do with balance than preference for male children. One woman laughs at herself: "I've got six grandsons, would you believe it, and no granddaughters. Talk about wanting a granddaughter!" Women believe that in contrast to most other cultures, Ukrainian boys were not spoiled or favored. During the Depression, when funds limited opportunity for most families, boys were sent to school more often than their sisters, but not because they were assumed to be intellectually superior or more valued human beings. Mariia explains:

> If anyone was going to break away from the farm and bring home wages for the family, it was certainly the boys. They were going to be the breadwinners and needed more education than the girls did. Like all girls at that time, we were led to believe that we were going to meet Prince Charming and get married; he would take care of us the rest of our life. Our importance was to raise children. So in that sense the males were favored, because they were allowed to get more education.

"We never had any sexist toys for our sons and daughter," recalls Khrystia. "We bought her graders and trucks. She had the choice—

if she wanted a doll, fine. The boys could choose dolls, graders, trucks, whatever." She and her husband encouraged all their children to help in the kitchen; he enlists all the children to dry the dishes: "The three-year-old is still young, but he encourages her to help Daddy in the kitchen."

Although children, especially girls, learned the traditional rural mainstays of canning, baking bread, making sauerkraut, and sewing, many Ukrainian women today have trouble finding time to practice these domestic arts or teach them to their children. And, like Inuit women whose mothers were reluctant to let them practice sewing seal or caribou skins in case they ruined them, sometimes Ukrainian women find that mothers do not easily give up control. As Sonia reflects, "I haven't baked bread for months. I know how to can, but my mother won't let me because I'm not good enough. She has to organize my kitchen: 'We're doing our sauerkraut today and the dill pickles tomorrow.' I'm not capable yet! But I'm happy as long as she's happy."

Anhelyna's experience is also typical. She moved four hours away from her parent's farm, so she had to learn to do everything on her own, including things that as a child she was told to watch and do: "Now I have to learn the hard way. I sew and mend. We can't afford the clothes, so I'm teaching my teenage daughter how to make them herself." Many women learned sewing in home economics classes or just taught themselves. Males also figure as teachers in the domestic realm. Jenny, a salesperson in a Ukrainian specialty market, learned to cook more from her father than from her mother. Her mother worked outside the home, and her father was an accomplished cook: "I always wanted to do things to please my dad, whereas my mother would find fault with my efforts. I learned to cook from my dad—I hope my mother never finds out!"

Ukrainian women proudly describe their grandsons and sons in terms of their cooking and cleaning ability. Growing up on the farm and later in town, both girls and boys learned that males and females shared equal responsibility. As Myrna explains, "All my children were in the kitchen; they shared chores. They *have* to share. My son enjoys cooking, and so does my grandson." She links present-day attitudes to how work was organized in a rural setting: "My husband's mom taught all her three sons about everything, 'men's work' *and* 'women's work.' So my husband helps the same as I do. We go fifty-fifty. If I'm canning, he's canning with me. He's in the garage, I'm helping him."

Lucy was raised during the Depression with two younger sisters. Her father taught school and farmed at the same time; her mother helped out with the farm and ran the house. Lucy and her sisters were raised to do both domestic and farm work: "We had no brothers to help, so we shared responsibilities. We were able to do a boy's job as well as a girl's job. I see nothing wrong in a sharing responsibilities if you enjoy it and can do it." In the ultimate test, some men change diapers, but others—"Forget it! Some wouldn't even give a bottle." Others take equal child care responsibilities, as Sonia describes: "We always do things together."

CONTEMPORARY POWERS: "WE FIND VERY LITTLE DIFFERENCE"

The sense of shouldering an equal share of responsibility that was the hallmark of rural life has persisted into urban life and affects the balance of power between men and women. Modern, younger couples share responsibility. Women speak in terms of male supportiveness for the female contribution, to the point of treating women as equals.

Social class distinctions create some variation in this pattern. For example, one retired educator comments that "as a rule, my acquaintances or my husband's are all professional people, and we find very little difference between men and women. In some instances, maybe on the farms or something, there might have been some degree of chauvinism. Males let their women be equal—if I can put it that way—they *gave* them this freedom, but also, they're chauvinists, they're no different than any male." She suspects that allowing women to live a more egalitarian life makes men feel superior and proud. Yet the two definitely shared power in important and routine ways.

The male has more power, some older women admit, but since women and men traditionally worked side by side, equally shared responsibilities produced relatively equal power. The tendency toward mutual respect and sustenance, evident among older couples, has intensified among many younger couples. Even among retired couples, the tendency to cross gender-based work lines grows.

Not all women are this sanguine about power relations in marriage, as Minnie argues: "I do believe that the man is still viewed as head of the household, even in this day and age. He makes the final decisions, and there's nothing wrong with that." Women still manipulate men into thinking they make decisions when women really have control.

Power balances out fairly evenly in Marusia's home, but "I still put my husband as the boss." If a decision must be made, she directs her children toward their father: "Go and ask Dad. Whatever he says, I'll agree. That's how I was brought up. When he was working and I wasn't, he gave me whatever I needed." Major decisions such as where to send children to school, where to live, or which new car to buy are generally shared equally. As a medical technician, Marusia describes herself as a "women's libber" and sees her relationship as equal:

> I don't think I would let anyone tell me what to do. When it came to buying a new vehicle, I don't know anything about it, so my husband did the research and the shopping around. I chose the color. When it came to buying the dishwasher and my sewing machine, which he doesn't know about, *Canadian Consumer* was our bible; I just went to that and decided. Why bother him? As far as money goes, we contribute equally. We know what the other is doing. Whoever needs whatever, we just go and buy it.

As noted earlier, most Ukrainian women have their own checking account, have equal control over a joint account, or split expenses equitably while reserving their own private funds for special purchases.

Love, Marriage, and Divorce: A Joining of Friends

"The Ukrainian wife is called *druzhyna*, which means friend . . . she is said to have been 'be-friended' with her husband. The same is said of the husband with respect to his wife. The *with* here stresses the equality and interdependence of their relationship."[31] Bohachevsky-Chomiak points out that the phrase "I take you as my helper" was used for both partners until 1646, when it was replaced by "I pledge you love, faith, consideration and obedience in marriage," reflecting the Russian emphasis on woman's obedience.[32]

Young girls learned from *The Sons of the Earth*, a book about Ukrainian settlers in Manitoba, that in the old country marriages were sometimes arranged, even though a female might dislike her parents' choice. Aleksandra remembers her grandfather and father taking turns reading the book around the fire on a winter's night: "We were supposed to be in bed, but we usually listened." Now women have greater scope in selecting their partner "for life," but family pressure toward marrying within the Ukrainian community remains strong.

For women, having children and having them young has always been a pivotal part of their role. Lidiia had her first at seventeen and realizes that by today's standards, she was a "teen mother." It just came naturally, she says: "I looked after the baby, and it was a very healthy baby. Coming from a family of eleven, I knew how to look after children." Michaelina married at fifteen years old because "the woman's career was to marry and have children. That's how they used to think." Like many Ukrainian brides of the early twentieth century, she married young to a man much older than herself because immigrant males far outnumbered females.[33] Her thirty-three-year old groom was a "nice bachelor" chosen by her mother and father. Michaelina's parents told her to make the best of it: "If you got married, you had to stay married, there was no place to turn. Where would you go? They needed ladies to help them to work, to start that farm going!"[34] As in the old country, many men regarded wives and children in economic terms: "Proverbs taught the peasant that a man who wished to become prosperous had to get married and have children to help with the work."[35] Parents selected a groom from the local men who were already established, which usually meant older.

Michaelina's father-in-law lived with her and her new husband. She was frightened of both men but remained married: "When I look at my great-granddaughter who is fifteen, it makes me shiver. I was just a child. I had to cook and do everything, learn if I didn't know." Milena's recollection of her sixteenth birthday reflects the childlike nature of many new brides: "We had a very heavy winter, and there was a snowbank beside our house. My husband stayed with the baby and I went out sledding on the snowbank, because I wanted to enjoy the fun. I was living my childhood. We didn't have any problems, though. Naturally, he was the boss, being older."

This pattern amplified the power differential typical of peasant societies. Milena lost her first husband during the Depression and raised a young son by herself. Since so many adolescent girls of her generation married established men twice their age, a fairly large age gap produced a high rate of early widows.[36]

Most women, though, married in their early twenties, chose their own husbands, and resisted complaining if the relationship turned sour. Weddings took place in one-room schoolhouses before churches began to dot the countryside. "We took the vows to heart, for better or for worse," Elzbieta recalls. She believes that the divorce rate soars now from lack of devotion and commitment:

> Then, you make your bed, you sleep in it. There was no divorce. We knew that. We made a choice and we didn't run back to our parents. Now it's too easy for them. With the first fight the daughter runs to the mother who says, "Stay here, you don't have to go back." There's so much divorce now, they get married and they're single already!

In the Ukrainian community, "The family unit is very strong," observes a Ukrainian minister who has seen few divorces in his parish. A marriage counselor says she is not surprised that Ukrainians account for very few of the 100,000 divorces in Canada annually. In her own practice, she has seen only one divorce; other counselors agree that the divorce rate in this community is remarkably low, as it is among the Mennonites: "We still have that pretty solid family life. It's waning, but it's still strong." A Ukrainian Catholic priest confirms that his parish contains only one divorcee and one widow. "We can count them on one hand." He attributes this unusually low rate of divorce by contemporary standards to a "much more positive and supportive home background." Lidiia agrees but stresses the commitment that marriage entails:

> A good marriage involves lots of hard, hard work. This new generation, it's different altogether: They want to have everything, but they don't want to work hard. That's the whole trouble. If something goes wrong, fffsssttt! She's gone already. They buy everything in the house, they want everything new, even if they can't afford it. They have a family, the wife can't work. Husband can't afford all this—pay the house, pay the furniture. Some young people cooperate, but lots don't, and that's where trouble starts.

"Years ago you wouldn't know of divorces in the Ukrainian community," declares Nadiia, who disapproves of "this cohabit stuff." She says her generation does not like divorce, cohabitation before marriage, or pregnancy outside of marriage. She admits that these things happened in her generation but either were hidden or brought tremendous shame down on the heads of the woman and her family: "Everything was covered up. Having a baby was the worst thing that could happen. You were ostracized for life. Now it's everywhere; the girls finish high school." This new openness strikes at the very heart of family life, Nadiia believes. Without sanctions, the Ukrainian family could become like families in other cultures: "It's a breakdown of our family, our social values, our whole social structure. We become a bit like the other people now! Some people might want to flower it up a bit, but the majority would tell you the same thing."

Ukrainian women hypothesize that divorce is more likely when women work for salaries and become more economically independent, because then a woman can afford to walk away from a bad relationship. "Divorce isn't good, but suffering isn't good either," an older woman argues. If a woman marries a man who becomes an alcoholic, and her well-being is jeopardized, "How are you going to put up with that? If they don't want to smarten up, get out!" Traditionally, one hedge against divorce was the fact that most women married Ukrainian men. Now women are reluctant to insist that their daughters marry a man of Ukrainian heritage, although they clearly would prefer it. Rose contrasts her views with those of a young non-Ukrainian woman:

> My husband and I were celebrating our fiftieth wedding anniversary, and our children were sending us to Hawaii. When I came to buy my American Express checks, I told the girl why we were going and she said, "How come you can live with one man that long!?" I said, "Just give and take, and it will last." And it sure will. It lasted fifty-two years before he died.

In the old country, the qualities of a good Ukrainian woman amounted to a formidable list: hardworking, a devoted mother, a family-type person yet independent in a way, able to stand on her own feet, and a religious woman who is concerned about everything in the community. Rose extends the list: "To all that you ladies have said, we may add the great devotion to family life—to the extreme! Keeping families together." Luba agrees:

> Most of our women are great volunteer workers in every community. They raise thousands of dollars for the church, the museums, and other worthwhile causes. They were very, very much aware of the need to educate the next generation and sacrificed for the young people. They built these institutions and the schools. That was the slogan of our life in Canada: Higher education for your children. Some of the younger women in our organization are even more aware of these things. They utilize their education and all the facilities that weren't available to us.

If you go to a Ukrainian woman's house, the saying goes, you will never go away hungry. At the heart of the home is the kitchen, redolent with the smells of *borsch* (beet soup), *holubtsi* (cabbage rolls), apple pies, and coffee. Sonia remembers how her best friend used to protest going to her house: "As soon as we were there, Mom would ask if we wanted something to eat. The same with my Baba [grandmother]. We would travel four hours to see her and barely walked in the door when she put chicken soup in front of us. She always had goodies. This is why Ukrainian people are always chubby; everyone's always eating!"

Eve, a home economist, traveled throughout Saskatchewan for the province's women's department conducting one-day schools. Women were asked to bring their lunch to the hall or school where lectures were held. In the Ukrainian districts, she says "the women made *banquets*—pies and roast chicken and *holubtsi* and salads of all kinds." By contrast, in the rich, mostly Anglo-Saxon districts, women brought bologna, white bread, lettuce, and tea. In the rural communities, women still put on a generous spread for every occasion: "A Ukrainian woman would be ashamed to serve anything smaller than a feast."

Men look for a good worker, not charm, when seeking a partner for life. A "good Ukrainian woman" takes care of herself, her children, and house (not to mention her husband). Beauty ranks far lower than being a superb and devoted mother. Trustworthiness and dependability, and keeping the core of family life, top the list of desirable traits. Adds Anhelyna, "A good woman knows how to manage the husband and son, too!" Furthermore, knowing Ukrainian, perhaps attending a Ukrainian church, and valuing Ukrainian culture make for an excellent mate. Says Sherry, who is twenty-six, "Women my age look for someone who feels strongly about Ukrainian tradition, the way we do. I am very emotional about our culture from long ago and the language." Women seek a partner who values family and cooperation. Men want a woman who has experience with bringing up children, is understanding, and is a good manager. A woman "should be a good Ukrainian patriot and a good Canadian. She should bring children up in the Canadian way, but always be proud of her background as Ukrainian—the best of both worlds. Canada is our country right now."

During the courting process, a Ukrainian woman traditionally protected her virtue by avoiding premarital sex. As Uliana says, "I was popular and I had fun—I liked boys, and they liked me—but I was a good girl." After marriage, the woman's role was so clearly cut out of the cloth of motherhood that "she was always pregnant." Now, Uliana says, "We all have careers *and* are having children boom, boom, boom. Before, our career was raising a family." Prior to oral contraception, some Ukrainian women used a homemade tampon saturated with vinegar, douched after intercourse with vinegar, used the rhythm method ("if they understood it"), or abstained from sexual relations. Their mothers were reluctant to discuss contraception, especially in an era when motherhood was expected and highly valued. Abortion or pregnancy outside of marriage were rare because of religious conviction and the fact that females typically married young. Although marriages occur later today, strong norms still exist against premarital sex and abortion, says Uliana:

> Say there's a pregnancy in a teenager. The family would probably just hide it to beat the band because of the embarrassment. Our women's group would be very solidly against abortion. Life is sacred, and family is, too. At the same time, we are not like the Catholic church that is against contraception. We believe that every child that comes into this world should be a wanted and loved child. We teach our daughters about the sacredness of family life.

Another side of love, marriage, and divorce lies in the expression of affection between partners. Women say that some men have great difficulty expressing affection and feelings, while others are very open. Education and how they were raised influence a man's ability to expose his softer side, but women describe Ukrainian men as "very affectionate." Although men are supposed to be tough, "it isn't unusual to see a Ukrainian man cry," says Gail:

> Ukrainian men are pretty open in communicating with their wives. They're very loving and open about expressing affection. They like dancing and partying. Still, women are *more* open about their feelings. Fewer things seem to be bothering the men than the women. Women will cry or become upset sooner than men; men will be crying on the inside but won't bring it out. It depends on the circumstance and the individual, but women seem to be softer-hearted than men.

Others say Ukrainian men "would give you the shirt off their back, or help in any way possible." Even when there was not much time for hugging, they felt loved, as Olha recalls: "Every night, Dad would read those little smiling Jerry Muskrat articles in the newspaper. Every night he'd read the newspaper to me." Ukrainian farm women were known as affectionate mothers in spite of the long hours of hard work. Many women remember their mothers singing or telling stories while they milked cows or tended the garden. Michaelina felt that her mother was always there for her except when she went into the fields: "It seems I was with her, and she was with me."

Challenges Confronting Women

What challenges do Ukrainian Canadian women face in the late twentieth century? "Oh, the same as you see across the border. We live in society. We're not ghettoed. Whatever happens out there happens to us." Ukrainian women face challenges not unlike those faced by women in the Blood, Inuit, Chinese, and Iroquois communities, including loss of cultural integrity that comes from assimilation into mainstream society and through intermarriage, and a language that fades further away with every generation. Earlier, the major challenge centered on women's education. However, other social problems (or symptoms) that plague native and Jamaican women—such as alcoholism, child abuse and neglect, wife battering, infidelity, desertion, non-support, and the poverty of single-parenting—appear "minimally, if at all" in this Ukrainian community. Counselors report that compared to other ethnic groups in the

Saskatoon area, Ukrainians have lower rates of most social problems. This is partially attributable to the heavy influence of not only the churches but also the Ukrainian heritage itself: "I suppose you have to look at the whole prospect of life. You understand your history, where you come from; you think you have a little part in the future generation's destiny," Lesia, age fifty-nine, hypothesizes.

EDUCATION AND SCHOOLING

Pioneers sought the freedom to be educated. Although early Ukrainian women played a significant role in founding educational institutions, by the early twentieth century, political turmoil in Ukraine meant that most immigrant women had never attended school. Women of the first and second waves speak of starting school at eight years old or leaving school by the eighth or ninth grade (while their brothers continued) because farm chores needed their attentions: "We couldn't go any further, because we had twelve cows to milk. We never had a chance!" Many taught themselves to read and write in English if they arrived in Canada as a teenagers. By the time children of pioneer parents reached school age during World War I, there was no money to buy them scribblers and pencils. Still, because Ukrainian women were determined to educate their children, many managed to complete a higher education in Saskatoon. Mary's story is typical of the older generation:

"Those days were the best years of my life . . ."
I was born in Saskatchewan on a farm. I went to one-room schools until grade eight, then to high school in Krydor, then to university in Saskatoon to study teaching. It was a hard life, but it was a beautiful beginning—a quiet, secluded, happy life—as a farm child. We were very, very close and very involved. Self-sufficient. We grew everything we needed.

We milked twelve cows every day and walked three miles to the little country school. The only time we didn't walk was in the wintertime when it was very cold. They were the best years of my life. I taught for ten years, even after we were married in 1952, between the little ones. I took a baby-sitter with me to the teacherage. When I was expecting a third one, I quit teaching.

Milena, now in her late eighties, took Ukrainian, Polish, and German in the open house schools. "That gave us a bit of a start. I had three years of schooling and learned three languages. We wouldn't dream of doing that now, but in Europe it was common." In Canada, women began earning degrees in home economics, education, music, and business as early as the 1930s. Although girls were often shortchanged in education, Sofiia says her father sold two railcar loads of wood in 1930 to pay for her schooling: "You know how hard he had to work? That's a lot of wood!" "Parents would long to send their children to high school if possible," recalls Aleksandra. "Since boys would be breadwinners for their wives later on, boys had the privilege"—an ironic twist, since Ukrainian women had long supported education for everyone. Says Anna, "I am proud to say that I am the first Ukrainian woman to graduate from the University of Saskatchewan. I was a teacher and married a schoolteacher."

KEEPING THE CULTURE

"After all these centuries, our artistic talents did not die," says Eleonora. "They carried on from generation to generation. A mother would be ashamed to have a little child wear an ordinary shirt without any embroidery. It would be a slur on her: What sort of a mother is she?" This true folk art threw a rainbow of brilliant colors and geometric or floral designs across a child's skirt or a husband's vest. Pioneer women gathered together in dimly lit, tiny living rooms to share a cultural evening of reading, embroidering, and passing along the oral legacy of songs and stories. This, too, was part of their role as keepers of the culture.

In the early years, talented, creative women who missed out on formal education pooled their memories of traditional arts and crafts, exchanging techniques and recipes, trying to hold on to the ancient culture of women. Some tasks grew wearisome, reflecting the restrictive nature of a mandated domestic role, as a grandmother says: "I used to make hundreds of *pirohare* [perogies, also known as *varenyky*]. I'm getting tired of perogies. I look like one!"

In the 1920s, Ukrainian National Houses sprung up across the Saskatchewan countryside. "Every community has one—a church and a hall where people could get together," Lidiia recalls. "There were always social gatherings, and the whole family participated. Our parents would go to dances, and the kids would be sleeping on the benches; as soon as we were big enough, we would be dancing, too. We have pictures of the drama circle, with my mom and dad in the middle." Evenings were filled with storytelling by grandfathers and grandmothers. Socializing may have been the only form of recreation, but it also helped preserve Ukrainian culture.

Ukrainian Canadian women still worry about whether their culture will be preserved, especially in church-related activities when young people show characteristically low attendance rates. Women encourage each other to carry on, even though they are getting older and preparing and serving food is hard work. Says Olga, who worked in a bakery, "They say this year we're not going to have the festival, and someone gets up and says we should hang on. Well, yesterday I was surprised. We had four young men doing all the cooking, and there were four young men serving and washing the pots! It was easy. It was long hours, and we were tired, but I don't think we'll give it up."

These women also see their culture becoming diluted with every generation of mixed marriages, Anna says: "We are losing, definitely. Some are dropping out completely, some are indifferent, but there's always the survival of the fittest. Some are going to lose the language, but teachers tell me that in these bilingual programs the majority of the students come from mixed marriages. There seems to be an upsurge in the language. Perhaps it hit rock bottom."

When pioneers came from the old country, they brought their beloved music with them, performing with mandolins, banduras, violins, dulcimers, and their voices. A senior-citizen mandolin orchestra echoes the sounds of long ago, and many young people are learning the bandura in a revival of old music, Anna adds: "You hear people playing the dulcimer—thirty-five years ago, nobody knew about it here!" Folk dancing groups rehearse steps that date back five thousand years, depicting the struggle for survival and life cycle events such as birth and death.[37] Ukrainian culture may shrink into the hands of a few dedicated traditionalists, but Anna believes that a viable culture must adapt to new realities: "We're going to be a new kind of Anglicized Ukrainians. You can't freeze-fix everything in time like you can a cabbage roll—make it and freeze it and have it next spring."

VIOLENCE, LIBERATION, AND ALCOHOL

In Ukraine, survival took precedence, as Lara, a shelter worker, explains: "There wasn't the money or time to become an alcoholic. The family unit was stronger. Values were important. Some spousal abuse related to alcohol occurred, but the most important source of women's oppression then was that they were losing their property and being exploited. These were national problems, not family problems." People were driven to drink out of frustration—not from family tension, but from political tension. "Even if a husband did hit his wife, no one would know about it," Lara reminds us. "You had to keep quiet, everything had to be covered up. The image of the home had to be kept intact."

Pioneer families could not afford alcohol or had little access to it in a wilderness that had not yet been punctured by airplanes and superhighways. More important than alcohol in triggering family violence was poor communication. If a couple had problems, they probably did not talk about them openly. As in other groups, boys learn to stifle their fears and tears. Lara describes how submerged feelings can twist into violence: "My ex-husband used to say to me, 'Well, if you want to cry, I'll give you something to cry about.' He couldn't stand people crying, because he could never cry as a little boy. He always had to win, no matter what, even if it meant beating me. That's power tripping." Some older women believe that men were warmer and more affectionate before they moved into urban areas: "You had your disputes, but you turned around and it was forgotten. Maybe the word was devotion. Understanding." Older women do not remember family violence in the pioneer or Depression days, yet historical records show that domestic violence was no stranger to the struggling pioneer families,[38] and women who work in Saskatoon's main shelter see similar rates of violence among Ukrainian families as with others.

Ukrainian women who head for the shelters tend to be in the older, middle-aged group and not to work outside the home. Lara says they represent the extreme cases who have accepted abuse for years. Some complain that they cannot tolerate the physical abuse as their bodies age; others feel that once their children have left the home, the reasons for staying in an abusive marriage start to slip away. ("They feel they've played their part.") Among the younger generation, women leave abusive men even more easily, Lara adds: "It's clash of personalities. You feel that life is too short to put up with something that isn't satisfactory. The young women are educated, so they can turn to a profession. They're more independent. They just don't have to tolerate any abuse." About 30 percent return to their partner and continue to be battered. Alcohol and drugs cause the most intractable problems, and abuse occurs across the social spectrum: "We see low-income families, and some middle income. Doctors and lawyers have everything in their names; when the wife leaves, she doesn't have access to money." Lara tells of a woman who came from the old country only to fall victim to battering by both her husband and her father-in-law:

> She thought that was the way it was supposed to be. Finally, when it dawned on her—and she was a big woman—she told them, "Either one of you lay a hand on me again and that will be *it*!" They figured that it was the same as some places in Europe where they can beat up a woman for anything, but she found out that in Canada that wasn't so.

The women's movement has helped enlighten immigrant women about the illegality and injustice of domestic violence: "We're becoming more educated and learning that we are worthwhile people. We don't have to put up with this kind of thing; it's not normal to be treated that way."

As in other communities, much domestic violence goes unreported and unpunished. A battered woman may talk about her problems only to her closest friend, if at all. On the positive side, once the family learns of a woman's distress, they are likely to swing into action to help her. Theoretically, a tight family and kinship structure should both insulate women from problems and provide effective coping mechanisms for dealing with those problems that inevitably arise. A counselor concludes:

> We have our problems, but because we're very proud people, we just don't like to expose them. Domestic violence is common. If a girl gets pregnant, it's all hush-hush. She wears a girdle the day of her wedding; when she has a baby seven months down the road, they say, "It was early." It's more open now. The family will take the daughter in and help raise this child rather than the daughter having an abortion or making a bad marriage.

Toward the Twenty-First Century

THE ROAD TO EQUALITY

"I left my husband at home painting the kitchen. I'm supposed to be helping him, but I'm over here talking to you. I guess I'm a liberated woman," Jean jokes during our discussion of women's liberation. "If you're both hard workers and you're striving for the same goal—survival and providing for your family—you don't need women's liberation," Martha argues.

Ukrainian Canadian women cite the title of Martha Bohachevsky-Chomiak's book on women in Ukraine, *Feminists Despite Ourselves*, as an apt description of their attitudes toward the women's movement. Anna explains:

> *"We were feminists in spite of ourselves . . ."*
> She's chosen a good title—we were always feminists in a sense, but despite ourselves. We are a little different category when you speak of the feminist movement. Any kind of women's movement among Ukrainian women was not a feminist movement in the sense of trying to achieve status, equality with men, or superiority to men. We were feminists in spite of ourselves, because the history of the Ukrainian people was very tragic and unfortunate in the last years in the old country. We were independent as a nation during the princely period and during the Cossack period.
>
> After the Bolshevik revolution of 1917, the Ukrainian people lost their independence. We were always subjugated as a group of people, husbands and wives, families and nation, under the Russians, under the Poles, under Romania. When it came to doing things, even when we came to this country, it automatically meant we had to do things together. Whether we went into an association of Ukrainian women or we organized a church group or a school, it appeared as a feminist "coming forward," but it really was part of that group idea of building ourselves up as a whole nation, as a people. That's why we got the support of the men.

Are Ukrainian women equal to Ukrainian men? "Nowadays they are, especially those who are born in Canada," says Jean. Who's the boss in her house? "Nobody . . . the cats!" Three factors contribute to this strain of "prairie feminism." First, as an oppressed people in the old country, Ukrainian women brought with them to Canada an unwavering desire to establish themselves as a progressive, respectable, educated community (often in the face of continued prejudice and discrimination in their new home[39]). Since men shared this vision, they supported the women in their attempts to improve the lot of pioneer descendants. Second, these women emphasize mutual help and cooperation, with equal sharing of responsibilities between men and women as necessity demands. The equation worked on the farm and carries over to urban life as the formula for a successful relationship. Third, many are convinced that the best way to keep the family together is for parents to stay home and raise their children. This last principle causes a great deal of consternation and debate, with some insisting that women at times must work outside the home or may prefer to do so, and others insisting that too many problems arise when "the home does not have a heart."

Ukrainian Women's Organizations and Male Support. Because men did not view women as "uppity" people who were trying to put them down, the attitude among Ukrainian women "is not quite the same thing as a feminist mood." "Since the women's liberation program came out," women's role in the church has progressed, says Mariia, who sings in the choir: "The work is all done by women, especially in our church. Maybe I shouldn't stick my tongue out like that, but women's liberation has made less work for women—it was about time women had our right!"

The Ukrainian women's movement started during World War I. Rumblings about having women organize were heard as early as the first stage of Ukrainian immigration (in the late 1890s), when "young Ukrainian girls were walking the streets in cities." The first fledgling organization started in Winnipeg in 1916, but like other attempts it failed. Finally the Saskatoon branch took hold in 1923, initiating a movement that quickly mushroomed all over Canada. In 1926 this core group was forced to organize nationally in order to coordinate and direct its work, becoming the Ukrainian Women's Association of Canada.

A leader points out that young girls at the Petro Mohyla Institute in Saskatoon first thought of founding a women's organization: "Many were training to teach in Ukrainian districts; it was their duty to organize women wherever they were placed as teachers. They organized the local, then the national, and of course that grew." Indeed, as young women matured, they were told that they should be leaders in the Ukrainian community: "We were to promote reading, enlightenment, books, organize drama clubs, and organize people. This was a broad movement. We all were part of it. Women started the museums, started the archives." Those who went to normal school "automatically knew we had to teach in Ukrainian districts, teach Ukrainian after school—we had to help the people, we had to organize a women's club." At eighteen, Martha had to go out into the country and establish a women's local: "We knew this was our mission, by the process of osmosis."

Gail completed her nursing degree after marriage and her first pregnancy. "In those days there was no such thing as a women's liberation movement, but I was a liberated woman. My husband encouraged and helped me because I studied at home. There was that urge among Ukrainians to rise, to be well established as educated people." Often, husbands and wives volunteer together in the women's association activities and in the museums. Those who have played significant leadership roles in the organizational life of Ukrainian women praise male supportiveness. Ukrainian women slipped easily and quickly into an "officially liberated" stance: "We all had good Ukrainian men. They never stood in our way. They encouraged, they helped. It was something wonderful. They babysat while we went to women's meetings. The educated kind, the priests, those upper- and middle-class men, they encouraged the women to organize. They supported the movement."

Martha volunteered for the Ukrainian Museum of Canada, traveling across the country to organize branches in major cities, always with her husband's support:

> At no time did he ever say that I shouldn't tour. Our husbands always have encouraged our work. You might get the odd one who might protest, but generally speaking the men felt that we were building a community life together. They gave us credit for what we were doing. Our men felt that we were equal; I don't think they dominated us.

Milena stresses that her strength as a woman derived in part from her husband's support: "I had very nice husband. He was just like mother to me, husband and midwife." Olenka explains how

Ukrainian women are not oppressed, even though on the surface some might think otherwise:

> Feminists might say that we just think we are equal but we're not, because men made some of the bigger decisions and certainly men's careers always came first. I don't think we felt oppressed; I know I certainly didn't. I had the freedom. Out of respect you considered him more important. If he had to move, we moved, yes. But the men were very proud of their wives and what they did, and we were loved very much.

Although many rural immigrant farmers resisted sending their children to school (for they were too important as economic laborers on the farm), the Ukrainians in Saskatchewan, led by both men and women, engaged in a far-reaching battle to educate rural children. Among the most important mechanisms for ensuring that farm children learned not only English but Ukrainian was the creation of private *narodni domy* (special Saturday classes in Ukrainian) and *bursy* (student residences).[40] Of the latter, the Petro Mohyla Institute became the flagship residence that enabled young rural Ukrainians to attend the city's high schools and university. It also encouraged them to pursue professional occupations, especially teaching, medicine, and law. The first teachers, women and men, helped build the rural communities. Compulsory classes in Ukrainian studies ensured that youths would advance their knowledge of the culture simultaneously. The Institute brought children in from the farms and small towns to attend high school in a supportive environment; now the Institute serves as home to university students in a new building close to the University of Saskatchewan, as well as to students attending technical and secretarial schools.

"We started a small collection in the Mohyla Institute, and we've grown," Anna says proudly of the impressive Ukrainian Museum of Culture, founded by the Ukrainian Women's Association of Canada. The association has already established branches in Winnipeg, Edmonton, Vancouver, and Toronto. The women brought the men along in the early days of hard work and dedication to preserving Ukrainian culture, she explains:

> Although the men are involved with this movement, our first board and committees were all women. Now we have men: first one man, then we added the others, up to about 20 percent of the board. So now we've

liberated the men, and that's a good joke! Still, the chairman of our board will always be a woman. We never had a penny. We went for grants to Ottawa, played politics, borrowed money, and the rest we collected.

Women built the museum's collection, staffed it, and persuaded the Canadian government to give them a small grant for training a university student as a museum worker, says Eve, a founding board member: "Up until then, we did everything ourselves. We had to collect all those artifacts that would otherwise have been lost in Canada. Let's thank our lucky stars that they weren't lost."

Sharing Work and Role Flexibility. Ukrainian women are feminists despite themselves in another sense as well: They were and are strong, spirited, and in many ways independent, but because of intense regard for preserving family life, they resist identifying with a movement that sometimes seems to require that women reject men. Ukrainian women describe their husbands as willing to pitch in with domestic chores—a line that seems much more difficult for men to cross in most other cultures. This appears to be the case for older as well as younger couples. Says Rozaliia, who is seventy-four, "If I was canning, my husband would roll up his sleeves and help me. He goes off picking wild mushrooms." When Mariia married, she and her husband worked together on their own small farm: "When we had cows to milk, we milked them together. We both went in the fields and worked. There were times that he had to work by himself—plowing or whatever—and I would stay home and do the chores and gardening. But if it was stooking or haying, we both were doing it."

Importantly, "women's work" and "men's work" represent useful categories for channeling daily activities, rather than rigid boundaries that neither gender may cross. As refugees from Germany after World War II, sixty-nine-year-old Nadiia cleaned an office building at night, and her husband washed dishes in a café. Now that he has retired, he helps her at home in the kitchen: "I come to help the head cook, full time!" Nadiia recalls: "My father helped, I can remember that. My sisters were always saying, when there was a wedding in the neighborhood, Mother was making dresses for the six girls, so Dad helped to stitch by hand." Mariia had to clean the house and cook, but her husband helped with washing dishes. She sees the division of labor as fairly equal. Liberation and responsibility must balance out, as Eleonora explains:

> In 75 percent of the things I am liberated! I don't have anything holding me back. There are still some things that I have hang-ups about, things that I don't think are proper or feminine. I *like* being a woman. I still like to respect a man. I like the male-female balance; I like my husband opening doors for me. My husband does the vacuuming, he cooks dinner—he happens to be there at those times, because his office is in our home. It works out better. If I didn't have a job, I wouldn't feel that I was oppressed if I had to do the vacuuming and cooking. When I have the time, I enjoy doing it.

Ukrainian women stress the combinational power of technological progress and the women's liberation movement as having a significant impact on their lives, despite the fact that (like women in the other cultures) few of them identify directly with the movement or attend movement meetings. Although Ukrainian Canadian women are extremely well organized in various women's groups, several ask why a women's liberation movement is necessary. On many crucial levels, Ukrainian women feel liberated in the first place: "We didn't have it [oppression]. We didn't feel degraded. We worked together with our men. It was a must to survive. You *had* to work." Furthermore, women also speak fondly of their fathers, who, in spite of their strictness, taught them to respect their elders and to work together. Hanna points out that burdens fell evenly across the shoulders of both sexes: "It was your home, and you both worked for the same thing. I don't think there was such a thing as a boss. The woman had to do those things because the man couldn't do everything. There was love, and you helped one another."

Technological progress continues to amaze older and middle-aged women. They suspect that younger women have too much freedom compared to the older generation, who lived through pioneer days, the Depression, and moving into the city. Liberation does not bother them so much as the related phenomenon of spoiled children who lack discipline and a sense of shared obligation to the family. "Women want too much," says Kateryna, "demanding too much from their husbands." They are never satisfied with their lives, these women think, because they have never learned responsibility.

Aleksandra supports equal opportunities for women in every way and has nothing but disdain for stereotypes: "It would be nice, if the car stalls, to know what's wrong with it—I don't see that as a man's exclusive domain. I have a screwdriver in the house. If he isn't around and something has to be done, why not?" She objects, though, to a woman "who is so liberated that she puts down her husband or other men." Kateryna supposes that some women want to be equal with men, and she tried to be equal in her marriage. ("Why not!") But she does not see women taking their share of homemaking responsibilities: "The center of the home isn't there the way it used to be. Many women want to be *more* than equal. Above." Marilyn counters that feminism and liberation are "fine as long as you don't overdo it." She believes that some women want to go too far: "It used to be that the men were dominant. Now women are dominant—domineering—and I don't think that's right either. It should be a happy medium, a balance."

Staying at Home to Raise Children. Olenka opens the debate:

> My family is very important to me. I was fortunate that my husband has a job that makes us very comfortable, so I didn't have to go out to work. I'm not a servant, but I do feel that my job is at home. I don't mind taking care of the house. I guess I'm not a liberated woman. Women should be able to express themselves and put their foot down as well as men, but I don't believe that women should be saying, 'No, I'm not staying home with my family, I'm going to work.' A mother staying home with her children is very important. I may be stereotyping, but if a woman has a child, her place is in the home, if permitted. I know that in some cases it isn't possible.

A woman should be able to pursue her career before, after, or even part-time during motherhood, Olenka argues.

Certainly Ukrainian Canadian women champion the concept of equality in the workplace, but they question when a woman should pursue the career to which she aspires. Jenny feels that "when children are young a mother can probably do more for them, unless she's definitely not the mother type and she'd have a nervous breakdown—then she shouldn't be a mother." Echoing the crossover between roles, however, these women also would accept a father staying home with children while the mother works for salary. Part of a *couple's* mission, they feel, is to raise children to be strong, confident, productive citizens, as with stooking, plastering walls, or making perogies, it does not matter whether male or female carries out the task. Sharing is the guiding principle. If a woman makes a better living, there is no reason why the father should not look after the children and house: "Children need their fathers just as much as they need their mothers." Karen, a law student, shares her feelings about women's liberation in the Ukrainian context:

"I really feel like a free spirit . . ."
With disintegration of the family unit, you get disintegration of all the other structures as well. All over the Western world we see a human cry for the women of the race—our women have been liberated for a thousand years. Western women are discovering that they have brains and can use them, after being cow-tied to an Anglo-Saxon mentality all this time. Eastern European women, especially, never had that. That's why in our church there is not this bloodcurdling cry for women priests or women clergy. There never has been and I doubt there ever will be, providing the family unit remains intact. Once we become assimilated, beyond where we are today, maybe things will change. Disintegration will bring out this kind of response, but up until that time, there's not even a hint of it.

There are many definitions of women's liberation. Women like myself have a career; I feel very successful with it. We have homes and families and feel successful there, too. It's a support system; the family has to work together. I also believe in equal pay for equal work. In some careers this is very easily done, but I don't like to see women as lumberjacks or working on oil rigs. I don't think just because we're fifty-fifty that certain jobs can be done equally well by both men and women. I have reservations about more extreme types of women's liberation.

Women perhaps should be feminine and not feminist. Perhaps I am coming from a more traditional role, but some of the feminist-type women I have met do not strike me as very happy people. I don't see them enjoying life. They seem to be very, very negative. This bothers me, because I don't like to see people who are hurting. Some of them are hurting themselves.

I am liberated in the fact that I can do whatever I want, whenever I want. My first obligation is to make sure my children are taken care of, but they haven't interfered with anything that I wanted to do. I don't feel oppressed, not in the least. I really feel like a free spirit. Life for us is beautiful. I get angry at these feminist movements. We've got the best of everything, and they're messing it up. Live, enjoy, love—take control of your lives. Don't always look for some kind of rainbow. The world doesn't owe us a living; we owe the world a living.

My mother is seventy-two years old this year. She was sixth in a family of twelve children. One of our favorite family stories is mother's birth. Baba [grandmother] was helping in the fields with haying. She started having labor pains, so she quietly left the field and went to the house. She delivered without the help of a midwife; an older daughter brought her hot water to wash the baby and herself. Baba had the baby in the afternoon; when the rest of the family came in from the field, there was supper on the table and a new baby sister in the cradle! When we talk about liberated women, we should look at those women—they were more than liberated.

WOMEN'S EMPOWERMENT

Ukrainian women see themselves as empowered and strong women, especially as keepers of the family, the community, and the culture. As Myrna says:

When you look at the embroideries, costumes, Easter egg designs, and our weaving from an artistic point of view, they were just ordinary women who created them, but they are beautiful, complicated designs.[41] I have never felt that our women were ordinary. Many were geniuses to do the things they did, especially when you consider that they were oppressed in the old country. But they survived; we're survivors.

She is teaching her daughters to paint Easter eggs. Other women keep up the tradition of making specialty breads, braiding and shaping them into baskets, animals, and complicated twists.

A Ukrainian proverb says, "Once you want to become a mushroom, you have to be prepared to go into the *borsch*." Anna laughs at the deep truth behind this saying: "Our Ukrainian *borsch* always has mushrooms in it, so once we're in here, that's it!" Supreme organizational architects, Ukrainian women know how to build grassroots groups around a common cause, then connect them into parallel district, provincial, national, and international organizations. The Ukrainian Women's Association of Canada provides a neat example. A woman becomes a member of the national organization simply by joining the local group. The local sends delegates to provincial conferences, which send delegates to the national conference, which in turn is a member of and sends delegates to the International Council of Women (ICW). The ICW gathers women's groups under its umbrella: church groups, service clubs, and multipurpose and specialized women's organizations.[42]

Lesia illustrates how being a local "mushroom" propelled her into international women's organizations: "First I joined the laws committee; my husband was a lawyer and all my children graduated in law, so I was very interested in it. Then I was economics chairman during World War II, then president, and then delegate to the International Council. The Canadian delegation visited the Canadian Embassy. That day we put on our little maple-leaf buttons and were given a Canadian flag. I was vice president of the International Council in the 1960s. I've been around the world twice, following the meetings." Various organizations link the individual to Ukrainian culture while she integrates into Canadian society.

A related source and reflection of empowerment is women's involvement in church life. "In a world of constant flux, it's nice to have a North Star," Khrystia declares. "You may wander, but the star will always be there. It's my point of orientation." For many Ukrainian women, the church (Orthodox or Catholic) is an important point of orientation.[43] The churches provide for many women a sense of well-being, security, and meaning. They also serve as a conduit into Ukrainian heritage and a bridge across generations. Youth choirs, women's associations, and summer camps generate endless opportunities for learning the culture. For example, altar boys and girls who never learned the language memorize Ukrainian liturgy. Some women see the church as a virtual extension of the family and see it as another way of keeping the culture and keeping the family at the same time.

Although women have not served as deacons since the twelfth century, the status of women in the church is a subject of heated discussion. Women, especially older women, form the backbone of the church; some advocate reestablishing a women's ministry. A thousand years ago Ukrainian women formed a clerical order of deaconesses. Ukrainian women take these early spiritual leaders as role models for their twentieth-century participation in the church. Khrystia asserts women's right to become fully involved in religious matters:

> The New Testament mentions deaconesses. Phoebe and Dorcas were ladies who ministered primarily to the women when they were ill or sick. They had a women's ministry. They catechized the women, taught them the faith, and assisted in the baptism of women. All of the spiritual needs of parish women were looked after by the deaconesses. Then, in the twelfth century, when the pressure on the Eastern Orthodox church was very great, these traditions were forced out.

Now women are not consecrated or blessed as spiritual leaders. Girls read the Apostles on occasion and participate in summer camp ceremonies. "We get them heavily involved," says a camp counselor, who stresses that priests' wives in rural areas often serve as cantors, reading and singing the ancient liturgy.

An Orthodox priest confirms that women are the basic support system for the church:

> If you go across Canada, you'll see a similar pattern coast to coast. We don't rely on bingos and casinos for raising funds. Our women make cabbage rolls and meals. This is how our churches exist! If you go to any parish, whatever size, where there's a thousand families or ten, the parish is held on the backs of the women. They do everything. They decorate the church. They provide the ecclesiastical embroideries.[44] They provide care for the children; they make sure the altar boys have their vestments and everything else. Their ministry is very, very supportive.

DREAMS FOR THEIR DAUGHTERS

Ukrainian women dream that their daughters will achieve the highest level of education possible. "Education was always very important," remarks Rose. "We've had three daughters. They're all university graduates. I have nine grandchildren now: seven go to university, and two are in high school. They wouldn't think of not going to university." Because of the extreme emphasis on education and women's long history in the old country in setting up community schools, Ukrainian women achieved relatively high levels of education and did in fact enter the work force after World War II.

Younger Ukrainian women are making it through university and into professional positions in record numbers, reflecting generations of stress on education, but they have absorbed the message passed down from great-grandmother to grandmother to mother that staying home to raise children is the noblest of all careers. Says Bettina, age nineteen: "If I decide to have a family, I will stay at home and raise my kids. It's important that you stay home with your children at least until they start school. They need a mother at home." Sixteen-year-old Cara plans to attend university. She wants to work, but when she has children she would like to stay home with them: "It's important to have a mother, instead of sending them to a day care center and have someone else look after them." As with Chinese Canadian women, juggling education, career, and family requires a delicate balancing act. Ukrainian Canadian women will try to finesse the two streams of activity in a way that favors motherhood and family life.

Sherry, who earned a bachelor's degree in education, took advantage of an exchange program through the University of Saskatchewan to visit Ukraine for six weeks. Although she learned to speak Ukrainian as a child, the trip was the first time she felt totally immersed in her culture. She dreams of taking her own children to the old country. Bettina is trying to learn how to make Ukrainian ritual breads from her mother; if they are good enough, she will take them to the next folk festival. Marusia, an active volunteer, speaks for many women of her generation: "We try to keep everything alive as much as possible; all the points of identity. We go overboard, but we're sensitive to giving our kids an identity, especially in today's untethered society. We feel that a solid sense of identity—of self-worth and self-respect—makes you a stronger person, a stronger woman. It affects your social behavior, even your politics."

Mothers express guarded optimism about their daughters' lives, however. What concerns them? "Jobs," several reply immediately. In a tight economy, many people in Saskatchewan work part-time or temporary jobs; many others move from job to job, seeking security. The unemployment rate runs higher in Saskatoon than in the province as a whole (12 percent as opposed to 6 or 7 percent). For women who can afford to stay at home while raising children, staying out of the public economy is a welcome relief.

For women whose traditional and contemporary roles spin centripetally toward home and family, the future depends heavily on a successful marital choice. Even though few relationships are made in heaven, happiness is relative, Olha, a widow of eight years observes: "My husband is gone. We were together forty-eight years. We raised five lovely children. I am alone now, but I still can do the work. I am just like Queen Ol'ha, all by myself in a big house, a big yard. It would have been nice if my husband could have lived, though. . . . Now I am four corners of the house."

The Last Day

Fifteen women sit around three long tables pushed end-to-end across a church basement. Most are over seventy and speak English through an interpreter. They wear kerchiefs loosely tied on their heads and flowing dark clothes, some for practicality and some for widowhood. This is the largest group interview I've conducted in all the communities. We talk and make cabbage rolls simultaneously. Great stainless steel bowls overflow with whole cabbage leaves boiled to perfection. Men rush out of the enormous and well-equipped kitchen to replenish the leaves and bring the women large pans of aromatic stuffing.

The air fills with the sweet cabbage and a choir of voices struggling with my questions, giggling, laughing, and sighing with equally sweet memories. Fingers fly to the bowl, to the table, to the pan, and back to the bowl, deftly wrapping each tasty morsel in its small blanket. Memories of the old country fly along the table almost as quickly, and a few tears make their way into the neat rolls. Valiantly, I drop a spoonful of stuffing on a leaf in front of me, but my fingers do not seem to find the same rhythm as those around me. My neighbors chuckle and gently show me again how to fold the leaves so the filling does not leak. They forgive my clumsiness when I tell them that my mother's father, George Billson, designed the flagship Ukrainian Orthodox Church in Hamilton; artist as well as architect, he also painted the onion-domed beauty in oils, a treasure I inherited many years ago.

Women are talking about how they always used to work like this in the old days, in large groups, side by side, whether it was stooking hay, planting, quilting, or cooking for the harvest workers, always singing Ukrainian folk songs to counterpoint their work. I ask if they would sing for me now. A few older women start out slowly, words tumbling over words, until fifteen voices swell into a medley of sweet, simple songs about life and women and love. More tears and fresh memories come into the next round of cabbage rolls and questions, followed by more songs and laughter. Somehow we have managed in the usual two hours to work through all the questions, a dozen lilting songs, and hundreds of tiny rolls. As the cabbage leaves run out, so does the afternoon and my time in Saskatoon.

After hugs and thank-yous, I head back to the airport for my last flight across Canada, this time across the golden girth of the prairies to the heart of the industrial East. As the plane heads from Saskatoon to Winnipeg to Toronto, I reflect on the generosity and honesty women have shared with me during this project. I settle into the seat, content, but a sudden asthma attack alerts me to the fact that I have inadvertently been seated in the last nonsmoking row on a smoking flight. Gasping for breath, and inhaler in hand, I am led to the only other open seat on the flight—first class!

For the next few minutes I chat about my project with an off-duty pilot. Suddenly he excuses himself and slips into the cockpit, then returns, beaming: "The pilot would like to meet you and hear about your research. Come up front." As I grope my way into the darkened cockpit and take one of the four seats, just behind the co-pilot, I am overwhelmed by a dazzling array of lights and switches. This is another world! I strap myself into the seat and chat about my findings. The three men seem fascinated and tell me proudly that their airline, one of Canada's subsidized companies, now has more than sixty female pilots, modern-day pioneers in their own right. The skies are one of the last frontiers for women to penetrate. They do well, the pilot reports, except when some passengers find out that a woman is at the controls of a 747. "That will change over time," he reassures me.

By now we are flying over the Thousand Lakes region of western Ontario, just past the Manitoba border. The cockpit windows wrap around three sides, enveloping us in air and sky. I wonder if I might have enjoyed this career had I known that it was open to me. The sun begins to set behind us, splashing pink across the mirrored lakes below and the gigantic popcorn clouds all around us. The sight etches into my memory. I, too, feel like Queen Ol'ha—strong, proud, and privileged.

9

Common Pain

Burdens Women Share

We're building another home for battered women and children here—
how many thousands of dollars are going to these homes? Maybe some
of that money could be given to research about what is causing all that
torment in the homes. What is happening to those people that they have
to fight all the time, that they have to beat up their wives, their children?
What's causing them to become the kind of people they are? There must
be something in our home life, something in our educational system.

—Lara

Sources of Confusion and Oppression

I began by asking the question, "Are women equally subordinated
everywhere?" After listening to the voices of women in these seven
cultural communities, I realize that the answer is not a simple one.
Women in some groups have more power, more opportunities,
more respect and decision-making authority, and more role balance
than women in other groups. Yet common threads run through all
the lives, threads that have more to do with being a woman than
with being a member of a particular culture.

These threads weave the tapestry of women's oppression. It is a
rough-woven cloth that pricks and binds, that wraps us together as
sisters, and that often makes it difficult for us to move or speak
freely. Sometimes we throw the tapestry off our shoulders and
march together; sometimes it feels too heavy to lift for more than a
flickering historical moment.

Monique Bégin, who provided two decades of leadership for the
Royal Commission on the Status of Women in Canada, reflected on
the common patterns she had discovered in women's lives:

What I discovered month after month, week after week, is how universal women's experiences were; this would be a lesson for life. Women in rural areas of Canada, women living and working in cities, native or immigrant women, young students as well as older women, Francophone and Anglophone women, all said the same things. They spoke of their aspirations and their lack of opportunities, the prejudices and stereotypes, the discrimination and injustice, the need to change marriages and families to attain real and equal partnership. They spoke of the children they cared for. They stress how the current political, economic, and social structures of Canada were an insult to their dignity as women. What they had to say was most empowering.[1]

Canadian feminists write from within a political culture that recognizes rather than denies the many differences among women.[2] Recognizing differences is essential, but recognizing the common patterns in the tapestry of women's oppression is equally important.

Patterns of Women's Oppression

The transformation to equal relations between males and females will be neither easy nor swift. Many factors (including the astronomical increase of domestic violence) indicate the tricky nature of attempts to change the status of women. Beyond amassing statistics on alcohol and drug abuse, spousal assault, child abuse, unemployment, suicide, and depression—all thought to be consequences of massive social upheavals—we must go one step further: How and why have these consequences occurred? What special problems affect male-female relationships? Can we find ways to mitigate such impacts in other eras, with other groups? How should we rethink policy and legislation to address these problems? What patterns run through this tapestry of women's oppression? The women in these communities spoke of six, each a powerful force in their lives.

THE PATTERN OF MALE SUPERIORITY

In cultures troubled by pervasive male chauvinist attitudes, male dominance, and violence or other abuse against women, both women and men observe that parents seem to spoil boys more than girls. Favoritism usually extends to large gaps between male and female education. The major exception, Ukrainians, report less favoritism toward males, greater role crossover, and more emphasis on education for females. Women in all cultures seem by and large to accept their roles, although younger women especially express deep resentment toward their parents for favoring the males.

Childhood male privilege spawns adult male superiority, expressed in implicit assumptions that men have the right to make final decisions about controversial issues for their wives and children as well as for themselves. Although most middle-aged and younger women assume that they will have some input into the decision-making process, married women vary on how assertive they are willing to be in order to make their opinions heard. Chinese, Blood, and Jamaican women struggle against traditional assumptions that more clearly favored male superiority; Mennonite, Ukrainian, and Inuit women benefit from traditionally more balanced roles. For the Iroquois, who were traditionally matriarchal, bringing men more equally into the decision-making process creates its own challenge.

Many women feel helpless about male dominance. This is the way it is, they feel, and there is nothing one can do about it except "get rid of the men," which many reject as a viable option *for them*. If a woman's culture abhors divorce, she may stay in an abusive relationship and not seek more liberating options. If her culture disapproves of abortion and contraception, then she believes she has little choice but to become pregnant and stay with her man—or risk being labeled deviant. Other women now find even the most minor expressions of male superiority to be offensive and cause for resistance.

THE PATTERN OF RELIGIOUS DIMINUTION

From the Mennonite concept of the godhead to missionaries preaching in native communities against divorce (regardless of personal victimization), women have been made smaller and lower than both God and men. Ironically, it is women who flock to the churches to hear the sermons that put them in their place and exhort them to obey, and it is women who keep the churches going with unstinting hours of volunteer work.

In the Mennonite faith, for example, women were historically not allowed to act as keepers of the book (that is, ministers), but they were expected to be keepers of the faith. Ukrainian women served as deaconesses hundreds of years ago, but they still cannot serve as priests. The major exceptions in this pattern—the medicine women, or faith keepers, among the Blood and Iroquois—continue to play significant roles in the spiritual lives of their communities. Even in their case, though, the overlay of Christianity has reduced their traditional religions and roles to peripheral and (some believe) outmoded spiritual expressions.

In almost every culture, if we dig back far enough, women were defined as sinful, as ritually impure, as evil personified, or as witches. This legacy dissolves slowly, as reflected in the persistent segregation of the sexes in many religious activities. Religions tend to transform the concept of female obedience to man (and a male-imaged god) into a pivotal sacred belief. Women speak angrily about the fact that some churches to this day uphold a double moral standard regarding prostitution, battering, adultery, and alcohol abuse. As women see themselves on more equal terms, they will continue to revise religious and church practices in ways that can help erase these ancient but persistent sources of oppression.

THE PATTERN OF EDUCATIONAL DISADVANTAGE

This long-standing and pervasive pattern cuts across cultures, often reflecting assumptions of male superiority and favoritism toward boys. Women also explain that the pattern of educating males first and females second (if at all) comes from the cultural imperative for males to be providers: For a male to be properly equipped to support a wife and children, he must receive as much education and training as possible. While this argument makes some economic sense, it begins to fall apart in agricultural settings, where both male and female skills support the family. For those who aspired to leave the farm, however, education often promised the only way out.

Whatever the reasons, women complain that their brothers are sent to better schools and for longer periods. This has been a particular bone of contention for urban Chinese women, but older Ukrainian women mention it as well. In the case of Inuit, Iroquois, and Blood women, residential schools established by missionaries or the government drew females and males alike. As elders recall, however, girls were taught domestic skills and boys were taught skills that would help them circulate in the public sphere.

Even when women have received adequate education, a tendency exists to track their brothers into career paths that will enable them to move up the career ladder and gain economic and political ascendancy and, conversely, to track females into domestic work, teaching, nursing, social work, and other courses that would make them better mothers and better nurturers of men. Jamaican women emphasize education for themselves and their children; many were highly educated before coming to Canada, having been spurred on by their families to use education as a way out of poverty.

Finally, informal socialization—a powerful type of education that occurs in the family, on the streets, and in the media—has in every community perpetuated stereotypical images of women as lesser, lower, weaker, or dependent. The highly positive messages Iroquois, Ukrainian, and Mennonite women receive about the value of their contributions (as girls, then as women) help counteract these negative messages.

THE PATTERN OF ECONOMIC AND POLITICAL SUBORDINATION

Women in almost all the communities spoke angrily of the ways in which men and men's laws or policies have prevented them from achieving economic security and finding their political voice. While not all women have been relegated to the weak and fragile feminine role pressed upon them in the Victorian era—in fact, many have traditionally been held in high esteem for their economic contributions to family and community—they all complain that men get the best jobs, receive more pay for the same work, or make the major decisions for both family and community. Jamaican women who head and provide for their families rankle at the lack of economic opportunity that plagues females everywhere.

Women mention severe restrictions on public sphere participation, either in the workplace or in political bodies. Even among Blood, Iroquois, and Inuit women, who have made outstanding leadership contributions to their communities, complaints surface about how difficult it still is to get elected to council or to gain equal access to jobs and housing. Many feel that women continue to suffer from pay inequities, differential benefits, the "glass ceiling" and lack of access to power structures, underemployment and unemployment, a lack of interesting work, or the inability to travel to where good work opportunities exist. Welfare dependency and

racial discrimination piled on top of gender discrimination combine to create especially recalcitrant economic problems for native
and minority women.

THE PATTERN OF FAMILY ENTRAPMENT

The fifth pattern, perhaps the most complex of all, women find the
most difficult to unravel. Across cultures, the tightly knotted economic and religious patterns described above define a woman's role
in the family, but the intensely emotional climate of family life further complicates that role. Whether she takes her place in a
male–female family system as daughter, wife, or senior mother or
heads her own single-parent household, people react violently to a
woman's attempts to be assertive, challenge authority, or choose reproductive, sexual, and financial freedoms.

Families form the key connective tissue of social life. As we have
seen, cultures vary on how they view women in the family—as the
heart in some, and as the outsider in others—but all families raise
common issues for women. Perhaps most importantly, they frame
the context in which a woman's "proper" role is debated. Families
are the home of the forced choice: children or work outside the
home, family or career, domesticity or public achievement. Many
women feel forced to choose the domestic sphere because of inade-
quate day care and the reluctance of many males to take on their
fair share of child care and housework.[3]

Women fall prey to the vision of female as heart and soul of a
family that needs her more than she needs herself. This pattern may
be less problematic for Mennonite women, who so clearly choose
this central family role, but even in that community a few women
grow depressed or cannot take the plunge into domesticity required by commitment to their faith. Even a woman who willingly
embraces motherhood and marriage may find herself caught in a
web of guilt and social pressure to meet the expectations of others,
often at her own expense. The "good woman" in every culture carries a heavy emotional load that women sometimes find overwhelming, leading to depression, drug and alcohol abuse, and attempts to escape the confines of tight definitions.

Where traditional cultures have emphasized male superiority
(even when these definitions are in the process of changing), family
life often presents a scene of violent and emotional power strug-

gles. Assumptions that women will nurse the sick, ease the aging process for elders, and tend the children—no matter what—sometimes add up to a very heavy burden. The woman who resists or rebels may find herself the victim of stony silence, angry outbursts, or violence.

Family entrapment also stems from the fact that the stigma of divorce or unmarried motherhood usually is visited more heavily upon women. The very fact of having a child may determine a young woman's life chances and her ability to make decisions for herself on her own terms. In this sense, our biology forms part of the trap. On the other hand, young women hear the biological clock ticking away as they try to finish their education and launch careers. The pressure to have children in spite of other aspirations restricts women's freedom to choose a lifepath that makes sense to them. Finding balance sometimes seems impossible, although many women devise creative means to solve this puzzle.

Finally, women in all cultures speak of the dilemmas of reproductive choice and access to adequate health care. From Inuit women in the Arctic who must be evacuated by plane when their due date approaches to teenagers who fear exposure to shame and parental wrath if they use birth control, women have not yet achieved liberation in regard to their bodies.

THE PATTERN OF PERSONAL VICTIMIZATION

For the most part, women fall victim to rape and battery not because they happen to be wealthy or impoverished, Chinese or Inuit, educated or illiterate, but simply because they are women. Rape crisis centers, shelters for battered women, and protective services for abused children stand out everywhere as important symbols of women's victimization. Women have been bitten, beaten, raped, and verbally assaulted—even burned at the stake—in order to keep them "in their place." Such patterns originated in ancient times, but they echo through more contemporary manifestations of control and abuse. Even today, systems of authority (such as police and courts) tend to minimize brutality against women as "a family matter," with the result that most violence against women goes unpunished.

Sadly, because violence breeds violence, women harmed in childhood may harm their own children and/or fall into the role of victims again themselves as adults. Mentally or physically abused women may find it difficult to leave their abusive partners, especially when they depend on them financially. In some cases this pattern comforts and reassures some females. (Robin Norwood argues that women who are deprived and harmed by their fathers in childhood may tend to seek abusive, distant males in their adulthood simply because these feel like familiar male-female interaction patterns.[4]) As women increasingly take on the role of provider, the likelihood of their being harmed increases also, as we saw in the cases of role reversal among Blood and Inuit couples.

Assault often lurks invisibly behind the facade of a "good" relationship, because many women will not discuss it even with families or friends. One woman characterized assault rates by saying offhandedly, "We hear about that once in a while. My sister's been beaten up by her husband before. I've heard other people. It is a problem for women here, as it is everywhere, but perhaps less so than in other communities." When I asked women in another community to name their most serious problem as a group, they immediately replied, "We're being assaulted by the men." Always, women implicate alcohol as a catalyst that lures both men and women toward the brink of interpersonal violence.

THE PARADOX OF CULTURE

Women suffer from diminished options because their cultures either approve of male dominance and violence or look the other way. Ironically, because these cultures also contain much that is worth preserving, women often lead efforts to protect them. Because culture includes everything from dancing and art to the rules for sharing wealth and power, however, preserving the more beneficial elements cannot be separated from preserving other elements, including age-old patterns that govern how males and females stack up in the power equation. Paradoxically, then, in seeking to keep their cultures, women may simultaneously perpetuate their subordination.

Worse yet, the laws and customs devised during centuries of male domination uphold these patterns and force them into women's subconscious thoughts. This exchange between two Jamaican teenage girls illustrates their power. Dagne and Susan say their friends want "looks and money . . . only looks, really" in a prospective beau. Dagne starts to say that she wants more:

Dagne: The kind of guy *I* would like to marry should be university educated, because I am going to be, and I think intellectually we should be on the same level. Mutual respect. He respects me, he lets me, you know, basically . . .

Susan (interrupting): "*Lets* you!?!" Listen to your words!

Dagne: Well, sure! I mean, I don't want to get involved with anyone like my boyfriend is now. I guess I got into that pattern of thinking. I feel like if I do something, he *lets* me do it.

Susan: You're being subordinate. Or you have to get around him.

Dagne: Yes. I guess I have fallen into that. I don't feel good about that at all.

Exchanges like this one occurred at some point during the interviews in every community, indicating a growing awareness of how deeply buried in the female psyche these old messages of male superiority still lie.

The lessons we learn from listening to the women in this book crystallize into a powerful statement about the impact of tradition on women's lives: *Male dominance threatens women, building layer upon layer of common pain.* Their stories also confirm that not all women are subordinate to men. If we imagine a continuum of oppression, some women in each community would fall closer to the extreme pole of total subordination, others toward total liberation. Similarly, if we place the cultures along the same continuum, some would lie closer to subordination, some closer to liberation. Each culture can point to significant changes that occurred historically in the status of women, or that are happening right now, that shift toward liberation or revert toward subordination. A step forward can be met very quickly by a backlash of forces to keep women "in their place." Conversely, generational differences that emerge during a period of rapid change sometimes wipe out centuries of tradition. Degrees of liberation need underscoring as much as degrees of subordination.

As with Dagne and Susan, we see that patterns of common pain slowly disintegrate as women begin to acknowledge how oppressed they have been. They develop scars to cover their wounds, work around the walls that constrict their lives, and find new ways to keep the positive sides of culture while reshaping the negative. As men begin to understand that oppressive, unbalanced patterns bind them as well, they join women in the struggle to weave a new and more comfortable fabric of gender relations. In the next chapter, I look at how the tapestry of oppression is fraying, even tearing apart, as women discover their uncommon strengths.

10

Uncommon Strengths

Women's Empowerment

I used to think that I was wasting my life, up until this point, but now I realize that I wasn't. It was okay for that to happen, that I had to raise my children by myself. That's what I feel most proud about in my life. But now, this time is for me.

—Velma

Searching for Identity in a Changing World

When women speak openly of their common pain, they portray one side of their lives, but the visible expressions of strength that emerge in every community equally deserve our attention. It is essential to underscore the positive aspects of female experience. While women paint a clear picture of hardship and frustration, they also describe their uncommon strengths and unique ability to survive in spite of traps and blocks.[1] As they craft individual identities and make sense of cultural identities, women display an impressive range of empowering strategies that go beyond just coping with pain. They shape the lives of children and communities. They learn new skills and harness the old. They work with other women to make things better in their small corner of the world. Some build strength through small, local groups and multiply their power by hooking into national and international women's organizations.

In the first chapter of this book I pictured women's issues as a tapestry woven from several patterns of oppression. Like all tapestries, there are lighter and darker areas, simpler and more complex figures, bold lines and subtle ones. When it comes to strengths and strategies, the imagery is similar. As the complex issues facing women intricately weave together, so do the solutions. Women's empowerment in one area (such as education) may render us powerful in another (such as work). Community solutions to lack of day care enable women to put educational and work skills to use. Support groups of all kinds appear to be a positive vehicle for expressing and reinforcing women's emotional openness, which in turn facilitates their ability to work creatively on other strategies.

Patterns of Strength and Wisdom

The patterns of women's power and strategies for change, as we have heard in these pages, spring from suffering and frustration, but also from hope and the ability to persist against the odds. Both women and men describe women's enormous ability to find meaning in chaos, to shine insight into the darkest corners, to rebound from the most trying circumstances, to endure emotional and physical pain, to hold families and communities together when things fall apart, and to reshape their lives doggedly until they make more sense. Their patterns of strength and wisdom include many variations on the following.

PATTERNS OF INDIVIDUAL ADAPTATION

I asked a group of Jamaican women in their thirties and forties, "What is the most significant thing that has happened to you in your life?" They replied without hesitating, "Raising my children by myself . . . and doing a good job of it." These strengths that stem from adversity contribute to their wisdom and help them achieve other dreams. For those who suffer from personal victimization, adaptations might mean establishing a shelter for battered women, seeking a college degree, going for counseling to lift the shawl of dependency, or seeking separation or divorce.

For women who fall into patterns of family entrapment, the struggle to achieve balance can be daunting. Many women cannot say, "I have to do something for myself." When they do achieve something for themselves, it often has to be within the context of the family role. Breaking out of old molds can be terrifying, but women do it. Melanie, a Ukrainian woman, talks about falling into a deep depression after her third child was born. Instead of prescribing antidepressants, her family doctor said, "I want you to go out and get a part-time job." She thought he was crazy when he insisted that her life was too oriented toward her family. His words seemed like a foreign language to her, totally antithetical to her upbringing. Melanie realized that he was right: She was trapped. She put her three-month-old baby into a play group for infants during the middle hours of each day and went to work in her older son's school cafeteria. She accepts this schedule because it fits into her role of wife and mother. She can still have the dishes done, beds made, and dinner prepared, and be there when the children leave in the morning and when they get home.

Suzanne, a Chinese Canadian woman who never worked outside the home, "found herself" after her last child left the nest ten years ago. She volunteers in an immigrant reception center, helping Chinese women from Hong Kong try their wings in a new environment. She makes sure she is home to make her husband's breakfast, lunch, and dinner, working her schedule in a way that does not compete with her primary role of homemaker. These individual strategies of finessing the balance between home and outside work suits some women very well. For others, though, nothing short of building a career outside the home will meet their need for independence and fulfillment.

PATTERNS OF ACHIEVEMENT AND HARNESSING ABILITIES

In every community, education serves as the main springboard for women to improve their chances of achieving independence, satisfying careers, and economic security. Among native people, female rates of high school and college completion often exceed male rates. Perhaps patience and conformity combine with sheer determination to propel them forward against the odds of lingering discrimination and family ties.

Ukrainian women have long viewed education as a necessity and have worked hard to build institutions that are open to both sexes. Jamaican and Chinese women embrace education as a clear advantage toward liberation. This pattern appears less often among the more conservative Mennonites, who define higher education as superfluous except for the few who will go into social work, teaching, or missionary work.

Theresa, a Ukrainian woman in her forties, was very excited when she finished her certification in elementary education and landed a contract for her first teaching job. ("This is a whole new phenomenon for us older women, you know.") Theresa divorced her abusive husband as soon as she was certain she could support herself. She says there are many older women like her in university seeking new lives: "After the children leave, we have to do something. We don't do the cooking we used to; time weighs heavily on our hands. Not all of us go to university, of course, but we have to do something."

PATTERNS OF ARTISTIC AND CULTURAL EXPRESSION

Blood women cook and help plan for Sun Dance, one reason this old tradition so central to Blood culture has persisted. They make velvet-soft pictures from dyed moose hair in a type of embroidery passed along by their mothers. Ukrainian women cultivate the arts of Easter egg painting, bread sculpture, weaving, and dancing, keeping the culture that helps define the community in spite of assimilation. Inuit women teach their children Inuktitut and the Scottish reels brought a century ago by whalers (now referred to as their "traditional dancing"). Chinese women learn the complicated recipes of their mothers and grandmothers and help prepare for the Great Chinese Dragon parade and other festivals.

Iroquois women, like the Blood, make the clothes for pow wows and painstakingly learn the slow, shuffling steps of traditional dances that would otherwise die out. Jamaican women dress up in every color of the rainbow for Caribana and make feasts of jerk chicken and goat meat stew. Mennonite women quilt and sew and keep the custom of visiting alive. In each of these acts—and many more—women affirm the beauty and uniqueness that keeps their cultures vibrant in a multicultural society.

PATTERNS OF POLITICAL PARTICIPATION AND COLLABORATIVE ACTION

Because the personal always accrues to the political, individual strategies ultimately make a collective statement. Beyond individual acts that preserve their cultures, women also contribute to the general political life of their communities. Inuit, Blood, and Iroquois women have fought hard to get elected to their tribal councils. Ukrainian and Chinese women have won seats in city elections. Women in all communities have supported candidates and championed positions through newspaper columns, letters to the editors, campaign work, and plastering broadsides throughout their neighborhoods.

The Mohyla Institute, the social and cultural institution associated with the Ukrainian Orthodox Church, was founded in 1916 by a small group of educated young men from Ukraine.[2] A community leader explains the original vision: "These men saw the problems that we faced adapting to Canadian life. They felt that there was a need for education; this was an idea transplanted from the old country." Ukrainian women made the institute work. It was an important answer to the urgent problem of placing children from the farms: "Where would they stay while they attended university or high school in the city?" Parents were anxious to give students a good home, so the institute was built as a hostel and a residential school. In keeping with the long-standing emphasis on education for girls, the institute was coeducational from the start. The first class (of 1917) included four females out of a couple dozen students, but the proportions became balanced later. This type of collaborative participation changed the face of education for generations of children of immigrants and farmers.

Using similar organizational strategies, but for a different cause, Inuit women have confronted the challenge of violence in their homes. Like other women in North America and elsewhere, they have looked to education as a way out of the problems generated by social upheaval. They also provide us with models of spousal assault support groups that include both the victim *and* the perpetrator, and that harness traditional values in bringing the couple to open communication and mutual respect. After trying shelters and safe houses, Inuit women realized that "mainstream" solutions might not fit their situation as well as innovative hybrid strategies.

Ukrainian women, like their Jamaican and Mennonite sisters, play central roles in Christian education, as Lara points out: "In church school we teach Ukrainian culture, traditions, and language. We teach catechism to the kids, a little bit of history and literature, and advise the youth groups. Without us, there wouldn't be a cultural program." Women sing in the choir, serve on the board of directors and trustees, and make mountains of food for fund-raising and other events. Mennonite women work together to serve missions overseas and to assist families at home who are going through hard times. Their tradition of service to others results in routine collaborative acts of generosity and tangible support.

Jamaican women help establish family planning clinics and help young women plan for education and careers. In every community, both women and men agree that women provide a sense of continuity with the past and hope for the future while dealing constructively with present problems. That women have always reached out to help one another, building cooperative alliances in times of need and in times of celebration, reflects a vital strength.

PATTERNS OF FAMILY RELIANCE

The opposite of family entrapment is the ability of women to rely on their families for mutual support and mutual responsibility.[3] Women in every culture, especially those under the age of sixty, speak of helping their sons to realize that caring for a home and children is not only women's work. A group of Jamaican women laugh as they compare notes on little victories: a boy of fourteen who loves to cook, and another who at thirteen automatically cleans up after meals and helps with his little brothers. They worry about the older teenage boys who seem to move away from domesticity when peer pressure sets in, but they support each other in reinforcing the boys' commitment to family. Otherwise all the domestic work reverts back to the mother, and these women have lost interest in that kind of entrapment.

Aside from establishing an understanding that women should be able to rely on their families, as well as vice versa, this pattern also means establishing respect for women's work. For Conservative and Old Order Mennonite women, strength means finding balance within the context of family and culture. They "keep the home fires burning" and keep their families together. Phrases like "she is the heart of the family," or the family's "spine" or "backbone," suggest the centrality of a woman's role. Yet their culture understands that a woman's work inside the home yields significant harvests, too.

Other women struggle successfully to define their work *outside* the home as being equally important as their spouse's. General Conference Mennonite couples talk before marriage about careers, jobs, and finances. Those who want to pursue their dreams of social work or missionary work, balancing them out with children at appropriate times, insist that their contributions as women cannot be placed second to those of men. The men agree. "She's her own person and I'm my own person," says one husband: "Fortunately we get to spend very special lives together, but we still can be individuals, and there are no strings attached to that." Although women might not always attribute their courage to change to the feminist movement, it is clear that messages of equality and liberation have filtered into their consciousness.

The Interplay of Domestic and Public Roles

In every culture, women's superior ability to adapt to tumultuous social change—or any change—defines their strength. Women seem to be coping better than men with the transformations that have swept through their communities. Whether change follows on the heels of immigration, being placed on reserves, or forced resettlement off the land, women seem to ride the upheavals more smoothly and easily. Why should this be so? I believe that the interplay of domestic and public roles actually helps shield women from the ravages of changing times.[4]

Anthropologists describe the insulating nature of women's role as keepers of the culture and the hearth, regardless of what happens around them. As Powers observes of the Lakota Sioux, "Women's participation in . . . Euramerican occupations in no way impinges on or detracts from their traditional roles, since in Lakota culture maternal and managerial roles are not regarded as antithetical."[5] In contrast, like Blood males, Oglala men have lost out on traditional and contemporary roles that have been usurped by government officials. Lurie agrees that "Indian women seemed to have held up better under the stresses of reservation life than men and are often in the forefront" of tribal affairs.[6] Men have in some ways suffered "greater identity dislocation" than women: Warriors, shamans, and hunters are obsolete, but mothering and domestic tasks remain.[7]

The following factors may also help explain the adaptive differential between males and females. First, even when women engage in nondomestic activities in traditional culture, their primary role is domestic. Second, women derive their primary sense of identity from the domestic role; for men this is at best a secondary source of identity or prestige. Third, this major part of the female role has remained consistent over time. Even if she works outside the home, a woman can still gain pleasure and prestige from being a good mother, wife, and homemaker. Fourth, in contrast, the major source of male role identity—the public sphere—has changed entirely and rapidly. Fifth, for women, engaging in paid work outside the home implies a liberating role expansion: Her paycheck gives her more power and authority at home, and she expands her social network. Sixth, with a man's inability to compete in the public sphere, staying at home implies a constrictive role contraction: He loses his paycheck (which usually means he must defer to his wage-earning partner), and his social network shrinks to traditionally lower-status members of his community (other unemployed men, housebound wives and husbands, and children).

Thus the woman's role as heart of the family helps protect her by providing continuity during times of change, and when she goes outside the home to work her horizons broaden. Conversely, when the man's role as provider dissipates (as has happened in native communities), staying at home—a place where his traditional role has been very limited—seems to narrow the boundaries of his world and make him more vulnerable to the upsetting aspects of change.

Balancing Power Between Women and Men

While one might expect women to acknowledge their "uncommon strengths," men in all the cultures also spoke, often in awe, of women's strength. They acknowledge that women have adapted to rapid change better than they have; they recognize women's superior capacity to juggle multiple roles; and they know that when men try to hold women down, men pay an emotional price as well. They understand women's central role in keeping the culture and how crucial this effort is to keeping their communities. Many men eagerly work side by side with women to achieve a better balance of power and shared roles in the home. Many advocate sharing both economic and political power—a position that would have shocked their fathers and grandfathers. They deplore the surge of family violence that seems to have flooded every community (except the Mennonites) as women have moved out of the domestic sphere.

Other men, of course, cling to the old ways, talking and living the language of male superiority. They thwart women's power at every opportunity. But in every community, women who are building organizations and new strategies for change actively seek out like-minded men as allies. Political strategies seem to work best when supportive men join dynamic alliances that challenge old power structures. Efforts to build or rebuild community and culture seem far more productive when the relationships between women and men proceed on an even keel.

Transforming Community and Society

As a Ukrainian leader points out, "We all know that if we didn't have women there wouldn't be a world." Women's strengths percolate to the surface through layers of domination, discrimination, and hardship. Below the "glass ceiling" lie many other ceilings, each one a challenge in its own right. Girls learn at an early age (although they might joke about it) that in order to succeed they will have to be twice as good as males. Women know that even when their achievements are not fully recognized, they must recognize themselves and forge ahead. Many women have learned that moving into the public sphere almost always means working two full careers, because they will continue to be the heart of the household. In a thousand creative ways, they find the time and energy to improve their economic well-being, support their friends and families, and have a few hours left to transform communities. Those who struggle against poverty and unemployment find myriad ways to feed the children and keep body and soul intact.

Together and alone, then, women possess an uncommon strength. This strength could be channeled into a powerful and empowering voice against violence, against discrimination and inequality, against sexism and racism, abuse and poverty. Women could present a united front that stands for healthy families and productive communities. Unfortunately, the feminist movement does not quite seize the imaginations of many women, in part because we fail to recognize the ways in which our unique strengths could be intertwined. Mobilizing our strength requires that we see our common ground while we respect our differences. The next chapter explores how diversity and the women's movement might come to terms with each other.

11

Diversity and the Future of the Women's Movement

We must not become disillusioned and hopeless at our difficulties at achieving unity. No group of men has been sufficiently foolhardy to attempt to embrace their entire gender in one homogenous consensus (except, perhaps, misogyny) and political will.

—Greta Hofmann Nemiroff[1]

A great deal has been accomplished by the multiple waves of feminist reform that have swept the world during the nineteenth and twentieth centuries. Continuing change will depend upon the ability of social movements to involve women who have been marginalized by the interlocking forces of gender, ethnicity, and social class. If positive social change is to touch the lives of a broad spectrum of women, though, political action must be based on recognition of cultural differences in female experience. In order to build effective coalitions against the injustices they suffer and toward strong communities, women have to discover their common ground. This means recognizing and respecting our diversity.

As we have seen throughout these chapters, messages about what it means to be a woman are conveyed from grandmother to mother, mother to daughter, down through the generations, giving birth to a uniquely female experience in each cultural community. Unfortunately, these messages can either empower or disempower women. Messages that mandate passivity and obedience in the private world of families tend to translate into female passivity and obedience in the public worlds of education, economics, and politics. Messages that define women as strong, competent, and brave—hardy perennials that bloom in all their splendor year after year, in spite of life's seasonal changes—help women move at will between the private and public worlds with grace and stamina.

Revitalizing the women's movement means learning to identify all the flowers in our female garden, and to appreciate each one for what she brings to the landscape. It means coming to terms with the subtle variations in how women feel about themselves. And it means overcoming our hesitation to connect with women whom we perceive as somehow "different."[2] A chrysanthemum looks and feels different from a daisy or a poppy, and each has its own roots; together, though, they splash brilliant color across the flowerbed.

A feminist movement that superimposes definitions of womanhood rooted in white, middle-class society will not attract women whose identity is complicated by ethnic or subordinate class status. A powerful women's movement will focus both on our *common* experience of gender oppression—daily expressions of abuse, sexual harassment, and discrimination that affect all women to some degree and form a springboard for action—and on the *unique* experience of gender oppression created by differences in social class, culture, race, or age.[3] Attending to both will elevate our political effectiveness in achieving shared goals.

Striving for inclusiveness could overload the women's movement by asking it to strike at the very core of all the ills and "isms" in our societies. It would be difficult for any movement to shoulder that burden competently. Failing to capitalize on both our commonality and our uniqueness, however, fragments our movement and diminishes our chances for cohesion and collaboration. Understanding, accepting, and leveraging our diversity is the key to a thriving women's movement.

Yet, although women in all walks of life are becoming more comfortable with the complexities of our female landscape, when I asked about women's liberation, many women said they do not agree with it and give it little thought. They perceive feminists as "uppity women" who want to be *too* independent and self-sufficient. They define "women's libbers" as strong, aggressive women who have no use for men, who refuse to have doors opened for them, and who reject being treated tenderly. Such perceptions signal a failing of the women's movement.

Many who acknowledge that liberated women may be doing something positive for themselves and for their children fear that achieving status and power equal (or superior) to men presents a dangerous threat to the stability of their relationships. Some women in each culture mentioned the failure of women who work outside the home to maintain the "keeper" role that in the past may have improved stability. Complaints about failure to discipline children, failure to pass on tradition, and failure of both genders to treat each other with consideration, respect, and trust are reflective of these deeper concerns about a changing and often bewildering society. A few women see day care—one of the centerpieces of the women's movement—as contributing to modern social pathology: If a woman gives her children to someone else to raise, how will she know what they are learning in terms of values, morals, skills, and culture? The question is not an idle one.

The chasms between middle- and lower-income women, and between those who were well and poorly educated, became painfully clear to me as I journeyed through various cultures. For some women, adopting a feminist attitude feels like adopting an adversarial position against men. This may be particularly true for minority, native, and immigrant women in their simultaneous struggle against racial or ethnic discrimination. And for a woman who feels trapped in a bad relationship for economic reasons, "liberation" threatens the security that she believes serves her better, at least for the time being. Feminism, with its alien ideas and strange expectations, asks her to give up too much before she in fact has the financial independence and cultural freedom to break away.

For all of these reasons, leveraging women's diversity presents a forbidding challenge. The women's movement falters when we take the radical intellectual position that anything short of full liberation is "false consciousness." Perhaps on some level *no* woman can break completely free from the negative effects of being socialized as a female in a male-dominated world, but it is intellectual arrogance to accuse women of false consciousness when they make choices within the context of their cultures.

Most of the women I spoke with are aware of the obvious and subtle oppressions they suffer every day. If false consciousness creeps in, it is not through lack of awareness or sophisticated definitions. For many women distancing themselves from notions of feminism reflects a persistent willingness to define exploitation or inequality as culturally acceptable, or even necessary. Women suffer from diminished options because they live in a world that either approves of male dominance and violence, or looks the other way. By preserving their culture—which may enhance survival in a rapidly changing world—women sometimes also perpetuate their subordination. That leaves many women between the proverbial rock and a hard place. For those caught in the grip of this dilemma, sisterhood becomes all the more important.

Women can achieve equality only if feminists start where each woman lives, giving her credit and respect for who she is, not putting her down for her willingness to assume the roles of housekeeper, kin keeper, or faith keeper that her culture may mandate and she may wholeheartedly embrace. Many women spoke of a disturbing association they have noticed in their communities between "women's liberation" on the one hand and divorce, battering, and alienation on the other. Whether the association exists or not—or exists in the reverse direction—for many women the price seems too high for a liberation they believe is already theirs, or is unattainable anyway.

Harnessing Diversity: Strategies for Collective Empowerment

What kind of movement could include rather than exclude women? What would make a broad range of women feel welcome and heard? What would empower women across cultures to work for their common interests while respecting their differences? I offer a few suggestions here—some of them obvious (but honored more in the breach than the observance), others not so obvious. I believe the women's movement will stand a better chance of gaining steam and solidifying old ground if we apply these guiding principles in both our scholarship and our activism.[4]

RESEARCH ON, WITH, AND BY WOMEN

How we see ourselves as women is inextricably interrelated to ethnicity, social class, and other factors that provide or restrict both interpersonal and public power. Analysis of data based on only one or two of these major social dimensions risks distorting the realities of women's lives.

- Research should be structured to take into account the impact of gender on race, class, and ethnicity, as well as the impact of these dimensions on ethnic identity.
- Theoretical and empirical investigations of women's oppression or power must take into account the definitions of reality held by women in cultural communities, rather than superimposing the definitions of academic or ideological communities.
- Theoretical and empirical investigations of marginalized groups, such as the native communities in this book, must be sensitive to the differential impact of cross-cultural contact on males and females.
- Feminists should reexamine their research and conceptual tools by asking the question, "Does this methodology exclude any group of women by its very structure or design?" If the answer is yes, they should invent a way to bring in those who would be left out. This means more community-based joint research or participatory research, helping women to learn emerging feminist research methods and adapt them to their own realities.
- Feminist research should result in coauthoring with women from different experiences and backgrounds, with a percentage of royalties returning to communities that participate in the project.

THEORIES ABOUT AND BY WOMEN

As I have tried to show in this book, while the theory of male domination and female subordination forces all women to examine their position vis-à-vis men, nonetheless it leaves out women for whom it is less true.

- While feminist theory is important to construct, it is also critical to reconstruct our basic assumptions about power, roles, subordination, oppression, and male domination. When the words women use to explain or describe our condition leave out the exceptions, they leave out women's power.
- Feminist theory, if it is to be powerful, must be inclusive. No theoretical system can simply ignore exceptions or redefine them as mere aberrations.
- Scholarly or rhetorical claims for multiculturalism must be tempered by recognition of gender stratification within cultural communities and in the society as a whole.

- Such claims must also be tempered by recognition of the differential status and access to resources accorded to certain groups, particularly racial minorities.
- We should not be in the business of belittling, dismissing or explaining away our power. Women are too quick to engage in "yes, but" discourse with each other. (For example: "Mohawk women enjoyed considerable power." "Yes, but that is because men allowed them to have power.") This type of thinking entraps women in a no-win maze of "logical inconsistencies": Even when we negotiate or take power from men, our sisters will not recognize it, let alone celebrate it. This tendency to disempower women conceptually must be rethought.
- Theories and research findings about women should be presented in accessible language and published in accessible outlets.

WOMEN'S ORGANIZATIONS

Greaves says that inclusiveness means organizations should "give up some old notions of operating and adopt, in the name of women and for the sake of the women's movement, some new ways of operating."[5] These new ways may be more burdensome and less efficient, but they are ultimately more authentic and more effective.[6]

- Women's organizations should consider using rotational, alphabetic, or other randomized means of filling at least half of their leadership positions. Women who are discriminated against because of race, culture, sexual orientation, or age may feel insecure about running for chair of a committee, or even volunteering to fill a minor position. If it is assumed that *all* members of an organization are expected to contribute in the ways they are able, and that they do not have to play games of "palace intrigue" or in-group politics, they will feel more at ease about participating.
- Women's organizations should make every effort to establish ties with other groups locally, regionally, nationally, and globally. Ukrainian women in Canada are extremely accomplished at this, sending representatives to multiple levels of organizations. Their connections to women's groups all over the continent and world strengthen their local base.

- Women's organizations should choose accessible activities and venues in terms of timing, physical challenge, and cost. Holding a monthly meeting at an expensive restaurant shuts out the majority of women, especially those with children and/or low income. The Women's Institute (founded in Canada, but with branches all over the free world) is a good example of how to involve as many people as possible. By rotating meetings from home to home and asking for a donation of only the change in one's purse, the majority of women in the community who wish to participate can do so. If a member's purse contains no change on meeting night, the hat is simply passed along; she can contribute another time.
- Women's organizations should make conscious efforts to hold "summits" for their leadership to share ideas, goals, and plans. Even if this means the leadership of local shelters, rape crisis centers, programs for women with disabilities, and political caucuses meet once a year in a park for an afternoon of talk, the movement will become more interwoven: Perspectives will be expanded, and ideas for collaborative future action will be generated. Summits that include users of services, service providers, and activist leaders will be particularly powerful.
- Organizations should make every effort to offer child care and transportation to those who need it so all interested women can join and participate.
- Larger organizations should "adopt" smaller ones. For example, women's organizations with newsletters can reach out to smaller groups and offer to publish articles and notices of mutual interest. Similarly, conference programs of larger, financially stable organizations can advertise upcoming events for less well-endowed groups.
- Every women's organization should examine its structure, modes of interaction, meeting formats and times, agendas, and tendencies toward hierarchy. They should ask: Whom are we serving? Can we shift toward more inclusiveness? Can we reach out to other kinds of women? Can we operate in a more egalitarian and circular fashion, rather than hierarchically? Can we dialogue and strive for consensus rather than argue, debate, vote, and win? Can we find power and strength in our diversity? (The answer is, of course, yes; some women's organizations already follow most or all of these modes.)

- The women's movement, through its various organizations, should "concentrate on improving the position of women less in relation to men than in relation to society as a whole."[7] In other words, women's place in society should be approached in terms of such issues as basic human rights, equity, access, and parity.

WOMEN'S CONFERENCES

Typically, women who attend regional and national conferences come from the universities. Those of us who teach, study, and write about women are a privileged class by virtue of our education and our position in the academy. So that our research and writing—which occasionally influences social policy and public understandings of women—will reflect the broader realities of women's lives, Greaves says that "we must constantly ask the ordinary woman, particularly the ordinary activist woman, what we should be doing. Failing to do this not only renders us irrelevant . . . [but] incomplete. Only by staying in touch with less privileged women's lives, dreams, and ideas will we be enabled to use our access to the academy and the movement effectively . . . for the benefit of [all] women."[8] Staying in touch means changing the ways in which conferences are typically planned.

- Women's conferences should be designed to include women of color, women outside academia, and women in all kinds of academic disciplines and institutions.
- Women's conferences should be carefully designed not only to present and draw women from a variety of worlds, but to desegregate them during conference activities. Too often there is a specific session or panel devoted to women of color (or native women, or Third World women), which tends to attract those who are specifically interested in the topic because of their own research agenda. While there may be value in offering sessions that focus on cultural or national differences, it is also necessary to reflect our diversity on virtually every panel. This is how we will learn from each other.
- Conference organizers should avoid using the "malestream" model: panels of multiple presenters who have fifteen minutes each to hit the high points of their work. This reinforces superficiality. By the time three or four speakers take fifteen minutes,

are introduced, and followed by a designated discussant's comments, there is usually little time left over for audience participation in a meaningful debate. What Greta Hofmann Nemiroff calls the "old patriarchal authoritarian 'talking heads' model" works against deeper understandings between women.[9] It should be replaced by more interactive models that invite participation from many women and stimulate dialogue.

- The classroom model itself—with presenters up front, and the audience in rows facing presenters—should be discarded. This model creates an intimidating atmosphere in which only the most daring will confront or challenge a panelist's assumptions. It also reinforces the myth of presenter as "expert" or authority.[10]

KEEPERS OF THE KEEPERS

Our ability to create new formats in which any woman can feel comfortable, heard, involved, and respected mirrors what women have struggled for in a male-dominated world. It is surprising that distancing and alienating models persist when so much as been written about women's unique ways of learning, knowing, and interacting. The women's movement, if it is going to succeed among anyone other than a select group of feminists, must take a very different tack. We must learn to appreciate women's different strengths, even when they may not be ours.

Although it will be difficult for women to exert enough pressure to overturn the prevailing ideologies and asymmetries of power that form the residue of centuries of male domination, we must keep in mind that humans create social institutions such as inequality between women and men—and that humans can change them as well.[11] In fact, convincing change will most likely be achieved by changing institutions rather than individuals,[12] which is precisely why it is so crucial for women's organizations to become inclusive, productive, and politically powerful.

For far too long women's contributions have been devalued by men; we as women must not shut each other out or in any way contribute to making each other smaller or less worthy. Mutual respect, inclusiveness, and shared power are the keys to making the women's movement stronger. Rather than fall into the trap of devaluing women who live different lives, we can be "keepers of the keepers," supporting each other in our common pain, harnessing our uncommon strengths, and celebrating our diversity every inch of the way.

Our uncommon strengths allow women to move beyond history toward a twenty-first century that, I predict, will be a bountiful one for women. I see strengths among women as individuals and in smaller groups, but the women's movement, which moves along crabwise, would benefit from our collective rethinking and reweaving.

We must think not only of women in the generic sense, but women with all of our colors and textures, our cultural idiosyncrasies and our individual styles. To be successful, the movement must be able to work with the "whole cloth" of women's experience. I hope *Keepers of the Culture* will bring us closer to that place.

End weaving . . .

I sit by the wood stove on a cold, starry night, reading the latest batch of letters from women in the communities. I can see from the range of comments that they have taken the review process seriously, although their corrections are few. Rather than the criticism I feared in moments of self-doubt, their comments convey the enthusiasm and delight that I hoped for in my most optimistic moments. This last stage of an eight-year project brings its own sweetness. A few comments suggest the commitment women feel to making their voices heard:

> Reading the entire book will be a pleasure. It was with some trepidation that I began to read our chapter. I wondered, "What did I say? Would I still feel the same or would I be embarrassed?" Well, I have to admit that my feelings and views are still the same, but today I would express them less vehemently. Yet, the ideas we expressed remain much the same today. Thanks for giving me the opportunity to review our chapter. It brought back many memories and much laughter. I look forward to receiving the final product and sharing it with my daughter and granddaughters.

> Thank you for giving me the opportunity to review and respond to your draft. I chuckle at the boldness of the words and ideas which I presented to you way back then. However, I was young, vibrant, and

determined, which allowed me to express my views as strongly as I did. Today, in comparison, I am much more mellow, mature, and wiser. My views haven't changed much, but I'm more cautious, experienced, and more family focused—and take into consideration wholeheartedly my husband's thoughts/opinions. I still am determined, though, and a little more aggressive in a constructive way. The book feels really powerful.

I think the book is going to be really nice for everybody in general to read.

It was certainly a very pleasant surprise hearing from you after such a spell. I am happy to see the years of your hard work are finally coming to fruition. I read through the material and I am happy to report that you did an excellent and very thorough job. I couldn't find any fault at all (even though I tried hard). We could even identify the parts that we contributed. So there!

Thank you for this opportunity to proofread these chapters. I've found them very interesting, informative, and enjoyable reading. I like the title for our chapter! We do have pleasant memories of the afternoon that we spent with you a number of years ago.

I have just completed reading the draft and enjoyed it. Our 13-year-old daughter also read it and enjoyed it. It was good to hear from you. We wish you well.

Enjoyed reading this copy! Hope you can get the drift of my thoughts on the back of the pages. Best wishes on your completion of this ambitious research project. I sure would like to read the book. Let us know where and when we can purchase it. Better yet, deliver some personally.

I am writing, not grammatically correct, but what lies in my heart. It is so much a matter of perspective: If equality means the equal distribution of men and women in any given vocation or club, society has a long way to go. But if we value male and female contributions equally (they may have very different vocations) and value each human as our equal, wouldn't that go a lot further in attaining a "just society"? Society is falling apart at the seams. Could we somehow restore worth to the "keeper of the home" so that woman's place as a chef, laundress, teacher, nurse, seamstress, chauffeur, and so forth, is properly valued? I'm not saying that all women may do is work at home, but can't we see the need to strengthen the social fabric of our society from the very basic institution, the home?

It was good to receive our chapter and so much better to have a talk on the phone! You certainly have captured the spirit of our life and our descendants. I'll be very pleased to read your book when it's available. Until I see you again, take care!

I curl up to the fire's warmth and read the letters again—letters from strangers who became colleagues and friends. Sisters. My journey is over, yet as women will now have the opportunity to hear each other's voices, it has just begun.

Appendix A
Basic Assumptions about the
Oppression of Women

Before embarking on this journey, I read widely about women and gender relations. I developed a set of basic premises or assumptions derived from feminist theory as laid out in Patricia Lengermann and Ruth Wallace's *Gender in America*, all of which relate to the over-riding hypothesis that women are universally subordinate to men.[1]

Different Status. "*Women's situation is different . . . from that of men in terms of material resources, power, valuation, and autonomy.*"

Inferior Status. "*Women's situation is not only different from but inferior to that of men.*"

Dominant/Subordinate Relationship. "*No documented case exists of a society in which women are dominant over men*"; only "*variations . . . in the degree of subordination.*"

Power and Control. "*Control over the means of production . . . is the primary source of power in society.*"

Liberation and Resistance. "*Powerlessness produces a counterforce, the wish for emancipation.*"

Categorization. "*Any member of a society can, from an early age, distinguish between males and females.*"

Functional Differentiation. "*All societies make clear distinctions between the activities and personality traits typically expected of individuals placed in the category 'female' and those placed in the category 'male.'*"

Segregation. "*All societies reserve certain spaces for 'males only' or 'females only.' Persons of the excluded gender who enter these spaces are subjected to severe social sanctions.*"

Access to Material Goods. "*Within any social class, gender arrangements in our society give women less access to money than men.*"

Differential Valuation. "*Almost all societies believe males are more important and more valuable than females.*"

Unequal Power. "*A variety of resources makes it easier for men to work their will in the world.*"

Barriers. *Gender inequality and* "*identity throw up massive barriers to free individual choice for both males and females.*"

Gender Impoverishment. "*Gender inequality impoverishes both women and men.*"

Pain and Anger. "*Our present gender arrangements create a situation of chronic psychic pain for both women and men.*"

Appendix B
Guideline for Interviews

After developing the logic of the basic assumptions in Appendix A, my next task was to create a set of questions—an interview guide—that would test the premises. The interview schedule included questions asked of women in all the communities, as well as questions tailored to each culture. It expanded to include questions raised by each group about their particular concerns.

I asked questions in public rather than personal terms. For example, the question "What are the major problems facing women in your community today?" maintains emphasis on public issues rather than personal troubles. This gives women a way of "grasping the social relations organizing the worlds of their experience" as they participate actively in a self-reflective dialogue.[2] A specific case is merely a point of entry into a larger social and economic analysis of the lives of women in general in each community.

Beyond interviewing, I also engaged in direct observation and participant observation throughout my stay of two to six weeks in each community (with return visits in some cases).

I. INTRODUCTION

1. (Introduction of the interviewer)
2. (Purpose of the interviews; informed consent agreement)
3. (Demographics/introductions)

II. GENDER/ETHNIC IDENTITY

1. Let's start with a very general question:
   What does being [Blood, Iroquois, etc.] and female mean to you?

397

2. What are the most significant things that have happened to you in your life?
3. What are the most significant things that you have done?
4. How has being [——-] affected what you have experienced or what you have done?
5. Who are the most important people in your life? How are they important?

III. GENDER INEQUALITY

Functional and Status Differentiation

1. What terms would you use to describe a good [——-] woman?
2. What about a good [——-] man?
3. How do these characteristics affect the kind of lifestyles women and men live here?
   —(probe for expectations for education, work, political and economic power)
4. How do you feel about those differences?

Inferior Status/Differential Evaluation

5. Some people say that a woman's situation in life is different from a man's.
   —Do you think that is true for [——-]?
   —If yes, in what ways is a woman's life different?
   —(probe for material resources, power, valuation, autonomy)
6. Are there ways in which the situation of the [——-] woman is *inferior* to that of the [——-] man?
7. Are there ways in which the situation of the [——-] woman is *superior* to that of the [——-] man?
   —If so, how and why?
   —How did that come about, historically?
   —Is that only for certain women, or for all?
   —Is that superiority true only for certain circumstances?
8. How do you think [——-] men feel about women's situation being superior in these ways?

Categorization

9. Are female and male babies valued equally?
   —How does that make you feel?
10. I'm wondering how these male/female differences get started in the first place.

—Are male and female babies dressed differently during the first year(s) of life?

—Are they treated differently in the first year(s)?

—What about later, during school years?

11. Are those traditions changing at all?

—have you raised your children in the "old way"?

—Why or why not?

12. Do you think the younger generation (the children) will pass the old attitudes and ways on to their children?

—Why or why not?

—What will persist?

Segregation

13. Are there places in the [————] community that are thought of as "men only" or "women only" places?

—Where (inside, outside the home)?

—How did this come to be?

—Are these informal rules followed?

—What happens if someone violates the rules?

14. What does that separation of males and females do for the community?

Work and Child Care/Gender Roles

15. Who is most likely to be the major breadwinner in a [————] home?

16. Is the woman likely to be working outside the home?

17. How do people react to women who work outside the home?

—Impact on male/female relations

—Impact on children

—Impact on lifestyle

—Impact on woman's well-being

18. Who does the household chores if the woman works outside the home?

19. Does the [————] man take over responsibility for child care if the woman works outside the home?

20. What about day care? Is this a reasonable alternative?

—(probe for quality, cost, accessibility)

Interpersonal Power

21. Who makes the decisions in most households?

—different areas of decision making

—How did that come about?

—Is it changing?

Access to Material Goods

22. Which resources do women have major control over?

—(probe for money: checkbooks, savings, investments, property, house, time, leisure activities, children, other)

23. When [———] women work outside the home, do you usually earn as much as the men?

—Should you?

—How do you feel about it?

24. Can you decide what happens to your earnings?

Unequal Power

25. Are there other ways in which men express power over women in your community?

—(probe for domestic violence, adultery, desertion, rape/sexual abuse, nonsupport, alcohol/drug abuse, other)

—Are there other ways in which women exert their power over the men?

26. What are the major problems facing women in your community today?

Barriers

27. Some women feel that inequality between the sexes throws up barriers to individual freedom of choice for both females and males. In other words, inequality hurts both genders, although in different ways. Do you agree with that?

—What kinds of barriers do you face (where do they come from)?

—What barriers do men face?

—How can these barriers be eliminated?

Gender Impoverishment

28. Would you say that [———] men are warm, loving, and able to express their feelings?

—(probe for why or why not, and under what circumstances)

29. Are the women like that?

—Why or why not, and under what circumstances?

30. Do [———] women see themselves as strong, competent, independent, and self-sufficient?

—(probe for why or why not, and under what circumstances)

31. Are the men like that?
    —(probe for why or why not, and under what circumstances)

Liberation and Resistance

32. If [——] women have less control and power, and if they feel frustrated, how do they react?
    —(probe for resistance, rebellion, submission, conforming to men's wishes, passing, tricking, retreating or giving up, other)

Pain and Anger

33. How do you feel about the situations we've been talking about?
    —What angers you the most?
    —How do you deal with your feelings?

34. Do you think the men ever feel guilty about the ways things are between men and women?

III. THE WOMEN'S MOVEMENT

Extent of Knowledge

1. What have you heard about the women's movement?
   —Feminism?
   —Liberation?

2. Where have you heard about it?

Extent of Participation

3. Have you ever been to any meetings or belonged to any movement organizations?
   —What about the Native Women's Association (etc.)?

4. What kind of experience was this for you?

Attitude

5. Are there ways in which you agree with the women's movement?
   —Disagree?

6. Would you say that [——] women are oppressed?

7. If so, do you think [——] need to be liberated?

8. Would that be a positive or a negative change?

Policies, Programs

9. Are there any public policies you would like to see changed?

10. Are there any public programs that would help [——] women?

11. Do you think these policies or programs will come about in your lifetime?
    —Or for your children?
    —Why or why not?

IV. CLOSURE

1. Any last ideas, or anything we left out?
2. What do you want for your children?
3. (Expression of appreciation)

Appendix C
Informed Consent Agreement

[Date]

I agree to participate voluntarily in this study of women in Canada. My participation involves an interview in which I will discuss my experiences in family, work, and community. I understand that the interview will take about two hours.

The interviews will be tape recorded and typed up so that the researcher can prepare course materials on women in Canada. Later, a book may result for use in women's studies courses. I will have the right to edit and correct the final manuscript of any article or book chapter on women in my community during a period of three months after it is returned to me. The material will be kept strictly anonymous and will not be linked directly with my name without my permission.

The (unlabeled) tapes and transcripts from this study will be available for use by students, scholars, and others who wish to understand better the lives of Canadian women. I authorize the researcher to publish quotations from the interviews (in written or taped form) for appropriate social scientific use.

I understand that this project is being conducted by a trained researcher for a serious scientific purpose and that careful attention to my general welfare will be provided throughout. Any questions I have about the project will be answered by the researcher to the best of her ability. I understand that I am free to "pass" on any questions that I do not feel entirely comfortable answering. I have read the above agreement, understand it, and am willing to participate in this project on women in Canada.

[Signatures of interviewee and interviewer]

Informed Consent Agreement

Appendix D
Sample Letter to Community

(Date)

Secretary Manager,
Pangnirtung Hamlet,
Pangnirtung, NWT

Dear Secretary Manager:

I will be visiting Pangnirtung in August for five weeks as part of a research project on Canadian women funded by the Canadian Government Faculty Enrichment Grant Program. As a Professor of Sociology at Rhode Island College, Providence, I am preparing course materials for "Women in Society: Focus on Canada," which will become part of our Canadian Studies Program. I plan also to write a book about women in Canada for use both in Canada and the United States.

Please accept this letter as my request for community permission and cooperation in interviewing women and men, taking photographs, and gathering background materials for a slide/tape presentation on changing roles among the Inuit. I am particularly interested in changes in male/female work, political, and economic roles. As you will see from my itinerary and proposal (attached), I am conducting this research with Chinese, Blood, Six Nations, Mennonite, Jamaican, and Ukrainian communities. I feel that it is very important to include a section on Inuit women in a course or book focused on women in Canada, and hope that your community will help me with this project.

I have written a letter requesting a research license from the Science Institute at Yellowknife [Northwest Territories]. If the Pangnirtung Council approves my request, please let the Science Institute know as soon as possible so the license can be issued by the

405

time I arrive. As you will see from the proposal, participants in the project will have an opportunity to engage in interpretative analysis and to read a draft of any article or book written from the interviews in their community.

If you need further information, please feel free to call me at any of the telephone numbers listed at various points of my itinerary. I appreciate anything you can do to facilitate this matter. Thank you in advance for your cooperation.

Janet Mancini Billson, Ph.D.,
Professor of Sociology
Rhode Island College
Providence, Rhode Island

Appendix E
Notes on the Interviewing Process

G enerally, women were eager to be interviewed and deeply concerned about being able to remember traditions, to communicate clearly, and to express themselves accurately. Some put down their own knowledge and a few questioned the necessity of studying women.

A few women in each community, when I asked if they had anything to add, would reply, "Well, nothing that so-and-so hasn't already said." After prefacing their remarks this way, they would then proceed to say something that had not already been said. Chinese and Inuit women were especially insecure about their ability to speak English. Although an interpreter was always present for older women, some in their middle years (the transitional generation) wanted to speak English, yet felt frustrated in attempting to get their ideas across precisely.

Inuit women were very forthcoming in the interview process, but they liked to be prompted with specific questions. Invited to tell a little about her life, one elder said, "Only if you ask me questions, then I'll remember." Her friend added, when I asked if there was anything else they would like to say: "It's hard. It's easier to answer when you ask a question."

Women in all communities seemed excited about the opportunity to share ideas with each other and with me. They threw themselves into the analysis of how things got to be the way they are, where they might be going, and trying to identify their problems and strengths as women. Because they questioned and challenged each other and even their own "mythologies," sometimes the interpretations shifted as we went along. For example, when I asked if there was anything else I should know in order to understand Inuit

407

women, an elder replied, "I don't know what I want you to know. I'm confused. Even I am still learning about Inuit ways sometimes." I reiterated that I considered her and the other women to be the experts on Inuit lives; I was only a midwife to help tell their stories. This helped her to bring out more of her own analysis.

Another elder said, "I really don't have much to say, but I'm sorry if I didn't answer your questions thoroughly." I replied that my questions might have sounded awkward to her; the interpreter said, "No, she says you have good questions, which is true." One Inuk said, "I have a lot to tell you. Maybe it would go on for days, if I had the time." In fact, because of her age (she was ninety-eight), I interviewed her in her home for two hours a day over four days. She seemed to thrive on the process and enjoyed reminiscing about the "time before."

A Blood woman told me that her people are suspicious of anthropologists and sociologists because they feel they have been studied too much without the results being checked with or communicated back to the community. Yet in searching through very extensive native collections at the University of Calgary, I found little research on the Blood tribe. A fairly large literature exists on the Plains Indians in general, on other tribes of the Plains Indians, or on the Blackfeet, but only a handful of pieces have been written about the Blood. The woman said her people feel that so many of them have completed higher education that they should be able to do research themselves. This was noted in a matter-of-fact, not hostile way. She added that the book *My People the Blood* by Adolf Hungry Wolf is accepted, "but it was written by a white man. He married a native woman and took her name." She was not aware of the extensive anthropological article from the 1940s by Esther Goldfrank. This suspicion may have something to do with the reluctance of some people on the reserve to be interviewed, at least initially until trust was established.

After an interview with five Jamaican women who live in the Toronto suburb of Mississauga—a lively session that was replete with characterizations of their husbands as loving but disengaged men who sometimes have affairs but do not let them disrupt their marriages—the women worried about the possibility that their "rantings and ravings" might throw a bad light on West Indian men. This interview followed one with three Jamaican women in their thirties who complained about their difficulties in finding a "good Jamaican man" who is not a playboy. They all agreed with the contrast between "intellectuals" and "scalawags" with very little in between, but felt they had painted a picture only of the men who were irresponsible: playboys, womanizers, macho men, and romeos. When I asked if they would like to broaden their characterizations, they declined. I reassured them that I would seek interviews from many different kinds of women, cutting across income levels and residence in various parts of the city, which they agreed would help. In fact, the characterizations did not change much from session to session.

This group also raised the question of stereotyping in ethnic terms, which is a risk in any cross-cultural research. Subtle and sometimes enormous differences exist among various types of Mennonites, or from one Inuit settlement to the next, or between the Mohawks and the Onondaga of the Six Nations Iroquois. Similarly, the Jamaican tradition is quite different from the Trinidadian, both in the islands and in Toronto. When I asked Jamaican women how they feel about being lumped together as West Indians given the extreme differences in culture, they admitted they did not like the stereotype in some ways, but that they use the term *West Indian* themselves—and with pride. They think some people might not understand who they are because they are "black" and "West Indian," but most identify with the term almost as a nationality. They agreed that differences are matched, if not overcome, by similar patterns of behavior and lifestyle.

In every community, I tried to interview women in protected environments where we would be free from interruptions. In most instances, however, it was easier during the evenings and more comfortable for women to invite others to their homes for the interviews. Inevitably, an occasional man or child appeared. In a Mennonite home, a thirteen-year-old boy happily took care of a six-week-old foster child as his mother participated in the interview in the next room. Teenaged daughters, sisters, female friends and neighbors who dropped by unexpectedly were invited to join in the discussions. This happened often in the smaller, tightly knit communities, where evening visits without appointments are commonplace. This natural process helped broaden the diversity of participants.

Two Mennonite couples who were interviewed said they were slightly self-conscious at first. One woman said, "For me, it was a little bit risky sitting across from a couple that we don't see too often. To sit here and say this is how we live life and not sound like this is the way life *should* be lived. Yet we have to recognize that we all have some fairly strong beliefs about these things. It's difficult not to put someone down that you want to stay close friends with—but I think we've managed! We all like talking about ideas."

Husbands and male partners were invariably cooperative, quietly absenting themselves as soon as they realized what was going on. When one Inuk husband came home and saw that we were taping an interview, he very quietly went over to the coffee maker (which they use for tea), emptied it, put some fresh water and tea bags in, and started the machine. This important gesture corroborated his wife's description of their relationship as being "fairly equal." We invited him to share his memories of the traditional male role; he seemed eager to talk and apologized that his English wasn't very good.

In contrast, one Inuk woman kept looking at the door of the room in the cultural center reserved for elders, as if she expected someone to intrude. When I asked if this was the case, she said, "Yes. We should interview the women where the men can't hear, because they would interrupt." She remarked that men's lives and women's lives were very different, but that they respected each other. In fact, the men, who typically use the same room for social and recreational activities, did not interrupt us during the two-hour discussion.

Another exception was at the Blood Sun Dance, when I interviewed an elder woman in her tipi between 11:00 P.M. and 2:00 A.M. (at her request). At least seven or eight times her husband, grandson, or nephew peeked in, ostensibly to get something but probably more out of curiosity. Nonetheless, the interview continued until we were satisfied that all the ground had been covered. She apparently did not feel pressured to break off our conversation.

The last significant exception was during an interview with nine women in the day room of a senior citizens' apartment in Vancouver's Chinatown. Although the interpreter invited only women to participate, two elderly Chinese men joined halfway through the interview. They were the only ones present who spoke English, albeit very little; the women seemed to relish the men's presence, but I had to work hard to keep the men from answering every question, raising their voices over the women. At one point, one of the men stood up to make his point in English. Preventing the men from taking over the interview was doubly difficult through an interpreter.

Ukrainian women introduced each other with great pride, but even they acknowledged that keeping their identities separate from men's is sometimes difficult. In one group interview, the convenor introduced the women who turned out to talk about Ukrainian women in Canada. In a feast of respect and admiration, she praised each woman's contribution to the community: "Mary Tkachuk, author of *Pysanka*, is past president of the Ukrainian Association of Canada and past president of the Ukrainian Museum. Mrs. Hnatyshyn is the mother of Ray (former Governor General of Canada). No, on second thought, she's not the mother of Ray— Ray is *her* son! You have no identity—you've got to make it!" The introductions continued: "Vera's mother was very artistic. She made the *pysanky* out of beeswax and dyes and many times by the case. She had that innate sense of color."

Women talked of insights they derived from our group interviews, as in this passage from the Ukrainian tapes:

When Anna phoned me, I had no idea what it was about. I had an idea we were supposed to meet somebody, so I phoned a few ladies and told them to phone somebody else, and this is how we got together. We have some of the older generation [several bragged about being in their eighties]. When she phoned me and said it was a sociologist, I thought it was someone like a social worker.

[Let me ask you then, how did you feel about being interviewed?] Stephania: "I think you bring out things you weren't even aware of. When you ask questions, things come out that you usually let sit there and don't think about." Mariia: "It's a good experience." Olha: "I think it was wonderful." Anna: "I've had the opportunity to talk to all kinds of women and the problems they have certainly make my eyes pop. I did say to a girl from Africa—she asked me what problems do women in Canada have—and foolishly I said I don't think we have a problem. Then I realize, where are you?! Then I qualified that. You know, I'm not saying there are *no* problems but when you look at the problems from some of those underprivileged countries, they really do have problems." Mariia: "But a lot of our problems are man-made. We make them ourselves sometimes." Sophia: "This was a wonderful revelation—things keep coming back. I think we all benefited . . . just by talking and sharing. Someone else thinks of something you didn't, because you have a way of asking questions, I think that's in itself an asset." Olha: "Maybe you did it the right way to bring it up to us. I found it very intriguing and very stimulating. But I suppose if you'd asked us these questions tomorrow we'd have had time to sort of . . . lie a little bit!" [laughter]

Similarly, I asked a male Blood elder for an appointment the next day. He replied with a grin, "OK, that's good. I've got twenty-four hours to think about what lies I'll tell you!" As an Inuk woman said, "I think the older ones tend to romanticize the past, forget about the negatives, but the negatives are there. You don't want to think about them, but for documentation you *can't* forget them."

Women took this project very seriously indeed. A Chinese woman in her forties, when asked how she and her husband divide household chores—since she works outside the home full-time— said, "Ah! If you put this in the book, my husband is going to kill me. He's a typical domineering male, so he doesn't do much." Another woman in the group admonished her quickly: "This goes into a book! A research book! So we must give our ideas here!"

Appendix F
The Research Process[3]

Intersecting Methodologies

Shulamit Reinharz, in describing "experiential research," says that "involvement in natural settings forces or allows one to be aware of environmental, architectural, climatic, botanical, etc., factors which are significant parts of people's experience, but not frequently asked about in other [positivistic] methods."[4] In addition to intensive interviewing in each community, I participate in daily life in the natural setting to help create the context that we need to understand women's experiences. In every community I have found women (and children!) to be eager teachers as we move through their routine activities.

A few weeks in a community using only traditional fieldwork methods of participant and passive observation would not yield enough data or an accurate basis for analysis. By combining these methods with intensive interviewing that progressively moves participants toward analysis of their situation (what I call the "Progressive Verification Method"), however, two to six weeks proves adequate. Historical and demographic data provide checks on my impressions; community reviews pick up glaring misinterpretations or errors in fact.

Although I have not interviewed a particularly large sample of women in any community, I make every attempt to talk with women across age and status groups. I ensure variety by a somewhat unorthodox technique for enlisting participants. Rather than employing the snowball or reputational technique—whereby people are asked to refer someone who might have expertise about a particular question—I ask participants to give me the names of others who might have a different experience from their own.

413

Progressive Verification

The point at which I know that I am getting a fairly accurate picture is the point at which I start hearing the same things over and over: Nothing new comes out in the interviews apart from personal anecdotal material. In each interview I think back to previous interviews and double-check what I have heard, either after I have completed the regular interview schedule or am in the process of doing so.

I ask participants to try to explain why women might *not* agree on a common analysis; this elicits subtleties that have to do with age, income, education, marital status, and unique situations shared by a few women in the community. When the analysis broadens until it is consistently verified by subsequent participants, I know that together we have achieved at least a basic understanding of male-female relationships and the roles of men and women in that culture, without obscuring their complexity and variability.

The Progressive Verification Method is a collaborative, phenomenologically oriented, interactive research method for and with women and their communities. It falls within guidelines issued by the Committee on the Status of Women in Sociology:[5]

1. *Theoretical Context.* The Progressive Verification Method makes it more likely that the "complexity of behavior and the diversity of within-gender experiences" will not be ignored.
2. *Research Assumptions.* The method makes assumptions explicit and builds on "empirically verified features of men's and women's social worlds."
3. *Research Design.* The method includes both "male and female subjects to allow meaningful analysis of subgroups," although the research clearly focuses on women.
4. *Operationalizing Major Concepts.* The research instruments are "equally appropriate for . . . members of various racial groups."
5. *Data Analysis.* Analysis of data proceeds within communities, leaving applicability of findings to the other sex and races "as an unresolved empirical issue."
6. *Discussion and Theory Building.* Generation of theories or concepts is based on "a variety of different perspectives (e.g., sociocultural, historical, structural, biological)."

The committee stressed that "gender should be conceptualized as a principle of sociocultural organization and a basic theoretical category, as well as a matter of individual differences," that may interact with other characteristics. The Progressive Verification Method can be used to build a theory of shifting gender roles that embraces the complexity of within-gender experiences, as mediated by other central sociocultural characteristics (such as race, class, age, and residence). It explicitly delineates the distinctions between men's worlds and women's worlds, with enough depth and breadth of data to make a meaningful analysis of differences between ethnic/racial groups, and it is inclusive of historical, structural, and sociocultural levels of analysis. The method conceptualizes gender as a critical dimension of sociocultural organization as well as a fundamental theoretical category.

Women as Collaborators

Because I am interested more in women's lives as reflections of women's position and power than in individual life histories, I prefer to interview women in groups of two to six whenever possible. Group sessions stimulate debate and generate multiple descriptions of reality and explanations of causality. They also help women to overcome structural isolation and to realize that their individual sufferings have social causes and are in some ways shared by other women.

In this study, a few interviews were conducted with males in each community in order to expand the female perspective of the male role. The Progressive Verification Method focuses on the experiences of women, however, echoing Eichler's concern that feminist research must "start from a female perspective which may or may not need to be modified when men are taken into consideration."[6] All interviews were taped and later transcribed; they ranged in length from one to four hours. Interpreters were essential in some cultures, especially for older women.

As an educated white woman of Protestant British- and French-Canadian background, I cannot fully comprehend the perspectives of women in other cultures. I stated at the beginning of each interview that I was simply holding a mirror up to the community; I would reflect back what I heard. Sessions were taped so the reflection would be as accurate as possible. Respondents received drafts and had three months to get back to me with ideas, revisions, additions, or clarification of misinterpretations. My mission was to learn, to explicate, and to draw connections.

I do not refer to the women and men who talk with me as interviewees. Rather, they served as consultants from the community who assisted me by participating in sessions and by providing contacts, housing, meals, cultural and historical background, and other information. Although I give participants the option of anonymity or credit, I guarantee that specific information or opinions will not be linked to them personally (see Appendix C).[7] Project consultants for this book are listed in the Acknowledgments, if they so desired. Their participation was extremely important to achieving an accurate and sensitive portrayal of changing gender roles in their communities.

Data Analysis

Conceptualization rests on insights or "key linkages." An overriding "pattern or story line that provides new insight into the situation investigated . . . may be expressed as a typology or as a principle of behavior that has relevance in a variety of settings."[8] These linkages are drawn out of our conversations, refined, and recorded in my field notes for each day. (Field notes also include any direct observations I am making, off-tape comments, and my responses to the research process.)

In order to achieve stability, hypotheses are developed, tested in the initial field experience, revised, tested against new data, revised again, and so on until all field data have been accounted for in the emergent hypotheses. This interactive process is conceptually parallel to the "constant comparative method" described by Glaser and Strauss for coding and building theory from qualitative data: "The analyst starts to achieve two major requirements of theory: (1) **parsimony** of variables and formulation, and (2) **scope** in the applicability of the theory to a wide range of situations."[9] In both cases, all data must be compatible with emergent categories, hypotheses, and theories. The difference between the Progressive Verification Method and "constant comparative method" lies in the fact that the former also addresses the data-gathering process, whereas the latter addresses the analysis of data. The qualitative data generated by intensive interviewing can achieve "stability" through such a reflexive process: "When the cumulative results of an intensive interview study continue to fall within a given range with interview after interview, despite attempts by the researcher to identify deviations from this range, the researcher senses the sort of stability that can inspire a high degree of confidence."[10] For this type of research, stability is parallel to traditional tenets regarding statistical reliability in quantitative research.

A Note to Other Feminist Researchers

In doing cross-cultural research, I have found it essential to follow some practical guidelines for interviewing: Be clear about the purpose of your presence; be passive and nonintrusive; learn the rules of the culture; don't take sides or offer advice; give something of yourself; don't play the expert (respondents are the experts); don't get too close to any faction or individual; take field notes every day, including on questions newly raised and as yet unanswered; tape everything; be patient; and treat respondents with the respect due collaborating colleagues.[11]

Notes and References

Preface

1. O'Brien 1981.
2. Most women who live in immigrant and native communities do not yet write prolifically about their experiences. Their educational levels are only beginning to make them comfortable writing for publication, especially women in those groups for whom English is a second (and recent) language. Furthermore, as the Immigrant Women's Editorial Collective (1987, 3–12) points out, economic realities squeeze out the luxury of taking time to reflect, document, theorize, write, and publish an article or book: "Unlike middle-class professional women and like their working class sisters, women who are active in the immigrant women's communities are themselves marginal: their jobs are unstable and sustained through short-term government grants; many have to hold down several jobs to survive financially; many of them are completely over-extended in their various organizing efforts; [and] the demands placed on them by other . . . immigrant women are great." It is in this sense that the methods used here facilitate communication by women whose lives are, in so many ways, lived on the edge.
3. Reinharz 1983 and Du Bois 1983.
4. In the absence of more appropriate terms, I use *domestic violence* for any assault between intimate partners, regardless of marital status or living arrangements. The terms *spousal assault* and *wife battering*, common in Canada and the United States, do not reflect violence toward women who are ex-wives, unmarried lovers, daughters, or friends of men who harm them. *Family violence* similarly might be construed to mean violence only in a legally constituted family group.
5. For a complete explanation of the research methodology, see Billson 1991b.
6. See Appendix B for the guideline for interviews.
7. Kieffer 1981 refers to this process as "dialogic retrospection."
8. Smith 1987, 142; see also Collins 1986.

Chapter 1

1. I focus in this book on power relations between females and males, how culture has shaped them, and how they have changed in the past century. Because

heterosexual power was my primary focus, my interview questions were not directed toward homosexual relationships and thus elicited little information in this area. Similar studies of power relations between intimate women would be useful and some have been conducted. See, for example, Rich 1980; Kurdek and Schmitt 1986; Fuss 1991; Kitzinger 1989; Stone 1990; and Valverde 1985.

2.   Because men are equally embedded in the same sex-biased cultures and until recently men wrote most history, anthropology, sociology, and psychology, the impact of oppressive traditions on women is probably understated.

3.   Women do most organization of holiday and ritual gatherings that "keep the kin" together.

4.   Billson 1991a, 1991c, 1990, 1988b.

5.   Collins 1990.

6.   See, for example, Blumberg 1989; Chafetz 1984; Huber 1986; Nielsen 1990; O'Kelly and Carney 1986; Demos and Segal 1994.

7.   Hoyenga and Hoyenga (1993) explore the origins of gender-related differences. Thorne (1993) discusses the bifurcation of gender roles manifested among schoolchildren.

8.   Faludi 1991.

9.   Wodak and Schulz 1986.

10.   Steinem 1992.

11.   See Rosaldo 1980; Sanday 1981; Edwards and Morrow 1985; Wodak and Schulz 1986; Bunch 1987; Andersen 1988; Kolenda 1988; Lorde 1992; Brettell and Sargent 1993; and Demos and Segal 1994.

12.   Silvera 1986, 195.

Chapter 2

1.   "Jay Silverheels" was born on the reserve as Harry Smith, son of Chief A. G. Smith.

2.   Johnson, 1943 (originally published in 1912). The internationally acclaimed poet was the daughter of nineteenth century Mohawk Chief George H. M. Johnson, who built Chiefswood, and Emily S. Howells, who came to Canada from Bristol, England. Born in 1861, she died in 1913 and was interred in Stanley Park, Vancouver, British Columbia. Iroquois stress the intimate relationship between living in harmony with Mother Earth and, in death, returning to the world of nature.

3.   Adapted from Hill, Gillen, and MacNaughton 1987, 52, and Mitchell and Barnes 1984, 3–4.

4.   Monture-Okanee 1992, 195.

5.   Hale 1969, 19, 49.

6.   Hewitt 1933, 475.

7.   Hale 1969, 31 fn.

8.   National Geographic Society 1979, 119.

9.   Canadians use the terms reserve and band; in the U.S., reservations and tribe are used.

10.   National Geographic Society 1979, 121.

11. Randle 1951, 172; also Tooker 1990, 114.

12. Shafer 1941, 71–132.

13. Shafer 1941, 79–82.

14. National Geographic Society 1979, 124.

15. Richards 1957.

16. Brown 1970. Very early accounts include: Beauchamp 1900; Carr 1887; and Hewitt 1933.

17. Monture-Okanee 1992, 200.

18. Monture-Okanee 1992, 200. The implication of "on the ground" rises from the specter of women lying dead after a raid on their village; until that happens, the tribe can persist.

19. National Geographic Society 1979, 129.

20. Hale 1969, 64–65.

21. Brown 1970, 164.

22. Interviewees differed in their interpretation of *nation*. Some argue that the term means the same as *tribe*. Thus, the Mohawk or Cayuga nation would be the same as the Mohawk or Cayuga tribe.

23. Hale 1969.

24. National Geographic Society 1979, 119. Other historically matriarchal societies in North America include, to some extent, the Wyandot of the Huron, the Montagnais-Naskapi of Labrador, the Cherokee, and the Arapaho. See Kolenda 1988, 3.

25. The Mohawks and the Cayugas were pro-British. The Oneidas and Tuscaroras favored the Americans; the Senecas and Onondagas were split on the issue. Dickason 1992, 185.

26. Based on entries in Marsh 1985, 903–904.

27. Marsh 1985, 904.

28. Johnson 1943, 95.

29. Monture-Okanee 1992, 196.

30. Iroquois women still play a key role in reserve life, as events illustrated among their Mohawk sisters at the Kanesatake Reserve near Oka, Quebec, in 1991. Clan mothers were instrumental in decision making as the crisis evolved, and it was a woman, Ellen Gabriel, who served as spokesperson.

31. Hale 1969, 92.

32. The Indian Act of 1876 (which has since been amended several times) devised the concept of "status Indian" in order to determine entitlement to reside in Indian reserves. The act outlawed Sun Dance (see chapter on the Blood Indians) and Potlatch (a custom among Pacific Northwest Indians). The act also made it illegal for an Indian women to maintain her status if she married a white man, hence the term nonstatus.

33. Nationally, about 50 percent of Indians marry Indians; 25 percent of Indian men marry white women; and 25 percent of Indian women marry white men.

34. Monture-Okanee 1992, 200. A Mohawk crisis center worker notes: "Take a First Nations woman growing up in Saskatchewan, sixteen years old. By the time she reaches twenty-five, she will have 131 times the chance of going to prison as a non-First Nations woman."

35. Monture-Okanee 1992, 199.

36. For a discussion of the role of contraception in enabling women to sequence career paths inside and outside the home, see Billson and Stapleton 1994.

37. Monture-Okanee 1992, 199.

38. Mackinnon (1992, 187) says of residential schools in Canada that "half of all Native children removed from their nations by white society were sexually abused, producing what some have called a lost generation of Native people. Here, sexual assault is a form of cultural genocide."

39. Monture-Okanee 1992, 198.

40. Monture-Okanee 1992, 197.

41. A similar pattern occurs among young African American males. See Majors and Billson 1992.

Chapter 3

1. Beverly Hungry Wolf 1980, 59ff.

2. Goldfrank 1944. The Indian Act outlawed Sun Dance, an annual two-week event in July. The Bloods persisted with this religious celebration in spite of the law, the only Plains tribe to do so without a break in their tradition.

3. Frank 1984, 17.

4. Many studies of the Blackfoot groupings emphasize the Peigan or the Blackfeet, both neighbors and probably original relatives of the Bloods, but the Bloods have evolved distinctly from their Blackfoot cousins in some important ways. See Parks, Liberty, and Ferenci 1980, 286; also Samek 1987, 11. As noted in Chapter 2, in Canada, the preferred terms are *reserve* and *band* rather than *reservation* and *tribe*, as in the United States.

5. Dempsey 1978. See also Ewers 1955, 36; and Haines 1976, 108, 146. A similar transformation is detailed for the Inuit in Billson 1988.

6. In 1877 the population of the newly created reserve was about 1,500 (Goldfrank 1944, 13); as of 1986 it was 5,781. Of 353,600 acres, 6,400 acres are devoted to Blood band farms; leased land farms, 32,000 acres; Blood band ranch, 30,000 acres; irrigated land, 4,500 acres; and timber limits land, 3,840 acres. It is the largest reserve in Canada in terms of area. The band owns the land, which is very fertile. People can build on the land and sell a house but they cannot sell the land with it. The Bloods receive two or three million dollars a year from natural gas in the forest reserve near the mountains; they use the funds for roads, schools, and the hospital. This amount was five million dollars in the early 1980s, but the economic downturn in Canada has affected Blood income. The modular home factory, crafts, and natural gas furnish at least three other sources of income beyond welfare.

7. Dempsey 1978, quoted in Frank 1984, 1.

8. Frank 1984.

9. Although his work focuses mainly on the Blackfeet of Montana, Ewers 1958 provides a detailed account of Blackfoot life in general, especially the woman's role (16–17, 102).

10. Schneider 1983, 101–121.

11. Ewers 1958, 17.
12. Ewers 1958, 11–12.
13. Grinnell 1962, 229.
14. Ewers 1958, 63, 75; Lewis 1942.
15. Ewers 1958, 109.
16. Lewis 1942, 38.
17. Medicine 1983, 269–270.
18. One of the problems of retrospective interviewing is that no Blood women alive today are old enough to remember traditional roles *prior* to the reserve period. The memories of elders who were children during the early reserve period (late 1890s to early 1920s) emerge from a time the government systematically attempted to transform their lives. Pool 1988 documents this for Wichita women (158–171). For this reason, anthropological and historical texts are especially important for native women, although they must always be viewed with some skepticism because of traditional white male dominance in these fields.
19. See Grinnell 1962, 216; Frank 1984; and McFee 1972, 41.
20. Ewers 1958, 100.
21. Ewers 1958, 99–100.
22. Frank 1984.
23. DeMallie 1983 (237–265), in his review of ethnographic reports on another Plains group, the Lakota, indicates that the division of labor was based on gender (and upheld more by the women than the men). Women had considerable power beyond the domestic circle, though, as they were important participants in religious ceremonies.
24. Medicine 1983, 267–280.
25. Goldfrank 1944, 13.
26. Wilson 1921; Goldfrank 1944, 14–15.
27. Frank 1984; see also Spindler and Spindler 1978, 73–85.
28. See, for example, Lithman 1984 and Grant 1985. As early as 1911, the Blood Pupils Association "complained to Ottawa that after having been taught the value of education and work they could find no employment on the reserves" (Samek 1987, 147).
29. L. Spindler 1977, 107–108.
30. Goldfrank 1944. See also Adolph Hungry Wolf 1977 and Beverly Hungry Wolf 1980. Sun Dance was outlawed in the late nineteenth century as a pagan ritual, but the Bloods defied the law and continued to engage in their summer activities.
31. Frank 1984, 18.
32. Adolph Hungry Wolf 1977, 4.
33. "Ceremonies," in Frank 1984, 27.
34. Beverly Hungry Wolf 1980, 56.
35. This was a common expression of grief. Frank 1984 (21) reports that a widow sometimes would also slash her legs and rub charcoal in the wounds.
36. Beverly Hungry Wolf 1980, 56.
37. Beverly Hungry Wolf 1980, 59.
38. See Ewers 1958, 34.

39. "Okan," by Jackie Red Crow in Frank 1984, 35.

40. Beverly Hungry Wolf 1980, 45.

41. Lurie 1972 (34) argues that many Native American women are receiving increasing recognition because "girls were educated in teaching, nursing and office work, and the work experience of Indian women in cities exposed them to the managerial side of white life. . . . they brought home skills that could be put to real use on the reservation to help them cope as an Indian community in a larger, white-dominated society."

42. Goldfrank 1944.

43. See also Native Women Publication Advisory Board (n.d.). Fowler 1987 reports that the Gros Ventres have been "remarkably successful in taking advantage of educational and other new opportunities" compared to other Plains Indians, but she does not comment on female versus male achievement.

Chapter 4

1. Inuk is the singular form of Inuit.

2. Bennett, Flannigan, and Hladun 1980, 3.

3. National Geographic Society 1979, 92–93, 95.

4. Lamphere 1993.

5. Billson 1990a, 1990b, 1990c, 1988b.

6. Billson 1990b; Billson and Mancini 1995.

7. Billson 1990b.

8. Billson 1988a.

9. Matthews (1983, 69–76) distinguishes between "transfer dependency" and "dependency theory." I intend the latter meaning here.

10. Hanley 1987.

11. Irwin 1989.

12. Finkler 1976, 46; McElroy 1977, 71.

13. In one home that I visited, the family dog urinated on the rug. The seventeen-year-old son, who just as easily could have found a piece of paper towel, said to his mother, "The dog peed on the rug," as if ordering her. She got the paper towel, cleaned it up, spanked the dog, rubbed his nose in it, and threw him out.

14. For details of "customary adoption" among Inuit families, see Billson and Mancini 1995; Billson and Stapleton 1994.

15. This argument is made also in Eber 1975.

16. This finding is supported by other research. For example, Endter-Wada, Robbins, and Levine 1992 report that native women in the Bristol Bay region of Alaska are "much more likely than men to process plants and berries . . . and less likely to process small game and big game. . . . More women are wage earners and work full-time, limiting their ability to engage in subsistence activities, while more men are involved in seasonal commercial fishing, which leaves the rest of the year free to hunt, trap, fish and process what they harvest." Similarly, Seyfrit and Hamilton 1992 found differences in men's and women's employment patterns as reported by high school students: "Only 6% of the students report that their fa-

thers hold professional or technical jobs . . . 10% of the students report that their mothers hold professional or technical jobs" (59).

17.   Skinner 1989; Inuit Committee on National Issues 1987; Lynge 1986.

Chapter 5

1.   Anthony 1989, 75.
2.   Walker 1984, 4.
3.   Walker 1984, 4.
4.   Walker 1984, 5–6.
5.   Yawney 1989.
6.   Yawney 1989, 186.
7.   Aho (1984) documents "macho" West Indian Calypsonians that sing about women in negative ways: "Women are either put high on a pedestal or dragged through the gutter. . . . Women are criticized for being too sexy, not sexy enough, reckless spenders, unclean persons, too smart or not smart enough." These images reflect the emotional distancing that intermittent relationships project and reinforce.
8.   Clarke 1973, 35.
9.   Clarke 1973, 57.
10.   Walker 1984, 8. As of 1984, there were 143,325 West Indians in Ontario, 46,170 in Quebec, and a few in other provinces.
11.   Walker 1984, 9.
12.   Walker 1984, 10.
13.   Walker 1984, 19.
14.   Walker 1984, 19.
15.   Walker 1984, 10.
16.   Quoted in Silvera 1981, 42.
17.   Cohen 1987.
18.   Smith 1967, 246–247.
19.   Smith 1967, 251.
20.   Smith 1967, 248.
21.   Smith 1967, 248.
22.   Smith 1967, 253.
23.   Quoted by Simms 1992, 177, from Wallace 1990 (1979).
24.   For a discussion of comparative perceptions of discrimination in Canada, see Breton 1981. He found that West Indians perceive lower rates of acceptance by "majority Canadian" groups than other groups such as Germans and Ukrainians (427). West Indians and Chinese feel "that present laws make it too difficult for people from their home country to come to Canada" (430). West Indians "are the only [group] with a large percentage who think that [discrimination] is either a very serious or a somewhat serious problem: 60 percent. Job discrimination is most frequently reported by Chinese and West Indians" (433). Breton adds that "West Indians perceive and experience problems in almost all areas except with regard to cultural maintenance: discrimination is mentioned by about three-fourths of the respondents; immigration laws and procedures by about two-thirds;

the actual experience of discrimination by over one-third. Problems of social acceptance either as neighbors or as relatives are also frequently mentioned. About the same percentage of Majority Canadians share this perception of the situation with West Indians. On the other hand, the propensity to favor ethnic organizational action to deal with problems appears to be low among W.I. respondents relative to perceived magnitude of the problems" (442).

25. Although social status distinctions exist in the West Indies based on skin color within the black community itself, McLaine 1986 confirms that "West Indians are not keenly aware that their 'Blackness' has negative connnotations until they immigrate to a White host country" (91). Because of the British educational system in Jamaica and their majority status in the Caribbean, women have adopted a strong belief in drive and determination that will eventually result in success. For an in-depth examination of racial discrimination and assimilation among West Indians in Canada since 1945, see Walker 1985, 16–22.

26. Immigrant Women's Editorial Collective 1987, 3. See also Ng and Estable 1987; hooks 1989.

27. The Loyalists, who supported the British during the American Revolution and headed for Canada in the decades that followed, included blacks as well as Iroquois, Mennonite, and British heritage families. See Walker 1992.

Chapter 6

1. Rich 1983, 21–23.

2. Fretz 1989, 7. Fretz also includes the Bohemian Brethren in Moravia and the Schwenckfelders in Silesia as Anabaptist splinter groups.

3. Van Braght 1976 documents many of these executions.

4. Fretz 1989, 9.

5. Rich 1983, 22.

6. Good and Good 1979, 12, 13.

7. Good and Good 1979, 10.

8. Rich 1983, 30.

9. Fretz 1989, 26.

10. Fretz 1989, 3. The land was sold first to an investor, Richard Beasley, in 1798, then sold to the Mennonites in 1800.

11. Fretz 1989, 29.

12. Kreider in Umrau 1986, 185.

13. The Amish separated from the Mennonites around 1700 under the leadership of Jacob Amman. He was distressed by the lack of enforcement of the *Meidung*, or shunning of excommunicated members. Other differences in dress and faith persist today, but these two strains of Anabaptists (the third being the Hutterites) share many key beliefs. See Kephart 1982, 49.

14. Kauffman and Driedger 1991, 27.

15. Kauffman and Driedger 1991, 38.

16. Fretz 1989, 54.

17. Fretz 1989, 51.

18. Fretz 1989, 54.

19. For an in-depth analysis of the Russian Mennonite Brethren who immigrated to Canada, see Hamm 1987.

20. According to Kauffman and Driedger (1991, 31), as of 1989 there were 856,000 baptized Mennonites world-wide, including 300,500 in North America—266,100 in the United States and 114,400 in Canada. They surveyed five major North American denominations: Mennonite Church ("Old Mennonites"), General Conference Mennonite Church, Mennonite Brethren Church, Brethren in Christ Church, and Evangelical Mennonite Church. They place the Conservative Mennonites in the middle of the spectrum and Old Order Mennonites at the conservative end (190).

21. Mary Ann Horst (1994), who was raised in the Old Order Mennonite Church in Floradale, Waterloo County, has written a small booklet about her decision to be baptized into the more liberal General Conference.

22. The concept of headship extends to men in general. For a single woman the order would be God, Christ, and then probably the church leaders (once she is of age) rather than brothers or fathers.

23. Shetler and Shank 1983, 16.

24. Rich 1983 documents the ebb and flow of women's participation (which has not been universally accepted) as deacons and missionaries in the formal work of the church.

25. For a discussion comparing Mennonite, Inuit, and Chinese women's attitudes toward abortion and contraception, see Billson and Stapleton 1994.

26. Fretz 1989, 134.

27. "Men are above" because they generally support the family.

28. This comment was written in response to the chapter review.

Chapter 7

1. The largest is San Francisco.

2. Based on Chang 1991 and stories told by the women I interviewed.

3. I am grateful to Catherine Lu for her suggestion of this title. Cathy, a political scientist, was born in China, lived in Hong Kong as a small child, and then emigrated to Vancouver, where she was educated.

4. Paul Yee 1988, 10. Canton, the province's capital city, was the only major port open to foreigners for a long period during the nineteenth century, so it became an ideal place for prospective emigrants trying to escape drought and famine to embark upon ships for North America. Chinese from the province refer to themselves as "Cantonese," after the city. See Wong 1972, 12.

5. Paul Yee 1988, 12.

6. Many Vancouverites blame their skyrocketing housing prices on the rapid influx of Hong Kong Chinese. See, for example, "Property Boom Fuels West-Side Tensions" 1989.

7. Li 1988, however, points out that racism during this period had more to do with structural issues (such as economic strain among the host population) than with individual racist attitudes.

8. Based on entries in Marsh 1985, 336–337. Li (1980) argues that restric-

tive Canadian immigration policies imposed unusual constraints on Chinese familial organization up until World War II.

9.   Anderson (1991) argues that the name "Chinatown" is a Western construction that reflects Western cultural domination. The term is retained here since Chinese and Chinese Canadian women in Vancouver freely refer to the old central Chinese-dominated neighborhood as "Chinatown." The more recent immigrants usually shop in Richmond and view Chinatown as somewhat "old fashioned." Some opium use and prostitution were linked with the associations, but that was not their primary purpose.

10.   Paul Yee 1988, 41.

11.   Paul Yee 1988, 21.

12.   Paul Yee 1988, 21.

13.   Lyman 1974, 86–92. Yung 1986 reports that during the California Gold Rush, "in 1850 there were only 7 Chinese women among 4,018 Chinese men in San Francisco. By 1860 the number had grown only to 1,784 among 33,149 men" (14).

14.   May Yee 1987 mentions the scarcity of primary and secondary material on Chinese women in Canada because men overshadowed women in both numbers and in historical attention. Nipp 1986 sheds light on the contributions of Chinese women.

15.   Paul Yee 1988, 49.

16.   Con et al. 1982, 167.

17.   Johnson 1983 describes the various stages of immigration in detail.

18.   Yung 1986, 10.

19.   Wolf 1985 shows that in the People's Republic of China, patriarchal thinking and the ideology of the men's family system persists long after the Cultural Revolution.

20.   Yu 1977 discusses the implications of residence rules for sex-role equality in China.

21.   Yung 1986, 10.

22.   Yung 1986, 10.

23.   Yung 1986, 13.

24.   Waley 1960, 283–284.

25.   For discussions of women and patriarchy in post-Communist China, see Stacey 1983 and Chow (n.d.). The current social policy of allowing only one child per family has led to some abortion of female fetuses and female infanticide, especially in rural areas.

26.   Yung 1986, 13.

27.   The staff members at SUCCESS, a program that offers education and counseling services to the Chinese community, shed light on traditional power relations between men and women in China and now in modern-day Canada. Members of the SUCCESS women's group all were born in either China or Hong Kong, but two or three of them had gone to Vietnam, Great Britain, or the United States before coming to Canada. Canada was their destination of choice, but either they could not get in when they wanted to or, for political reasons, they could not move freely.

28. "Traditions Then . . . and Now," unpublished pamphlet, Chinese Cultural Center, Vancouver, BC, n.d.

29. Paul Yee 1988, 12.

30. Man 1994, 12.

31. This account was written by an ESL student in Richmond, a suburb of Vancouver, and is used with her permission.

32. Man 1994 (14) found that astronaut wives worry about their husbands' possible infidelity between visits to Vancouver.

33. Eng, a very successful real estate broker, proves the point that the availability of female role models can inspire younger women and girls; several mentioned her by name as evidence that Chinese women can make it in Vancouver.

34. Yee 1988, 67.

35. Geschwender 1990, 6.

Chapter 8

1. Sometimes spelled Olha. Ukrainian Women's Association of Canada, 612 24th Street East, Saskatoon, SASK, S7K 0L1: Card produced in honor of the Millennium of the Baptisms of Ukraine into the Holy Orthodox Faith, 988–1988. Ol'ha's grandson, Prince Volodymyr the Great, baptized his people into the faith in 988.

2. See, for example, Swyripa 1988; Owechko, Kuchar, and Tatchyn 1985, 42.

3. Tkachuk, Kishchuk, and Nicholaichuk 1987, 19.

4. Tkachuk, Kishchuk, and Nicholaichuk 1987, 20.

5. Bohachevsky-Chomiak 1988, 5.

6. Chykalenko-Keller 1920, 1a.

7. Bohachevsky-Chomiak 1988, 22.

8. Bohachevsky-Chomiak 1988, 33–34.

9. Martynowych 1991, 4–11.

10. Petryshyn 1978, 75.

11. Hryniuk 1990 challenges the assumption that the farmers were escaping poverty, arguing that eastern Galicians were in fact accomplished agriculturists with the ability to become prosperous in their adopted homeland. Ukrainian Canadian women have been more likely to live on farms than the general Canadian population; see M. Petryshyn 1980, 192.

12. W. R. Petryshyn 1978, 76.

13. Keywan 1977 tells the pioneer story.

14. Martynowych 1991, 79. See also Czumer 1981 and Tesarski 1987.

15. Martynowych 1991, 80.

16. Martynowych 1991, 81.

17. Women and men built these ovens with clay from the land they homesteaded. Many families in Saskatoon who have enough room in their backyards still have a *pich* for baking bread.

18. Saskatoon, now with a population of over 150,000, was the largest of these centers. From Saskatoon, approximately 200 miles (320 kilometers) south-

east lies Yorkton; 85 miles north lies Prince Albert; 60 miles east lies Humboldt. Ukrainians were given land in bloc settlements near each of these budding communities and along either the North Saskatchewan River, the Canadian National Railway (CNR) lines, or the Canadian Pacific Railway (CPR) lines. Saskatoon lies at the intersection of the South Saskatchewan River and the CPR.

19.   Stooking was low-paid, backbreaking labor that consisted of "gathering eight to ten sheaves of wheat, dropped by a horse-drawn self-binding reaper, and stacking them into piles" (Martynowych 1991, 82). This process protected the grain from rotting and weather damage until it was ripe enough to thresh.

20.   Wolowyna 1980, 163–164.

21.   Two early feminist treatments of Ukrainian women note this matriarchal tradition: Potrebenko 1977 and Kostash 1977.

22.   Kinnear 1988.

23.   Working in the 1890s and early part of the twentieth century, long after the major cross-continental lines had been completed, Ukrainian men helped lay the spurs that connected outlying districts.

24.   Balan 1984, 88.

25.   Sharing work across genders may have been common, but when it came to inheriting the family farm the oldest male usually had the distinct advantage. See also Swyripa 1991.

26.   Recipes for Ukrainian specialty foods can be found in (among others) Ukrainian Women's Association of Canada 1984.

27.   Owechko, Kuchar, and Tatchyn 1985, 39.

28.   Ukrainian women wear the coral necklaces with their traditional dress for dances and festivals. See Faryna 1976, 21, for a full description of their costume.

29.   Petryshyn 1978, 83. These figures are for all of Canada. The rural-to-urban migration sped up during World War II and peaked during the 1950s and 1960s. The shift toward urban population occurred also because the post-World War II Ukrainian immigrants tended to go directly toward such eastern Canadian cities as Hamilton.

30.   These observations echo the conclusions of sociologists and anthropologists who have long believed urban life to be more alienating than rural life. See, for example, the work of Georg Simmel, Robert Redfield, and Louis Wirth.

31.   Owechko, Kuchar, and Tatchyn 1985, 39.

32.   The old version resurfaced in Volyn in the 1920s, however, when the fall of Tsarist rule removed the "major prop of the Russian Orthodox Church" (Bohachevsky-Chomiak 1988, 5).

33.   Wolowyna 1980, 163.

34.   Martynowych 1991, 92–93.

35.   Martynowych 1991, 92–93.

36.   Swyripa 1988 confirms that Ukrainian women during this period married men several years their senior, more so than women in other groups.

37.   Faryna 1976, 28.

38.   See Balan 1984 and Martynowych 1991, 92–94, for various newspaper accounts of family violence.

39. See especially Martynowych 1991 and Balan 1984 for discussions of evidence that the early immigrants were given less fertile farmland than British and northern European groups. Later, during World War I, Ukrainians were sometimes accused of being "enemy aliens"; the later immigrants, refugees of World War II, often were turned away from homes, jobs, and other opportunities with the slur "DP's" (displaced persons).

40. For a detailed discussion of bilingual education in Saskatchewan, see Martynowych 1991, 340–380; the Mohyla Institute is mentioned on p. 371.

41. Weaving of flax and hemp is an old art in Ukraine, passed through to women in Canada by their great-great-grandmothers. The *kylym*, a tapestry used for walls, beds, and floors, exists throughout Eastern Europe, but the Ukrainian version is known worldwide for its rich color and high quality (Faryna 1976, 12–13). Ukrainian weaving patterns appear in Bilash and Wilberg 1989.

42. Founded in Washington, DC, in 1888, the ICW is headquartered in New York. More than seven hundred women from seventy-five countries joined in celebrating the organization's hundredth birthday in 1988.

43. The structure and dogma of the church have not changed radically in the last millennium of the Ukrainian Orthodox Church, a minister acknowledges: "We've adapted methodology in some areas, but if you leave the church and come back three years later, it's the same church. The church that was yours as a child is still there for the person who is in a state of flux and can't put her feet on the ground yet."

44. Women use this specialized and difficult form of embroidery to decorate priest's robes, for altar cloths, and other church articles. See Faryna 1976, 8.

Chapter 9

1. Bégin 1992, 33.
2. Vickers 1992, 43, citing work of Roberta Hamilton and Michele Barrett.
3. See Luxton 1988.
4. Norwood 1985.

Chapter 10

1. Focusing on "uncommon strengths" does not imply that women in these communities do not, like women everywhere, succumb to self-destructive mechanisms of self-deprecation, depression, alcohol and drug abuse, withdrawal, hardening of the emotional arteries, suicide, and other hurtful coping styles. Nor does it imply that they never take their hurt and anger and loneliness out on children or partners.

2. For a detailed discussion of the complex relationship between the Ukrainian Catholic Church and the Ukrainian Greek Orthodox Church (later renamed the Ukrainian Orthodox Church)—and the role of the Mohyla Institute in the conflict—see Balan 1984, 90–120.

3. Hall 1994 explores this possibility in detail.
4. Excerpted from Billson 1991.
5. Powers 1986, 2–3.

6. Lurie 1972, 29–36.
7. Powers 1986, 3.

Chapter 11

1. Nemiroff 1992, 287. She adds that "we must develop coalitions on the numerous issues which concern us all, such as class-ism, racism, heterosexism, ethnicity, and all the injustices women suffer."
2. As Vickers 1992 points out, the relationship of mainstream to smaller, culturally based women's movements has not been ideal. For example, "the relationships of the [Canadian] women's movement with the Native women's movement remain a failure of tragic proportions." This is true even though "Canada's general political culture is growing in its understanding of diversity, and our women's movements remain dynamic spurs to that growth" (60).
3. Simms 1992 notes that "the two most oppressed groups of women are Black women and aboriginal women" (176).
4. See Wolf 1993a and 1993b.
5. Greaves 1992, 154.
6. See Wine and Ristock 1991.
7. Vickers 1992, 58.
8. Greaves 1992, 155.
9. Nemiroff 1992, 286.
10. See Flaherty and Backhouse 1992 and Billson 1992.
11. Chafetz 1988, 5.
12. Risman and Schwartz 1989, 8

Appendices

1. Derived from Lengermann and Wallace 1985, 2, 3, 15, 16, 21, 22, 23, 25, 26, 27, and 29.
2. Smith 1986, 6.
3. This discussion is adapted from Billson 1991, 201–215.
4. Reinharz 1983, 178.
5. Committee on the Status of Women in Sociology 1983, 178.
6. Eichler 1977, 410.
7. The informed consent agreement provides an overview of the research and states that a draft of findings on the community will be sent to consultants for suggestions, factual corrections, and updating. When interpretive disagreements arose, I reviewed the transcripts and other data, called those who raised the questions, and tried to reach consensus. Ultimately, I am responsible for my own interpretative risks. Anthropologist Fluehr-Lobban (1990, 1994) has written extensively on the importance of informed consent agreements, which are often overlooked in social science research.
8. Williamson 1982, 206.
9. Glaser and Strauss 1967, 111.
10. Williamson 1982, 172.
11. First seven adapted from Williamson 1982, 200–201.

Bibliography

Preface

Billson, Janet Mancini. 1991b. The progressive verification method: Toward a feminist methodology for studying women cross-culturally. *Women's Studies International Forum*, 14 (3):201–215.

Immigrant Women's Editorial Collective. 1987. Immigrant women in Canada: The politics of sex, race and class. *Resources for Feminist Research* (May):3–12.

Collins, Patricia Hill. 1991. Learning from the outsider within: The sociological significance of Black feminist thought, in Mary Margaret Fonow and Judith A. Cook, eds., *Beyond methodology: Feminist scholarship as lived research*. Bloomington and Indianapolis: Indiana University Press.

Du Bois, Barbara. 1983. Passionate scholarship: Notes on values, knowing and method in feminist social science. In Gloria Bowles and Renate Duelli Klein, eds., *Theories of women's studies*. London: Routledge and Kegan Paul.

Immigrant Women's Editorial Collective. 1987. Immigrant women in Canada: The politics of sex, race and class. *Resources for Feminist Research* (May):3–12.

Kieffer, Charles. 1981. The emergence of empowerment: The development of participatory competence among individuals in citizen organizations. Unpublished doctoral dissertation, University of Michigan.

O'Brien, Mary. 1981. *The politics of reproduction*. London: Routledge and Kegan Paul.

Reinharz, Shulamit. 1983. Experiential analysis: A contribution to feminist research. In *Theories of women's studies*, Gloria Bowles and Renate Duelli Klein, eds. London: Routledge and Kegan Paul.

Smith, Dorothy E. 1987. The everyday world as problematic: A feminist methodology, in Dorothy E. Smith, *The everyday world as problematic*. Boston: Northeastern University Press.

Chapter 1

Alba, Richard D. 1990. *Ethnic identity: The transformation of white America*. New Haven, CT: Yale University Press.

433

Andersen, Margaret L. 1988. *Thinking about women: Sociological perspectives on sex and gender*, 2nd ed. New York: Macmillan.

Berkowitz, S. D., ed. 1984. *Models and myths in Canadian sociology*. Toronto: Butterworths.

Billson, Janet Mancini. 1991a. Interlocking identities: Gender, ethnicity and power in the Canadian context. *International Journal of Canadian Studies* 3:49–67.

————— 1991c. Standing tradition on its head: Role reversal among [Alberta] Blood Indian couples. *Great Plains Quarterly* 11 (Winter): 3–21.

————— 1990. Opportunity or tragedy? The impact of Canadian resettlement policy on Canadian Inuit families. *American Review of Canadian Studies* 20 (Summer): 187–218.

————— 1988a. No owner of soil: The concept of marginality revisited on its sixtieth birthday. *International Review of Modern Sociology* 18 (Autumn): 183–204.

————— 1988b. Social change, social problems, and the search for identity: Canada's northern native peoples in transition. *American Review of Canadian Studies* 18 (Autumn): 295–316.

Bolaria, B. Singh, and Peter S. Li, eds. 1988. *Racial oppression in Canada*, 2nd ed. Toronto: Garamond.

Blumberg, Rae Lesser. 1989. *Women and the wealth of nations: Theory and research on gender and global development*. New York: Praeger.

Brettell, Caroline B., and Carolyn F. Sargent. 1993. *Gender in cross-cultural perspective*. Englewood Cliffs, NJ: Prentice-Hall.

Bunch, Charlotte. 1987. Bringing the global home. In *Passionate politics: Feminist theory in action, essays 1968–88*. New York: St. Martin's.

Burt, Sandra. 1986. Women's issues and the women's movement in Canada since 1970. In *The politics of gender, ethnicity and language in Canada*, Alan Cairns and Cynthia Williams, eds. Toronto: University of Toronto Press.

Cannon, Lynn Weber, Elizabeth Higginbotham, and Marianne L. A. Leung. 1988. Race and class bias in qualitative research on women. *Gender and Society* 2 (4): 449–462.

Chafetz, Janet Saltzman. 1988. *Feminist sociology: An overview of contemporary theories*. Itasca, IL: Peacock.

————— and A. G. Dworkin. 1986. *Female revolt: Women's movements in world perspective and historical perspective*. Totowa, NJ: Rowman & Littlefield.

————— 1984. *Sex and advantage: A comparative macro-structural theory of sex stratification*. Totowa, NJ: Rowman and Allenheld.

————— 1983. *The changing position of women in the family: A cross-national comparison*. Leiden, the Netherlands: Brill.

Collins, Patricia Hill. 1990. *Black feminist thought: Knowledge, consciousness, and the politics of empowerment*. Boston: Unwin Hyman.

Demos, Vasilikie, and Marcia Texler Segal. 1994. *Ethnic women: A multi-layered status*. Bayside, NY: General Hall.

Dill, Bonnie Thornton. 1983. Race, class, and gender: Prospects for an all-inclusive sisterhood. *Feminist Studies* 9:131–150.

Du Bois, Barbara. 1983. Passionate scholarship: Notes on values, knowing and method in feminist social science. In *Theories of women's studies*, Gloria Bowles and Renate Duelli Klein, eds. London: Routledge and Kegan Paul.

Edwards, Mary I., and Margot Dudbey Morrow, eds. 1985. *The cross-cultural study of women*. Old Westbury, NY: Feminist Press.

Eichler, Margrit. 1992. Not always an easy alliance: The relationship between women's studies and the women's movement in Canada. In *Challenging times: The women's movement in Canada and the United States*, Constance Backhouse and David H. Flaherty, eds. Montreal: McGill-Queen's University Press.

———— 1977. Sociology of feminist research in Canada. *Signs* 3 (2): 409–422.

Eitzen, D. Stanley, and Maxine Baca Zinn. 1991. *In conflict and order: Understanding society*, 5th ed. Needham Heights, MA: Allyn and Bacon.

Elliott, Jean Leonard. 1983. *Two nations, many cultures: Ethnic groups in Canada*, 2nd ed. Scarborough, Ontario: Prentice-Hall.

Epstein, T. Scarlett, Janet Zollinger Giele, and Audrey Chapman Smock, eds. 1977. *Women: Roles and status in eight countries*. New York: Wiley.

Faludi, Susan 1991. *Backlash: The undeclared war against American Women*. New York: Crown.

Fuss, Diana, ed. 1991. *Lesbian theories, gay theories*. New York: Routledge.

Goyder, John. 1990. *Essentials of Canadian society*. Toronto: McClelland & Stewart.

Greenglass, Esther R. 1982. *A world of difference: Gender roles in perspective*. Toronto: Wiley.

Hartsock, Nancy C. M. 1983. *Money, sex, and power*. Boston: Northeastern University Press.

Hess, Beth B. 1990. Beyond dichotomy: Drawing distinctions and embracing differences. *Sociological Forum* 5 (1):75–93.

———— and Myra Marx Ferree, eds. 1987. *Analyzing gender: A handbook of social science research*. Newbury Park, CA: Sage.

Hiller, Harry H. 1991. *Canadian society: A macro analysis*. Toronto: Prentice-Hall Canada.

Hoyenga, Katherine Blick, and Kermit T. Hoyenga. 1993. *Gender-related differences: Origins and outcomes*. New York: Allyn and Bacon.

Hraba, Joseph. 1979. *American ethnicity*. Itasca, IL: Peacock.

Huber, Joan. 1986. Trends in gender stratification, 1970–1985. *Sociological Forum* 1: 476–496.

———— 1976. Sociology. *Signs* 1 (3): 685-697.

Immigrant Women's Editorial Collective. 1987. Immigrant women in Canada: The politics of sex, race and class. *Resources for Feminist Research*, May, 3–12.

Jaggar, Alison M., and Paula Rothenberg Struhl. 1978. *Feminist frameworks: Alternative theoretical accounts of the relations between men and women*. New York: McGraw-Hill.

Joy, Annamma. 1984. Sexism in research: Anthropological perspectives. In *Taking sex into account: The policy consequences of sexist research*, Jill McCall Vickers, ed. Ottawa: Carleton University Press.

Kanter, Rosabeth Moss, and Marcia Millman, ed. 1975. *Another voice: Feminist perspectives on social life and the social sciences*. Garden City, NY: Double-day.

Kelly, M. Patricia Fernandez. 1992. A chill wind blows: Class, ideology, and the reproductive dilemma. In *Challenging times: The women's movement in Canada and the United States*, Constance Backhouse and David H. Flaherty, eds. Montreal: McGill-Queen's University Press.

Kelly-Gadol, Joan. 1976. The social relation of the sexes: Methodological implications of women's history. *Signs* 1 (4): 809–823.

Kieffer, Charles. 1981. The emergence of empowerment: The development of participatory competence among individuals in citizen organizations. Unpublished doctoral dissertation, University of Michigan.

Kim, Hyun Kyung. 1990. The changing status of women, 1965–1980: A cross national analysis. Paper presented at the annual meeting of the American Sociological Association, Washington, DC.

Kitzinger, Celia. 1989. *The social construction of lesbianism*. Newbury Park, CA: Sage.

Kolenda, Pauline. 1988. *Cultural constructions of "woman."* Salem, WI: Sheffield.

Kurdek, L. A., and J. P. Schmitt. 1986. Interaction of sex-role self-concept with relationship quality and relationship belief in married, heterosexual cohabiting, gay, and lesbian couples. *Journal of Personality and Social Psychology* 51:365–370.

Lengermann, Patricia Madoo, and Ruth A. Wallace. 1985. *Gender in America: Social control and social change*. Englewood-Cliffs, NJ: Prentice-Hall.

Lipman-Blumen, Jean. 1984. *Gender roles and power*. Englewood Cliffs, NJ: Prentice-Hall.

Lipset, Seymour Martin. 1989. *Continental divide: The values and institutions of the United States and Canada*. Toronto: Canadian-American Committee.

Lorde, Audre. 1992. Age, race, class, and sex: Women redefining difference. In *Women, culture, and society: A reader*, Rutgers University Women's Studies Program. Dubuque, IA: Kendall/Hunt.

Mackie, Marlene. 1987. *Constructing women and men: Gender socialization*. Toronto: HBJ-Holt.

Mandell, Nancy, and Ann Duffy, eds. 1988. *Reconstructing the Canadian family: Feminist perspectives*. Toronto: Butterworths.

Matheson, Gwen, ed. 1976. *Women in the Canadian mosaic*. Toronto: Peter Martin Associates.

Matthews, Ralph. 1983. *The creation of regional dependency*. Toronto: University of Toronto Press.

Matthiasson, Carolyn J., ed. 1974. *Many sisters: Women in cross-cultural perspective*. New York: Free Press.

Nielsen, Joyce McCarl. 1990. *Sex and gender in society: Perspectives on stratification*. Prospect Heights, IL: Waveland.

Nemiroff, Greta Hofmann ed; 1987. *Women and men: Interdisciplinary readings on gender*. Toronto: Fitz Henry and Whiteside.

O'Kelly, Charlotte G., and Carney, Larry S. 1986. *Women and men in society:*

Cross-cultural perspectives on gender stratification, 2nd ed. Belmont, CA: Wadsworth.

Porter, John. 1965. *The vertical mosaic: An analysis of social class and power in Canada*. Toronto: University of Toronto Press.

Pryke, Kenneth G., and Walter C. Soderlund. 1992. *Profiles of Canada*. Toronto: Copp Clark Pitman.

Reinharz, Shulamit. 1992. *Feminist methods in social research*. New York: Oxford University Press.

—— 1983. "Back into the personal" or: Our attempt to construct "feminist research." In *Theories of women's studies*, Gloria Bowles and Renate Duelli Klein, eds. London: Routledge and Kegan Paul.

—— 1983. Experiential analysis: A contribution to feminist research. In *Theories of women's studies*, Gloria Bowles and Renate Duelli Klein, eds. London: Routledge and Kegan Paul.

—— 1979. *On becoming a social scientist: From survey research and participant observation to experiential analysis*. San Francisco: Jossey-Bass.

Rich, Adrienne. 1980. Compulsory heterosexuality and lesbian existence. *Signs* 5:4.

Richardson, Laurel. 1988. *The dynamics of sex and gender*. New York: Harper & Row.

Richmond-Abbott, Marie. 1983. *Masculine and feminine: Sex roles over the life cycle*. Reading, MA: Addison-Wesley.

Risman, Barbara J., and Pepper Schwartz. 1989. *Gender in intimate relationships: A microstructural approach*. Belmont, CA: Wadsworth.

Roberts, Elizabeth. 1984. *A woman's place*. Oxford, England: Basil Blackwell.

Rosaldo, Michelle Z. 1980. The use and abuse of anthropology: Reflections on feminism and cross-cultural understanding. *Signs* 5.

—— and Louise Lamphere, eds. 1974. *Women, culture, and society*. Palo Alto, CA: Stanford University Press.

Rosser, Sue V. 1988. Good science: Can it ever be gender free? *Women's Studies International Forum* 11 (1): 13–19.

Sanday, Peggy. 1981. *Female power and male dominance: On the origins of sexual inequality*. Cambridge, England: Cambridge University Press.

Sandoval, Chela. 1984. Comment on Krieger's "Lesbian identity and community: Recent social science literature." *Signs* 9:725–729.

Saunders, Eileen. 1988. Women and Canadian society: The sociological frame. In *Social issues: Sociological views of Canada*, Dennis Forcese and Stephen Richer, eds. Scarborough, Ontario: Prentice-Hall Canada.

Scanzoni, Letha Dawson, and John Scanzoni. 1981. *Men, women, and change: A sociology of marriage and the family*. New York: McGraw-Hill.

Silvera, Makeda. 1986. How far have we come? In *Fireworks: The best of Fireweed*, Makeda Silvera, ed. Toronto: Women's Press.

Smith, Dorothy E. 1986. Institutional ethnography: A feminist method. *Resources for Feminist Research*, May, 6–13.

—— 1977. Some implications of a sociology for women. In *Woman in a man-made world: A socioeconomic handbook*, Nona Glazer-Malbin and Helen Youngelson Waehrer, eds. Chicago: Rand McNally.

Stacey, Judith, and Barrie Thorne. 1985. The missing feminist revolution in sociology. *Social Problems* 32 (April): 301–316.

Steinem, Gloria. 1992. *Revolution from within: A book of self-esteem.* Boston: Little Brown.

Stockard, Jean, and Miriam M. Johnson. 1980. *Sex roles: Sex inequality and sex role development.* Englewood Cliffs, NJ: Prentice-Hall.

Stone, Sharon Dale. 1990. *Lesbians in Canada.* Toronto: Between the Lines.

Thorne, Barrie. 1993. *Gender play: Girls and boys in school.* New Brunswick, NJ: Rutgers University Press.

Turner, Jonathan H. 1984. *Oppression.* Chicago: Nelson Hall.

Valverde, Mariana. 1985. *Sex, power and pleasure.* Toronto: Woman's Press.

Vickers, Jill. ed. 1984. *Taking sex into account: The policy consequences of sexist research.* Ottawa: Carleton University Press.

Wallace, Ruth A., ed. 1989. *Feminism and sociological theory.* Newbury Park, CA: Sage.

Whyte, Martin King. 1978. *The status of women in preindustrial societies.* Princeton, NJ: Princeton University Press.

Wilson, S. J. 1986. *Women, the family, and the economy.* Toronto: McGraw-Hill Ryerson.

Wodak, Ruth, and Muriel Schulz. 1986. *The language of love and guilt: Mother-daughter relationships from a cross-cultural perspective.* Philadelphia: Benjamins.

Zinn, Maxine Baca. 1982. Mexican-American women in the social sciences. *Signs* 8:259–272.

Chapter 2

Beauchamp, William M. 1887. Iroquois women. *Journal of American Folk-Lore,* 13 (49): 81–91.

Billson, Janet Mancini, and Martha Stapleton. 1994. Accidental motherhood: Reproductive control and access to opportunity among women in Canada. *Women's Studies International Forum* 17 (July–August): 357–372.

Boyd, Monica. 1977. Occupational attainment of native born Canadian women: Results from the 1973 Canadian National Mobility Study. Working Paper No. 77-26. Madison: University of Wisconsin, Center for Demography and Ecology.

Brown, Judith K. 1970. Economic organization and the position of women among the Iroquois. *Ethno-History* 17: 151–167.

Campbell, Maria. 1973. *Half-breed.* Toronto: McClelland and Stewart.

Carr, Lucien. 1884. *On the position of women among the Huron-Iroquois tribes.* Peabody Museum of American Archaeology and Ethnology, 16th annual report, vol. 3, Cambridge, MA.

Chartrand, Larry. 1981. Women against patriation. *Native People,* 12 (March 20): 1–2.

Cheda, Sherrill. 1981. Indian women: An historical example and a contemporary view. In *Women in Canada,* Marylee Stephenson, ed. Don Mills, Ontario: General Publishing.

Department of Indian Affairs and Northern Development (DIAND), 1969. *White paper: Statement of the Government of Canada on Indian policy*. Ottawa: Author.

Dickason, Olive P. 1992. Canada's First Nations: A history of founding peoples from earliest times. Toronto: McClelland & Stewart.

Fels, Julie. 1980. *Ontario native women: A perspective*. Thunder Bay, Ontario: Guide Printing (for the Ontario Native Women's Association).

Fenton, William N. 1975. The lore of the longhouse: Myth, ritual and Red Power. *Anthropological Quarterly* 48 (3): 31–147.

Fisher, Robin, and Kenneth Coates. 1988. *Out of the background: Readings on Canadian Native History*. Toronto: Copp Clark Pitman.

Frideres, James S. 1988. Native people. In *Racial oppression in Canada*, 2nd ed., B. Singh Bolaria and Peter S. Li, eds. Toronto: Garamond.

——— 1988. *Native peoples in Canada: Contemporary conflicts*. Scarborough, Ontario: Prentice-Hall Canada.

Foreman, C. T. 1966 (1954). *Indian women chiefs*. Muskogee, OK: Hoffman.

Foster, W. Garland, Mrs. (Mohawk Princess). 1931. *Being some account of the life of Tekahion-Wake (E. Pauline Johnson)*. Vancouver, BC: Lion's Gate.

Freilich, Morris. 1963. Scientific possibilities in Iroquoian studies: An example of Mohawks past and present. *Anthropologica* 5 (2): 171–186.

Frisch, Jack A. 1970. Tribalism among the St. Regis Mohawks: A search for self-identity. *Anthropologica* 12 (2): 207–220.

Goldenweiser, A. A. 1915. Function of women in Iroquois society. *American Anthropologist* 17.

Grant, Gail. 1985. *The concrete reserve: Corporate programs for Indians in the urban work place*. Halifax, Nova Scotia: Research on Public Policy Communication Services.

Hale, Horatio. 1969 (1883). *The Iroquois Book of Rites*. New York: AMS.

Hewitt, J. N. B. 1933. *Status of women in Iroquois polity before 1784*. Smithsonian Institution Annual Reports. Washington, DC: Government Printing Office.

Hill, Bruce, Ian Gillen, and Glenda McNaughton. 1987. *Six Nations Reserve*. Markham, Ontario: Fitzhenry and Whiteside.

Hunsberger, Bruce. 1978. Racial awareness and preference of white and Indian Canadian children, *Canadian Journal of Behavioural Sciences* 10 (2): 176–180.

Jackson, Michael. 1979. The rights of the native people. In *The practice of freedom*, R. St. J. MacDonald and J. P. Humphrey, eds. Toronto: Butterworths.

Johnson, Charles M. 1964. *The valley of the Six Nations: A collection of documents on the Indian lands of the Grand River*. (The Champlain Society for the Government of Ontario). Toronto: University of Toronto Press.

Kirkness, Verna. 1986. Emerging native women. *Canadian Journal of Women and the Law* 2 (2): 408–415.

Kolenda, Pauline, ed. 1988. Cultural construction of 'women'. Salem, Wisconsin: Sheffield.

Krotz, Larry. 1990. *Indian country: Inside another Canada*. Toronto: McClelland & Stewart.

Lurie, Nancy Oestreich. 1972. Indian women: A legacy of freedom. *American Way*, April, 28–35.

Mackinnon, Catharine A. 1992. Feminist approaches to sexual assault in Canada and the United States: A brief retrospective. In *Challenging times: The women's movement in Canada and the United States*, Constance Backhouse and David H. Flaherty, eds. Montreal: McGill-Queen's University Press.

Majors, Richard, and Janet Mancini Billson. 1992. *Cool pose: Dilemmas of Black manhood in America*. New York: Lexington.

Marsh, James H., ed. 1985. *The Canadian encyclopedia*, vol. 2. Edmonton, Alberta: Hurtig.

McKenzie, J. 1896. *The Six-Nations Indians in Canada*. Toronto: Hunter Rose.

Miller, J. R. 1991. *Skyscrapers hide the heavens: A history of Indian-white relations in Canada*. Toronto: University of Toronto Press.

Mitchell, Mike, and Barbara Barnes. 1984. *Traditional teachings*. Cornwall, Ontario: North American Indian Travelling College.

Mohawk Women of Caughnawaga. 1980. The least members of our society. *Canadian Women's Studies/Les Cahiers de la Femme* 2 (2): 64–66.

Monture-Okanee, Patricia. 1992. The violence we women do: A First Nations view. In *Challenging times: The women's movement in Canada and the United States*, Constance Backhouse and David H. Flaherty, eds. Montreal: McGill-Queen's University Press.

———— 1989. A vicious circle: Child welfare and the First Nations. *Canadian Journal of Women and the Law* 3 (1).

———— 1986. Ka-Nin-Heh-Gah-E-Sa-Nonh-Yah-Gah. *Canadian Journal of Women and the Law* 2 (1).

Morgan, Lewis Henry. 1969. *League of the Iroquois*. New York: Corinth.

Nagler, Mark. 1970. *Indians in the city: A study of the urbanization of Indians in Toronto*. Ottawa: Saint Paul University, Canadian Research Centre for Anthropology.

National Geographic Society. 1979. *The world of the American Indian*. Washington, DC: author.

Ontario Native Women's Association. 1975. *Ontario native women: A perspective*. Thunder Bay, Ontario: Author.

———— n.d. *Breaking the cycle of aboriginal family violence: A proposal for change*. Thunder Bay, Ontario: Author.

Osennontion (Marlyn Kane) and Skonaganlehra (Sylvia Maracle). 1989. Our world. *Canadian Woman Studies* 10 (2–3): 7–19.

Randle, Martha C. 1951. Iroquois women, then and now. In symposium on local diversity in Iroquois culture. *Bulletin of the Bureau of American Ethnology*, 149. Washington, DC: United States Government Printing Office.

Richards, Cara E. 1974. *The Oneida people*. Phoenix: Indian Tribal Series, VI.

———— 1974. Onondaga women: Among the liberated. In *Many sisters: Women in cross-cultural perspective*, Carolyn J. Matthiasson, ed. New York: Free Press.

———— 1957. Matriarchy or mistake: The role of Iroquois women through time. In *Cultural stability and cultural change*, Verne F. Ray, ed. Seattle: University of Washington Press.

———— 1957. The role of Iroquois women. Unpublished Ph.D. dissertation, Cornell University.

———— Richardson, Karen. 1981. No Indian women . . . no Indian nation. *Ontario Indian* 4 (May): 10–12.

Samek, Hana. 1986. Evaluating Canadian Indian policy: A case for comparative historical perspective. *American Review of Canadian Studies* 16 (Autumn): 293–299.

Sanders, Douglas E. 1975. Indian women: A brief history of their roles and rights. *McGill Law Journal* 21 (4):667ff.

Schwartz, Mildred A. 1991. Canadian society: Trouble in paradise. *Current History*, December, 417–421.

Shafer, Ann Eastlack. 1941. The status of Iroquois women, MA Thesis, University of Pennsylvania. In *Iroquois women: An Anthology*, W.G. Spittal, ed. Ohsweken, Ontario: Iroqrafts.

Shorten, Lynda. 1991. *Without reserve: Stories from urban natives*. Edmonton, Alberta: NeWest Press.

Six Nations Agricultural Society. n.d. *Six Nations Indians, yesterday and today, 1867–1942*. Author.

Spittal, W. G., ed. 1990. *Iroquois women: An anthology*. Ohsweken, Ontario: Iroqrafts.

Tooker, Elizabeth. 1990. Women in Iroquois society. *In Iroquois Women: An anthology*, W.G. Spittal, ed. Ohsweken, Ontario: Iroqrafts.

Turpel, Ellen. 1990. Aboriginal peoples and the Canadian Charter: Interpretive monopolies, cultural differences. *Canadian Human Rights Yearbook 1989–1990*, 3–45.

Weaver, Sally M. 1983. The status of Indian women. In *Two nations, many cultures: Ethnic groups in Canada*, J. L. Elliott, ed. Scarborough, Ontario: Prentice-Hall Canada.

———— 1981. *Making Canadian Indian policy: The hidden agenda, 1968–70*. Toronto: University of Toronto Press.

White, Pamela M. 1986. *Native women: A statistical overview*. Ottawa: Native Citizens Directorate.

United Nations Human Rights Commission. 1981. Rights violated. *Native People* 14 (September): 2.

Chapter 3

Ahler, Janet Goldenstein. 1980. The formal education of Plains Indians. In *Anthropology on the Great Plains*, W. Raymond Wood and Margot Liberty, eds. Lincoln: University of Nebraska Press.

Albers, Patricia, and Beatrice Medicine, eds. 1983. *The hidden half: Studies of Plains Indian women.* Washington, DC: University Press of America.

Billson, Janet Mancini. 1988. Social change, social problems, and the search for identity: Canada's Northern Native peoples in transition. *American Review of Canadian Studies* 18 (3):295–316.

Cameron, Anne. 1981. *Daughters of Copper Woman.* Vancouver, BC: Press Gang.

Cardinal, Harold. 1979. Native women and the Indian Act. In *Two nations, many cultures*, Jean Leonard Elliott, ed. Scarborough, Ontario. Prentice-Hall Canada.

DeMallie, Raymond J. 1983. Male and female in traditional Lakota culture. In Patricia Albers and Beatrice Medicine, eds. *The hidden half: Studies of Plains Indian women.* Washington, DC: University Press of America.

Dempsey, Hugh A. 1978. *Charcoal's world, 1856–1896.* Saskatoon, Saskatchewan: Western Producer Prairie Books.

Dingman, Elizabeth. 1973. Indian women—the most unequal in Canada! *Chatelaine* 46 (February): 38–39, 78, 80–82.

Ewers, John C. 1958. *Blackfeet: Raiders on the northwestern Plains.* Norman: University of Oklahoma Press.

——— 1955. *The horse in Blackfoot Indian culture.* Smithsonian Institution, Bureau of American Ethnology Bulletin 159. Washington, DC: U.S. Government Printing Office.

Fisher, Anthony D. 1966. The perception of instrumental values among the young Bloods of Alberta. *Dissertation Abstracts* (27:2231B UM 66-14, 660).

Fisher, Robin, and Kenneth Coates. 1988. *Out of the background: Readings on Canadian native history.* Toronto: Copp Clark Pitman.

Fowler, Loretta. 1987. *Shared symbols, contested meanings: Gros Ventre culture and history, 1778–1984.* Ithaca, NY: Cornell University Press.

Frank, Lois, ed. 1984. *Niitsitapi: "The real people"—a look at the Bloods.* Standoff, Alberta: Ninastako Cultural Center, Blood Indian Reserve.

Frideres, J. S. 1988. *Native peoples in Canada: Contemporary conflicts*, 3rd ed. Scarborough, Ontario: Prentice-Hall Canada.

——— 1974. *Canada's Indians.* Scarborough, Ontario: Prentice-Hall Canada.

Goldfrank, Esther S. 1944. *Changing configurations in the social organization of a Blackfoot tribe during the reserve period (The Blood of Alberta, Canada).* Seattle: University of Washington Press.

Goodwell, Jean, ed. 1975. *Speaking for ourselves.* Ottawa: Secretary of State.

Grant, Gail. 1985. *The concrete reserve: Corporate programs for Indians in the urban work place.* Halifax, Nova Scotia: Research on Public Policy Communication Services.

Grinnell, George Bird. 1962. *Blackfoot lodge tales.* Lincoln: University of Nebraska Press; New York: Charles Scribner's Sons [1892].

Haines, Francis. 1976. *The Plains Indians.* New York: Crowell.

Henry, Alexander, and David Thompson. 1897. *New light on the early history of the greater Northwest: The manuscript journals of Alexander Henry and David Thompson, 1799–1814,* Elliott Coues, ed. New York: n.p.

Hungry Wolf, Adolph. 1977. *The Blood people: A division of the Blackfoot Confederacy*. New York: Harper and Row.

Hungry Wolf, Beverly. 1980. *The ways of my grandmothers*. New York: Morrow.

Jamieson, Kathleen. 1979. Multiple jeopardy: The evolution of a native women's movement. *Atlantis* 4 (Spring): 157–178.

———— 1978a. *Citizens minus: Indian women and the law in Canada*. Advisory Council on the Status of Women. Hull, PQ: Government Printer.

———— 1978b. Advisory Council on the Status of Women. *Indian women and the law in Canada*. Ottawa: Supply and Services Canada.

Kehoe, Alice B. 1976. Old woman had great power. *Western Canadian Journal of Anthropology* 6:68–76.

———— 1970. The function of ceremonial sexual intercourse among the northern Plains Indians. *Plains Anthropologist* 15:99–103.

Lachapelle, Caroline. 1982. Beyond barriers: Native women and the women's movement. In *Still ain't satisfied! Canadian feminism today*, Maureen Fitzgerald et al., eds. Toronto: Women's Press.

Landes, Ruth. 1969. *The Ojibwa woman*. New York: AMS.

Lavallee, Mary Ann. 1970. Yesterday's Indian women. *Tawow* 1 (Spring):6–7.

Lewis, Oscar. 1941. Manly-hearted women among the South Peigan. *American Anthropologist* 43:173–187.

———— 1942. *The effects of white contact upon Blackfoot culture*. Monographs of the American Ethnological Society, No. 6. Seattle: University of Washington Press.

Liberty, Margot. 1980. The Sun Dance. In *Anthropology on the Great Plains*, W. Raymond Wood and Margot Liberty, eds. Lincoln: University of Nebraska Press.

Lithman, Yngve Georg. 1985. *The practice of underdevelopment and the theory of development: The Canadian Indian case*. Stockholm: University of Stockholm.

———— 1984. *The community apart: A case study of a Canadian Indian reserve community*. Winnipeg: University of Manitoba Press.

Lurie, Nancy Oestreich. 1972. Indian women: A legacy of freedom. In *Look to the mountain top*, Charles Jones, ed. San Jose, CA: Gousha.

Lyon, Louise, and John W. Friesen. 1969. *Culture change and education: A study of Indian and non-Indian views in southern Alberta*. Calgary, Alberta: University of Calgary.

MacLean, Hope. 1982. *Indians, Inuit, and Metis of Canada (Blackfoot)*. Toronto: Gage.

McIntyre, Mary Margaret. 1974. Attitudes of Indian and non-Indian girls. Master's thesis, University of Calgary (Canadian Theses No. 21310).

McFee, Malcolm. 1972. *Modern Blackfeet: Montanans on a reservation*. New York: Holt, Rinehart and Winston.

———— 1968. The 150% man, a product of Blackfeet acculturation. *American Anthropologist* 70:1096–1103.

Meadows, Mary Lea. 1981. Adaptation to urban life by Native Canadian women. Master's Thesis, University of Calgary (Canadian Theses No. 52414).

Medicine, Beatrice. 1983. "Warrior women"—sex role alternatives for Plains In-
dian women. In *The hidden half: Studies of Plains Indian women*, Patricia
Albers and Beatrice Medicine, eds. Washington, DC: University Press of
America.

Mountain Horse, Mike. 1979. *My people the Bloods*. Calgary: Glenbow-Alberta
Institute.

Native Women Publication Advisory Board. n.d. *Speaking together: Canada's native women*. Ottawa: Secretary of State.

Parks, Douglas R., Margot Liberty, and Andrea Ferenci. 1980. Peoples of the
Plains. In *Anthropology on the Great Plains*, W. Raymond Wood and Margot
Liberty, eds. Lincoln: University of Nebraska Press.

Pierre-Aggamaway, Marlene. 1983. Native women and the state. In *Perspectives
on women in the 1980s*, Joan Turner and Lois Emery, eds. Winnipeg: University of Manitoba Press.

Poole, Carolyn Garrett. 1988. Reservation policy and the economic position of
Wichita women. *Great Plains Quarterly* 8 (Summer): 158–171.

Powers, Marla N. 1986. *Oglala women: Myth, ritual, and reality*. Chicago: University of Chicago Press.

Regular, W. Keith. 1986. *Red backs and white burdens: A study of white attitudes
towards Indians in southern Alberta, 1896–1911*. Ottawa: National Library of
Canada.

Rosaldo, Michelle A., and Louise Lamphere, eds. 1974. *Women, culture, and society*. Palo Alto, CA: Stanford University Press.

Samek, Hana. 1987. *The Blackfoot Confederacy, 1880–1920*. Albuquerque: University of New Mexico Press.

Sanders, Douglas. 1975. Indian women: A brief history of their roles and rights.
McGill Law Journal 21 (4):656–672.

——— 1974. Indian Act—status of Indian woman on marriage to person without
Indian status. *Saskatchewan Law Review* 38:234ff.

Schneider, Mary Jane. 1983. Women's work: An examination of women's roles in
Plains Indian arts and crafts. In *The hidden half: Studies of Plains Indian
women*, Patricia Albers and Beatrice Medicine, eds. Washington, DC: University Press of America.

Spector, Janet D. 1983. Male/female task differentiation among the Hidatsa: Toward the development of an archaeological approach to the study of gender.
In *The hidden half: Studies of Plains Indian women*, Patricia Albers and Beatrice Medicine, eds. Washington, DC: University Press of America.

Spindler, George D., and Louise S. Spindler. 1978. Identity, militancy, and
cultural congruence: The Menominee and Kainai. *Annals of the American
Academy of Political and Social Science* 436 (March): 73–85.

——— 1965. Researching the perception of cultural alternatives: The instrumental activities inventory. In *Context and meaning in cultural anthropology*,
Melford Spiro, ed. New York: Free Press.

Spindler, Louise S. 1977. *Culture change and modernization*. New York: Holt,
Rinehart and Winston.

Van Kirk, Sylvia. 1988. "Women in between": Indian women in fur trade society in Western Canada. In *Out of the background: Readings on Canadian native history*, Robin Fisher and Kenneth Coates, eds. Toronto: Copp Clark Pitman.

Walters, Cyril M. 1970. Indian children's perception of sex roles. Unpublished master's thesis, University of Alberta.

Weist, Katherine M. 1980. Plains Indian women: An assessment. In *Anthropology on the Great Plains*, W. Raymond Wood and Margot Liberty, eds. Lincoln: University of Nebraska Press.

Willis, Jane. 1973. *Giniesh: An Indian girlhood*. Toronto: New Press.

Wilson, R.N. 1921 (April). *Our betrayed words*. Ottawa: Author.

Wissler, Clark. 1918. *The Sun Dance of the Blackfoot Indians*. Anthropological Papers of the American Museum of Natural History, vol. 16, no. 3. New York: American Museum of Natural History.

—— 1913. *Societies and dance associations of the Blackfoot Indians*. Anthropological Papers of the American Museum of Natural History, vol. 11, no. 4. New York: American Museum of Natural History.

—— 1912. *Ceremonial bundles of the Blackfoot Indians*. Anthropological Papers of the American Museum of Natural History, vol. 7, no. 2. New York: American Museum of Natural History.

—— 1911. *The social life of the Blackfoot Indians*. Anthropological Papers of the American Museum of Natural History vol. 7, no. 2. New York: American Museum of Natural History.

—— 1910. *Material culture of the Blackfoot Indians*. Anthropological Papers of the American Museum of Natural History, vol. 5, no. 1. New York: American Museum of Natural History.

Zentner, Henry. 1973. *The Indian identity crisis*. Calgary, Alberta: Strayer.

Chapter 4

Alexander, Bryan. 1993. *Inuit*. Austin, TX: Raintree Steck-Vaughn.

Alia, Valerie. 1991. Aboriginal perestroika. *Arctic Circle*, November/December, 23–29.

Anders, G., ed. 1966. *The east coast of Baffin Island: An area economic survey*. Ottawa: Industrial Division, Department of Indian Affairs and Northern Development.

Annaqtuusi, Ruth, and David F. Pelly. 1986. *Tulurialik*. Toronto: Oxford University Press.

Armstrong, Terrence. 1966. The administration of northern peoples: The USSR. In *The Arctic frontier*, Ronald St. J. MacDonald, ed. (Canadian Institute of International Affairs and the Arctic Institute of North America.) Toronto: University of Toronto Press.

Asch, Michael. 1984. *Home and native land: Aboriginal rights and the Canadian constitution*. Toronto: Methuen.

—— 1977. The Dene economy. In *Dene Nation—the colony within*, Mel Watkins, ed. Toronto: University of Toronto Press.

Atkin, Ronald. 1973. *Maintain the right: The early history of the North West Mounted Police, 1873–1900.* Toronto: Macmillan.

Baikie, Margaret. n.d. *Labrador memories: Reflections at Mulligan.* Grand Falls, Newfoundland: Robinson-Blackmore.

Balikci, Asen. 1964. *Development of basic socio-economic units in two Eskimo communities.* Ottawa: National Museum of Canada.

——— 1960. Ethnic relations and the marginal man in Canada: A comment. *Human Organization,* 170–171.

——— 1978. The Netsilik Eskimo today. *Etudes/Inuit/Studies* 2 (1): 111–119.

Bell, Jim. 1992. Nunavut: The quiet revolution. *Arctic Circle,* January/February, 13–21.

Bennett, Allan C., William E. Flannigan, and Marilyn P. Hladun. 1980. *Inuit community.* Don Mills, Ontario: Fitzhenry and Whiteside.

Billson, Janet Mancini. and Kyra Mancini. 1995. *Inuit women: A century of change.*

——— and Martha Stapleton. 1994. Accidental motherhood: Reproductive control and access to opportunity among women in Canada. *Women's Studies International Forum* 17 (July-August): 357–372.

——— 1990a. Changing role of Inuit women and their families: New choices for a new era. In *Gossip: A spoken history of women in the North,* Mary Crnkovich, ed. Ottawa: Canadian Arctic Resources Committee.

——— 1990b. Opportunity or tragedy? The impact of resettlement policy on Canadian Inuit families. *American Review of Canadian Studies* 20 (Summer): 187–218.

——— 1990c. Violence toward Inuit women and children. In *Gossip: A spoken history of women in the North,* Mary Crnkovich, ed. Ottawa: Canadian Arctic Resources Committee.

——— 1988a. No owner of soil: The concept of marginality revisited on its sixtieth birthday. *International Review of Modern Sociology* 18:183–204.

——— 1988b. Social change, social problems, and the search for identity: Canada's northern native peoples in transition. *American Review of Canadian Studies* 18 (Autumn): 295–316.

Blodgett, Jean. 1980. *Cape Dorset (artists and the community).* Winnipeg: Winnipeg Art Gallery. (Comments by Houston, Eber, Ryan, Pootoogook, and Blodgett).

Boas, Franz. 1901. The Eskimo of Baffin Land and Hudson Bay. *Bulletin of the American Museum of Natural History* 15.

Briggs, Jean L. 1974. Eskimo women: Makers of men. In *Many sisters: Women in cross-cultural perspective,* Carolyn J. Matthiasson, ed. New York: Free Press.

——— 1970. *Never in anger: Portrait of an Eskimo family.* Cambridge, MA: Harvard University Press.

Brody, Hugh. 1975. *The people's land: Eskimos and whites in the eastern Arctic.* Markham, Ontario: Penguin.

Bruemmer, Fred, et al. 1985. *The Arctic world.* Toronto: Key Porter.

Burns, John F. 1974. Eskimo males said to be battling "lib" by beating wives. *New York Times,* November 20.

Cairns, Alan, and Cynthia Williams. 1985. *Constitutionalism, citizenship and society in Canada*. Toronto: University of Toronto Press.

Canadian Arctic Resources Committee. 1989. *Nunavut: Political choices and manifest destiny*. Ottawa: Author.

Chamberlin, J. E. 1975. *The harrowing of Eden: White attitudes toward North American natives*. Toronto: Fitzhenry and Whiteside.

Clark, Bruce. 1990. *Native liberty, crown sovereignty: The existing aboriginal right of self-government in Canada*. Montreal: McGill-Queen's University Press.

Clark, Joe. 1991. Completing the circle of confederation—aboriginal rights. *Canada Today*/d'aujourd'hui 22 (2): 14–15. Washington, DC: Canadian Embassy (Excerpts from a speech by the Minister Responsible for Constitutional Affairs, Queen's University, Kingston, Ontario, September 9).

Coates, Kenneth, and Judith Powell. 1989. *The modern North: People, politics, and the rejection of colonialism*. Toronto: Lorimer.

Condon, Richard G. 1987. *Inuit youth: Growth and change in the Canadian Arctic*. New Brunswick, NJ: Rutgers University Press.

———— 1981. Inuit behavior and seasonal change in the Canadian Arctic. *Studies in Cultural Anthropology* 2.

Cowan, Edward. 1978. Canadian Eskimos are adopting the white man's ways. *New York Times*, August 8.

Cox, Bruce, ed. 1988. *Native people, native lands: Canadian Indians, Inuit and Metis*. Ottawa: Carleton University Press.

Cox, Marlene Joan. 1979. A cross-cultural study of sex differences found in drawings by Canadian Inuit and American children. Unpublished doctoral dissertation, Illinois State University.

Creevy, Ian. 1993. *The Inuit (Eskimo) of Canada*. London: Minority Rights Group.

Crowe, Keith J. 1991 [1974]. *A history of the original peoples of Northern Canada*. (Arctic Institute of North America). Montreal: McGill-Queen's University Press.

Cruikshank, Julia Margaret. 1976. Matrifocal families in the Canadian North. In *The Canadian family*, K. Ishwaran, ed. Toronto: Holt, Rinehart and Winston of Canada.

———— 1969. The role of northern Canadian women in social change. Unpublished master's Thesis, University of British Columbia.

Dacks, Gurston, ed. 1990. *Devolution and constitutional development in the Canadian North*. Ottawa: Carleton University Press.

———— and Ken Coates, eds. 1989. *Northern communities: The prospects for empowerment*. Edmonton, Alberta: Canadian Circumpolar Institute/University of Alberta Press.

Danglure, Bernard Saladin. 1978. Man (*angut*), son (*irniq*) and light (*qau*), or the circle of masculine power in the Inuit of the Central Arctic. *Anthropologica* 20 (1–2): 101–144.

Department of Indian Affairs and Northern Development. 1974. *Arctic women's workshop*. Ottawa: Author.

——— 1986. *The Inuit*. Ottawa: Author.

——— 1985. *The North*. Ottawa: Author.

——— 1982. *Native peoples and the North: A profile*. Ottawa: Author.

——— 1980. *The Inuit*. Ottawa: Author.

Department of the Secretary of State: 1975. *Speaking together: Canada's native women*. Ottawa: Author.

Derman, William, and Scott Whiteford, eds. 1985. *Social impact analysis and development planning in the Third World*. Boulder, CO: Westview.

Dewey, Kathryn. 1985. Nutrition, social impact, and development. In *Social impact analysis and development in the Third World*, William Derman and Scott Whiteford, eds. Boulder, CO: Westview.

Dickerson, Mark O. 1992. *Whose North? Political change, political development, and self-government in the Northwest Territories*. Vancouver: University of British Columbia Press.

Duffy, R. Quinn. 1988. *The road to Nunavut: The progress of the Eastern Arctic Inuit since the Second World War*. Montreal: McGill-Queen's University Press.

Eber, Dorothy. 1990. *When the whalers were up North: Inuit memories from the Eastern Arctic*. Montreal: McGill-Queen's University Press.

——— 1975. *People from our side*. Seattle: University of Washington Press.

——— 1972. *Pitseolak: Pictures out of my life*. Montreal: Design Collaborative Books.

Elias, Peter Douglas. 1991. *Development of aboriginal people's communities*. North York, Ontario: Centre for Aboriginal Management Education and Training and Captus Press.

Environment Canada. 1983. *Environment Canada and the North: The perceptions, roles and policies of the Department of the Environment regarding development north of 60*, Discussion Paper. Ottawa: Author.

Finkler, Harold W. 1976. *North of 60: Inuit and the administration of criminal justice in the Northwest Territories—the case of Frobisher Bay*. Ottawa: Department of Indian Affairs and Northern Development.

Franks, C.E.S. 1989. Indian self-government: Canada and the United States compared. Paper presented to the annual meeting of the Western Social Science Association, Albuquerque, NM.

Freeman, Minni Aodla. 1978. *Life among the Qallunaat*. Edmonton: Hurtig.

Freuchen, Peter. 1961. *Book of the Eskimos*. New York: Fawcett.

Garber, Clark N. 1962. Sex and the Eskimo. *Sexology* (March).

——— 1947. Eskimo infanticide. *Scientific Monthly* 64 (February):98–102.

Giffen, Naomi Musmaker. 1930. *The roles of men and women in Eskimo culture*. Chicago: University of Chicago Press.

Goar, Carol. 1991. The constitution: Why Ottawa plan has natives angry. *Toronto Daily Star*, September 28, p. D5.

Goldhar, Harry. 1970. Ottawa wants education to aid Eskimo integration. *Toronto Daily Star*, June 22.

Graburn, Nelson H. H. 1987. Inuit art and the expression of Eskimo identity. *American Review of Canadian Studies*, 17 (1): 47–66.

———— 1972. *Eskimos of Northern Canada*, 2 vols. New Haven, CT: Human Relations Area Files.

———— 1969. *Eskimos without igloos: Social and economic development in Sugluk*. Boston: Little, Brown.

Grant, Shelagh D. 1989. *Sovereignty or security: Government policy in the Canadian North, 1936–1950*. Vancouver: University of British Columbia Press.

Goudie, Elizabeth. 1973. *Woman of Labrador*. Toronto: Peter Martin Associates.

Guemple, D. L. 1961. *Inuit spouse exchange*. Chicago: Department of Anthropology, University of Chicago.

Hahn, Elizabeth. 1990. *The Inuit*. Vero Beach, FL: Rourke.

Hancock, Lyn. 1975. A good woman in the North. *North* 22 (September-October): 12–15.

Hanley, Charles J. 1987. Tomorrow slowly encroaches on harsh, scenic Arctic (Pond Inlet, NWT) *Los Angeles Times*, October 11, pp. 2ff.

Harper, Kenn. 1986. *Give me my father's body: The life of Minik, the New York Eskimo*. Frobisher Bay, Northwest Territories: Blacklead.

Harrington, Lyn. n.d. *Ootook: Young Eskimo girl*. Toronto: Nelson.

Hawkes, David C., ed. 1989. *Aboriginal peoples and government responsibility: Exploring federal and provincial roles*. Ottawa: Carleton University Press.

Hobart, Charles W. 1984. Impact of resource development projects on indigenous people. In *Resource communities: A decade of disruption*, Don D. Detomasi and John W. Gartrell, eds. Boulder, CO: Westview.

———— 1982. Industrial employment of rural indigenes: The case of Canada. *Human Organization* 41 (1): 54–63.

Hunt, Constance. 1977. Fishing rights for Inuit women. *Branching Out* 4 (March-April): 6–7.

Hyde, Deborah. 1980. Women, production and change in Inuit society. Unpublished thesis, Carleton University.

Inuit Committee on National Issues. 1987. *Completing Canada: Inuit approaches to self-government*. Kingston, Ontario: Institute of Intergovernmental Relations.

Inuit Tapirisat of Canada. 1983. Nunavut—"our land." In *Two nations, many cultures: Ethnic groups in Canada*, 2nd ed., Jean Leonard Elliott, ed. Scarborough, Ontario: Prentice-Hall.

Irwin, Colin. 1989. Lords of the Arctic, wards of the state: The growing Inuit population, Arctic resettlement, and their effects on social and economic change—a summary report. *Northern Perspectives* 17 (1): 2–12.

Jenness, Diamond, 1966. The administration of Northern peoples: America's Eskimos—pawns of history. In *The Arctic frontier*, Ronald St. J. Macdonald, ed. Toronto: University of Toronto Press. (Canadian Institute of International Affairs and the Arctic Institute of North America.)

Jull, Peter. 1981. Aboriginal peoples and political change in the North Atlantic area. *Journal of Canadian Studies* 16 (2).

Kallso, Josephine. 1984. *Taipsumane*. Nain, Labrador: Torngasok Cultural Centre.

Keenleyside, D. 1975. *The land beyond*. Toronto: Nelson, Foster and Scott.

———— 1977. *Where the mountain falls*. Toronto: Nelson, Foster and Scott.

Kleivan, Inga. 1976. Status and role of men and women as reflected in West Greenland petting songs to infants. *Folk* 18:5–22.

Krech, Shepard III, ed. 1984. *The subarctic fur trade: Native social and economic adaptations*. Vancouver: University of British Columbia Press.

Krosenbrink-Gelissen, Liliane E. 1991. *Sexual equality as an aboriginal right: The Native Women's Association of Canada and the constitutional process on aboriginal matters, 1982–1987*. Saarbrucken, Ft. Lauderdale, FL: Verlag Breitenbach.

Labarge, Dorothy. 1975. Femme traditionnelle, femme nouvelle. *North* 22 (September):8–11.

Lamphere, Louise. 1993. The domestic sphere of women and the public world of men: The strengths and limitations of an anthropological dichotomy. In *Gender in cross-cultural perspective*, Caroline B. Brettell and Carolyn F. Sargent, eds. Englewood Cliffs, NJ: Prentice-Hall.

Lange, Lynda. 1986. The relation between the situation of Dene women and the changing situation of elders, in the context of colonialism: The experience of Fort Franklin, 1945–1985. Paper presented at conference on Knowing the North, Boreal Institute for Northern Studies, Edmonton, Alberta.

Lantis, Margaret. The administration of Northern peoples: Canada and Alaska. In *The Arctic frontier*, Ronald St. J. Macdonald, ed. Toronto: University of Toronto Press.

Leacock, Eleanor. 1982. Relations of production in band society. In *Politics and history in band societies*, Eleanor Leacock and Richard Lee, eds. New York: Cambridge University Press.

Lerou, Odette, Marion E. Jackson, and Minnie Aodla Freeman, eds. 1994. *Inuit women artists*: Voices from Cape Dorset. Vancouver: Douglas and McIntyre; Hull, Quebec: Canadian Museum of Civilization; Seattle: University of Washington Press.

Lopez, Barry. 1986. *Arctic dreams: Imagination and desire in a northern landscape*. Toronto: Bantam.

Lowenstein, Tom. 1994. *Ancient land, sacred whale: The Inuit hunt and its rituals*. New York: Farrar, Straus, and Giroux.

Lubart, J. M. 1970. *Psychodynamic problems of adaptation: Mackenzie Delta Eskimos*. Ottawa: Department of Indian Affairs and Northern Development.

Lynge, Finn. 1986. An international Inuit perspective on development in the Arctic. *Northern Raven* 6 (Summer): 1–3.

Mackie, Marlene. 1983. *Exploring gender relations: A Canadian perspective*. Toronto: Butterworths.

Manue, George, and Michael Posluns. 1983. The Fourth World in Canada. In *Two nations, many cultures: Ethnic groups in Canada*, 2nd ed. Scarborough, Ontario: Prentice-Hall Canada.

Marcus, Alan R. 1992. *Out in the cold: The legacy of Canada's Inuit relocation experiment in the high Arctic*. Copenhagen: IWGIA.

Markoosie. 1974. *Harpoon of the hunter*. Montreal: McGill-Queen's University Press.

Marsh, Donald B. 1987. *Echoes from a frozen land*, Winifred Marsh, ed. Edmonton, Alberta: Hurtig.

Matthews, Ralph. 1983. *The creation of regional dependency*. Toronto: University of Toronto Press.

Matthiasson, John S. 1992. *Living on the land: Change among the Inuit of Baffin Island*. Peterborough, Ontario: Broadview.

—— 1976. Northern Baffin Island women in three cultural periods. *Western Canadian Journal of Anthropology* 6 (3): 201–212.

McAlpine, Phyllis J., and Nancy E. Simpson. 1976. Fertility and other demographic aspects of the Canadian Eskimo communities of Igloolik and Hall Beach. *Human Biology* 48 (February):113–138.

McElroy, Ann. 1977. *Alternatives in modernization: Styles and strategies in the acculturative behavior of Baffin Island Inuit*, 3 vols. New Haven, CT: Human Relations Area Files, Ethnography Series.

—— 1976. The negotiation of sex-role identity in Eastern Arctic culture change. *Western Canadian Journal of Anthropology* 6 (3):184–200.

—— 1975. Canadian Arctic modernization and change in female Inuit role identification. *American Ethnologist* 2 (November):662–686.

McGhee, Robert. 1977. Ivory for the Sea Woman: The symbolic attributes of a prehistoric technology. *Canadian Journal of Archaeology* 1:141–149.

McMahon, Kevin. 1988. *Arctic twilight*. Toronto: Lorimer.

McNiven, Jean. 1975. La femme et la Nord. *North* 22 (October): 62–63.

Mead, Margaret. 1959. *The Eskimos*. (Based on the fieldwork of Franz Boas in Cumberland Sound, Baffin Island, NWT, 1883) (n.p.)

Merritt, John, Terry Fynge, Randy Ames, and Peter Jull. 1989. *Nunavut: Political choices and manifest destiny*. Ottawa: Canadian Arctic Resources Committee.

Minior, Kit. 1992. *Issumatuq: Learning from the traditional helping wisdom of the Canadian Inuit*. Halifax, Nova Scotia: Fernwood.

Mowatt, Farley. 1975. *People of the deer*. Toronto: Seal.

Munro, Mary. 1975. Pangnirtung women carvers. *North* 22 (October): 46–49.

Myers, Marybelle. 1975. Remembering (Eskimo Women's Crafts Workshop). *North* 22 (October):26–29.

National Geographic Society. 1979. *The world of the American Indian*. Washington, DC: Author.

Newman, Shirlee. 1993. *The Inuits*. New York: Watts.

Northwest Territories Bureau of Statistics. 1988. *NWT vital statistics 1977–1986*. Yellowknife, Northwest Territories: Author.

—— 1987. *Statistics quarterly* 9, 4 (Dec.). Yellowknife, Northwest Territories: Author.

Nungak, Zebedee. 1988. *Inuit stories: Povungnituk*. Hull, Quebec: Canadian Museum of Civilization.

Palliser, Annie. 1975. Annie, jeune Inuk en transition. *North* 22 (October): 50–51.

Petrone, Penny. 1988. *Northern voices: Inuit writing in English*. Toronto: University of Toronto Press.

Raine, David F. 1980. *Pitseolak: A Canadian tragedy*. Edmonton, Alberta: Hurtig.

Remie, C. H. W. and J.M. Lacroix, eds. 1991. *Canada on the threshold of the 21st century*. Amsterdam: Benjamins.

Research Branch, P.R.E., Indian and Inuit Affairs Program. 1979. *A demographic profile of registered Indian women*. Ottawa: Department of Indian and Northern Affairs.

Révillon Frères. 1983. *Eskimo life of yesterday*. Surrey, BC: Hancock House. (Originally published in 1922).

Reynolds, Jan. 1993. *Frozen land: Vanishing cultures*. San Diego, CA: Harcourt Brace.

Roy, Gabrielle. 1961. *The hidden mountain*. Toronto: McClelland and Stewart.

Samek, Hana. 1986. Evaluating Canadian Indian policy: A case for comparative historical perspective. *American Review of Canadian Studies* 16 (Autumn): 293–299.

Shannon, Robert F. J., ed. 1985. Salute to women in the North! *North* (October): 1–63.

Skinner, Neil C. 1989. Foundations of aboriginal sovereignty in North America: A comparative review. Paper presented to the annual meeting of the Western Social Science Association, Albuquerque, NM.

Smith, Gordon W. 1966. Sovereignty in the North: The Canadian aspect of an international problem. In *The Arctic frontier*, Ronald St. J. Macdonald, ed. Toronto: University of Toronto Press.

Steltzer, Ulli. 1982. *Inuit: The North in transition*. Vancouver, BC: Douglas and McIntyre.

Struck, Doug. 1985. Among the people (series). *Baltimore Sun*, January 13–17.

Thomas, Lewis H. 1970. *The North-West Territories 1870–1905*. Booklet No. 26. Ottawa: Canadian Historical Association.

Upton, L. F. S. 1988. The extermination of the Beothucks of Newfoundland. In *Out of the background: Readings on Canadian native history*, Robin Fisher and Kenneth Coates, eds. Toronto: Copp Clark Pitman.

Valentine, Victor F., and Frank G. Vallee, eds. 1978. *Eskimo of the Canadian Arctic*. Toronto: Macmillan.

Vallee, Frank G. Differentiation among the Eskimo in some Canadian Arctic settlements. In *Eskimo of the Canadian Arctic*, Victor F. Valentine and Frank G. Vallee, eds. Toronto: Macmillan.

Van Raalte, Sharon. 1975. Inuit women and their art. *Communique* 8 (May): 21–23.

van Steensel, Maja, ed. 1966. *People of light and dark*. Ottawa: Department of Indian Affairs and Northern Development.

Vanstone, James W. 1966. Influence of European man on the Eskimos. In *People of light and dark*, Maja van Steensel, ed. Ottawa: Department of Indian Affairs and Northern Development.

Vesilind, Priit J. 1983. Hunters of the lost spirit. *National Geographic* 163 (February): 151–197.

Watts, Ronald L., and Douglas M. Brown. 1991. *Options for a new Canada*. Toronto: University of Toronto Press.

Weick, Edward. 1988. Northern native people and the larger Canadian society—emerging economic relations. *American Review of Canadian Studies* 18 (Autumn): 317–329.

Weller, Geoffrey R. 1988. Self-government for Canada's Inuit: The Nunavut proposal. *American Review of Canadian Studies* 18 (Autumn): 341–358.

Wenzel, George W. 1981. Clyde Inuit adaptation and ecology: The organization of subsistence. Canadian Ethnology Service, Paper No. 77, National Museum of Man Mercury Series. Ottawa: National Museums of Canada.

Whittington, Michael S. 1986. *Native economic development corporations: Political and economic change in Canada's North*. Ottawa: Canadian Arctic Resources Committee.

Wilkinson, Doug. 1965. *Land of the long day*. New York: Holt.

Wonders, William C., ed. 1989. *Knowing the North: Reflections on tradition, technology and science*. Edmonton, Alberta: Canadian Circumpolar Institute/University of Alberta Press.

———— 1988. Overlapping native land claims in the Northwest Territories. *American Review of Canadian Studies* 18 (Autumn): 359–368.

Young, E. A. 1995. *Third World in the First: Development of aboriginal peoples of remote Canada and Australia*. New York: Routledge.

Zaslow, Morris. 1984. *The Northwest Territories 1905–1980*. Booklet No. 38. Ottawa: Canadian Historical Association.

Chapter 5

Aho, William R. 1984. The treatment of women in Trinidad's calypsoes, 1969–1979. *Sex Roles* 10 1–2: 141–148.

———— 1981. Sex conflicts in Trinidad's calypsoes, 1969–1979. *Revista/Review* Interamericana 11 (Spring): 76–81.

Alberro, Ana, and Gloria Montero. 1976. The immigrant woman. In *Women in the Canadian Mosaic*, Gwen Matheson, ed. Toronto: Peter Martin Associates.

Andre, Jacques. 1985. The cock and the jar: Sexuality and femininity in Afro-Caribbean societies. *L'homme* 25 (4): 49–75.

Anthony, Suzanne. 1989. *West Indies*. New York: Chelsea House.

Bannerji, Himani. 1987. Introducing racism: Notes towards an anti-racist feminism. *Resources for Feminist Research*, May, 10–12.

Barbalsingh, Frank. 1986. West Indians in Canada: The Toronto novels of Austin Clarke. *Journal of Caribbean Studies* 5 (2): 71–77.

Barber, Marilyn. 1980. The women Ontario welcomed: Immigrant domestics for Ontario homes, 1870–1930. *Ontario History* 72:148–172.

Boyd, Monica. 1976. Occupations of female immigrants and North American immigration statistics. *International Migration Review* 10 (Spring):73–80.

———— 1975. Status of immigrant women in Canada. *Canadian Review of Sociology and Anthropology* 12 (November):406–416.

Brand, Dionne. 1984. A working paper on black women in Toronto: Gender, race and class. *Fireweed* (Summer/Fall).

Breton, Raymond. 1983. West Indian, Chinese, and European ethnic groups in Toronto: Perceptions of problems and resources. In *Two nations, many cultures: Ethnic groups in Canada*, J. L. Elliott, ed. Scarborough, Ontario: Prentice-Hall Canada.

Brodber, Erna. 1982. *Perceptions of Caribbean women: Towards a documentation of stereotypes*. Institute of Social and Economic Research (Eastern Caribbean). Cave Hill, Barbados: University of the West Indies.

Brothers, Don. 1988. *West Indies*. New York: Chelsea House.

Carter, Edward H. 1967. *History of the West Indian peoples*. London: Nelson.

Clarke, Austin. 1975. *The bigger light*. Boston: Little, Brown.

——— 1973. *Storm of fortune*. Boston: Little, Brown.

Cohen, Rina. 1987. The work conditions of immigrant women live-in domestics: Racism, sexual abuse and invisibility. *Resources for Feminist Research*, May, pp. 36–38.

Cracknell, Basil E. 1974. *The West Indians*. Newton Abbott, UK: David and Charles.

Dabydeen, Cyril. 1986. Outside El Dorado: Themes and problems of West Indians writing in Canada. *Journal of Caribbean Studies* 5 (2): 79–90.

Diebel, Linda. 1973. Black women in white Canada: The lonely life. *Chatelaine* 46 (March):84, 86–88.

D'Oyley, Enid F. 1984. *The bridge of dreams*. Toronto: Williams Wallace.

——— and Rella Braithwaite, eds. 1973. *Women of our times*. Toronto: Canadian Negro Women's Association for the National Congress of Black Women.

Epstein, Rachel. 1980. West Indian domestic workers on employment visas: "I thought there was no more slavery in Canada!" *Canadian Women's Studies/Les Cahiers de la Femme* 2 (1): 22–29.

Estable, Alma. 1986. *Immigrant women in Canada—current issues*. Ottawa: Canadian Advisory Council on the the Status of Women.

Evans, Lancelot O. 1973. *The Caribbean (the English-speaking islands) in pictures*. New York: Sterling.

Farkas, Edie. 1979. Victimizing domestic workers. *Multiculturalism* 11 (4):17–18.

Gipson, Joella H., ed. 1977. *Impetus, the black woman: Proceedings of the Fourth National Congress of Black Women of Canada*.

Greene, J. Edward. 1970. Political perspectives on the assimilation of immigrants: A case study of West Indians in Vancouver. *Social and Economic Studies* 19 (September): 406–423.

Gregory, Frances. 1979. Immigrant domestics speak out. *Wages for Housework Campaign Bulletin* 4 (2): 2–3.

Gulbinowicz, Eva. 1979. *Problems of immigrant women, past and present: A bibliography*. Mimeo. Toronto: Ontario Ministry of Labour.

Gupta, Nila, and Makeda Silvera, eds. 1989. The issue is 'ism: Women of colour speak out. *Fireweed* 16.

Harney, Robert F., ed. 1985. *Gathering place: Peoples and neighborhoods of Toronto, 1834–1945*. Toronto: Multicultural History Society of Ontario.

Henry, Frances. 1968. The West Indian domestic scheme in Canada. *Social and*

Economic Studies 17 (March):83–91.

hooks, bell. 1989. *Talking back: Thinking feminist, thinking black.* Boston: South End.

———— 1984. *Feminist theory from margin to center.* Boston: South End.

Hull, Gloria, Patricia Bell Scott, and Barbara Smith. 1982. *All of the women are white, all of the men are white, but some of us are brave.* Old Westbury, NY: Feminist Press.

Immigrant Women's Editorial Collective. 1987. Immigrant women in Canada: The politics of sex, race and class. *Resources for Feminist Research*, May, 3–12.

Klotman, Phyllis, and Willmer H. Baatz. 1978. *The black family and the black woman.* New York: Arnot.

Ladner, Joyce A. 1971. *Tomorrow's tomorrow: The black woman.* Garden City, NY: Doubleday.

Lash, Ronnie, and Gwen Morgan. 1979. Immigrant women fight back: The case of the seven Jamaican women. *Resources for Feminist Research* 8 (November):23–24.

Lenskyj, Helen. 1980. Social change affecting women in urban Canada, 1890–1930, and its impact upon immigrant women in the labour force. Unpublished master's thesis, University of Toronto.

Leo-Rhymie, Elsa. 1993. *The Jamaican family: Continuity and change.* Kingston, Jamaica: Grace Kennedy Foundation.

McClaine, Paula Denice. 1986. Political alienation: Some social/psychological aspects of the political culture of Afro-Canadians. *Journal of Caribbean Studies* 5 (2): 91–116.

Moraga, Cherrie, and Gloria Anzaldua, eds. 1981. *This bridge called my back: Writings by radical women of color.* Watertown, MA: Persephone.

Mordecai, Pamel, and Mervyn Morris, eds. 1980. *Jamaican woman: An anthology of poems.* Kingston, Jamaica: Heinemann Educational.

Morgan, Gwen, and Michael David. 1980. Caribbean women and immigration. *Rikka* 7 (Spring):20–22.

Naylor, Gloria. 1983. *The women of Brewster Place.* New York: Penguin.

Ng, Roxana, and Alma Estable. 1987. Immigrant women in the labour force: An overview of present knowledge and research gaps. *Resources for Feminist Research*, May, 29–33.

Ramirez, Judith, ed. 1983. *Implementation of the special policy on foreign domestic workers: Findings and recommendations for change.* Toronto: Intercede International Coalition to End Domestics' Exploitation.

Rodman, Selden. 1968. *The Caribbean.* New York: Hawthorn.

Romero, Mary. 1992. *Maid in the U.S.A.* New York: Routledge.

———— 1988. Sisterhood and domestic service: Race, class, and gender in the mistress-maid relationship. *Humanity and Society* 12:318–346.

Scarborough Board of Education. 1976–1977. *West Indians in Toronto.* Filmstrip. Toronto: Author.

Seydegart, K., and G. Spears. 1985. *Beyond dialogue: Immigrant women in Cana-*

da, 1985–1990. Mimeo, Erin Research.

Shafer, Suzanne M. *Escape from racism, sexism, and poverty for minority women.* Association paper. Tempe: Arizona State University.

Sherlock, Philip M. 1967. *The land and people of the West Indies.* Philadelphia: Lippincott.

———. 1966. *West Indian folk-tales.* Toronto: Oxford University Press.

Silvera, Makeda. 1990. Broken dreams: West Indian women in Toronto. *Rikka* 7 (Spring): 17–19.

———, ed. 1986. *Fireworks: The best of Fireweed.* Toronto: Women's Press.

——— 1983. *Silenced (Oral histories of West Indian women working as domestic servants in Canada).* Toronto: Williams-Wallace.

——— 1981. Immigrant domestic workers: Whose dirty laundry? *Fireweed* 9 (Winter): 53–59.

Simms, Glenda. 1992. Beyond the white veil. In *Challenging times: The women's movement in Canada and the United States,* Constance Backhouse and David H. Flaherty, eds. Montreal: McGill-Queen's University Press.

Smith, Michael G. 1967. *West Indian family structure.* Seattle: University of Washington Press.

Spelman, Elizabeth V. 1988. *Inessential woman: Problems of exclusion in feminist thought.* Boston: Beacon.

Stack, Carol B. 1974. *All our kin: Strategies for survival in a black community.* New York: Harper and Row.

Stasiulis, Daiva. 1987. Rainbow feminism: Perspectives on minority women in Canada. *Resources for Feminist Research,* May, pp. 5–9.

Tennant, Madge. 1980. Canadian experience. *Rikka* 7 (Spring): 46–48.

Turrittin, Jane Sawyer. 1979. We don't look for prejudice: Migrant mobility culture among lower status West Indian women from Montserrat. In *Two nations, many cultures: Ethnic groups in Canada,* J. L. Elliott, ed. Scarborough, Ontario: Prentice-Hall Canada.

Valverde, Mariana. 1992. "The mothers of the race": Race in the sexual and reproductive politics of first-wave feminism. In *Gender conflicts: New essays in women's history,* Franca Iacovetta and Mariana Valverde, eds. Toronto: University of Toronto Press.

——— 1992. Racism and anti-racism in feminist teaching and research. In *Challenging times: The women's movement in Canada and the United States,* Constance Backhouse and David H. Flaherty, eds. Montreal: McGill-Queen's University Press.

Walker, James W. Saint George. 1992. *The Black Loyalists: The search for a promised land in Nova Scotia and Sierra Leone, 1783–1870.* Toronto: University of Toronto Press.

——— 1985. *Racial discrimination in Canada: The Black experience.* Ottawa: Canadian Historical Association.

——— 1984. *The West Indians in Canada.* Ottawa: Canadian Historical Association.

Wallace, Michele. 1990. *Black macho and the myth of the superwoman.* New

York: Routledge, Chapman & Hall.

Yawney, Carole. 1989. To grow a daughter: Cultural liberation and the dynamics of oppression in Jamaica. In *Feminism in Canada: From pressure to politics*, 2nd ed., Geraldine Finn and Angela Miles, eds. Montreal: Black Rose.

Chapter 6

Billson, Janet Mancini, and Martha Stapleton. 1994. Accidental motherhood: Reproductive control and access to opportunity among women in Canada. *Women's Studies International Forum* 17 (4): 357–372.

Cooper, Charlotte Sloan. 1978. *The Mennonite people*. Saskatoon, Saskatchewan: Western Extension College Educational Publishers.

Correll, Ernst H., and Harold S. Bender. 1955–1959. Marriage. In *Mennonite encyclopaedia*, vol. 3, pp. 502–510. Hillsboro, KS: Mennonite Brethren Publishing House.

Driedger, Leo. 1983. Changing Mennonite family roles: From rural boundaries to urban networks. *International Journal of Sociology of the Family* 13 (2): 62–81.

Driedger, Otto H. 1968. Mennonite family stress in the city. *Mennonite Life* 23 (October): 176–178.

Epp, Frank H. 1982. *Mennonites in Canada, 1920–1940*. Scottsdale, PA: Herald.

―――― 1977. *Mennonite peoplehood: A plea for new institutions*. Waterloo, Ontario: Conrad.

―――― 1974. *Mennonites in Canada, 1786–1920: The history of a separate people*. Toronto: Macmillan of Canada.

Ferguson, Mary Louise. 1981. The role participation and life satisfaction of married women in a rural Ontario community. Master's thesis, University of Guelph.

Flint, Joanne. 1980. *The Mennonite Canadians*. Toronto: Van Nostrand Reinhold.

Fretz, Joseph Winfield. 1989. *The Waterloo Mennonites: A community in paradox*. Waterloo, Ontario: Wilfred Laurier University Press.

―――― 1974. *Mennonites in Ontario*, 2nd. ed. Waterloo: Mennonite Historical Society of Ontario.

Gingerich, Orland. 1972. *The Amish in Canada*. Waterloo, Ontario: Conrad.

Good, Merle, and Phyllis Good. 1979. *Twenty most asked questions about the Amish and Mennonites*. Lancaster, PA: Good Books.

Good, Phyllis. 1993. *A Mennonite woman's life*. Intercourse, PA: Good Books.

Hamm, Peter M. 1987. *Continuity and change among Canadian Mennonite Brethren*. Waterloo, Ontario: Wilfred Laurier Press.

Horsch, John. n.d. *Mennonite history*. Scottdale, PA: Mennonite Publishing House.

Horst, Mary Ann. 1984. *My Old Order Mennonite heritage*. Kitchener, Ontario: Pennsylvania Dutch Craft Shop.

Hostetler, J. A. 1983. *Mennonite life*. Scottdale, PA: Herald.

———— 1983. *Amish life*. Scottdale, PA: Herald.

Kauffman, J. Howard. 1979. Social correlates of spiritual maturity among North American Mennonites. *Sociological Analysis* 40 (1): 27–42.

———— and Leo Driedger. 1991. *The Mennonite mosaic: Identity and modernization*. Scottdale, PA: Herald.

Kephart, William M. 1982. *Extraordinary groups: The sociology of unconventional life-styles*, 2nd ed. New York: St. Martin's.

Klaassen, Walter. 1973. *Anabaptism: Neither Catholic nor Protestant*. Waterloo, Ontario: Conrad.

Lederach, Paul M. 1971. *Mennonite youth*. Scottdale, PA: Herald.

Loewen, Harry. 1980. *Mennonite images: Historical, cultural, and literary essays dealing with Mennonite issues*. Winnipeg, Manitoba: Hyperion.

Martin, Isaac G. 1975. *The story of Waterloo-Markham Mennonite Conference*. Unpublished paper, Conrad Grebel College, Waterloo, Ontario.

Mennonite Brethren. 1969–1973. *Mennonite encyclopedia: A comprehensive reference work on the Anabaptist-Mennonite movement*. Hillsboro, KS: Mennonite Brethren Publishing House.

Moorsel, Greg Van. 1986. Mennonites in Ontario. *London* (Ontario) *Free Press*, July 14, pp. 1, 6–7.

Murdie, R. A. 1971. The Mennonite communities of Waterloo County. In *The Waterloo County area selected geographical essays*, A. G. McLelland, ed. Waterloo, Ontario: University of Waterloo.

Poettcker, Henry, and Rudy A. Regehr, eds. 1972. *Call to faithfulness: Essays in Canadian Mennonite studies*. Winnipeg, Manitoba: Canadian Mennonite Bible College.

Redekop, Calvin H. 1969. *The Old Colony Mennonites: Dilemmas of ethnic minority life*. Baltimore: Johns Hopkins University Press.

Rich, Elaine Sommers. 1983. *Mennonite women: A story of God's faithfulness, 1683–1983*. Scottdale, PA: Herald.

Shetler, Sanford G., and J. Ward Shank. 1983. *Symbols of divine order in the Church: A compendium on I Corinthians 11:2–16*. Harrisonburg, VA: Sword and Trumpet.

Sommerville, E. 1971. Waterloo County: A population profile, 1951–1971. In The Waterloo County area selected geographical essays, A. G. McLelland, ed., Waterloo, Ontario: University of Waterloo.

Springer, Nelson P. 1977. *Mennonite bibliography, 1631–1961*. Scottdale, PA: Herald.

Umrau, Ruth, ed. 1986. *Encircled: Stories of Mennonite women*. Newton, KS: Faith and Life.

Van Braght, Thieleman J. 1986. *Martyr's mirror*. Scottdale, PA: Herald.

Wiebe, Bernie. 1972. Canadian Mennonite families: Foundations and launching pads. In *Call to faithfulness: Essays in Canadian Mennonite studies*, Henry Poettcker and Rudy A. Regehr, eds. Winnipeg, Manitoba: Canadian Mennonite Bible College.

Chapter 7

Anderson, Kay J. 1991. *Vancouver's Chinatown: Racial discourse in Canada, 1875–1980*. Montreal: McGill-Queen's University Press.

Buxbaum, David C. 1978. *Chinese family law and social change in historical and comparative perspective*. Seattle: University of Washington Press.

Baker, Hugh D. R. 1979. *Chinese family and kinship*. New York: Columbia University Press.

Bingham, Marjorie Wall, and Susan Hill Gross. 1985. *Women in modern China*. St. Louis Park, MN: Glenhurst.

Chan, Anthony B. 1983. *Gold mountain: The Chinese in the New World*. Vancouver, British Columbia: New Star.

Chang, Jung. 1991. *Wild swans: Three daughters of China*. New York: Simon & Schuster.

Chow, Esther Ngan-Ling. 1993. *Women, the family, and policy: A global perspective*. New York: State University of New York Press.

Con, Harry, et al. 1982. *From China to Canada: A history of the Chinese community in Canada*. Ottawa: Canadian Government Publication Center.

Epstein, Rachel, Roxana Ng, and Maggi Trebble. 1978. *Social organization of family violence: An ethnography of immigrant experience in Vancouver*. Vancouver, BC: Women's Research Centre.

Family Planning Services. 1978. *Family planning and the Chinese community*. Division Bulletin No. 9. Mimeo. Vancouver, British Columbia: Author.

Geschwender, James A. 1990. Racial stratification, gender, and the social location of Chinese-Canadians in British Columbia. Unpublished paper.

Glenn, Evelyn Nakano. 1986. *Issei, Nisei, war bride: Three generations of Japanese American women in domestic service*. Philadelphia: Temple University Press.

Gough, Barry M. 1988. Gold miners and settlers. In *A history of British Columbia: Selected readings*, Patricia E. Roy, ed. Toronto: Copp Clark Pitman.

Gross, Susan Hill, and Marjorie Wall Bingham. 1985. *Women in traditional China*. St. Louis Park, MN: Glenhurst.

Hong, Lawrence K. 1976. The role of women in the People's Republic of China: Legacy and change. *Social Problems* 23 (June): 545–557.

Huang, Lucy-Jen. 1976. The family and the communes in People's Republic of China: Retrospect and prospect. *Journal of Comparative Family Studies* 7 (Spring): 97–109.

———— 1971. Role stereotypes and self-concepts among American and Chinese students. *Journal of Comparative Family Studies* 2 (Autumn): 215–234.

Institute of Ethnology. 1985. *The Chinese family and its ritual behavior*. Nan-Kang, Taipei: Academia Sinica.

Johnson, Graham E. 1983. Chinese Canadians in the '70s: New wine in new bottles. In *Two nations, many cultures: Ethnic groups in Canada*, J. L. Elliott, ed. Scarborough, Ontario: Prentice-Hall Canada.

Keyes, Susan. 1984. Measuring sex-role stereotypes: Attitudes among Hong Kong Chinese adolescents and the development of the Chinese sex-role inventory. *Sex Roles* 10 (January): 129–140.

Lai, David. 1988. *Chinatowns*. Vancouver: University of British Columbia Press.

Lang, Olga. 1968. *Chinese family and society*. Hamden, CT: Archon.

Levy, Howard S. 1966. *Chinese footbinding*. New York: Rawls.

Li, Peter S. 1988. *The Chinese in Canada*. Toronto: Oxford University Press.

——— 1980. Immigration laws and family patterns: Some demographic changes among Chinese families in Canada, 1885–1971. *Canadian Ethnic Studies* 12, 1:58–73.

Lim, Sing. 1979. *West Coast Chinese boy*. Montreal: Tundra.

Lyman, Stanford. 1974. *Chinese Americans*. New York: Random House.

Man, Guida Ching-Fan. 1994. The astronaut phenomenon: Consequence of the diaspora of the Hong Kong Chinese. Paper presented at the annual meeting of the American Sociological Association, Los Angeles.

Marsh, James H., ed. 1985. *The Canadian encyclopedia*, vol. 2. Edmonton, Alberta: Hurtig.

McCallan, N. J., and Katherine Roback. 1980. *An ordinary life: Life histories of women in the urban core of Vancouver*. Vancouver, British Columbia: Canadian Research Institute for the Advancement of Women.

McLaren, Ian F. 1985. *The Chinese in Victoria: Official reports and documents*. Ascot Vale, British Columbia: Red Rooster.

Morton, James W. 1974. *In the sea of sterile mountains*. Vancouver, British Columbia: Douglas.

Naidoo, Josephine C. 1980. Women of South Asian and Anglo-Saxon origins in the Canadian context. In *Sex roles: Origins, influences and implications for women*, Cannie Stark-Adamec, ed. Montreal: Eden.

Ng, Roxana. 1986. Immigrant women in Canada: A socially constructed category. *Resources for Feminist Research*, May, pp. 13–15.

——— 1981. Constituting ethnic phenomenon: An account from the perspective of immigrant women. *Canadian Ethnic Studies* 13 (1): 97–108.

——— and Judith Ramirez. 1981. *Immigrant housewives in Canada: A report*. Toronto: Immigrant Women's Centre.

——— and Tania Da Gupta. 1981. Nation builders? The captive labour force of non-English-speaking immigrant women. *Canadian Women's Studies/Les Cahiers de la Femme* 3 (1): 83–85.

——— and Janet Sprout. 1978. *Services for immigrant women: Report and evaluation of a series of four workshops conducted in the summer, 1978*. Mimeo. Vancouver, British Columbia: Women's Research Centre.

Nipp, Dora. 1986. But women did come: Working Chinese women in the interwar years. In *Looking into my sister's eyes*, J. Burnet, ed. Toronto: MHSO.

Ng, Winnie. 1982. Immigrant women: The silent partners of the women's movement. In *Still ain't satisfied! Canadian feminism today*, Maureen Fitzgerald et al., eds. Toronto: Women's Press.

Ono, Dawn Kiyoye. 1978. White male supremacy and the "Oriental Doll." *Asianadian* 1 (3): 24–25.

Property boom fuels west-side tensions. 1989. *Vancouver Province*, April 9, p. HK6–7.

Roy, Patricia E. 1988. *A history of British Columbia: Selected readings.* Toronto: Copp Clark Pitman.

Royal Commission on Chinese Immigration. 1978. *Report of the Royal Commission on Chinese Immigration.* New York: Arno.

Stacey, Judith. 1983. *Patriarchy and socialist revolution in China.* Berkeley: University of California Press.

Waley, Arthur. 1960. *Book of songs.* New York: Grove. Warburton, Rennie. 1988. British Columbia's fear of Asians, 1900–1950. In A History of British Columbia: Selected readings, Patricia E. Roy, ed. Toronto: Copp Clark Pitman.

Ward, W. Peter. 1988. Class and race in the social structure of British Columbia, 1870–1939. In A History of British Columbia: Selected readings, Patricia E. Roy, ed. Toronto: Copp Clark Pitman.

Wolf, Margery. 1985. *Revolution postponed: Women in contemporary China.* Stanford, CA: Stanford University Press.

Wong, Aline K. 1974. Women in China: Past and present. In *Many sisters: Women in cross-cultural perspective*, Carolyn J. Matthiasson, ed. New York: Free Press.

Wong, Karen C. 1972. *Chinese history in the Pacific Northwest.* : Author.

Wright, Richard. 1988. *In a strange land.* Saskatoon, Saskatchewan: Western Producer Prairie Books.

Wynne, Robert E. 1978. *Reaction to the Chinese in the Pacific Northwest and British Columbia, 1850–1910.* New York: Arno.

Yao, Esther S. Lee. 1983. *Chinese women, past and present.* Mesquite, TX: Ide House.

Yee, May. 1987. Out of the silence: Voices of Chinese Canadian women. *Resources for Feminist Research*, May, pp. 15–16.

Yee, Paul. 1988. *Saltwater City: An illustrated history of the Chinese in Vancouver.* Vancouver, British Columbia: Douglas and McIntyre.

Yu, Elena. 1977. Kinship structure, post-marital residence and sex-role equality in China. *Sociological Focus* 10 (2): 175–188.

Yung, Judy. 1986. *Chinese women of America: A pictorial history.* Seattle: University of Washington Press.

Yu-Ning, Li, ed. 1992. *Chinese women through Chinese eyes.* Armonk, NY: Sharpe.

Chapter 8

Balan, Jars. 1984. Salt and braided bread: Ukrainian life in Canada. Toronto: Oxford University Press.

Bilash, Radomir, and Barbara Wilberg, eds. 1989. *Tkanyna: An exhibit of Ukrainian weaving*. Edmonton, Alberta: Canadian Institute of Ukrainian Studies Press.

Billson, Janet Mancini. 1993. Review essay, Challenging Times: The Women's Movement in Canada and the United States (C. Backhouse and D. Flaherty, eds.). *Canadian Review of American Studies*, Special Issue, Part II: 317–325.

Bohachevsky-Chomiak, Martha. 1988. *Feminists despite themselves: Women in Ukrainian community life, 1884–1939*. Toronto: University of Toronto Press.

Canadian Council on Rural Development. 1979. *Rural women: Their work, their needs, and their role in rural development*. Ottawa: Minister of Supply and Services Canada.

Canadian Department of the Secretary of State, Women's Programme Summary of Issues. 1975. *Rural women*. Ottawa: Author.

Cape, Elizabeth. 1982. Aging women in rural society: Out of sight, out of mind. *Resources for Feminist Research* 11 (July): 214–215.

Cavanagh, Judy. 1982. The plight of women farmworkers. *Resources for Feminist Research* 11 (March): 6–7.

Chykalenko-Keller, Hanna. 1920. Memorandum prepared for the International Women's League of Peace and Freedom, Geneva, June. 1920.

Crocker, Olga. 1982. Stress of farm women related to the changing economy. *Resources for Feminist Research* 11 (March): 182–184.

Czumer, William A. 1981. *Recollections about the life of the first Ukrainian settlers in Canada*. Edmonton, Alberta: Canadian Institute of Ukrainian Studies Press.

Djao, Angela W., and Roxana Ng. 1986. Structured isolation: Immigrant women in Saskatchewan. In *Women—isolation and bonding: Readings in the ecology of gender*, Kathleen Storried, ed. Saskatoon: University of Saskatchewan.

Fairbanks, Carol. 1986. *Prairie women: Images in American and Canadian fiction*. New Haven, CT: Yale University Press.

——— and Sara Brooks Sundberg. 1983. *Farm women on the prairie frontier: A sourcebook for Canada and the United States*. Metuchen, NJ: Scarecrow.

Faryna, Natalka, ed. 1976. *Ukrainian Canadiana*. Edmonton, Alberta: Ukrainian Women's Association of Canada.

Gerus, O. W., and J. E. Rea. 1985. *The Ukrainians in Canada*. Ottawa: Keystone.

Haly, Theresa, Angela Djao, and Lily Tingley. 1985. *Doubly disadvantaged: The women who immigrate to Canada*. Mimeo. Saskatoon: Immigrant Women of Saskatchewan.

Hedley, Max J. 1982. Normal expectations: Rural women without property. *Resources for Feminist Research* 11 (March): 15–17.

Hryniuk, Stella. 1990. *Peasants with promise: Ukrainians in Southeastern Galicia, 1880–1900*. Edmonton, Alberta: Canadian Institute for Ukrainian Studies Press.

Kinnear, Mary. 1988. "Do you want your daughter to marry a farmer?": Women's work on the farm, 1922. *Canadian Papers in Rural History* 6:137–153.

Keywan, Zonia. 1977. *Greater than kings*. Montreal: Harvest House.

Kordan, Bohdan S. 1985. *Ukrainians and the 1981 Canada Census: A data handbook*. Edmonton, Alberta: Canadian Institute of Ukrainian Studies.

Kostash, Myrna. 1977. *All of Baba's children*. Edmonton, Alberta: Hurtig.

Krawchuk, Peter. 1972. Ukrainian women in early history. *Ukrainian Canadian*, March, pp. 15–19.

Lupul, Manoly R., ed. 1982. *A heritage in transition: Essays in the history of Ukrainians in Canada*. Toronto: McClelland and Stewart.

—— 1978. *Ukrainian Canadians, multiculturalism, and separatism. An assessment*. Proceedings of a conference by the Canadian Institute of Ukrainian Studies. Edmonton: University of Alberta Press.

Martynowych, Orest T. 1991. *Ukrainians in Canada: The formative period, 1891–1924*. Edmonton, Alberta: Canadian Institute of Ukrainian Studies Press.

Owechko, Iwan, Roman V. Kuchar, and Roman O. Tatchyn. 1985. *Ukraine and Ukrainians*, 2nd ed. Greeley, CO: Ukrapress.

Petryshyn, Marusia K. 1980. Changing status of Ukrainian women in Canada, 1921–1971. In *Changing realities: Social trends among Ukrainian Canadians*, W. Roman Petryshyn, ed. Edmonton, Alberta: Canadian Institute of Ukrainian Studies Press.

Petryshyn, W. R., ed. 1980. *Changing realities: Social trends among Ukrainian Canadians*. Edmonton, Alberta: Canadian Institute of Ukrainian Studies Press.

—— 1978. The Ukrainian Canadians in social transition. In *Ukrainian Canadians, multiculturalism, and separatism: An assessment*, Manoly R. Lupul, ed. Edmonton: University of Alberta Press.

Potrebenko, Helen. 1977. *No streets of gold: A social history of Ukrainians in Alberta*. Vancouver, BC: New Star.

Redekop, Mary. 1972. Looking back on fifty years (Women's Branches of the Association of United Ukrainian Canadians). *Ukrainian Canadian*, March, 7–14.

Swyripa, Frances. 1991. *Wedded to the cause: Ukrainian-Canadian women and ethnic identity, 1891–1991*. Toronto: University of Toronto Press.

—— 1988. From Princess Olha to Baba: Images, roles and myths in the history of Ukrainian women in Canada. Unpublished doctoral dissertation, University of Alberta.

Tkachuk, Mary, Marie Kishchuk, and Alice Nicholaichuk. 1987. *Pysanka: Icon of the universe*. Saskatoon, Saskatchewan: Ukrainian Museum of Canada.

Tesarski, Felix. 1987. *Son of pioneers*. Winnipeg, Manitoba: Hignell Printing.

Thompson, Elizabeth. 1991. *The pioneer woman: A Canadian character type*. Montreal: McGill-Queen's University Press.

Ukrainian Women's Association of Canada. 1984. *Ukrainian daughter's cookbook*. Regina, Saskatchewan: Daughters of Ukraine.

Wolowyna, Jean E. 1980. Trends in marital status and fertility of Ukrainians in Canada. In *Changing realities: Social trends among Ukrainian Canadians*, W. Roman Petryshyn, ed. Edmonton, Alberta: Canadian Institute of Ukrainian Studies Press.

Chapter 9

Bégin, Monique. 1992. The Royal Commission on the Status of Women in Canada: Twenty years later. In *Challenging times: The women's movement in Canada and the United States*, Constance Backhouse and David H. Flaherty, eds. Montreal: McGill-Queen's University Press.

Luxton, Meg. 1988. The gendered division of labour in the home. In *Social inequality in Canada: Patterns, problems, and policies*, James Curtis et al., eds. Scarborough, Ontario: Prentice-Hall Canada.

Norwood, Robin. 1985. *Women who love too much.* NY: St. Martin's Press.

Vickers, Jill. 1992. The intellectual origins of the women's movement in Canada. In *Challenging times: The women's movement in Canada and the United States*, Constance Backhouse and David H. Flaherty, eds. Montreal: McGill-Queen's University Press.

Chapter 10

Balan, Jars. 1984. *Salt and braided bread: Ukrainian life in Canada.* Toronto: Oxford University Press.

Billson, Janet Mancini. 1991. Standing tradition on its head: Role reversal among Blood Indian couples. *Great Plains Quarterly*, 11 (Winter): 3–21.

Lurie, Nancy Oestreich. 1972. Indian women: A legacy of freedom. In *Look to the mountaintop*, Charles Jones, ed. San Jose, CA: Gousha.

Nickles, Elizabeth. 1981. *The coming matriarchy: How women will regain the balance of power.* New York: Seaview.

Powers, Marla N. 1986. *Oglala women: Myth, ritual, and reality.* Chicago: University of Chicago Press.

Turner, Joan, ed. 1990. *Living the changes.* Winnipeg: University of Manitoba Press.

Vickers, Jill. 1992. The intellectual origins of the women's movement in Canada. In *Challenging times: The women's movement in Canada and the United States*, Constance Backhouse and David H. Flaherty, eds. Montreal: McGill-Queen's University Press.

Chapter 11

Backhouse, Constance, and David H. Flaherty, eds. 1992. *Challenging times: The women's movement in Canada and the United States.* Montreal: McGill-Queen's University Press.

Chafetz, Janet Saltzman. 1988. *Feminist sociology: An overview of contemporary theories.* Itasca, IL: Peacock.

Greaves, Lorraine. 1992. What is the interrelationship between academic and activist feminism? In *Challenging times: The women's movement in Canada and the United States*, Constance Backhouse and David H. Flaherty, eds. Montreal: McGill-Queen's University Press.

Hess, Beth B. 1990. Beyond dichotomy: Drawing distinctions and embracing differences. *Sociological Forum* 5 (1): 75–93.

Nemiroff, Greta Hofmann. 1992. That which divides us; that which unites us. In

Challenging times: The women's movement in Canada and the United States, Constance Backhouse and David H. Flaherty, eds. Montreal: McGill-Queen's University Press.

————— 1984. "CANADA: The Empowerment of Women." In *Sisterhood is global: The international women's movement anthology*, Robin Morgan, ed. Garden City, NY: Anchor/Doubleday.

Risman, Barbara J., and Pepper Schwartz. 1989. *Gender in intimate relationships: A microstructural approach*. Belmont, CA: Wadsworth.

Simms, Glenda. 1992. Beyond the white veil. In *Challenging times: The women's movement in Canada and the United States*, Constance Backhouse and David H. Flaherty, eds. Montreal: McGill-Queen's University Press.

Vickers, Jill. 1992. The intellectual origins of the women's movement in Canada. In *Challenging times: The women's movement in Canada and the United States*, Constance Backhouse and David H. Flaherty, eds. Montreal: McGill-Queen's University Press.

Wine, Jeri, and Janice Ristock, eds. 1991. *Women and social change: Feminist activism in Canada*. Halifax: James Lorimer.

Wolf, Naomi. 1993a. *Gender-quake: How to change feminism so women can change the 21st century*. New York: Random House.

————— 1993b. *Fire with fire: The new female power and how it will change the 21st century*. New York: Random House.

Appendices

Billson, Janet Mancini. 1991. The progressive verification method: Toward a feminist methodology for studying women cross-culturally. *Women's Studies International Forum* 14 (3):201–215.

Committee on the Status of Women in Sociology. 1988. The treatment of gender in research. *Footnotes*, January, pp. 10–11.

Eichler, Margrit. 1977. Sociology of feminist research in Canada. *Signs* 3 (2):409–422.

Fluehr-Lobban, Carolyn. 1994. Informed consent in anthropological research: We are not exempt. Unpublished manuscript.

————— ed. 1990. *Ethics and the profession of anthropology: Dialogue for a new era*. Philadelphia: University of Pennsylvania Press.

Glaser, Barney G., and Anselm L. Strauss. 1967. *The discovery of grounded theory: Strategies for qualitative research*. Chicago: Aldine.

Lengermann, Patricia Madoo, and Ruth A. Wallace. 1985. *Gender in America: Social control and social change*. Englewood-Cliffs, NJ: Prentice-Hall.

Reinharz, Shulamit. 1983. "Back into the personal" or: Our attempt to construct "feminist research." In *Theories of women's studies*, Gloria Bowles and Renate Duelli Klein, eds. London: Routledge and Kegan Paul.

Smith, Dorothy. 1986. Institutional ethnography: A feminist method. *Resources for Feminist Research*, May, pp. 6–13.

Williamson, John B., et al. 1982. *The research craft: An introduction to social research methods*, 2nd ed. Boston: Little, Brown.

Index